# FRIEDRICH
# SCHILLER

*Poet of Freedom*

## Volume II

Schiller Institute
Washington, D.C.
1988

The translators wish to acknowledge the help of three native German-speaking members of the Schiller Institute, for their work in ensuring the accuracy of the translations in this volume, and for the encouragement and support that they extended to this effort—Ralf Schauerhammer, Stephanie Pauls, and Wolfgang Lillge.

Cover design: Alan Yue
Book design: Paul Arnest
Project editors: Christina Huth, Marianna Wertz, Ronald Kokinda
Composition: World Composition Services, Inc., Sterling, Virginia

Please direct all inquiries to the publisher:
Schiller Institute, Inc.
P.O. Box 20244
Washington, D.C. 20041-0244

# CONTENTS

# FOREWORD

> "It is beauty, through which one proceeds to freedom."
>
> —Friedrich Schiller
> *Letters On the Aesthetical Education of Man*

This second volume of English translations of the works of Friedrich Schiller by members of the Schiller Institute is released at a crucial moment in world history. Humanity is faced with an apocalyptic crisis, which can and will be solved in an enduring way only to the extent that the realm of beauty is brought into existence within individual souls and among the people of sovereign nations. As Schiller wrote in his *Letters On the Aesthetical Education of Man*, "One, in order to solve the political problem in experience, must take the path through the aesthetical, because it is beauty, through which one proceeds to freedom."

Today we are faced with a conjunctural crisis similar to, but far greater than, that which Schiller himself experienced at the time of the American and French revolutions. Today as then, humanity is faced with a choice. If man does not act to solve such crises as the AIDS epidemic, and the financial and economic crises, and if the free world does not act to defend itself against the Russian imperial threat, then, as Schiller said at the time of the French Revolution, a great moment will have found a little, unresponsive people.

However, if sufficient individuals act in accordance with natural law to solve these crises, to create a new world economic order founded on justice, to defend the inalienable right of all men to life, liberty and the pursuit of happiness, then the potential which Schiller saw in the American Revolution, to free man from the ugliness of barbarism, can yet be realized, and the Age of Reason achieved.

The Schiller Institute, and those who participated in doing the translations in this book, are no detached spectators in this battle to determine the direction that humanity will take over the next century.

The Schiller Institute was founded by Helga Zepp-LaRouche in 1984, with the support and collaboration of her husband Lyndon H. LaRouche, for the purpose of strengthening the Western Alliance and of defending world peace, based upon the economic development of the developing sector nations.

Precisely because of these republican policy principles, Lyndon and Helga LaRouche, and their collaborators in the Schiller Institute, have been subjected to massive human rights violations demanded by the Russian empire and carried out in large part by elements of the U.S. government, in violation of the U.S. Constitution. This attack on the Schiller Institute merely confirms the power of Schiller's ideas and poetry in the service of republicanism in its war against the oligarchical world outlook. The enemies of humanity realize that humanity, ennobled by beauty, is invincible.

## WHY TRANSLATE SCHILLER?

This is the reason why the Schiller Institute has committed itself to translating the collected works of Schiller into English. In order to prevent the creation of a cultural renaissance in America, British intelligence moved quickly to establish a monopoly over the translation of Schiller's work. To distort the content and thus delimit the effect of Schiller's work on an English-speaking audience, British oligarchical interests centered in Edinburgh, Scotland launched a major effort during his lifetime to mistranslate Schiller, to portray him as a poet inferior to his contemporary Wolfgang Goethe, and to mischaracterize him as a follower of Immanual Kant, Schiller's arch intellectual enemy.

The operation against Schiller in this respect was fourfold:

First, in 1800, Samuel Coleridge, who had earlier toyed with the idea of translating "all the works of Schiller," completed translating Schiller's dramas, *The Piccolomini* and *Wallenstein's Death*. As evidence of how little Coleridge and his circle truly appreciated Schiller, according to Coleridge himself, who freely altered the original, the play was "full of long speeches," it "wasted and depressed" his spirits and "left a sense of wearisomeness and disgust which unfitted" him for "anything but sleeping or immediate society." Coleridge, who became an opium addict, later came to look upon his translation of Schiller as the source of his subsequent "intellectual barrenness." Although his translation was a financial failure, it represented a major effort on the part of the British Romantic school to distort one of the major works of the antiromantic Schiller. No wonder the romantic feudalist Sir Walter Scott considered Coleridge's translation superior to the original.

The second step in this process was the publication in 1813 of the book *Germany* by Madame de Staël, niece of the Swiss banker Jacques Necker, whose financial policies brought about the French Revolution. In this book, purportedly popularizing Schiller, de Staël criticized Schiller and his work as inferior to the genius of Goethe.

As a third step, this same misestimation of Schiller was reenforced in 1823 with the publication of Thomas Carlyle's *Life of Schiller*. Carlyle, a protégé of the East India Company's John Stuart Mill, falsely claimed that Schiller lacked a sense of humor and "could not have written one good poem if he had not met Goethe."

Far from sharing Schiller's republican views, Carlyle was a literary agent of the British empire. His major writings, commissioned by John Stuart Mill, covered up the British role in fomenting the Jacobin mob of the French Revolution, advocated a revival of the pagan belief in the racial superiority of the Nordic race, and lamented the emancipation of blacks in the British West Indies. In his later years, Carlyle was an ally of Giuseppe Mazzini and his anarchist Young Europe movement. Carlyle's work was well received by Karl Marx's collaborator Friedrich Engels, and he acquired two disciples—John Ruskin and William T. Stead, founders of the oligarchic British Round Table.

Finally, in 1842, Sir Edward Bulwer-Lytton had his translations of the *Poems and Ballads* of Schiller published in the pages of Blackwood's *Edinburgh Magazine*. Bulwer-Lytton, like Carlyle, was of a world outlook directly opposite to Schiller. The British colonial secretary during the British Opium Wars against China and later imperial high commissioner in India, Bulwer-Lytton was an outspoken promoter of the pagan Isis cult. His first novel provided the theme for Richard Wagner's first opera, *Rienzi*, which was a major inspiration for Hitler's doctrine of Nordic racial supremacy. Bulwer-Lytton's translations of Schiller's poetry were thus a transparent attempt on the part of the British Colonial Office to peremptorily distort and rob Schiller of his power to mobilize republican forces against imperial rule.

Other translations of Schiller's work have been published, but the above operations, conducted by agents of British intelligence, helped to establish a cultural climate, in terms of accepted literary standards, antagonistic to Schiller, and thus succeeded in blunting the impact of Schiller's work in America. This contributed to the failure of America, the "beacon of hope and temple of liberty," to become a new Athens.

As a necessary first step to reversing the damage done to republicanism by the oligarchy's slander that Schiller is inferior to Goethe, this volume contains a definitive essay by Helga Zepp-LaRouche, "Poetry and *Agapē*: Reflections on Schiller and Goethe." Zepp-LaRouche elaborates that, like Kant, who bases his aesthetics on subjective feelings of pleasure and pain, Goethe is the poet of *Eros*—lust. In contrast, Schiller's poetry expresses the higher notion of love (*agapē*) for God, truth, beauty and humanity, as an objective principle of the universe. This quality of mind, so crucial to the establishment of a New World Economic Order based upon sovereign republics, is precisely the quality of mind in Schiller which the oligarchy is committed to destroy and subvert. It is for that reason that Madame de Staël, Thomas Carlyle and other enemies of humanity preferred Goethe and his Faustian pact with the devil.

## SCHILLER VS. KANT

This volume also contains, in Schiller's own words, the definitive refutation of the claim that Schiller was a Kantian. As indicated above, a major feature of the cultural warfare carried out against Schiller was the disinformation, that Schiller's aesthetics are based upon the views of Immanuel Kant. It is indeed true, that Schiller studied and mastered Kant's work, but only for the purpose of *refuting* his aesthetics, as they were elaborated in Kant's *Critique of Judgment*. In this work, Kant argued that aesthetical judgment is subjective, and based upon a feeling of pleasure or pain. In doing so, Kant, who doubted the existence of the Creator, denied that there are knowable objective laws, which apply both to the creation of the physical universe and to the creation of beauty by man. This gnostic denial of man's capacity to participate intelligibly in creation is what makes Kant's philosophy evil, a fact forcefully emphasized by Lyndon LaRouche, who, along with his wife Helga and the Schiller Institute, have relaunched Schiller's attack on Kantian immorality.

Schiller explicitly rejected Kant's subjectivism. In a letter written to his friend Gottfried Körner on December 21, 1792, Schiller wrote, "I believe I have found the objective concept of the beautiful, which is in itself qualified to be an objective principle of taste and of which Kant doubted." In another letter to Körner on January 25, 1793, Schiller rejects Kant's notion that taste would unavoidably always remain an empirical question, and counterposes to Kant's "subjective rational" notion of the beautiful his own "sensuous objective" theory.

This volume includes translations of a student's transcript of a lecture series on aesthetics given by Schiller during the 1792–93 winter semester at the University of Jena, and also Schiller's correspondence with his friend Körner between January 25 and February 28, 1793, titled *Kallias, or, On the Beautiful*. Both the lecture series and *Kallias* reflect Schiller's rejection of Kant's *Critique of Judgment* and the evolution and elaboration of his own theory of beauty. As such, they lay the basis for Schiller's two more famous writings, *On Grace and Dignity* (translated in this volume), and the *Letters On the Aesthetical Education of Man* (translated in Volume I), which were composed later the same year.

In the *Critique of Judgment*, Kant argues that art differs from science, because beauty is a matter of subjective taste. By basing his aesthetics on feelings of pain or pleasure, Kant is led to deny, that the capacity for producing beautiful art is knowable and therefore reproducible. Thus, Kant writes in his *Critique of Judgment* as follows: ". . . a Homer . . . cannot show how his ideas, so rich in fancy and yet so full of thought came together in his head, simply because he does not know and therefore cannot teach others . . . . artistic skill cannot be communicated; it is imparted to every artist immediately by the hand of nature; and so it dies with him."

It should thus be obvious that, if one wished to prevent Schiller's writings on aesthetics from generating a renaissance, one need only convince the reader that Schiller is merely a Kantian and, as Kant said, "there is no science of the beautiful," and "no industry can learn 'artistic genius.'"

In *Kallias, or, On the Beautiful*, Schiller makes absolutely clear his philosophical differences with Kant in enunciating an alternative theory of beauty. In contrast with Kant, who, like Aristotle, limits reason to mere logic, Schiller places himself in the tradition of Plato and the Socratic method. Thus, while agreeing with Kant that beauty is not based upon logical concepts, Schiller points out that Kant fails entirely, to identify the actual basis of beauty, which Schiller locates in that higher form of reason, which supercedes the merely logical.

As Schiller stresses, beauty is the "form of a form," i.e., beauty is that form which is not determined from the outside by logical concepts, but rather is determined through itself. As such, the beautiful, according to Schiller, is analogous to the form of practical reason, i.e., freedom. Thus, although the beautiful is not based upon merely logical concepts, it nonetheless is, contrary to Kant, intelligible from the standpoint of what Plato refers to as the hypothesis of the higher hypothesis, or creative reason.

Schiller maintains that nature or sensuous existence, insofar as it stands under the law of self-determination, which characterizes the creative human mind, is objectively and not merely subjectively beautiful. The beautiful is thus the objective nature of sensuous existence, insofar as its form is determined through itself and not imposed from the outside. This, then, is the scientific basis for Schiller's contention, that it is through beauty, that political freedom is achieved. The individual, who through perception of beauty becomes beautiful and therefore capable of producing beauty, is, by the very nature of the beautiful, free from within, and thus truly free.

In this volume of translations, there are several additional works by Schiller, which directly address Schiller's opposition to Kant and the Romantics. These include *On Grace and Dignity*, which is a thorough refutation of Kant's oppressive notion of the categorical imperative, the two critiques, *On Bürger's Poems* and *On Matthisson's Poems*, and *Of the Aesthetic Estimation of Magnitude*.

Also included is Wilhelm von Humboldt's intellectual biography of Schiller, published as an introduction to a volume of the Schiller-Humboldt correspondence. Humboldt takes explicit note of the fact that Schiller's aesthetic writings are a refutation of Kant:

. . . Schiller found that according to his way of thinking, the sensuous powers of man were in part offended against, in part not sufficiently recognized, and the possibility in those powers of voluntary harmony with the unity of reason through the aesthetic principle was not sufficiently emphasized. So it happened that, when he first expressed Kant's name in print in *On Grace and Dignity*, Schiller appeared as Kant's opponent.

For Schiller, a beautiful soul is he who obeys reason with joy. The emotions of such a person are so in harmony with Reason that the guidance of the will may be abandoned to the emotions, and never run the danger of being in contradiction with Reason. On the other hand, as Schiller emphasizes, Kant's conception of duty, his categorical imperative, in attempting to repress the sensuous part of man rather than transform it, so as to harmonize sensuousness and Reason, is incompatible with beauty and freedom. Echoing the New Testament argument in behalf of agapic love, that the law alone strengthens sin, Schiller writes, "The enemy merely cast down can arise again, whereas the reconciled is truly vanquished."

The purpose of Schiller's dramas and poetry is to bring about such a reconciliation in the audience, and thus to create the beautiful souls capable of creating and enjoying durable political freedom. In his tragedies, Schiller explores those strategic crises in which individuals such as Spain's Prince Don Carlos and the Marquis of Posa fail to act, at the *punctum saliens*, the crucial turning point, in a manner coherent with natural law. In every case, their failure to act in a way that effectively challenges those axiomatic, logical assumptions embedded in the play's action, which lead to a self-destructive conclusion, reflects their own lack of such a beautiful soul.

This does not mean, however, as some Romantics would suggest, that Schiller had a tragic outlook. To the contrary, Schiller's world outlook is Promethean optimism. Man, insofar as he educates himself aesthetically, is capable of overcoming even death—and only thus is he truly free.

## THE INALIENABLE RIGHTS OF MAN

In this volume, the Schiller Institute presents new translations of two plays written late in Schiller's life, neither of which is a tragedy—*Wilhelm Tell* and *The Parasite, or, The Art of Self-Advancement*. Although the latter is a translation and adaptation of a play by the French playwright Picard, both plays properly locate Schiller's poetic work in the tradition of Aeschylos on the one hand, and Dante and his *Divine Comedy* on the other.

In *Wilhelm Tell*, although the Swiss republican forces are nearly defeated as a result of their failure to act in a timely fashion, they are saved by Tell, who, at the *punctum saliens*, acts out of self-defense against the tyrant, who would violate natural law. Tell acts not for selfish personal reasons, as does the Duke of Austria, who kills his uncle, the Emperor, but rather as an instrument of the Creator above, in behalf of the inalienable rights of man. Tell acts in behalf of the universal good, against the hubris of oligarchical tyranny. The natural law basis for his action is expressed in the famous *Rütli oath* taken by his countrymen:

> No, there's a limit to the tyrant's power
> When the oppressed can find no justice, when
> The burden grows unbearable—He reaches
> With hopeful courage up into the Heavens
> And seizes hither his eternal rights,
> Which hang above, inalienable
> And indestructible as stars themselves—
> The primal state of nature reappears,
> Where man stands opposite his fellow man—
> As last resort, when not another means
> Is of avail, the sword is given him—
> The highest of all goods we may defend
> From violence.—We stand before our country,
> We stand before our wives, before our children!

Moreover, as Walter Fürst rightly concludes:

Were there 'tween us and Austria an umpire,
So then would justice and the law decide,
But he who doth oppress us, is our Emp'ror
And highest judge—so therefore God must help us
Through our own arm.


## SOLON VS. LYCURGUS

Unlike so many today, who falsely define the political spectrum in terms of "left," "right," and "center," Schiller in his historical writings, particularly his lecture entitled *The Legislation of Lycurgus and Solon*, correctly saw history as a conflict between two opposing philosophies of law, the one exemplified by the republican reforms of Solon of Athens and the other the oligarchical system of Lycurgus, the mythical founder of Sparta.

The republican form of government epitomized by Solon's Athens exists for the purpose of developing the mind of the individual citizen, so that that citizen may contribute to the improvement of the nation and, by extension, to the improvement of humanity as a whole. Because the citizen was not sacrificed to the state, but rather the state served the people in Athens, "all virtues matured, industry and art flourished, the blessings of diligence abounded, all fields of knowledge were cultivated."

Not accidentally, the first act with which Solon began his work was the famous edict, whereby all debts were annulled. Thus Solon, like the Schiller Institute today, insisted upon the primacy of human life, and conditioned the right to private property upon its employment in behalf of human life. In contrast, as Schiller writes, Lycurgus "worked against the highest purpose of humanity, in that through his well thought out system of state, he held the minds of the Spartans fast at the level where he had found them and hemmed in all progress for eternity. . . . All industry was banned . . . all science neglected. . . ." In short, Lycurgus reduced Sparta to an environmentalist slavocracy, contrary to the negentropic nature of the universe and of the human mind.

In this work, as well as the other historical pieces translated in his volume, including *The Mission of Moses, The Jesuit Government in Paraguay,* and his lecture on *Universal History,* Schiller accurately describes the political conflict which has defined Western European history to this day. Moreover, Schiller's view is not a Manichean one, pitting darkness and light, goodness and evil, in eternal battle. Schiller believed that the Spartan model can be defeated, a new Athens can be created, but only to the extent that the artist, wielding the weapon of poetry as Solon did, ennobles the human soul. But if this fails to occur, then indeed, the consequences will be tragic.

## The Song of the Bell

The purpose of the Schiller Institute in issuing this book is, thus, to contribute to creating a new Athens on these American shores, a development the oligarchy has always been committed to preventing. To that end, we conclude this foreword by considering Schiller's poetry. The translations of Schiller's poems in this volume and in Volume I, represent the only English translation of his poetry generally available today. In part, the reason for this is that the nineteenth century Romantic propaganda, to the effect that Schiller is a mediocre poet compared to Goethe, continues to prevail in academia to this day. Certainly the mistranslations of Schiller's poetry by Sir Edward Bulwer-Lytton, among others, have contributed to this deliberate effort to detract from Schiller's primary importance as a poet.

Without denying Goethe's technical gifts as a poet, it is undeniably the case that Goethe's poetry is limited in quality by his own erotic flaws, as Helga Zepp-LaRouche amply demonstrates. It is indeed the case that a poet's product can only be as beautiful as that poet's soul, and in the case of Goethe, the erotic obsessions of his soul prevent him from expressing the Promethean agapic love, which characterizes a beautiful soul. Schiller, on the other hand, consistently writes poetry from this standpoint, because his is a beautiful soul. Thus it is fair to say, that Schiller is the poet of love (*agapē*), because he has succeeded in educating his emotions aesthetically, and that therefore his poetry has the capacity to transform the emotions of his audience in the same way. This is a power, which Goethe unfortunately does not exhibit, and it is for this reason, that the Romantics have attempted to use Goethe against Schiller.

The twenty-five poems which appear in this volume are all translated in the same meter, rhythm, and rhyme scheme as the original German. Every effort has been made to maintain literal accuracy in translation, so that the reader can be assured, that he is reading a translation as true as possible to the original.

Of the poems in this volume, none is more clearly an expression of Schiller's beautiful soul and republican outlook than *The Song of the Bell*. *The Song of the Bell* is, on the one hand, a celebration of the republican principles of the American Revolution, and on the other, a denunciation of the dionysian romantic destructiveness of the French Revolution. In it, Schiller develops the theme that man, though merely mortal, is capable of contributing through his labor to eternal *concordia*, the name which Schiller gives the bell. But, says the poet, this can happen only to the extent that freedom, in contrast to the anarchy of the French Revolution, is premised on natural law. Man is free through his industry and his art, not merely to construct some earthly paradise, which will pass away, but rather, to promote the welfare of humanity. It is this work, and this alone, the work of love (*agapē*), which makes man worthy of his Creator.

In a commentary on the French Revolution, the historical subject of *The Song of the Bell*, Schiller clearly presents the relationship between beauty and political freedom: "Freedom, political and civil, remains ever and always the holiest of all possessions, the worthiest goal of all striving, the great rallying point of all culture; but this glorious structure can be raised only upon the firm basis of an ennobled character and before a citizen can be given a constitution, one must see that the citizen be himself soundly constituted."

Indeed, it is to develop just such a sound constitution in this nation's citizenry, which is our purpose in publishing these works of Friedrich Schiller in America today.

—William F. Wertz, Jr.
August 14, 1988

# POETRY AND *AGAPĒ*

## *Reflections on Schiller and Goethe*

BY HELGA ZEPP-LAROUCHE
CHAIRMAN, SCHILLER INSTITUTE

About the immortality of our national poet Friedrich Schiller there can be no doubt. So it is quite possible for us to imagine that, since he is immortal, he might be alive today, and that he is just now looking around in Germany. What he thought of the potential of the German people, he let us know in the sketch for his poem, *German Greatness*, for example. To judge from this high idea, he would probably be horrified about the German reality of today. He would find all too many of the maladies once again in exacerbated form, which he had written about in the *Aesthetical Letters*, especially the coincidence of an enervation of leading strata and a degeneration of entire population groups.

What advice would Schiller give us today? Without any doubt, Germany today is in a confounded situation, and the country's special strategic and geographical position is certainly one of the most difficult conceivable in the world. It is therefore not entirely incomprehensible if many of its better, thinking citizens are threatening to succumb to

---

This article was originally published in the German-language magazine *Ibykus, Zeitschrift für Poesie, Wissenschaft und Staatskunst,* first quarter 1988, No. 23.

resignation when they have to watch as the decision-makers pay obeisance in their unprincipled mediocrity to the presumed new masters.

Yet, the greatest problem does not lie primarily in the admittedly alarming, objective reality, but rather more in the personal, subjective realm. Most Germans today are cut off from those sources which could give them the inner power in this hour of need, to seek positive solutions even in the midst of the most adverse circumstances—German humanist culture and especially the heritage of the German classical period. And it would grieve Schiller the most, that his work is so little alive in the population today—not for his own sake, but because there are so many treasures there which could help our poor, shattered people.

More than ever before, Germany today needs its Schiller, despite the *Zeitgeist* which is apparently aimed in the other direction. Just now, we need the beneficent effect which ensues from occupying ourselves with his image of man, and never before was it so urgent that we rise up to his high ideals. The German classics, but especially Schiller's poetry and philosophy, are the soul of the German nation, and if we awaken them to new life today, then all of the laws of the universe speak in favor of a new, magnificent Renaissance issuing from them.

It is only at such extraordinary moments that a person realizes that it is not the things of the mind which move history, but rather the emotions underlying thinking, which determine both the method of thinking, as well as the objects thought about. In this respect, the two emotions of *Agapē* and *Eros* may be considered to be the two fundamental motive forces of all human action and structures of thought. It is either the love of humanity, *Agapē*, which inspires an epoch as its general orientation, or it is self-deification, *Eros*, with all of the emotions which issue from it, which dominates the spirit of an era. And if one looks back, it may easily be established, that all progress in the history of humanity always depended upon the action, often of a single person, moved by *Agapē*, regardless of whether this "action" was a cultural, political, or religious work. As soon as the work of this individual has begun to take effect upon his contemporaries, or even upon many successive generations, we see that the moral character of the people was improved. And, vice-versa, it was often the influence of a single person, whose self-love was displayed as a model by those wielding power, who cast the human species back into barbaric conditions once more.

Of all thinkers who ever expressed themselves in the German language, Friedrich Schiller is the one out of whose work there speaks the most grand and most beautiful love of humanity, indeed, in whose work and life there is nothing to be found, which were not determined by the passionate desire to ennoble the character of people. Schiller is the poet of *Agapē*, in the most primordial sense of the word. Schiller was uniquely capable of combining the interests of virtue stylistically, and in the most playful way, with poetry, so that, although establishing the highest of ideals in the process, naturalness was never violated in the representation. No other poet has been capable of portraying man in greater beauty, nor has any other been in more perfect agreement with the most existential truths of Christian-humanist philosophy. Schiller was able to portray the things most sacred to man, at once with the same inner necessity and freedom, as Raphael with his Madonnas. He was the genius who knew how to draw other persons aloft to his own heights.

If the German population of today has strayed from Schiller, that is not progress, as is sometimes said; it is rather an infinite loss, but, as we may hope, not an irreparable one. For Schiller demanded of poetry nothing less than that it should treat only of universal subjects, those which would lose nothing of their truth in coming centuries. Is it conceivable that we might rediscover those riches for the people of our day, that culture in which

Schiller's work is but the most beautiful jewel, but by no means the only treasure?

## SCHILLER'S VIEW OF HUMANITY

One of Schiller's most lovable character traits, and also the key to understanding the immense power which went forth from him, was his genuinely childlike innocence, which, despite all of the later storms in his life, he never lost. This was the source of his unshakable faith in a better mankind. He had a very happy childhood, as he felt himself, and saw himself frankly as a "favorite of happiness," in contrast to Rousseau and Kant, whose childhood he suspected to have been very unhappy, to judge from their philosophies as adults.

At the end of his stay at the Karlsschule, Schiller said: "The first years of youth perhaps determine the facial features of a person for his entire life, just as they are the foundation of his moral character on the whole." Schiller had the good fortune not only to grow up in a loving family, but he also experienced a spiritualized religiosity, imparted especially by his teachers Jahn, Moser, and Abel, in the tradition of Leibniz's *Theodicy*, which was to form the foundation of his philosophical views throughout his life. While as a youth he had first wanted to become a pastor, he quite soon rejected the narrowness of Lutheran dogmatism. But what stayed with him was a deep and childlike piety, and so in *The Robbers*, he has the character Karl Mohr say: "It was a time when I could not fall asleep if I had not said my prayers at night."

Schiller also had the advantage of studying at one of the best Württemberg Latin schools in the city of Ludwigsburg, particularly through the method of dialogue of his teacher Jahn, who used the Latin texts not only as a means of teaching grammar, but in order to let the world of thought and the conditions of life of antiquity come alive once again. In these early years, Schiller's enthusiasm for classical antiquity, the heroic, and greatness of character, were awakened.

Schiller posed his own idea of history against that of Rousseau. For Rousseau, the golden age of humanity was long past; this innocent childhood had been destroyed by culture, so that this happy condition could only be regained by turning away from culture and returning to a state of nature. Schiller, on the other hand, pointed up the importance of the powers awakened in childhood, and actually saw, in the repetition of childhood at a more mature age, the possiblity of overcoming the inner fragmentation of modern man, and creating a new man, reconstituted in his wholeness. Schiller himself was the best example for this new ideal of humanity, of the person who, with the ideals of his childhood, consciously becomes a personality perfecting itself as life progresses.

It is astounding, with what clarity Schiller set forth the philosophical principles in his first dissertation in the Karlsschule, principles which would later blossom in such rich form from all of his poetry and works. The ideas developed in this dissertation, which, by the way, was rejected because of its content, show Schiller to be a worthy successor to Nicolaus of Cusa and Leibniz, even if their works were imparted to him only indirectly. Thus, in the introduction to his *Philosophy of Physiology,* in the first chapter on the "Determination [*Bestimmung*] of Man," he wrote: "This much, I think, is sufficiently demonstrated, that the universe is the work of an infinite mind, and is designed according to a magnificent plan. Likewise, as through the omnipotent influence of divine power, the universe ran from the plan into reality, and all forces work, and work into one another, like the strings of an instrument running together with a thousand voices into one melody; so should the minds of men, ennobled with the forces of the divinity, discover from the individual effects their cause and intent, from the connection of causes and intentions, to discover the entire grand plan of the whole, to recognize the Creator out of the plan, to love Him, exalt Him, or more briefly, to hear Him

sublimely ringing in our ears: Man exists, that he may strive
to match the grandeur of his Creator, with his very vision
to encompass the world as the Creator encompasses it.—
Godlikeness is the determination of Man. This, his ideal, is
indeed infinite, but the spirit is eternal. Eternity is the
measure of infinity, i.e., it will eternally grow, but never
achieve it."

What would have been more characteristic for Schiller's
thinking than to point to the divine determination of mankind in an essay on physiology in conclusion of his study of
medicine at the Karlsschule? He places the answer to the
question of the meaning of human life foremost, that is,
being like God as the determination of Man, and demands
at the same time, that the person adopt this manner of vision
of his Creator when he looks upon the world. This motif
resounds throughout Schiller's works, according to which
man is only truly man when "he has absorbed the divinity
into his will." And Cusa's idea, too, of the coincidence of
the macrocosms of the created world with the microcosms of
the knowing mind, is addressed, an idea we will encounter
often, worked up in poetic form, for example in the poems
*The Artists* and *Columbus*.

Schiller furthermore writes, "A soul, says one wise man
of this century, enlightened to the degree that it has the
plan of divine providence as a whole before its eyes, is the
happiest of souls. An eternal, grand, and beautiful law has
bound perfection to delight, discontent to imperfection.
That which brings a person closer to that atonement, be it
directly or indirectly, will delight him. That which brings
him away from it, will grieve him, and what grieves him,
he will avoid, but what delights him, for that he will strive.
He will seek perfection, because imperfection causes him
pain; he will seek it because it delights him himself. . . .
Thus it is as much whether I say: The person exists to be
happy; or he exists to be perfect. He is only then perfect,
when he is happy. He is only then happy, when he is
perfect."

Nicolaus of Cusa expressed the same idea when he said the person is entirely human only when he develops all of the capacities with which he is endowed, but if he does not do this, his existence would be diminished.

And Schiller's words once more: "Yet another law, one beautiful and wise, a branch of the first, bound the perfection of the whole with the happiness of the individual human being with human being, yea, human being with animal, by the bond of universal love. Love, therefore, the most beautiful and most noble force in the human soul, the great chain of sentient nature, is nothing but the exchange of myself with the being of a fellow human being. . . .

"And why universal love: Why all the delights of universal love?—Alone out of this latter fundamental intent, to promote the perfection of one's fellow man. And this perfection, comprehension, research, admiration of the great plan of nature. Yea, ultimately all the delights of the senses, of which one ought to speak in its place, incline themselves, through many bends and apparent contradictions, finally back to the same point. Immutably, the truth remains ever identical to itself: The human being is destined to comprehend, to research, to admire the great plan of nature."

The highest summit worthy of man's aspirations, for Schiller, is perfection, the atonement of the individual with the "great plan of nature." Love is thus nothing else than that we make that person, whom we love, better, because only thereby do we make him happy. Thus, the motive force which promotes both the perfection of the whole as well as the happiness of the individual, is love—*Agapē*. If, accordingly, we win a fellow human being to better understand the universe through the development of his own intellectual capacities, he will come closer to his purpose, to be more similar to God, and thus our love, understood as *Agapē*, has the effect of permitting him to become happier.

Schiller again treated love as the motive force of all progress in the universe in *Theosophy of Julius*, which was first published in a revised form in the *Thalia* in May 1786. There he described it as the calling of all thinking beings in the universe to rediscover its lawfulness. He writes: "Harmony, truth, order, beauty, excellence give me joy, because they transform me into the active condition of their inventor, because they reveal to me the presence of a reasoning, sentient being, and permit me a presentiment of my kinship with this being."

The affinity of the human being with the Creator thus permits him to find joy in the truth, beauty, and so forth, but love is the emotion which permits him to take part in all of this. Schiller goes even further, and says: "I frankly confess that I believe in the existence of an unselfish love. I am lost if it does not exist, I surrender divinity, immortality, and virtue. I have left no proof of these hopes if I cease to believe in love. A spirit which loves itself alone is an atom swimming in immeasurable empty space."

Here, Schiller develops the idea contained in all of his poems. "Thus love—the most beautiful phenomenon in creation endowed with soul, the omnipotent magnet in the world of mind, the source of devotion and of the most sublime virtue—love is but the reflected appearance of this single primal force, an attraction of the excellent, founded upon a momentary exchange of the personality, an exchange of beings.

"If I hate, I deprive myself of something; if I love, I am the richer for that which I love. Forgiveness is to find once again a lost possession—misanthropy is extended suicide; egoism is the supreme poverty of an enervated being."

This "attraction of the excellent" makes it easier for the human being to grow, to develop himself, and, in history, to progress as a species. In the poem *The Artists*, Schiller explains the whole of human history out of this principle. The third strophe reads:

Nur durch das Morgentor des Schönen
Drangst du in der Erkenntnis Land.
An höhern Glanz sich zu gewöhnen,

Übt sich am Reize der Verstand.
Was bei dem Saitenklang der Musen
Mit Süßem Beben dich durchdrang,
Erzog die Kraft in deinem Busen,
Die sich dereinst zum Weltgeist schwang.

Was erst, nachdem Jahrtausende verflossen,
Die alternde Vernunft erfand,
Lag im Symbol des Schönen und des Großen
Voraus geoffenbart dem kindischen Verstand.
Ihr holdes Bild hieß uns die Tugend lieben,
Ein zarter Sinn hat vor dem Laster sich gesträubt,
Eh noch ein Solon das Gesetz geschrieben,
Das matte Blüten langsam treibt.
Eh vor des Denkers Geist der kühne
Begriff des ew'gen Raumes stand,
Wer sah hinauf zur Sternenbühne,
Der ihn nicht ahndend schon empfand?

(Only through beauty's morning-gate did you penetrate
the land of knowledge. Before it becomes accustomed to
greater brilliance, the understanding must practice on allure-
ments: the sound of the muses' strings courses through you
with sweet trembling, nourishing the strength within your
breast that later soars to the soul of the world.

What aging reason found only once millennia had run
their course, already lay revealed to the childish mind in the
symbol of the beautiful and great. Her lovely image bid us to
love virtue; the gentle soul did battle against evil before some
Solon ever wrote down laws, whose methodical cultivation
yields colorless blossoms. Long before the idea of infinite
space stood clearly in the philosopher's mind, who could gaze
at the starry theater, and not immediately intuit it?)

The beauty of nature facilitates our love of the Creator,
the grandeur of the stellar heaven awakens the power of
imagination for the intellectual comprehension of infinity.
There is thus an intimate relationship between the capacity
for emotions and thinking. Just as love reveals all riches to
the human being, its contrary is what severs him from
everything, makes him impoverished. Thus, the question

of intelligence has implicitly become a question of morality, for that for which the person is ready to take responsiblity, that too is what he understands.

Schiller brings this chain of thought to its ultimate decisive point: ". . . Egoism and love divide mankind into two absolutely dissimilar species, the borders between which never flow together. Egoism establishes a mid-point in itself; love plants it outside itself in the axis of rotation of the eternal whole. Love is the co-governing citizen of a flourishing free state. Egoism is a despot in a devastated creation. Egoism plants its seeds for gratitude, love for ingratitude. Love makes gifts, egoism only lends—regardless whether before the throne of adjudicating truth, whether for the pleasure of the next moment, or upon the prospect of a martyr's crown, regardless of whether the interest is to be paid in this life or the other!"

This idea comes up in Schiller's drama, *Don Carlos,* as the Marquis of Posa finds the prince Don Carlos in a pitiful state of mind, because he had forgotten the great ideals of his youth and only pines over his hopeless love for his stepmother. Posa accuses him: "Oh Carlos, how poor you are, how destitute, since you love none but yourself!"

Schiller's early writings, today unfortunately forgotten for the most part, contain hidden within them the key to the poet's thinking, in whatever form it may later be expressed. Schiller's beautiful ideal of humanity has its basis in nothing else than in love, in the sense of *Agapē*. This is that love of God, of humanity, of one's neighbor, whom a person ought to love as he loves himself. It is that tender love for the great idea that mankind will achieve the age of reason, but this tenderness is bound together with that passion, without which nothing great can ever be created. This pure, unselfish love brings Schiller, as if self-evidently, to lay out an image of man in which moral beauty is the maximum of the perfection of character. Since this love is true, its expression is free and natural, it issues from that state of emotion where reason and sensuousness, duty and inclination, coincide, when duty has become nature.

## THE BEAUTIFUL SOUL

About such a person, Schiller says, that he has a beautiful soul. By no means is this the moralizing Kantian, who obtains virtue only in rigid battle against his inclinations pulling him in the contrary direction. Thus, as Schiller was occupying himself with Kant's work, in a letter to his friend Körner on February 19, 1793, he wrote: "Clearly the violence which practical reason [for Kant] exerts, in the moral determination of the will against our instincts, has something insulting and embarrassing about it. Now, we want to see compulsion nowhere, not even when reason exerts it, and we want to know the freedom of nature, too, is respected, because we consider every being from the standpoint of aesthetic judgment to be an end in itself, and because for us, to whom freedom is supreme, it is loathsome and disgraceful that something should be sacrificed to anything else and serve as a means. For that reason, a moral deed can never be beautiful, if we observe the operation through which it is wrested from the distress of sensuousness."

The only use which Schiller allows for Kant's conception of morality is when it briefly comes into effect, when as-yet uneducated emotions threaten to set themselves in opposition to the demands of reason. But that is only a negative assessment: Why, Schiller correctly asks, did Kant write only for the serfs, and not for the beautiful souls? The beautiful souls are beautiful, not because of anything they do, but because they are. For the same reason, Schiller rejected every visible moral utility of a work of art, for this utility could never contribute anything to the beauty of a work; this must instead issue forth out of the nature of an object freely and without compulsion. In *Kallias, or, On the Beautiful*, Schiller describes a moral deed by portraying five variations of the help of a passerby for a person hurt and lying on the side of the road. Schiller lets only the behavior of the very last traveller stand as an example of a morally beautiful deed, because he came to the help of the person stranded and hurt at the wayside, unbidden and without reflection, although it cost him something, and because he did what was his duty with such ease, as if it had been merely his instinct to act that way.

Schiller sees the way toward ennoblement of the individual, upon which all improvement in political affairs depends, in the education of emotions up to those airy heights where those emotions correspond with reason. Only if the individual person perfects himself, will the character of the nation be improved, and only then does political progress occur. In *The Legislation of Lycurgus and Solon*, Schiller writes: "The state itself is never the purpose, it is important only as the condition under which the purpose of mankind may be fulfilled, and this purpose of mankind is none other than the development of all the powers of people, i.e., progress."

And further, "In general, we can establish a rule for judging of political institutions, that they are only good and laudable, to the extent that they bring all forces inherent in persons to flourish, to the extent that they promote the progress of culture, or at least do not hinder it." Schiller's sole motive for publishing his journal, *Die Horen*, was "to promote true humanity." In the Eighth Letter on *Don Carlos*, he wrote about the fundamental ideas on which the drama is based, as the favorite subject of the century, "the most perfect condition of mankind, achievable as it is contained in its nature and in its powers," as "the greatest possible freedom of the individual together with the highest flourishing of the state," or simply, "the proliferation of a more pure, more tender humanity."

## SCHILLER AND THE STUDY OF HISTORY

Schiller, after all, occupied himself intensively for ten years with the study of history, and, in addition to poetry and philosophy, he made accomplishments of genius in this field. His inaugural address as professor of history at the

University of Jena, on the subject of *What Is, and to What End Do We Study, Universal History?* is exemplary, and surpassed all existing theories of history. For Schiller, history was neither the dry chronology of events, nor an academic end in itself. Precisely because of its universal character, Schiller saw the study of history as an excellent means for shaping the personality, in direct contrast to the specialist education even of his time. In the inaugural address, he says: "But one destiny you all share in the same way with one another, that which you brought with you into this world—to educate yourself as a human being—and history addresses itself to this human being."

Schiller's independent historical works were intended not only to impart to the readers knowledge of the great freedom-fighters of various times in history, but also to give them courage for the present. Schiller's great historical dramas are based on this study of history, and added "the infallible key to the most secret accesses of the human soul" to the knowledge of the power of theater. Schiller compared the moral power of theater with religion, with which it shared the task of forming the character of people.

In the foreword to *The Bride of Messina*, Schiller says: "True art does not aim at portraying a transitory play, it seriously intends not merely to transpose a person into a momentary dream of freedom, but to make him really and truly free, and to achieve this by awakening in him a force, exercising and educating it to push the sensuous world, which otherwise weighs upon us but as raw matter, pressing upon us as a blind power, into an objective distance, to transform it into a free world of our mind, and to dominate the material world through ideas."

How else should a person be able to develop himself than through just this power awakened in him; what permits him to grow as a person; what raises him above the intellectual feebleness of mediocrity, and "permits him to love the truth more than any system"? That art has this effect, can be confirmed by anyone who has experienced the potential effect of great dramas or works of music upon an audience, on condition that the artists step back behind the work itself and are able to communicate the same *agapic* excitment which inspired the poet or the composer. The artist who knows how to move the hearts of his audience in that way, makes the people who are his audience free, in fact.

If such a work of art is a tragedy, for example, the viewer sees himself confronted with realities which pose to him questions more profound than those he usually faces in his own life. By identifying himself with the main characters and the theme of the tragedy, he grows beyond himself. The chief characteristic of tragedy is that it demonstrates that the human being is not the sole master of his own fate. Even if he does everything necessity demands of him, summoning up all of his powers, violent developments may intervene, which destroy all of his efforts, and perhaps even his very existence.

Schiller, however, employs just these tragic situations to show that these blows of fate may indeed be capable of destroying a person externally, but, in doing so, they awaken in the character of the drama, and in the viewers, powers of self-assertion and of moral resistance against unjust conditions. It is these extraordinary situations which first demonstrate the true greatness of a person, because they crush those who are only apparently great, just as necessity can bring forth unforeseen heroes. In the *Xenia* dialogue of *Shakespeare's Shadow*, Schiller polemicizes against the pettiness of the poets of his time, and asks: "Whence do you take grand, gigantic fate, which elevates the person when it crushes him?"

So, human greatness lies not in the enjoyment of extraordinary power or a special reputation by virtue of advantages of birth or possessions. It lies instead in that personal heroism which is characteristic of that person who prescribes to himself a great idea, and does not deviate from it even under the most adverse circumstances, or in the behavior of a simple citizen, who, in an emergency, suddenly understands that whether the course of fate can be altered, depends upon his own action.

Such heroic traits are found in individual leading characters in all of Schiller's dramas, from Karl Mohr, through
Posa and Elizabeth, Max and Thekla, down to Gertrud
and Wilhelm Tell. The most beautiful example and most
successful representation of the "warrior angel," however,
is without any doubt the *Maid of Orleans,* Schiller's representation of Joan of Arc: a simple shepherd girl who courageously saves a nation in danger.

It is no coincidence that such heroic figures are found in
all of Schiller's dramas, because they represent the standard
which Schiller thought to be the only one worthy of human
beings, one which he demanded be met by the poet himself,
by the figures he conceived, as well as by people in real
life. Thus, in the *Aesthetical Letters,* he wrote about the
requirements of his own time: "Particularly now, it is creative political work that occupies nearly all spirits. The
events in this last decade of the 1700's are, for philosophy,
no less demanding and important, than is trading for the
man of the world. . . .

"A law of the wise Solon condemned the businessman
who chose no party in a revolt. Always when there had been
an incident, in response to which this law could have been
used, it seemed to be like the present, where the great
destiny of mankind is brought into question, and where
man, therefore, as it seems, cannot remain neutral, without
being guilty of indifference to what must be most holy for
mankind, to be responsible. . . ."

For Schiller, the idea that someone could be neutral,
or hide his views out of cowardly duplicity with respect to
the great issues of history, was an outrage. In this respect,
he took the biblical standpoint, that "the Devil will take
those who are 'lukewarm.' " This may well be one of the
reasons why the liberals of our day like Schiller so little.

## GOETHE, POET OF *EROS*

When one speaks about the German classical period,
Schiller and Goethe are the first names which come to mind

as far as poetry is concerned, although there are other personalities who contributed more than Goethe to shaping the humanist spirit of the classical period, such as Wilhelm von Humboldt, who was much, very much closer to Schiller with respect to his ideal of humanity.

At first glance, one might be inclined to attribute tragic elements to Schiller's life: He died young, at the age of 45; he had to fight his entire life against hard, objective circumstances; and all too often, illness made his work difficult. Goethe, on the other hand, lived a long life, was always well provided with material goods, could do and let lie whatever he wanted, and everything seemed easier for him. And yet, Schiller was the happier of the two, and Goethe by far the poorer.

It is well known that Goethe was heartlessly indifferent to the fate of the nation, and Solon's wise law certainly applied to him. At the time when Germany was threatened with utter defeat under the assault of Napoleon's imperialist war campaigns, Goethe, unmoved, wrote the *Affinities,* a rather uninteresting piece about an exchange of partners, which appears in a favorable light only in comparison with today's soap operas. In 1811 he was still praising Napoleon, while during the entire scope of the Liberation Wars, he had nothing to say about this most sublime moment in German history, and remained utterly cut off from the general excitement.

What was the reason for this coolness toward ideals, for which the heart of every ardent patriot was inflamed? Goethe is the perfect example of an extraordinarily gifted person, who had the talent to become a genius, but who lacked the moral strength to realize this potential. What stood in his way was, quite simply, his vanity. The beauty of many of his lyric poems is incontestable, but what source does this beauty draw on? It was love, but not in the sense of *Agapē,* but of *Eros.* According to Goethe's view, informed by his study of antiquity, *Eros* was the heavenly, productive power of life, the drive for pleasure and pain, to whose impulses one must at once surrender, as if to a higher authority.

   This is why Goethe generally felt inspired to compose poetry only when he had just been overcome by a new infatuation, or had received some other external impulse which satisfied his need for attention. As a consequence, his poetic production was somewhat left to chance. If there were no external impulse, he often had to go through "dry periods," as long as twelve years (!) before his acquaintance with Schiller inspired him once again. That Goethe composed beautiful poems, especially in the lyrics of his youth, cannot be denied. One such beautiful poem which shows Goethe from his sympathetic side is the *May Festival*, one of the *Sesenheimer Lieder*, the poems written just as he had fallen in love with Friedericke Brion.

Wie herrlich leuchtet
Mir die Natur!
Wie Glänzt die Sonne!
Wie lacht die Flur!

Es dringen Blüten
Aus jedem Zweig
Und tausend Stimmen
Aus dem Gesträuch.

Und Freud' and Wonne
Aus jeder Brust.
O Erd', O Sonne!
O Glück, O Lust!

How splendidly doth nature
Shine forth to me!
How glistens the sun!
How laugh the fields!

Blossoms burst from
Every branch
And a thousand voices
From the bush.

And joy and bliss
From every breast.
O Earth, O Sun!,
O happiness, O delight!

The *May Festival* expresses supreme jubilation. The soul and nature (O Erd', O Sonne, O Glück, O Lust) are moved by the same fundamental force, a pantheistic idea, which is to be found in all of Goethe's work. The last lines, too, sound quite beautiful:

Wie ich dich Liebe
Mit warmem Blut,
Die du mir Jugend
Und Freud' und Mut

Zu neuen Liedern
Und Tänzen gibst.
Sei ewig glücklich,
Wie du mich liebst!

As I love you
Warm-bloodedly,
You who give me youth
And joy and hearten [me]

To new songs
And dances.
Be ever happy,
As you love me!

But, unfortunately, there is no truth in them, since just because the girl who inspired this poem was so dumb to have loved Goethe, she was to be unhappy all her life, when he left her soon thereafter. That the crucial point for Goethe was not so much the happiness of the beloved as the pleasure of the conquest, becomes clear from another well-known poem, written in the same year. And there we read:

Und der wilde Knabe brach
's Röslein auf der Heiden.
Röslein wehrte sich und stach,
Half ihm doch kein Weh und Ach,
Mußt' es eben leiden.
Röslein, Röslein, Röslein rot,
Röslein auf der heiden.

And the rough boy picked
The little rose on the heath.
The rose defended herself and pricked,
But her woes and ahs were in vain,
She just had to bear it.
Rose, rose, little red rose,
Little rose on the heath.

As if the reference were necessary, Goethe suddenly speaks of Röslein (little rose) no longer as "it," but as "she," no "woe" or "ah" could help her—the poor girl. You see, *Eros* can be quite brutal.

What anguish and desperation erotic perplexity may lead to, was hardly given more accurate artistic expression than by Schubert in his musical composition to *Gretchen at the Spinning Wheel* from Goethe's *Faust*. Gretchen speaks these words after Faust has seduced her, and the other side of the coin of erotic emotion makes its appearance, i.e., the inner strife, anxiety, and desperation. The immense tension expressed in the music of Schubert's song betrays more than the words alone ever could, and the song reveals an astonishing depth of comprehension of the composer, who had just reached his nineteenth year!

Meine Ruh' ist hin,
Mein Herz ist schwer;
Ich finde sie nimmer
Und nimmermehr.

My peace is gone
My heart is heavy;
I will find it never
And nevermore.

Goethe himself commented on *Eros* as the driving force of all action in an explication of the poem *First and Last Words. Orphic*, and wrote to explain the strophe titled *Eros*: "By this notion, everything one might possibly conceive of is comprehended, from the most quiet inclination to the most passionate frenzy; here, there join together the individual Daimon and the seducing Tyche; the person seems to be obeying only himself, allowing sway to his own desires, pandering to his own instincts, and yet there are fortuitous elements which intercede, extraneous things which divert him from his way; he believes he has grabbed hold of something, yet he is the one captured; he believes he was won, yet he is already lost."

For Goethe, the demonic in a person was his inborn character, which is his fate, and which he must necessarily obey. If one investigates the deeper layers of Goethe's character, one discovers that *Eros*, "pandering to his instincts," "up to passionate frenzy," and the demonic, are closely connected—*Eros* is the emotion corresponding to the satanic.

Schiller perceived this character trait of Goethe's very precisely, and often spoke about it. In a review in the journal *Allgemeine Literatur-Zeitung*, of Goethe's drama *Egmont*, in which the demonic in human beings is graphically portrayed, Schiller correctly remarked, that *Egmont* was no masterpiece. He noted that the historical Egmont was far more tragic and passionate than what Goethe had made of him. Goethe had sinned "against nature and truth."

The reason for Schiller's criticism lay in the utterly contrary notions the two had of poetry and their image of man. Schiller wrote to Körner on September 12, 1788: "And his entire character is different from mine from the outset, his world is not mine, and the way we think appears to be utterly different." Although he respected Goethe's all-encompassing education, he remained ever critical of what Goethe produced, and repeatedly said, that "Goethe never had a moment of effusion" even toward his closest friends. He would make his existence known, Schiller said, charitably, but only as a god, without giving of himself, which was egotistical to a very high degree, and calculated entirely toward the enjoyment of self-love. This was a state of mind, Schiller wrote, in which it was impossible that Goethe was happy, but it would make him, too—Schiller—unhappy to be often in Goethe's company.

Once he went so far as to write the following to Körner: "Mankind ought not allow one with such a character to appear among it. He is despicable to me for that, although I love his mind with all my heart and think highly of him." Another time, after a visit with Goethe, he wrote again to Körner, that Goethe, as a human being, utterly lacked the sympathetic way of being committed to an idea. To Goethe, wrote Schiller to his friend, philosophy was something too subjective, and that is where argument and conviction stopped. Goethe's way of thinking was too sensuous, and "he fingers too much."

The picture resulting from his work and the reflections of his contemporaries, shows Goethe to be in fact, and in more than one respect, Schiller's counterpole. Of course, one must understand the relationship between the two poets from the standpoint of the time in which they lived, and take as a measure for each of them the immense accomplishments in language and comprehensive education. But what did each of them create on the basis of this background, in the face of the moral decadence of their time?

While Schiller demanded of the artist that he ennoble himself to become the ideal which he portrays before he might dare to have an effect upon his audience, Goethe made no such demands upon himself. For Schiller, the character of a human being was more important than the poet, while Goethe enjoyed being celebrated as the "prince of poets," captivating people with his multifaceted talents.

The judgment on Goethe must be even more crushing, when one considers the totality of his dramatic work. While Schiller, exclusively, brought only "the great issues of mankind" upon the stage, all of the themes which Goethe treated were outright petty. The male characters in particular cast a very desolate light upon their author. There is no single hero figure. Instead, debauched milksops are put on the stage for the first time; yes, in a certain way, Goethe is the great grandfather of the sentimental Don Juans who have dominated modern poetry since then.

Goethe's main male characters, Werther, Wilhelm Meister, Faust, Egmont, Weißlingen, Ferdinand, Tasso, and so on, are all narcissistic, effeminate Don Juans, who really only need women to bolster their vanity. In reality, they are puffed-up weaklings. And Goethe's female figures are either victims, or manipulative or silly characters, suitably setting the witty male egoists in the right light. No, nothing great can be found in such characters, and so, from Goethe's effeminate self-adulating creatures to today's "softies" and "wimps" of our contemporary so-called authors, there was a clear path: one heading steeply downhill.

## GOETHE'S *FAUST*

More than anything else, however, the key to understanding Goethe is the *Faust* poem, which Goethe worked on for a number of decades. It is, and, among other things, a documentation of his own self-image. Goethe himself is Faust, and he is talking about himself when he says to Wagner:

FAUST: Du bist dir nur des einen Triebs bewußt;
O lerne nie den andern kennen!
Zwei Seelen wohnen, ach! in meiner Brust,
Die eine will sich von der andern trennen.
Die eine hält, in derber Liebeslust,
Sich an die Welt mit klammernden Organen;
Die andre hebt gewaltsam sich vom Dunst
Zu den Gefilden hoher Ahnen.
O gibt es Geister in der Luft,
Die zwischen Erd' and Himmel herrschend weben,
So steiget nieder aus dem goldnen Duft
Und führt mich weg, zu neuem, buntem Leben!

You are possessed by only one passion;
Oh learn to know no others!
Two souls are housed, ah! in my breast,
And one seeks to sever me from the other.
The one holds, in rude pleasure of love,
Onto the world with clasping organs;
The other lifts itself forcefully from the haze
To the fields of lofty heritage.
Oh if there be spirits in the air,
Swaying in potency between earth and heaven,
Come down below from the golden vapor
And lead me on the way, to new, colorful life!

Now, the one soul speaks for itself, the image of "rude pleasure of love" with "clasping organs" is ugly enough, and the other turns toward magic with the appeal for new excitements, new titillations for those smothered by boredom, who wish to live only for the pleasure of the moment. Goethe had also written:

Kannst dem Schicksal widerstehen;
Aber manchmal gibt es Schläge.
Will's nicht aus dem Wege gehen,
Ei, so geh du aus dem Wege!

You can resist fate;
But sometimes there are blows.
If it won't get out of your way,
Oh, then you get out of its way!

Get out of fate's way—That is not a proposal made to heros, but it is indeed one for *schlemiehls*. And he also wrote:

Willst du dir ein hübsch Leben zimmern,
Mußt dich ums Vergangne nicht bekümmern;
Das wenigste muß dich verdrießen;
Mußt stets die Gegenwart genießen,
Besonders keinen Menschen hassen
Und die Zukunft Gott überlassen.

If you wish to make a beautiful life for yourself,
You must not worry about the past;
Vex yourself the least;
You must instead enjoy the present,
Particularly hate no men
And leave the future to God.

When the pleasure of the moment becomes a value, the moral standard is obviously lost. Even more problematic is a side of Goethe's philosophy expressed in the following lines:

Geh! gehorche meinen Winken,
Nutze deine jungen Tage,
Lerne zeitig klüger sein!
Auf des Glückes großer Waage
Steht die Zunge selten ein:
Du mußt steigen oder sinken,
Du mußt herrschen und gewinnen,
Oder dienen und verlieren,
Leiden oder triumphieren,
Amboß oder Hammer sein.

Go! Listen to my advice,
Utilize your youthful days,
Learn early to be cunning!
On Fortune's great scales
The tongue is seldom a guarantee:
You must rise or sink,
You must conquer and win,
Or serve and lose,
Suffer or triumph,
Anvil or hammer be.

"Anvil or hammer be"—this is a thoroughly oligarchical way of looking at things. It is crude Darwinism, and the same dubious worldview of the mafia and all totalitarian regimes. It is the same mentality which attracted Goethe more to Napoleon than to the patriots of 1813. To pledge oneself only to the pleasure of the moment, and to enter a pact with the devil to that purpose, is that not the core of the immorality of all times, then, as much as today? It is the essence of that which makes satanism in the world possible.

Even if the Faustian pact with the devil seems at first glance to have no connection with the existentialist thirsting for pleasure and the liberal accommodation to the path of least resistance (just get out of the way), the inner connection is yet all the more obvious. For the name of Satan is temptation, and that is precisely the form Mephistopheles' appearance takes. It is the problem of oligarchical power-elites, who want to stay on the side of the hammer at any price, and their only concern is to get out of the way of anything which might endanger this position and reduce the pleasure of the moment.

Since this kind of thinking refuses to acknowledge the existence of a natural law as a higher lawfulness, the consequences of arbitrary power appear to be fortuitous, and as a result, there is a greater propensity to believe in "luck," astrology, and magic. This is especially the case when one has the machinery of deception under one's own control, as Schiller describes this in *The Ghost-Seer* (*Der Geisterseher*), for example.

That Goethe worked up the legend of Faust in this way, rather than doing it differently, is doubtlessly a reflection of his character, for the story had been known for a good 300 years, and was originally intended to be a comparison with the fall of Lucifer, in which Faust ends in disgrace. In the second part of *Faust*, Goethe abolishes just this disgrace, saves Faust in a mystical way, and lets Faust challenge God with impunity, and even glorifies the deed.

Goethe's version of *Faust* thus corresponded directly to the philosophy of the modern Enlightenment, but also that of the Romantics, which was aimed not only at exterminating the moral influence of the Church, but also the image of mankind of so-called German idealism, based on similar principles.

Already in the legendary version, Faust represented intellectually anti-church science and education, a trait which was to become dominant in Goethe's version. Goethe thereby created one of the most crucial points of reference for the gnostic satanism of today, and since then the battle between humanism and scientific materialism, or so-called "pure" science, has taken on many forms. It appeared, though not for the last time, in the form of Nazi ideology against the German classics, but just as much in the form of communism against Christianity.

The crucial point at issue in all of these succeeding forms is that of the image of man and the question of morality in social life, as well as in politics. Either the person is moved by *Agapē*, and acts as a beautiful soul for the improvement of the conditions of mankind, or he lets himself be driven by *Eros*, and does everything to satisfy his own self-love— even if he has to sell his soul to the devil. How present this problem is, becomes abundantly clear from an interview which the liberal foreign minister of the Federal Republic of Germany, Hans-Dietrich Genscher, gave on the subject. There still are people, Genscher said, who speak of the Soviet Union as "the Empire of Evil," but the Germans have something Faustian about them in any case, and so they might as well try to make a deal.

The fateful question for the German nation today can indeed be put in the following context: Whether we decide, under extremely precarious circumstances, to enter a Faustian pact with the devil; or whether there is still an echo of the greatness of Schiller among us, and whether moral resistance stirs in us, precisely in these times of need, from which alone that heroic courage can emerge, which is necessary to save a nation which has succumbed. It is an occasion of hope, that the power of love is richer than the poverty of self-love, and we owe it to our Schiller, that we not prove to be a small species in this situation.

## Scenes in Schiller's Life

*Solitude, the military academy in Baden-Würtemberg where Schiller spent his youth under tyrannical conditions. Here he wrote* The Robbers.

*A plaster cast of Friedrich Schiller and his wife Charlotte in the small church where they were married in Jena.*

*A bust of Schiller outside the classroom where he delivered his first lecture on Universal History at Jena.*

*The two-story tower which served Schiller as his study while professor at Jena Univerity.*

*The Schiller house in Weimar, which has been restored since German reunification.*

*Statue of Schiller and Wolfgang von Goethe in front of the theater in Weimar.*

*The Jena gravesite of Schiller, to which his remains were moved to protect them during World War II. After the war, his remains were returned to Weimar where he was buried in a crypt next to Goethe.*

## The Beloved Poet of Freedom—in Germany . . .

*This Schiller statue stands outside the Berlin Theater.*

*Schiller statue in Mannheim, where his early dramas were performed.*

*This Schiller statue graces the theater grounds in Wiesbaden, Germany.*

## ... and in America

*Schiller statue in a Chicago park. German settlers in America brought their Poet of Freedom with them.*

*The New York Central Park bust of Schiller.*

*A copy of the statue of Schiller and Goethe from Weimar stands in the German Cultural Garden in Cleveland, Ohio.*

*Celebrating Schiller's 225th Birthday in 1984 . . .*

*At its founding in 1984, the Schiller Institute called for worldwide celebrations of Schiller's 225th birthday, on Nov. 10.*

*Planting a linden tree in Mannheim in the park where the statue of Schiller stands.*

*Joan of Arc in downtown Washington, D.C. joins the festivities.*

*In Chicago, a Schiller birthday parade in the land of Lincoln.*

*and ten years later, his 235th birthday*

*A wreath is laid at the poet's statue in New York's Central Park celebration in 1994.*

*Reciting the "Ode to Joy" in Leesburg, Va.*

*Schiller is recited in downtown Chicago as part of a demonstration during the 235th birthday festivities.*

Wilhelm Tell *was staged by the Schiller Institute in Stockholm, Sweden . . .*

*and in Seattle, Washington, at the Institute's 1984 celebration of Schiller's birthday.*

The Parasite *was performed in Virginia and New Hampshire by a Schiller Institute cast in 1988, using the translation in this volume.*

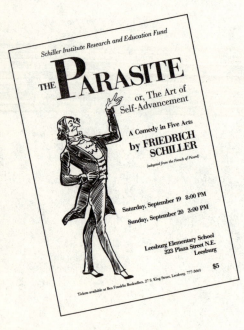

# FRIEDRICH
# SCHILLER
## *Poet of Freedom*

# POETRY

# POETRY

# *From the Anthology of 1782*

## TO THE SPRING

Be welcome, beauteous stripling!
Thou bliss of nature's vale!
With thy full flower basket
Be welcome, on the dale!

Oh! Oh! thou art returning!
And art so fair and sweet!
And heartily we're gladden'd,
To hasten thee to meet.

Rememb'rest still my maiden?
Oh, dear, indeed must thou!
There I was lov'd by the maiden,
And the maiden loves me now!

For the maiden many a flower
Requested I from thee—
I come once more entreating
And thou?—thou giv'st it me?

Be welcome, beauteous stripling!
Thou bliss of nature's vale!
With thy full flower basket
Be welcome, on the dale!

*William F. Wertz, Jr.*

# HYMN TO THE INFINITE

'Twixt the Heaven and earth, high in the airy sea,
In the cradle o'th' storm borne am I by a peak,
 Storm clouds tower
 'Neath me to loose their power,
Dizzily round me my glances run,
And I think of thee, Eternal One.

Thine own shuddering pomp lend to the finite now,
Terrible Nature! Thou, who art infinitude's
 Giant daughter,
 Be my mirror o' Jehovah!
Of his God to the rational worm
Sing like an organ superbly, storm!

Hark! it singeth—On th' rocks, how it resounds below!
Howling the hurricane utters Zebaoth's name.
 Here 'tis written
 With the stylus o' th' lightning:
O ye *creatures, do you know* me?
Spare us, Master! we do know thee.

*William F. Wertz, Jr.*

# FLOWERS

Children of the sun arisen,
Flowers of the deck'd out plain,
Ye for joy and mirth are risen,
Nature's love ye did obtain.
Beauteous robe with light embroider'd,
Beauteous Flora hath you broidered
With the hues of godly light.
Lovely springtime children, moan ye!
Living *soul* to you denied she,
And ye dwell yourselves in night.

Nightingale and lark are singing
To you love's delightful prize,
Juggling sylphs are also swinging
On your womb in loving wise.
Did the daughter of Dione
Not incurve your cup's corona
Swelling to the seat of love?
Tender springtime children, weep ye!
*Love*, alas, to you denied she,
To you feelings blest above.

But hath mother's words, stern spoken,
Banish'd me from Nanny's view,
When to her as love's soft token
In my hands I gather you,
Language, spirit, heart, existence,
Silent heralds of sweet grievance,
To you pours this harmony,
And the mightiest God in heaven
To your silent leaves hath given
His sublime divinity.

                              *William F. Wertz, Jr.*

## THE PLAGUE
### A *Fantasy*

    Ghastly praise the strength of God
Pestilences, infection wreaking,
That with their gruesome brotherhood
    Through empty gravenight's vale are sneaking.

    Fear lays hold o'th' pulsating heart,
Jerky wince the tendons groaning,
Ghastly smiles the madness in its fearful moaning,
    In howling of trills doth the pain flowing start.

Fury doth roll into bedrooms raving—
Pois'nous fog is 'round deserted cities waving,
    Men—all haggard—dull and wan—
    Swarm into the gloomy land.

Brooding death on muggy air is lying,
Treasure in the filling graves is plying—
    Pestilence thy jubilee.
Deadly silence—grave's full measure
Changes with the roars of pleasure,
    God doth praise Plague dreadfully.

                       *Marianna Wertz*

## 1782–1788

## THE CONFLICT

No, longer with this fight I'll not be striving,
    With Duty's giant task.
Canst thou not quench the heart's own ardent driving,
    Then, Virtue, for this off'ring do not ask.

A vow I've taken, yes, a vow I've taken,
    To tame myself within;
Here is thy wreath, forever have I it forsaken,
    Accept it back and leave me free to sin.

What we've determined, now be torn asunder!
    She loves me—forfeit be this crown of thine!
He's blessed, who, in blissful rapture buried under,
    So swift survives the fall as I have mine.

She sees the worm that gnaws upon my youthful
        blooming,
    And how my springtime flees,
She wonders at the hero's self-denial I'm assuming,
    And my reward she gen'rously decrees.

Mistrust, O beautiful soul, this angel's graces!
    To the offense thy pity armeth me.
Is there in this existence's unmeasured spaces,
    Is there a lovelier reward than *thee*?

Than the offense, that I would e'er be shunning?
    O tyrant destiny!
The sole reward, that ought my virtue to be crowning,
    Is to my virtue's final moment see.

                        *William F. Wertz, Jr.*

# RESIGNATION

I, too, was in Arcadia engender'd,
    There, too, by Nature's art
Upon my cradle oaths of joy were render'd,
I, too, was in Arcadia engender'd,
    Yet tears were all my short spring did impart.

The May of life blooms once, there are no others,
    The bloom doth fade 'fore me.
The silent God—oh weep for me, my brothers—
The silent God my torch's light now smothers,
    And doth the vision flee.

Already on thy darksome bridge I'm standing,
    Dreadful Eternity.
To thee my fortune's warrant I am handing,
Receive it from me with unbroken banding,
    I know naught of felicity.

Before thy throne I my laments am laying,
    Thou Justice, veil enthrall'd.
On yonder star did go a happy saying,
Thou art here thron'd with scales of judgment weighing
    And by thyself Requiter call'd.

Here, 'tis said, terrors are on evil closing,
    And joys for honest men do wait.
The windings of the heart thou'll be exposing,
The enigmatic Providence disclosing
    And reck'ning with the sorrowful create.

Here open house to refugees bestowing,
    Here ends at last the thorny path of strife.
A godlike child, the name of *Truth* avowing,
The many fled, the few were really knowing,
    Restrain'd the ardent bridle of my life:

"In 'nother life I'll give thee compensation,
    Give me thy very youth!
Naught can I give thee but this wise instruction."
I took the the other life as my instruction,
    And all my youthful joys I gave to Truth.

"Give me the woman, to thy heart so tender,
    To me give Laura thine!
Beyond the grave your pains will interest render."
Then, bleeding from a wounded heart I rent her
    And cried aloud and gave her mine.

*"You see that time to yonder shore is flying,
    Fair Nature blooming forth
Stays 'hind her here—a wither'd body—lying.
When earth and heaven crumble, at each other flying,
    By this know thou that now's fulfill'd the oath."

"The debtor's note is drawn upon the dying,"
    The world doth mock anew,
"The Liar, who's on despot's pow'r relying,
Hath shadows for the Truth on thee been plying,
    Thou art no more, when this note doth fall due."

The serpent-band doth mock in brash derision:
    " 'Fore this deceit, that aging consecrates,
Thou tremblest now? What mean thy gods, creation
Of cunning plan, the sick world's sly salvation,
    That wit of man alone necessitates?

*"A conjurer, mere vermin lacking powers
    That might alone allows,
A fire most dreadful, kindl'd in high towers,
To lay a siege to fantasies of dreamers,
    Where torch of lawfulness but darkly glows.

---

* This stanza was eliminated by Schiller in his final edition of the poem

"What future is't, from us the grave's concealing?
    Th' Eternal, with whom thou hast vain discourse?
Rever'd alone, because sly veils are it concealing,
The giant shadow of our fearful feeling
    In hollow glass of conscience's remorse.

"An image false of living form engender'd,
    Time's mummy it be,
By hoping spirit's balm it now is render'd
In lodgings cold beneath the grave it's tender'd,
    This, calls thy fever—immortality?

"For hopes—by their decay the lie is given—
    Thou didst a *certain* good renounce?
Six thousand years has death in silence striven,
Has e'er a corpse from out the tomb arisen?
    Who aught of the Revenger did announce?"

I saw that time to yonder shore is flying,
    Fair Nature blooming forth
Stayed 'hind her here, a withered body, lying,
No dead one came from out his tomb arising,
    And still I trusted in your godly oath.

All of my joys for thee I've sacrificed,
    I throw myself on judge's throne 'fore thee
The scorn of crowds I've heartily despised,
*Thy* goodness only have I greatly prized,
    Requiting one, I claim what's due to me.

"With equal love I love all of my children!"
    An unseen Genius then exclaim'd.
"Two flowers," cried he, "hear ye, mankind's children—
Do bloom for the wise seeker in my garden.
    'Tis *hope* and *pleasure* they are nam'd.

"Who of these flowers *one* doth pluck, be sharing
    The other sister not.
Let him enjoy, who no faith can be bearing.
This truth's old as the world. Who faith hath, be
        forbearing.
    The world's whole hist'ry is the world's just court.

"Thou *hope* hast known, art duly compensated,
    Thy *faith* it was, the fortune given thee.
Thou couldst the wise men have interrogated:
What man hath from the Minute abrogated,
    Gives back then no Eternity."

*Marianna Wertz*

*1788–1805*


## THE FAMOUS WIFE
### An Epistle from One Married Man to Another

I should lament for thee? Curse thou the bond of Hymen
With bitter tears of thy regret?
Why so? Since faithless is thy woman
Who seeks in other's arms to get
What thou to her hast been denying?
Friend, hear another's sorrow and
Now learn how light *thine* own's abiding.

It pains thee, that a second's sharing,
In thine own right?—Oh, enviable man!
*My* wife, to all the human species is belonging.
From Belt up to the Moselle strand,
E'en where the Appenine does stand,
E'en in the father town of fashion,
Will she be sold at ev'ry booth in auction,
Art-critic-like permit inspection,
Must she upon each parcel bearing transport
From every pedant, every coward,
Before the gaze of Philistines must she,
And, as each filthy Aristarch gives orders,
To walk on fired coals or flowers
To honor's temple or to pillory.
One Leipzig man—wish for him God's rebuking!
Takes detailed measurement as she were fortress high,
And offers regions to the populace to buy,
Where 'tis my right *alone* to speak of what they're
    viewing.

*Thy* wife,—Thanks to the canon laws of Justice!—
Thy wife doth know *thy* title is still precious,
She knows *wherefore?* and this is goodly known.
*I'm* but as *Ninon's* husband known.
Thou weepest, that i'th' parterre, and at the Faro-table,
When thou appearest, all tongues sizzle?
O Man of Bliss! Who one day this might be
A cause for praising!—Me, lord brother, me,
At last on me's bestowed a wheysome-cure,
That rare good luck, on her left side I'm sitting—
No eye marks *me*, and every gaze is flitting
Upon my haughty half for sure.

Scarce comes the morningtide,
Yet, now the stairway cracks with blue and yellow
     jackets,
With letters, bales of unpaid postal packets,
All marked: 'Tis to the *Famous* Wife!
How sweet she sleeps!—Yet *dare* I spare her never.
"The newspapers, Madam, from Jena and Berlin!"
The gracious sleeper's eye with lightning opens then,
Her first glance falls—upon the critics' word.
This beautiful blue eye—*to me*
Not e'en one blink!—through wretched paper wanders
     she
('Til one hears from the nursery loud crying),
At last she lays it down, and for her children's calling.

Now the vanity is set,
Yet only half a glance bestows she on her mirror.
A surly and impatient threat
She hurls unto her maid with terror.
The Graces from her dressing table have now left,
In place of graceful angels ever loving,
One sees Erinyes there her locks attending.

Now carriages start rattling near,
And springing from their steps are hired footmen,
The odorous Abbott, the realm's Baron, the Briton,
(Who naught of German can read clear),
Grossing and Company, the Man of Wonder Z**————,
The *Famous* one to hear them now are begging.
A thing, that humbly pushed itself in corner tight,
And husband called, is fashion'bly in sight.
Here, dares to her—be *thy* housefriend so daring?—
The dullest *fool*, the poorest wight,
*How much he doth admire her,* saying;
And doth so right before my sight!
I stand nearby, and wish to be thought courteous,
To beg him dine, which I now must.

At dinner, friend, my first distress begins,
It breaks out over my dear bottles!
With wine from Burgundy, which me my health forbids,
Must for applauses, now wash I their throttles,
My hard-earned bits of bread so fine,
Are spoils for parasites' addiction;
Oh, this unpleasant, cursed malediction,
This *Immortality* doth kill my Rhinegau wine!
The worm upon all fingers, what a printing!
What, thinkst thou, be my thanks?—A shoulder
    shrugging,
A pantomime, an ill-bred, unrefined complainer—
Canst not thou guess?—O, I see clear as life!
That this precious gemstone of a wife
One such orangutan away did cart her.

The springtime comes. On meadows and on pastures
As Nature spreads her colored carpet there,
The flowers dress themselves in freshest green so fair,
The lark doth sing, all life the forest captures—

To her the springtime's void of bliss.
The songstress of the sweetness of sensation,
The beauteous grove, which views our recreation,

Ne'er more speaks to her heart of this.
For nightingales have never learned of reading,
The lilies *do admire* not,
The universal cries for Being
Inspire *her*—a verse of wit is sought.
But no! The season is but fine—for *touring*.
Yet now the Pyrmont must be crowded full!
All over Carlsbad one can hear the raving.
Quick is she there!—'mid crowds so colorful,
Where orders' ribbons and scholastic necklets,
Celebrities of *every* kind,
Like in that barge of Charon, they combined,
To'th' play to pose and bear themselves to markets,
Where secretly from miles they're lured,
From their own injuries, their chastity is cured,
There, friend—Oh, learn to praise thine own
    misfortunes!
There wandered my dear wife, and left me seven
    orphans.

Oh, sparkling was my love's first wedded year!
How soon—alas, away thou fled'st so quickly!
A wife, as none there be nor ever were,
For me enchantment's goddesses bred sweetly,
With lightning soul, with wide-awakened mind
And gently fragile, changeable sensation—
So saw I her, whom hearts held fast entwined,
Like May's day at my side in recreation;
That sweetened word: I love but thee!
Spoke from those pair of eyes so lovely.
So led I her to marriage truly—
Oh, happier could no man be!

Those enviable years, a field flow'ry,
From out this mirror looked on me and smiled,
To me my heaven opened wide.
Soon saw I lovely children 'round me jesting,
Among the ring the fairest *she*,
The happiest of all was *she*,
And *mine* by spirit's harmony,
Through everlasting heart's firm binding.
And then appeared—Oh, may our God condemn him!
A man so *great*, a *real fine wit*.
This man so great did one fine deed!—And ripped
My house of cards completely down from Heaven.

What have I *now*?—Lamentable exchange!
Now 'wakened from delight's far range,
For me, what of this angel is remaining?
A spirit *strong* within a body *soft*,
'Tween man and wife a creature crossed,
Unskillful both in ruling and in loving;
A child with one gigantic weapon,
A thing between baboons and men of wisdom!
So wretchedly unto the *stronger* crawling,
From *beauty's* species did she flee,
From 'top her throne cast downwardly,
Enchantment's holy mysteries from her escaped,
From Cytherea's *Golden Book* erased
For—Just one paper's charity!

*Sheila Jones*

# THE PROVERBS OF CONFUCIUS

## I.

Threefold is the stride of time:
Hesitantly is the future nighing,
Arrow swift the now is flying,
Stands the past in still eternal clime.

No impatience can e'er speed it
In its stride, if it delay.
Neither fear, nor doubt impede it
In its course, if it runs 'way.
No remorse, no magic saying
Can move that which e'er is staying.

Wouldst thou wisely and with pleasure
End the days of life's brief measure,
Take the hesitant to heed,
Not as tool to serve thy deed.
Ne'er as friend the fleeting know,
Nor the ling'ring choose as foe.

## II.

Threefold is the span of space:
Ceaselessly with restless pace
Strives the *length*; i'th' distance soaring
Endlessly the *breadth* is pouring;
Bottomless the *depth* descends.

Thee as image these are given:
Restless forth must thou be driven,
Ne'er stand still and weary be,
Wilt thou the completion see;
Thou in breadth must be extended,

Shall the world be apprehended;
In the depth must thou be going,
Shall the essence thou be knowing.

But persistence guides to th' goal,
But the full to clearness guideth,
In th' abyss the truth resideth.
                    *William F. Wertz, Jr.*

## PEGASUS IN YOKE

Once to a horses mart—to Haymarket maybe,
Where other things to merchandise as yet be changing—
Did bring a poet most hungry
The Muses' steed, to be exchanging.

The Hippogriff did neigh so bright
And in parade did prance with pomp so pretty,
Astonished stood each one and cried:
"The noble, kingly animal! But pity,
That doth an ugly pair of wings its figure fair
Deform! The fairest mailtrain were it gracing.
The breed, the people say, be rare,
Yet who will through the air be racing?
And no man will his coin be losing."
At last a daring farmer stood.
"The wings, indeed," says he, "not useful does one find
      them;
Yet man can always either clip or bind them,
Then is the horse for pulling ever good.
A twenty-pound, on this to risk I'm willing."
The shyster, much amused, the wares now cheaply
      selling,

Agrees at once. "One man, one word!"
And Hans trots freshly with his booty for'd.

The noble beast is now in yoke restrained.
Yet feels it scarce the burden so unwonted,
So runs it forth with flight desires undaunted,
And flings, from noble wrath enflamed,
To chasm's edge, all that the cart contained.
"All right," thinks Hans. "I may be to this beast confiding
Alone no cart. Experience doth cunning make.
Come morn will passengers be riding,
I'll hitch it to the cart the lead to take.
Two horses shall this lively crab for me be saving,
And with the years will fade its raving."

At first it went quite well. The lightly-winged horse
Enlives the old nag's step, and swift the cart is flying.
But now what's this? With one look at the clouds turned
    course,
And 'customed not, the ground with solid hoof to plying,
Forsaking soon the safer cart-wheel trail,
And true to nature's stronger call,
It runs clear through the swamp and moor, tilled field
    and hedges;
An equal frenzy doth th' entire post-team seize,
No call doth help, no rein its haste doth ease,
At last, to wand'rer's fearful ledges,
The wagon, smashed apart from endless jolts,
On steepest summit of the mountain halts.

"That just is not the right way ever,"
Says Hans with face contorted much by doubt.
"So will it be successful never;
Let's see, if this mad dog be brought
Through meager food and work to tether."
The trial will be made. Soon beast with beauty rare,
Before three days did fade around it,

To shadow was reduced. "I have, I have now found it!"
Cries Hans. "Now quick, and hitch it here,
Before the plough beside my strongest steer."

'Tis said, 'tis done. In ludicrous procession,
One sees on plough an ox and winged stallion.
Unwilling mounts the griff and strains with final might
It sinews forth, to take as old to flying.
In vain, delib'rate doth the neighbor stride
And Phoebus' steed so proud to steer must be
    complying.
'Til now, consumed by long resistant course,
The strength from all its limbs is thinning,
From grief, now breaks the noble, godly-horse
To earth it falls and in the dust is spinning.

"Accursed beast!" at last breaks Hans' abuse
Loud scolding out, whilst from him flies a beating.
So you then e'en for ploughing are no use
The rogue sold you to me was cheating.

While yet in him doth rage of anger last,
The whip doth swing, comes cheerful now and fast
A merry fellow on the street with footsteps fleeting.
The zither sounds so nimbly in his hand,
His hair an ornament of yellow
Is plaited through with golden band.
"Whereto, that pair astonishing, my fellow?"
He calls the peasant from afar.
"The bird and ox a *single* rope is binding,
I ask of you, what is that pair!
If for a while you'd be confiding
The horse, to make a test, to me,
Look out, you shall a marvel see!"

The Hippogriff unyoked doth stand,
And smiling doth the young man swing upon its
    haunches.
Then barely feels the beast the master's certain hand,
So gnashes it, the bridle's band
And climbs, and light'ning flashes from inspired glances.
No more the former creature, kingly-wise,
A god, a spirit, doth arise,
Unfurls with sudden stormy splendor
Its grandeur winged, shoots roaring to the sky—
And 'fore a glance can follow nigh,
It glides into the high blue yonder.

*Marianna Wertz*

## THE PLAYING BOY

Frolic, child, in the mother's womb! On the heavenly
    island
Findeth the turbid grief, findeth the sorrow thee not.
Lovingly o'er the abyss do the arms of the mother thee
    hold
And in the effluent grave smilest thou guiltlessly down.
Frolic, innocence lovely! Still is Arcadia 'round thee,
And the nature uncurbed, followeth merry desire;
Still the opulent power createth fictional limits,
And the courage that wills wanteth still duty and aim.
Frolic! Soon shall the labor arrive, the haggard, the
    earnest,
And what the duty commands, courage and joyfulness
    lack.

*Becky Jones*

## IDEALS

So wilt thou faithless from me sever
With thine endearing fantasy,
With thine afflictions, and thy pleasure,
With all relentlessly now flee?
Can nothing, fleeting one, delay thee,
Oh! golden time of life to me?
But vainly, do thy waves now hurry
On down to the eternal sea.

Extinguished are the suns so cheering,
Which once my youthful pathway lit,
Ideals now are disappearing,
Which swelled the heart inebriate.
It is gone by, the sweet believing
In essences my dream did bear,
The raw reality is thieving,
What once so fair, so godly were.

As once, with most imploring raptures
Pygmalion embrac'd the stone,
'Til on the marble's icy features
Sensations glowing sudd'nly shone,
So I with arms of love enwreathing,
In youthful passion Nature press'd,
'Til she herself began to breathing,
To warm upon my poet's breast,

And, sharing in my impulse burning,
The silent one a language found,
The kiss of love to me returning,
And understood my heartbeat's sound;
There liv'd for me the trees, the roses,
To me the silver fount did sing,
And for himself then felt the soulless
From my life's resonating ring.

There issu'd with almighty striving
From narrow breast, a circling All,
To tread forth boldly into living
In deed and word, in shape and call.
So greatly was this world thus moulded
As long the bud kept it in thrall;
So little, ah! has it unfolded,
This little one, how poor and small!

So sprang, bewing'd by courage daring,
Exub'rant in his dreamer's craze,
And unrestrain'd by any caring,
The youthful one into life's ways.
Up to the aether's faintest starlet
Uplifted him the great plan there,
Naught was so high and naught so distant,
Whereto its wings did not him bear.

So was he thence transported lightly,
Naught's for the happy hard to do!
So danc'd before life's cart so brightly
The light and airy retinue!
The Love was there with charming payment,
And Fortune with her wreath of gold,
'Twas Glory, too, in starcrown raiment
And Truth in sunny splendor bold!

But ah! scarce at the journey's midway,
Dispersed all the retinue,
They wander'd faithless from my pathway
And each did other course pursue.
Light-footed Fortune fast was flying,
The thirst for knowledge linger'd on,
A gloomy cloud of doubts was nighing
Around the Truth bedeck'd in sun.

I saw the holy wreath of Glory
Profan'd upon the vulgar crown.
Ah, after brief bloom, all too quickly,
The beaut'ous loving time had flown!
And stiller e'er it grew and ever
More lonely on the rugged road,
Scarce was a single pallid shimmer
By Hope on that dim path bestow'd.

Of all the rustling crowd so merry,
Who waited by me lovingly?
Who solace at my side doth tarry
And to the dark house follows me?
Thou, the thou for all wounds art caring,
Art Friendship's gentle, tender hand,
Life's burden lovingly art sharing,
Thou, whom I early sought and found.

And thou, who happ'ly with her marries,
As she the stormy soul doth charm:
Thou Labor, that which never wearies,
Which slow creates, yet ne'er doth harm,
Which to the edifice eternal
By sandgrain but by sandgrain nears,
Yet surely from Time's debt supernal
Doth cancel minutes, days, and years.

  *Renee Sigerson and Marianna Wertz*

## DIGNITY OF WOMEN

Honor the women! They're roses celestial
Twining and weaving in lives terrestrial,
Weaving the bond of the most blessed love,
Veiled in the Graces' most modest attire
Nourish they watchful the e'erlasting fire
Of lovely feelings with hand from above.

To truth's limits ever endless
Man with wild force doth flee,
Thoughts do drive him ever restless
Onto passion's stormy sea.
Greedy grasps he the eternal,
Silent will his heart be ne'er,
Restless through the stars supernal
Hunts he his dream's image e'er.

But with their glances so magic'ly chaining,
Beckon the women the fug'tive restraining,
Warning him back in their presence anew.
In the mother's most moderate quarters
They have remained yet with modesty's manners,
Nature's daughters, with piety true.

Hostile e'er the man is striving,
With a crushing force doth roam,
Wildly through his life surviving,
Without rest and without home.
What he builds, he ruins later,
Never rests the wishes' strife,
Never, as the head of Hydra
Falls and e'er renews its life.

But they, contented with quieter honor,
Pluck now the women the moment's fine flower,
Nourish it loving and diligently,
They have in their bounded work greater freedom,
Richer than man, too, in districts of wisdom
And in the unending sphere, poetry.

Stern and proudly self-depending,
Knoweth man's cool breast thereof,
Heartily to heart though bending,
Not the godly joy of love,
Knows he naught of souls exchanging,
Not in tears melts he e'er hence,
Steels he in life's battles raging
Harder yet his hardened sense.

But, just as softly from zephyr doth shiver,
Quick as Aolian harp-string doth quiver,
Thus so the feeling-full woman's soul, too.
Image of pain makes her tenderly fearful,
Heaves then the e'er-loving bosom, and tearful,
Beaming the eyes are from heavenly dew.

In the realm where men are ruling
Might defiant right doth have,
With his sword the Scyth'an's proving
And the Persian will enslave.
War be they in fury waging,
The desires both wild and rude,
Eris' voice is hoarsely raging,
Governing, where Charis fled.

But now, so softly, persuasively pleading,
Women with scepter of morals are leading,
Smother they discord, all raging enlight,
Teach they the powers, that hateful develop,
Each in a more loving form to envelop,
And what forever would flee, they unite.

*Marianna Wertz*

# THE VEILED IMAGE AT SAÏS

A younger man, whom Learning's fiery thirst
Propelled to Saïs in far Egypt, there
To master hidden wisdom of the priests,
Already had with hasty mind traversed
A few degrees; his seeker-lust e'er tugged
Him on, and hardly could the hierophant
Appease th' impatient striver. "What have I,
If I've not everything," the youngster spoke.
"Is there perhaps a Lesser here and More?
Then is thy truth, like to the senses' bliss,
Naught but a sum, that one can more or less
Possess and ne'ertheless possess it still?
Is't not unique and indivisible?
Take any tone from out a harmony,
Take any hue from out the rainbow—And
All, that remains to thee, is naught, so long
The tones and colors lack the lovely All."

As they so spoke, they stood alone and still
In a remote rotunda, where unto
The younster's eyes there fell an image, veiled,
Of giant stature. He, in wonderment,
Then glances to the leader and exclaims:
"What is it, that behind this veil doth hide?"
"The truth," is the reply.—"What?" shouts the lad,
"I strive for truth alone, and this is it
Before me, that one thus conceals from me?"

"Discuss that with the Deity," retorts
The hierophant. " 'No mortal man,' says she,
'May raise this veil, 'til I do so myself.
And who with sacrilegious, guilty hand
Doth lift the pure, forbidden veil too soon,
He,' says the Goddess"—"Well?"—

" 'He *sees* the truth.' "
"A most peculiar oracle! And thou,
Then thou hadst never lifted it thyself?"
"I? Truly not! Nor was I tempted to."
—"I grasp it not. If nothing but this thin
Partition separates me from the truth—"
"That, and a law," his leader interrupts.
"More weighty is this flimsy gauze, my son,
Than thou believest—For thy hand 'tis light
No doubt, yet very heavy for thy conscience."

The youth went to his home, all full of thought.
The burning appetite for knowledge steals
His sleep, he tosses feverishly upon
The couch and then at midnight rouses up.
Involuntarily his timid tread
Conducts him to the temple. There he scales
The wall with ease, a plucky leap transports
The daring one to the rotunda's midst.

Now here he stands, the solitary one
Embraced so foully by the lifeless hush,
That only hollow echoes of his steps
Disrupt within the secret, private vaults.
From over through the cupola's op'ning casts
The moon a pallid shine of silver-blue,
And frightful, like a god attending, gleams
The figure in its lengthy veil throughout
The gloomy darkness of the central vault.

He treads up toward it with uncertain step,
Already will the brazen hand go touch
The Holy One, when hot and cool convulse
Throughout his bones and he is thrust away
By unseen arm. "Thou wretch, what wilt thou do?"
So calls a faithful voice within his soul.
"Wilt thou then the All-Holy One thus tempt?
'No mortal man,' proclaimed the oracle's mouth,

'May raise this veil, 'til I do so myself.'
But ne'ertheless did not this same mouth add:
'Who raises up this veil, shall see the truth?' "
"Behind it be, what may! I'll raise it up."
He shouts it with loud voice—"I want to see it."
See it!
Long after him a mocking echo yells.

He speaks it and has stripped away the veil.
"And now," you ask, "what shows itself to him?"
I do not know. Insensible and pale,
The priests discovered him upon the morn
Outstretched before the pedestal of Isis.
And that which he had seen and come to know,
His tongue has ne'er confessed. Eternally
Departed was his life's serenity,
His grief swept him into an early grave.
"Woe unto him," this was his warning word,
When pressed by questioners impetuous,
"Woe unto him, who comes to truth through guilt:
For him 'twill be delightful nevermore."

*Daniel Platt*

## THE PHILOSOPHICAL EGOIST

Hast thou the suckling beheld, who, is of love yet
  unconscious
That doth warm him and rock, sleeping from arm into
  arm,
Wand'ring, 'til by the call of the passions youth doth
  awaken
And with consciousness flash dawning doth light up his
  world?
Hast thou the mother beheld, when she dear one's sweet
  slumber

Buys with her very own sleep and for the dreaming one
    cares,
With her very own life she feedeth the flame as it
    trembles
And with the care itself caring is for her reward?
And thou blaspheme the Nature so great, that, now babe
    and now mother,
Now receiving, now gives, but through necess'ty
    persists?
Self-sufficient want thou from beaut'ous ring to withdraw
    thee,
That each creature to creature arrays in intimate band?
Wilt, thou poor one, stand thee alone and through
    thyself only,
When with the pow'rs' exchange, stands the eternal
    itself?

*Janet West*


## TO A YOUNG FRIEND
### As He Dedicates Himself to Philosophy

Many difficult trials the young man of Greece had to pass
    through,
Ere the Eleusian house, welcomed the one who's been
    tried.
Art thou matured and prepared, to enter the holy
    temple,
Where the suspected great wealth, Pallas Athene
    secures?
Know'st thou yet, what thee there awaits? How dear is
    thy purchase?
That for an uncertain good, payest thou with what is
    sure?
Feelest thou power enough, to fight the most difficult
    battles,
When thy reason and heart, senses and thoughts
    disunite?

Courage enough, to wrestle with doubt, the immortal
  Hydra,
And to manly attack, th' enemy inside thyself?
With an eye that is healthy, a heart of innocence holy,
To unmask the deceit, tempting thee as if the truth?
Flee, if thou art not secure with the leadership in thine
  own bosom,
Flee, the enticing abyss, ere be consumed in the maw!
Several went for the light and only in deep night have
  fallen;
There in the twilight's glow childhood wanders secure.

Bruce Director

## THE GUIDES OF LIFE
### (*Originally titled* The Beautiful and the Sublime)

Two kinds of genius there be, which thee through life do
  accompany.
Good for thee, if as one helping they stand at your side!
With enjoyable play the one for thee shortens the
  journey,
Lighter for thee becomes duty and fate on his arm.
'Twixt discussion and jokes he escorts thee up to a
  chasm,
Where at eternity's sea shudd'ring mortality stands.
Here receives thee determined and grave and silent the
  other,
With a gigantic arm carries he thee o'er the deep.
Never trust thee to *either* alone! Entrust to the former
Thine own *dignity* not, nor to the latter thy *luck*!

Dennis Speed

# THE MAIDEN FROM AFAR

Within a vale, a herdsman's dwelling
Appeared with every fresh new year
Soon as the first lark's song was swelling,
A maiden, wonderful and fair.

She was not born within the valley,
Whence she did come, that no one knew,
And quick her traces hence did sally,
So soon the maiden once withdrew.

Exalting was her blessed presence,
All hearts grew wide, that her did see,
Yet dignity, a lofty essence
Discouraged close proximity.

She brought with her both fruits and flowers,
Grown ripe upon another plain,
And in another sunlight's showers,
In nature's far more joyful reign.

And to each one a gift was sharing,
To one the fruit, the blooms to some,
The youngster and the graybeard faring,
Each one went gifted to his home.

And welcome were all guests there present,
Yet when approached a loving pair,
To them she gave the finest present,
The loveliest of flowers there.

*William Ferguson*

## CERES' LAMENT

Is the lovely spring appearing?
Has the earth again grown young?
Sunny hills new green are bearing,
And the crust of ice is sprung.
In the river's sky-blue mirror
Zeus doth laugh without a cloud;
Mildly blows the winged zephyr,
Tender sprig with buds is proud.
Songs awaken in the bowers
And the Oread speaks fair;
Once again return thy flowers,
Daughter thine returneth ne'er.

Ah, how long 'tis, that I wander
Seeking over hill and dale!
Titan, all thy beams from yonder
Sent I down the cherished trail;
Yet to me proclaim'd one never
Of the dear beloved face,
And the day, that findeth ever,
Of the lost one found no trace.
Hast thou, Zeus, then from me snatched her?
Hath, by her attractions drawn,
To the swarthy Orkus' river
Pluto with him dragged her down?

Who will on those dismal beaches
Message of my grief relay?
From the land the skiff e'er pushes,
Yet but shades doth it convey.
On no blessed eye's bestowed
That nocturnal region e'er,
And so long the Styx hath flowed,
It no living form did bear.
Deep are thousand paths descending,

None ascendeth back to light,
Of her tears no witness sending
For the anxious mother's sight.

Mother, who of Pyrra's mortal
Stem art born into this world,
May, through grave's e'er-flaming portal
Follow the beloved child;
Only who Jove's dwelling shareth,
Neareth not the gloomy strand,
Only holy ones e'er spareth,
Fates, your stern and stringent hand.
Hurl me into night of darkness
Out of heaven's gold domain!
Honor not my rights as goddess,
Ah! they are the mother's pain!

Where she is with husband dreaded,
Joyless throned, climb'd I e'en,
There with gentle shades I treaded
Gently 'fore the ruling queen.
Ah, her eye, with teardrops weighing,
Seeks the golden light for naught,
Into distant regions straying,
On the mother falls it not—
Till the joys she doth discover,
Till her breast with breast allies
And, as sympathy wins over,
E'en the rugged Orkus cries.

Idle wish! Lamenting empty!
Quiet in the track so sure
Rolls the day's safe carriage stead'ly,
Zeus's rulings e'er endure.
He doth from that dark obscureness
Turn his blessed head away;
Once seized hold of in night's darkness,
Ravish'd from me she doth stay,

Till the river's darkened billows
From Aurora's colors glow,
Iris into Hell's midst follows
Drawing on her lovely bow.

Is there naught of her remaining?
No sweet pledge reminding me,
That the distance love's retaining,
Of her hand no trace there be?
Fasten there no knots of loving
Twixt the mother and the child?
Twixt the dead ones and the living
Is no bond uniting styled?
No, she's not escaped fully!
No, we are not full in breach!
For the ever-highest duly
Hath to us yet granted speech!

When the springtime's young do wither,
When from northern air's cold rush
Leaf and flower lose their color,
Sadly stands the naked bush,
Take I then the highest living
From Vertumnus' bount'ous horn,
Offered that the Styx be giving
Me the seeds of golden corn.
Sad, I sink it in earth's bosom,
On the child's heart is it lain,
That from it a word doth blossom
Of my love, and of my pain.

Now the hours' even dancing
Happ'ly doth the spring renew,
From the sunshine's love-filled glancing
Will the dead be born anew;
Germs, which perished to the viewing
In the cold womb of the earth,
In bright color's realm renewing,

Fight to free themselves with mirth.
When the stem to heaven guideth,
Seeks the timid root the night,
Equally her care divideth
'Tween the Styx, the Aether's might.

Rest they half among the perished,
Half among the living sphere—
Ah they are my heralds cherished,
Voices sweet from Coc'tus drear!
Held like she herself in prison
In the dreadful gorge's sway,
From the shoots of spring arisen
Lovely mouth to me doth say:
Far from golden daylight's greeting,
Where the shadows sadly go,
Loving bosoms yet are beating,
Hearts yet tenderly do glow.

O, so may you greet with pleasure,
Children born of pastures new,
May your cup be over measure
From the nectar's purest dew.
I will dip you in the beaming,
With the light-filled Iris' grace
I will paint your leaves with gleaming
Like unto Aurora's face.
In the springtime's happy glitter
Gather tender breasts again,
In the autumn's garland bitter
Glean my pleasure and my pain.

                              *Marianna Wertz*

## TO EMMA

Far off in the mist grey reaches
Lies my bliss of former days,
Only on *one* star so beaut'ous
Lingers still with love my gaze.
But, just as the star's bright light,
Is it but a glow by night.

Did a lengthy sleep oppress thee,
In which death had closed thine eyes,
Still my sorrow had possessed thee,
Thou didst live in my heart's sighs.
But! thou liv'st in light above,
No more liv'st thou for my love.

Can sweet longing by love nourished,
Emma, can it fleeting be?
What has passed away and perished,
Emma, can that love e'er be?
Is her flame in heaven high,
Like an earthly good, to die?

*Bruce Director*

## THE MAIDEN'S LAMENT

The clouds are flitting, the oakwood roars,
The maid is sitting upon green shores,
The waves they are breaking with might, with might,
And she sighs out into the sombre night,
Her eyes are from crying grown turbid.

"The heart is now deadened, devoid's the world,
And ne'er again be my wishes fulfilled.
Thou holy one, summon thy child back home,
For I have the fortune terrestrial known,
For I have full lived and have loved!"

The tears running down do in vain their course take,
Lamenting, 'twill never the dead one awake;
Yet name it, what comforts and healeth the breast,
After sweetest love all its pleasure has lost,
I, the heavenly, won't be denying.

"Let run down the teardrops in vain do they break,
The dead one lamenting 'twill never awake!
The sweetest of balms for the sorrowful breast,
After beautiful love all its pleasure has lost,
Are but love's lamenting and sighing."

*Marianna Wertz*


## WILHELM TELL

When powers raw break hostilely asunder,
And courage blind ignites the flames of war,
When in the battle furious factions thunder,
The voice of justice can be heard no more,
When every vice sets shamelessly to plunder,
When bold caprice the Holy throweth o'er,
The anchor's loos'd, on which the nation's clinging:
That is no proper theme for joyful singing.

But when a people, herds devoutly tending,
Content with self, nor other's goods desires,
The yoke throws off, unworthy 'neath it's bending,
Though angered, still humanity admires,
In victory, its modesty's unending;
That is immortal and to song inspires
And such a view may I with joy have shown thee,
Thou knowest it, for all that's great thine own be.

*Becky Jones*

# THE SONG OF THE BELL

*I call the living · I mourn the dead · I break the lightning*

Walled up in the earth so steady
Burned from clay, the mould doth stand.
This day must the Bell be ready!
Fresh, O workmen, be at hand!
    From the heated brow
    Sweat must freely flow,
That the work may praise the Master,
Though the blessing comes from higher.

Our work in earnest preparation,
Befitteth well an earnest word;
When joined by goodly conversation,
Then flows the labor briskly forw'd.
So let us now with care consider,
What through a frail power springs forth:
The wicked man one must have scorn for,
Who ne'er reflects, what he brings forth.
This it is, what all mankind graceth,
And thereto his to understand,
That he in inner heart so traceth,
What he createth with his hand.

    Take the wood from trunk of spruce tree,
    Yet quite dry let it abide,
    That the flame compressed so tightly
    Strike the gullet deep inside!
        Cook the copper brew,
        Quick the tin in, too!
    That the glutinous bell-metal
    Flowing rightly then will settle!

What in the dam's dark cavern dour
The hand with fire's help did mould,
High in the belfry of the tower
There will our story loud be told.
Still will it last as years are tolling
And many ears will it inspire
And wail with mourners in consoling
And harmonize devotion's choir.
What here below to son terrestr'al
The ever-changing fate doth bring,
Doth strike the crown which made from metal,
Uplifting it doth sound its ring.

Bubbles white I see creating,
Good! the mass doth flow at last.
Now with potash permeating,
Let us hasten quick the cast.
    And from lather free
    Must the mixture be,
That from metal pure abounding
Pure and full the voice be sounding.

For with its joyful festive ringing
It doth the child beloved greet
On that first step his life is bringing,
Which starts in arms of slumber sweet;
For in the womb of time's attesting
His fortune black or bright is resting,
The mother's tender cares adorning
With love, to guard his golden morning.—
The years they fly like arrows fleet.
From maiden breaks the lad so proudly,
And into life so wild doth roam,
Throughout the world he wanders widely.
As stranger, seeks his father's home,
And glorious, in youthful splendor,
Like creature from the heav'nly land,

With cheek so modest, shy and tender
Sees he the maid before him stand.
Then seized by nameless longing, aching,
The young lad's heart, alone he leaves,
From out his eyes the tears are breaking,
His brothers' ranks so wild he flees.
Her steps he blushingly doth follow
And is by her fair greeting blessed,
The fairest seeks he in the meadow,
With which by him his love is dressed.
Oh! gentle longing, sweetest hoping,
The first love's time of goldenness!
The eye doth see the heavens op'ning,
So feasts the heart in happiness—
Oh! that it last forever greening,
The beaut'ous time of love's beginning!

How indeed the pipes are browning!
This small staff do I dip in:
When its glaze to us is shining,
Will the casting time begin.
Now, men, lively be!
Test the mix for me,
If the brittle with the nimble
Join together 'tis good symbol.

For where the rough is with the supple,
Where strong itself with mild doth couple,
The ringing will be good and strong.
So test therefore, who join forever,
If heart to heart be found together!
Delusion is short, remorse is long.
In the bridal locks so lovely
Plays the virgin's modest crown,
When the churchbells pealing brightly
To the festive gleam call down.
Ah! Life's fairest celebrating

Doth the May of life end, too,
With the girdle, with the veiling
Tears delusion fair in two.

The passion doth fly.
Love must be enduring;
The flowers fade by,
Fruit must be maturing.
The man must go out
In hostile life living,
Be working and striving
And planting and making,
Be scheming and taking,
Through hazard and daring,
His fortune ensnaring.
Then streams in the wealth in an unending measure,
The silo is filled thus with valuable treasure,
The rooms are growing, the house stretches out.
And indoors ruleth
The housewife so modest,
The mother of children,
And governs wisely
In matters of family,
And maidens she traineth
And boys she restraineth,
And goes without ending
Her diligent handling,
And gains increase hence
With ordering sense.
And treasure on sweet-smelling presses is spreading,
And turns 'round the tightening spindle the threading,
And gathers in chests polished cleanly and bright
The shimmering wool, and the linen snow-white,
And joins to the goods, both their splendor and
    shimmer,
And resteth never.

And the father with joyful glance
From the house gable's view oh so vast
Surveying his fortune's enhance,
Seeth the posts of trees that are tow'ring
And the rooms of his barns o'erflowing
And the silos, bent low from the blessing,
And the billows of corn unceasing,
Boasting with haughty mouth:
"Firm, as the soil o' th' earth,
'Gainst all misfortune's pow'r
Splendid my house doth tow'r!"—
Yet with mighty fate supernal
Is entwined no bond eternal,
And misfortune strideth fast.

    Good! now be the cast beginning,
    Finely jagged is the breach.
    Yet before it start to running,
    Let us pious verses preach.
        Make the tap eject!
        God our house protect!
    Smoking in the handle's hollow
    Shoots with fire-brownéd billow.

Benef'cent is the might of flame,
When o'er it man doth watch, doth tame,
And what he buildeth, what he makes,
For this the heav'nly powers he thanks;
Yet fright'ning Heaven's pow'r will be,
When from its chains it doth break free,
Embarking forth on its own track,
Nature's daughter, free alack.
Woe, when it is liberated
Growing such that none withstand,
Through the alleys populated
Rolls the monstrous firebrand!

For by elements is hated
The creation of man's hand.
From the heavens
Blessing's teeming,
Rain is streaming;
From the heavens, unforeseen,
Strikes the beam!
Hear in belfry whimpers form!
That is storm!
Red as blood
Heavens broil,
That is not the daylight's flood!
What a turmoil
In the roads!
Steam explodes!
Climbs the fire column glowing,
Through the streets' long rows it's going
Forth it goes with wind's speed growing,
As in jaws of ovens cooking
Glows the air, the beams are cracking,
Pillars tumble, windows quav'ring,
Children wailing, mothers wand'ring,
Whimp'ring cattle
Under rubble,
All is running, saving, flying,
Bright as day the night is shining.
Through long chain of hands, not resting
As contesting
Flies the bucket, lofty bowing
Spouts the fountain, water flowing.
Howling comes the storm a-flying,
Which doth seek the roaring flames.
Crackling in the well-dried grains,
Falls it, in the roomy silo,
On the wood of rafters hollow,

And as if it would by blowing
With itself the earth's full weight
Drag it, in its vi'lent flight,
Into Heaven's summit growing
Giant tall!
Hopeless all
Yields the man 'fore God's great powers,
Idle sees he all his labors
And amazed to ruin going.

All burnt out
Is the setting,
Of the savage storm's rough bedding;
In the empty window op'ning
Horror's living,
And high Heaven's clouds are giving
Looks within.

Just one peek
To the ashes
Of his riches
Doth the man behind him seek—
His wanderer's staff then gladly seizes.
Whatever fire's rage has cost,
One solace sweet is e'er unmovéd:
He counts the heads of his belovéd
And see! not one dear head is lost.

   In the earth it is receivéd
   Full the mould is happ'ly made;
   Will its beauty be perceivéd,
   So be toil and art repaid?
      Should the cast not take?
      Should the moulding break?
   Ah! perhaps, whilst we are hoping,
   Harm is us already gripping.

To holy earth's e'er-dark'ning bosom
Do we entrust our hands' true deed,
The sower doth entrust his seed
And hopes, indeed, that it will blossom
To bless, as Heaven hath decreed.
Still costlier the seed we've buried
With sorrow in the womb of earth
And hope, that from the coffin carried
'Twill bloom to fairer fortune forth.

From cathedral,
Anxious, long,
Bell is sounding
Funeral song.
Earnestly its doleful toll doth carry
Some new wanderer on the final journey.

Ah! the wife it is, the dear one,
Ah! it is the faithful mother,
Whom the swarthy Prince of Shadeland
Carries off from arm of husband,
From the group of children dear,
Whom she blooming to him bare,
Whom she on her breast so true
Watched with pleasure as they grew—
Ah! the bonds of home so giving
Will forevermore be loose,
For in shadowland she's living,
Who was mother of the house,
For her faithful rule now ceases,
No more keepeth watch her care,
Henceforth in the orphaned places
Rules the foreign, loveless e'er.

Till the Bell be cooly laying,
Let no stringent work ensue;
As the bird in leaves is playing,
May each person goodly do.
　　Nods the starlit sky,
　　Duty's all foreby,
Hears the lad the vespers sounding,
For the Master toil's abounding.

Briskly hastens he his paces
Far in forest wild the wand'rer,
To the lovely cottage-places.
Bleating homeward draws the sheep herd,
And the cattle
Broad-foreheaded, flocks so glossy,
Come in lowing
To accustomed stalls they're going.
Heav'ly in
Shakes the wagon,
Harvest-laden,
Colored brightly
On sheaves sightly
Garlands lie,
And the young folk of the reapers
Dancing fly.
Street and market-place grow stiller,
Round the social flame of lighting
Gather those in household dwelling,
And the town gate closes creaking.
Black bedighted
All the earth be
Yet the burgher is affrighted
Not by night,
Which the wicked has excited,
For the watchful law's clear eye keeps sight.

Holy Order, blesséd richly,
Heaven's daughter, equals has she
Free and light and glad connected,
City buildings hath erected,
Who herein from country dwelling
The uncivil savage calling,
Ent'ring into human houses,
Gentler custom she espouses,
With the dearest band she's bound us,
Love for fatherland weaves 'round us.

Thousand busy hands in motion
Help in cheerful unity,
And in fiery commotion
Will all forces public be.
Master and the men take action
Under freedom's holy care,
Each is pleased with his position,
Scorn for every scoffer share.
Work's the burgher's decoration,
Labor's prize is to be blest;
Honor kings by royal station,
Busy hands *us* honor best.

Peace so gentle,
Charming concord,
Tarry, tarry
Friendly o'er this city be!
May the day be ne'er appearing,
When the rugged hordes a-warring
Through this quiet vale are storming,
When the heavens,
Which the evening's blushes pretty
Paint so fine,
From the village, from the city
Wildly burning frightful shine!

Now for me break up the building,
Its intent is filled a-right,
That our hearts and eyes be feasting
On the most successful sight.
    Swing the hammer, swing,
    'Til the mantle spring!
If the Bell be now awoken,
Be the frame in pieces broken.

The Master can break up the framing
With wisen'd hand, at rightful hour,
But woe, whene'er in brooks a-flaming
Doth free itself, the glowing ore!
Blind-raging with the crash of thunder,
It springs from out the bursted house,
And as from jaws of hell asunder
Doth spew its molten ruin out;
Where senseless powers are commanding,
There can no structure yet be standing,
When peoples do themselves set free,
There can no common welfare be.

Woe, when in womb of cities growing,
In hush doth pile the fiery match,
The people, chains from off it throwing,
Doth its own help so frightful snatch!
There to the Bell, its rope-cord pulling,
Rebellion, doth it howling sound
And, hallowed but for peaceful pealing,
To violence doth strike aloud.

Liberty, Equality! Men hear sounding,
The tranquil burgher takes up arms,
The streets and halls are all abounding,
And roving, draw the murd'ring swarms;
Then women to hyenas growing
Do make with horror jester's art,
Still quiv'ring, panther's teeth employing,

They rip apart the en'my's heart.
Naught holy is there more, and cleaving
Are bonds of pious modesty,
The good its place to bad is leaving,
And all the vices govern free.
To rouse the lion, is dang'rous error,
And ruinous is the tiger's bite,
Yet is most terrible the terror
Of man in his deluded state.
Woe's them, who heaven's torch of lighting
Unto the ever-blind do lend!
It lights him not, 'tis but igniting,
And land and towns to ash doth rend.

Joy unto me God hath given!
See there! like a golden star
From its husk, so blank and even,
Peeleth out the metal core.
From the crown to base
Like the bright sun plays,
And escutcheons' decoration
Builder's skill gives commendation.

Come in! Come in!
Ye workmen all, do come ye close in,
That we commence the Bell to christen,
*Concordia* its name be given,
To concord, in an intimate communion,
The loving commons gathers she in union.

And be her purpose thus fulfilled,
For which the Master did her build:
On high above low earthly living,
Shall she in heav'n's blue tent unfurl'd,
Be thunder's neighbor, ever-pending,
And border on the starry world,
A single voice from high she raises
Like constellations' band so bright,

Which its creator wand'ring praises,
And leads the wreathéd year a-right.
Alone to grave, eternal singing
Her metal mouth be consecrate,
And hourly with all swiftness winging,
Shall she be moved by time in flight,
Her tongue to destiny is lending,
*Herself* has heart and pity not,
With nothing but her swing attending
The game of life's e'er-changing lot.
And as the ring in ears is passing
Sent by her mighty sounding play,
So let her teach, that naught is lasting,
That all things earthly fade away.

Now with rope's full power bringing
Rock the Bell from vault with care,
That she in the realm of ringing
Rises, in the Heavens' air.
    Pull ye, pull ye, heave!
    She doth move, doth wave.
Joy be she this city bringing,
*Peace* be the first chime she's ringing.
                                    *Marianna Wertz*

## THEKLA
### A *Spirit-Voice*

Where be I, and whither have I wended,
When my fleeing shadow from thee moved?
Have I not concluded and thus ended,
Have I never lived and never loved?

Art thou for the nightingales inquiring,
Who enchanted thee in springtime's day
With their melody so soul inspiring?
Only just so long they loved, were they.

Have I then the lost one found forever?
Trust in me; I am with him now wed,
Where those bound as one, no more do sever,
There, where no more tears are ever shed.

Yonder wilt thou us again be finding,
When thy love with our love doth compare;
There's my father, free of sin abiding,
Bloody murder does not reach him there.

And he feels, him no delusion's cheated,
When he looked unto the stars on high;
For as each one metes, to him is meted,
Who believes it, hath the holy nigh.

Vows are kept within those spaces yonder
To the feelings fair that ne'er betray;
Venture thou, to dream and wrongly wander:
Lofty sense lies oft in childish play.
                              *Patricia Noble Schenk*

# THE YOUTH AT THE BROOK

By the fountain sat the stripling,
Flowers wove he in a wreath,
And he saw them ripped asunder,
Driven by the waves beneath:—
And my days are so escaping
As the fountain flows away!
And so pales my youth before me,
As the wreath does fast decay.

Question not, wherefore I sorrow
In the bloomtime of my life!
All is hopeful and rejoicing,
When the spring renews itself.
But these thousand sounds of nature,
Which awakens on the plain,
Rouse within my deepest bosom
Only heavy cries of pain.

What to me are all the pleasures,
Which the lovely spring awards?
One there is, for whom I'm searching,
She is near and ever far.
Stretch I wide my arms with longing
For the precious silhouette,
Ah, I cannot yet attain it
And my heart's unstilled as yet!

Come below, thou beaut'ous darling,
And thy castle proud depart!
Flowers, born of springtime's bounty,
Will I on thy lap impart.
Hark, the woods resound with singing,
And the fountain ripples fair!
Room is in the smallest shelter
For a happy loving pair.

*Christine Douglas*

# DITHYRAMB

Never, believe me, appear the Divine Ones,
Never alone.
Scarce have I Bacchus, the one who's beguiling,
But then comes Amor, the boy who is smiling,
Phoebus, the lordly one, makes himself known.
They're nearing, they're coming, now all the celestial,
With Deities fills up the hallway terrestrial.

Say, how receive I, who's born a mere worldling,
Choirs from on high?
    Grant unto me your existence immortal,
    Gods! What to you can he give who is mortal?
Lift me unto your Olympian sky!
    This joy, it dwells only in Jupiter's palace,
    O fill me with nectar, O pass me the chalice!

Pass him the chalice! Pour for the poet,
Hebe, pour free!
Sprinkle his eyesight with heaven's bedewing,
That he the Styx, the detested, ne'er's viewing,
One of our own let him seem to be.
    It rushes, it sparkles, the font of the numinous,
    The bosom grows peaceful, the eye becomes
        luminous.

*William F. Wertz, Jr.*

# DRAMA

# WILHELM TELL

## DRAMA

*New Year's Gift for 1805*

TRANSLATED BY WILLIAM F. WERTZ, JR.

## DRAMATIS PERSONÆ

HERMANN GESSLER,
  *Imperial Governor in*
  *Schwyz and Uri*
WERNER, BARON VON
  ATTINGHAUSEN,
  *Standard-bearer*
ULRICH VON RUDENZ, *his*
  *nephew*

*Countrymen from Schwyz*
WERNER STAUFFACHER
KONRAD HUNN
ITEL REDING
HANS AUF DER MAUER
JÖRG IM HOFE
ULRICH DER SCHMIED
JOST VON WEILER

---

*Wilhelm Tell*, Schiller's last and greatest republican drama, was written at the end of his life, from 1803–4, when Schiller was at the peak of his artistic genius. The play was first performed in Weimar on March 17, 1804, and first put in print in October of that year, by Cotta at Tübingen. It was dedicated, as the title indicates, as a New Year's Gift to the World.

59

*From Uri*
WALTER FÜRST
WILHELM TELL
RÖSSELMANN, *the priest*
PETERMANN, *the sacristan*
KUONI, *the herdsman*
WERNI, *the hunter*
RUODI, *the fisherman*

*Peasant women*
ARMGARD
MECHTHILD
ELSBETH
HILDEGARD

*Tell's boys*
WALTER
WILHELM

*From Unterwalden*
ARNOLD VOM MELCHTAL
KONRAD BAUMGARTEN
MEIER VON SARNEN
STRUTH VON WINKELRIED
KLAUS VON DER FLÜE
BURKHARDT AM BÜHEL
ARNOLD VON SEWA

*Mercenary soldiers*
FRIESSHART
LEUTHOLD

RUDOLF DER HARRAS,
  *Gessler's horsemaster*
JOHANNES PARRICIDA,
  *Duke of Schwabia*
STÜSSI, *the game keeper*
THE STEER OF URI
AN IMPERIAL MESSENGER
TASKMASTER
MASTER STONEMASON,
  JOURNEYMEN and
  LABORERS
PUBLIC CRIERS
BROTHERS OF MERCY
HORSEMEN OF GESSLER
  AND LANDENBERG
MANY COUNTRYMEN, MEN
  AND WOMEN FROM THE
  FOREST CANTONS

PFEIFER VON LUZERN
KUNZ VON GERSAU
JENNI, *fisher boy*
SEPPI, *herdsman boy*
GERTRUD, *Stauffacher's
  wife*
HEDWIG, *Tell's wife,
  Fürst's daughter*
BERTA VON BRUNECK, *a
  rich heiress*

# ACT I

## SCENE I

*High rocky shore of the Vierwaldstättensee, opposite Schwyz.*

*The lake makes a cove in the land, a hut is not far from the shore, fisherboy conveys himself in a boat. Across the lake one sees the green meadows, villages and farms lie in the bright sunshine. To the left of the spectator the peaks of the Haken show themselves, surrounded by clouds; to the right in the distant hinterground one sees the ice-covered mountains. Even before the curtain rises, one hears the cowherd's dance and the harmonious chime of the cattle bells, which continues for some time even during the opening scene.*

FISHERBOY *(sings in the boat):*
  *(Melody of the cowherd's dance.)*
  The lake it doth smile, to bathing it calleth,
  The boy asleep on the verdant shore falleth,
    There hears he a ringing,
    Like flute-tones so nice,
    Like voices of angels
    In Paradise.
  And as he awakens in happiness blest
  There waters are washing him round the breast,
    And it calls from the bottom:
    Th'art *mine*, laddy dear!
    Entice I the sleeper,
    I pull him in here.
HERDSMAN *(upon the mountain):*
  *(Variation of the cowherd's dance.)*
    Ye pastures farewell!
    Ye meadows aglowing!
    The herdsman is going,
    The summer is hence.
  We go to the mount, return we'll be making,

When the cuckoo calls, when the songs are awaking,
When with flowers the earth itself new doth array,
When the fountains flow in the loveliest May.
    Ye pastures farewell,
    Ye meadows aglowing!
    The herdsman is going,
    The summer is hence.

ALPINE HUNTER (*appears opposite upon the top of the rock):*
(*Second Variation.*)
    The heights are athund'ring, now trembles the bridge,
    Nor feareth the archer on dizzying ridge,
    He strideth undaunted
    O'er ice-covered fields,
    No spring there is flaunted,
    No shoot there green yields;
And under the footsteps a mist-covered sea,
No longer the cities of man doth he see,
    Through the rift of clouds only
    He glimpses the world,
    Deep under the water
    Green fields are unfurl'd.

(*The landscape is altered, one hears a muffled crack from the mountains, shadows of clouds move across the region.* RUODI *the fisherman comes out of the hut.* WERNI *the hunter climbs from the rocks.* KUONI *the herdsman comes, with the milkpail on his shoulder.* SEPPI, *his handyman, follows him.*)

RUODI:  Be speedy, Jenni. Haul the boat ashore.
  The grizzled Vale-Lord comes, dull roars the glacier,
  The Mythenstein is drawing on his cap,
  And from the weather cleft a cold wind blows,
  The storm, I think, will be here, ere we know't.
KUONI:  Rain's coming, Ferryman. My sheep are eating
  The grass with greed, and Watcher paws the earth.
WERNI:  The fish are springing, and the waterfowl

Dives down below. A storm is now approaching.

KUONI *(to his boy):*
   Look, Seppi, that the cattle have not strayed.

SEPPI: I recognize brown Liesel by her bell.

KUONI: So we are missing none, she goes the farthest.

RUODI: A pretty peal of bells there, Master Herdsman.

WERNI: And handsome cows—They're yours,
   compatriot?

KUONI: I'm not so rich—they are my gracious Lord's,
   Of Attinghausen's, and to me entrusted.

RUODI: How fair the band appears on that cow's neck.

KUONI: That knows she too, that she doth lead the
   herd,
   And took I it from her, she'd cease to feed.

RUODI: That makes no sense! A cow devoid of reason—

WERNI: That's easy said. The beast hath reason too,
   That's known to *us*, we men who hunt the Chamois,
   Who shrewdly post, when they to pasture go,
   A sentinel, who pricks his ears and warns
   With piercing whistle, when the hunter nears.

RUODI *(to the herdsman):*
   You drive them home?

KUONI:                    The Alp is grazed quite bare.

WERNI: Safe journey home, my friend!

KUONI:                                That wish I you,
   Not all your trips are ended in return.

RUODI: There comes a man who rushes with great
   haste.

WERNI: I know him, it is Baumgart of Alzellen.

(KONRAD BAUMGARTEN *rushing in breathless.*)

BAUMGARTEN: May God be willing, Ferryman, your
   boat!

RUODI: Now, now, what is the hurry?

BAUMGARTEN:                          Cast off now!
   You must save me from death! Set me across!

KUONI: Compatriot, what's wrong?

WERNI:                           Who follows you?

BAUMGARTEN (*to the fisherman*):
Haste, haste, e'en now they're close upon my heels!
The Gov'rnor's troopers are in hot pursuit,
I am a man of death, if I am seized.
RUODI:  Why are the troopers in pursuit of you?
BAUMGARTEN:  First rescue me, and then I'll talk to you.
WERNI:  You are defiled with blood, what hath occurred?
BAUMGARTEN:  The Emperor's cast'llan, who at Rossberg
    sat—
KUONI:  The Wolfenschiessen? *He's* pursuing you?
BAUMGARTEN:  *He'll* harm no man again, I've struck him
    dead.
ALL (*fall back*):
May God forgive you! What is it you've done?
BAUMGARTEN:  What any free man in my place had
    done!
I've exercised my household right against
Him who'd defile mine honor and my wife's.
KUONI:  The Cast'llan hath your honor then impaired?
BAUMGARTEN:  That he did not his evil lust fulfill,
Hath God and my good axe alone prevented.
WERNI:  You've split his head in two then with your axe?
KUONI:  O, let us hear, you've time enough, before
He hath the boat unfastened from the shore.
BAUMGARTEN:  I had been felling timber in the woods,
When ran my wife toward me in mortal fear.
The Cast'llan quartered in my house, he had
Commanded her, to get a bath prepared.
And when he had indecencies of her
Demanded, she escaped, to search for me.
Then ran I brisk thereto, just as I was,
And with the axe I've blessed his bath for him.
WERNI:  You've acted well, no man can blame you for it.
KUONI:  The maniac! Now hath he his reward!
'Twas long deserved from Unterwalden's people.
BAUMGARTEN:  The deed was noised about, I am
    pursued—
And while we're speaking—God—the time is flying—

*(It begins to thunder.)*

KUONI: Quick, Ferryman—convey this man across.

RUODI: It can't be done. A violent storm is now
Approaching. You must wait.

BAUMGARTEN:             Oh, Holy God!
I can not wait. The least delay is death—

KUONI *(to the fisherman):*
Set out with God, one must assist his neighbor,
The like can happen to each one of us.
*(Roaring and thundering.)*

RUODI: The Föhn is loose, see how the waters rise,
I can not steer against the storm and waves.

BAUMGARTEN *(embraces his knees):*
So help you God, as you now pity me—

WERNI: His life's at stake, have mercy Ferryman.

KUONI: He is a father, and hath wife and children!
*(Repeated peals of thunder.)*

RUODI: So what? I have a life as well to lose,
Have wife and child at home, like he—Look how
It surges, how it heaves and whirlpools draw,
And all the water rouses from the depths.
—I would be glad to save this worthy man,
Yet it's impossible, you see yourself.

BAUMGARTEN *(still on his knees):*
So must I fall into the tyrant's hands,
The shore of rescue now so near to sight!
—Lies yonder! I can reach it with mine eyes,
My voice's sound can make its way across,
Here is the boat, that would convey me thence,
And must I lie here, helpless, and forlorn!

KUONI: Look, who is now come here!

WERNI:             'Tis Tell from Bürglen.

(TELL *with crossbow.)*

TELL: Who is the man, who here implores for help?

KUONI: It's an Alzeller man, he hath his honor
Defended, and the Wolfenschiessen slain,
The Cast'llan of the King, who sat at Rossberg—

The Governor's troopers are upon his heels,
He begs the boatman carry him across,
But he's afraid o'th' storm and will not go.
RUODI: Now here is Tell, he steers the rudder too,
He'll be my witness, should the trip be dared.
TELL: If need be, Ferryman, all may be ventured.
*(Violent peals of thunder, the lake surges up.)*
RUODI: Am I to plunge into the jaws of hell?
That none would do, who did possess his senses.
TELL: The valiant man thinks of himself the last,
Put trust in God and rescue the distressed.
RUODI: Secure in port 'tis easy to advise,
Here is the boat and there the lake! Attempt it!
TELL: The lake can pity, but the Governor will not,
Attempt it, Boatman!
HERDSMAN AND HUNTER: Save him! Save him!
Save him!
RUODI: And 'twere my brother and my very child,
It can not be, 'tis Simon-Judä day,
Here raves the lake and wants to have its victim.
TELL: With idle talk will nothing here be done,
The hour insists, the man must now be helped.
Speak, Boatman, wilt thou take him?
RUODI:                              No, not I!
TELL: I' th' name of God then! Give the boat to me,
I will attempt it, with my feeble strength.
KUONI: Ha, valiant Tell!
WERNI:                    That is the hunter's way!
BAUMGARTEN: You are my savior and mine angel, Tell!
TELL: I'll save you from the pow'r o' th' Governor,
From per'l of storm another must give aid.
Yet better is't, you fall into God's hands,
Than into men's! *(to the herdsman)* Compatriot,
console
My wife, if something human falls to me,
I've done, but what I could not leave undone.
*(He springs into the boat.)*

KUONI (*to fisherman*):
    You are a master of the helm. What Tell
    Hath dared to do, that could not *you* have ventured?
RUODI: Far better men do not take Tell's example,
    There are not two, like he is, in the mountains.
WERNI (*hath climbed upon the rock*):
    He pushes off. God help thee, valiant swimmer!
    See, how the bark is reeling on the waves!
KUONI (*on the bank*):
    The surge is passing thence—I see't no more.
    Yet wait, here it appears again! Robustly
    The valiant man is working through the breakers.
SEPPI: The Governor's troopers come now at full gallop.
KUONI: God knows, they are! And that was help in
    need.

    (*A troup of Landenberg troopers.*)

FIRST TROOPER: Give up the murderer, you have
    concealed.
SECOND: *This* way he came, in vain you're hiding him.
KUONI AND RUODI: Whom mean you, trooper?
FIRST TROOPER (*discovers the boat*):
                        Ha, what see I! Devil!
WERNI (*above*):
    Is't he in yonder boat, you seek?—Ride on!
    If you lay quickly to, you'll haul him in.
SECOND: Accurs'd! He hath escaped.
FIRST (*to herdsman and fisherman*): You've helped him
    to escape,
    You'll pay us for it—Fall upon their herds!
    Tear down the cottage, burn and strike it down!
    (*Rush off.*)
SEPPI (*Rushes after them.*):
    O my poor lambs!
KUONI (*follows*): O woe is me! My herds!
WERNI: O these berserkers!
RUODI (*Wrings his hands.*): Righteousness of Heaven,

When will the savior come into this land?
*(Follows them.)*


### SCENE II

*At Steinen in Schwyz.*

A *linden tree in front of* STAUFFACHER's *house on the
country road, near the bridge.*

WERNER STAUFFACHER, PFEIFER VON LUZERN
*enter in conversation.*


PFEIFER: Yes, yes, Lord Stauffacher, as I told you.
Swear not to Austria, if you can help it.
Hold firmly to the Empire as before,
God shield you in your ancient freedom!
*(Presses his hand cordially and wants to go.)*
STAUFFACHER: Yet stay, until my wife returns—You are
My guest in Schwyz, I in Luzern am yours.
PFEIFER: Much thanks! I must reach Gersau yet today.
—What difficulties you may have to suffer
From arrogance and greed of governors,
Bear it with patience! It can alter, quickly,
Another Emperor can gain the throne.
Are you once Austria's, you're hers forever.
*(He exits.)*

*(*STAUFFACHER *sits down sorrowfully upon a bench under
the linden tree. Thus is he found by* GERTRUD, *his wife,
who places herself along side him and observes him for a
long time silently.)*

GERTRUD: So grave, my friend? No longer do I know
thee.
For many days in silence I observe,
How gloomy spirits furrow in thy brow.

Upon thine heart a silent grief is weighing,
Confide in me, I am thy faithful wife,
And I demand my half of all thy sorrow.
(STAUFFACHER *extends his hand to her and is silent.*)
What can oppress thine heart, tell it to me.
Thine industry is blest, thy fortunes bloom,
Full are the barns, and now the herd of oxen,
The breed of horses sleek and fully fed
Is safely from the mountain brought back home
To winter in their comfortable stalls.
—Here stands thy house, rich, like a nobleman's,
From beauteous timber is it newly built
And fit together with the standard gauge,
From many windows shines it pleasant, bright,
With colored coats of arms is it adorned,
And proverbs sage, the which the wanderer
Delaying reads and at their meaning wonders.
STAUFFACHER: The house stands well constructed and
    well joined,
But ah—the ground, on which we built it, rocks.
GERTRUD: My Werner, tell me, what thou mean'st by
    that?
STAUFFACHER: Of late I sat as now beneath this linden,
With joy reflecting on what's fairly done,
When came from Küssnacht, from his citadel,
The Gov'rnor riding with his mercenaries.
Before this house he halted in surprise,
Though I rose quickly, and submissively,
As is becoming, I approached the Lord,
Who represents the Emperor's judicial
Power i'th' land. To whom belongs this house?
He asked maliciously, for well he knew't.
But thinking quickly thus I answered him:
This house, Lord Gov'rnor, is my Lord's the Emp'ror's
And yours and mine in fief—then he replies:
"I'm regent in the land i'th' Emp'ror's stead
And will not, that the farmer's house be built
With his own hand, and he thus freely live,

As if he were the master in the land.
I shall make bold, to hinder you in this."
This saying rode he thence defiantly,
But I remained behind with doleful soul,
Considering the evil man's remarks.

GERTRUD:   My dearest Lord and husband! Wouldst thou
      take
An honest word of counsel from thy wife?
I boast to be the noble Iberg's daughter,
A much-experienced man. We sisters sat,
There spinning wool, throughout the lengthy nights,
When round our father leaders of the people
Convened themselves, and there the parchments read
Of ancient emp'rors, and the country's weal
Considered in judicious conversation.
Heedful I heard there many prudent words,
What intellectuals think, what good men wish,
And silently I've kept them in my heart.
So listen to me then and heed my speech,
For what thee pressed, behold, I long have known.
—The Governor resents thee, would thee harm,
Because thou art an hindrance to him, that
The men of Schwyz will not subject themselves
To th' upstart prince's house, but true and firm
Adhere unto the realm, just as their worthy
Forefathers have resolved and have performed.—
Is't not so, Werner? Tell me, if I lie!

STAUFFACHER:   So is it, that is Gessler's grudge against
      me.

GERTRUD:   He envies thee, since thou dost dwell in
      bliss,
A free man on thine own inheritance,
—For he hath none. From Emperor and realm
Thou hold'st this house in fief, thou may'st it show,
So well as any prince displays his land,
For over thee thou recognize no lord
Except the highest in all Christendom—
He merely is his house's younger son,

Naught calls he his except his knightly cloak,
He therefore sees each honest man's good fortune
With squinting eyes of poisonous disfavor,
*Thee* hath he long ago destruction sworn—
As yet thou art uninjured—Wilt thou wait,
Until he wreaks his evil will on thee?
The smart man thinks ahead.

STAUFFACHER:                     What's to be done!

GERTRUD (*steps nearer*):
So hear what I advise! Thou know'st, how here
In Schwyz all honest men do now complain
About this Gov'rnor's greed and tyranny.
So have no doubt, that they there yonder too
In Unterwalden and in Uri land
Are weary of oppression and the yoke—
For just as Gessler here, there yonder o'er
The lake the Landenberger is as brazen—
There comes no fishing boat across to us,
Which doth not tell of some new mischief and
Beginning-violence from the governors.
Therefore it would be wise, if some of you,
Of sound intent, did quietly confer,
How we might free ourselves of this oppression,
So know I well, that God would not desert you
And would be gracious to a righteous cause—
Dost thou not have a friend in Uri, speak,
To whom thou may'st thine heart sincerely open?

STAUFFACHER: I know of many men of courage there
And men of high repute and eminence,
Who are my trusted friends and confidants.
(*He stands up.*)
Wife, what a storm of dangerous ideas
Awak'st thou in my quiet breast! My innermost
Thou bring'st from me into the light of day,
And what I secretly forbade myself
To think, thou boldly speak'st with easy tongue.
—Hast thou considered well, what thou advisest?
The savage discord and the clang of arms

Thou callest forth into this peaceful vale—
Dared we, a feeble folk of herdsmen, go
To battle with the master of the world?
'Tis only for some pretext, that they wait,
In order to unleash on this poor land
Their savage hordes of military might,
Therein to govern with the victor's rights
And 'neath the show of righteous punishment
To extirpate our ancient freedom's charter.

GERTRUD: You *too* are men, know how to wield your
   axe,
And God gives help unto courageous men!

STAUFFACHER: Oh wife! A fearful raging scourge is war,
   It strikes at once the shepherd and his herd.

GERTRUD: One must endure, whatever heaven sends,
   Inequity endures no noble heart.

STAUFFACHER: This house delights thee, that we newly
   built.
But war, the monster, burns it to the ground.

GERTRUD: Thought I my heart to temp'ral goods
   enslaved,
I'd throw the torch with mine own hand thereto.

STAUFFACHER: Thou dost believe in human kind! But
   war
Spares not the tender infant in its cradle.

GERTRUD: The innocent in heaven have a friend!
—Look forward, Werner, not behind thee now!

STAUFFACHER: We men can perish bravely sword in
   hand,
And yet what destiny will fall to you?

GERTRUD: The final choice is left e'en to the weakest,
A spring from yonder bridge doth make me free.

STAUFFACHER (*falls into her arms*):
Who presses such a heart unto his bosom,
He joyfully can fight for hearth and home,
And fears he not the hosts of any king—
To Uri shall I post without delay,
There lives a friend of mine, Lord Walter Fürst,

Who thinks the same as I about these times.
There too I find the noble Banneret
Of Attinghaus—although of lofty stock
He loves the people, honors ancient customs.
With both of these I shall confer, how one
May bravely fight against the country's foes—
Farewell—and while I am away, bear thou
With prudent sense the regiment o' th' house—
To th' pilgrim, wand'ring to the House of God,
To th' pious monk, collecting for his cloister,
Give richly and dispatch him well cared for.
Stauffacher's house is not concealed. It stands
Out by the public way, a welcome roof
For all the wanderers, who take this road.

*(While they exit toward the hinterground,* WILHELM TELL
*enters downstage with* BAUMGARTEN.*)*

TELL *(to* BAUMGARTEN*):*
Now you will have no further need of me,
Go into yonder house, wherein resides
Stauffacher, who's a father to th' oppressed.
—Yet see, there's he himself—Come, follow me!
*(Walks toward him, the scene changes.)*

## SCENE III

*Public place near Altorf.*

*On an eminence in the hinterground one sees a fortress
being constructed, which is already so far advanced, that
the form of the whole is evident. The back side is finished,
the front is being built even now, the scaffolding is still
standing, on which the workmen are climbing up and down,
upon the highest part of the roof hangs the slater.—Everything is in motion and work.*

TASKMASTER. MASTER STONEMASON. JOURNEYMEN
*and* LABORERS.

TASKMASTER *(with stick, drives the workers):*
Not long be idle, brisk! The building stones

This way, the lime, the mortar bring up here!
If the Lord Governor comes, that he may see
The work's advanced—It saunters just like snails.
*(To two laborers, who bear loads)*
Call that a load?  At once go double it!
O how these laggards shirk their very duty!

FIRST JOURNEYMAN:  Yet it is hard, that we should bear
    the stones
To build a keep and dungeon for ourselves!

TASKMASTER:  What's that you murmur?  That's a
    wretched people,
To naught adroit except to milk their cows,
And saunter idly all around the mountains.

OLD MAN *(takes a rest)*:
I can no more.

TASKMASTER *(shakes him)*:  Get up, old man, to work!

FIRST JOURNEYMAN:  Have you no viscera at all, that you
    Would drive the aged man to hard forced labor,
Who scarce can haul himself?

MASTER STONEMASON AND JOURNEYMEN:
                        It cries to heaven!

TASKMASTER:  Look to yourselves, I do, what is my
    office.

SECOND JOURNEYMAN:  Taskmaster, how's the fortress to
    be named,
That we build here?

TASKMASTER:          *Keep Uri* it is called,
For underneath this yoke you will be bowed.

JOURNEYMEN:  Keep Uri!

TASKMASTER:          Well, what's there to laugh about?

SECOND JOURNEYMAN:  With this small hut you want to
    humble Uri?

FIRST JOURNEYMAN:  Let's see, how many of such
    molehills one
Must place upon another, ere a mountain
Is made therefrom, that's like the least in Uri!
*(Taskmaster goes toward the hinterground.)*

MASTER STONEMASON:  I cast the hammer in the
    deepest lake,
  That served in building this accursed structure!

(TELL *and* STAUFFACHER *enter.*)

STAUFFACHER:  O had I never lived, to look at this!
TELL:  Here 'tis not good to be. Let us proceed.
STAUFFACHER:  Am I in Uri, in the land of freedom?
MASTER STONEMASON:  O Lord, if you at first had seen
    the cellars
  Beneath the towers! Yes, who lives in *there*,
  Will never hear the rooster crow again!
STAUFFACHER:  O God!
STONEMASON:        Behold these flanks, these buttresses,
  They stand, as built for all eternity!
TELL:  Whatever hands have built, hands can destroy.
  (*Pointing toward the mountains.*)
  That house of freedom God hath built for us.

(*One hears a drum, people enter, who carry a hat upon
a pole, a crier follows them, women and children press
tumultuously thereafter.*)

FIRST JOURNEYMAN:
  What means the drum?  Give your attention!
MASTER STONEMASON:                                Why
  A carnival parade and why the hat?
CRIER:  I' th' Emperor's name! Hear ye!
JOURNEYMEN:                          Be quiet! Hear ye!
CRIER:  You see this hat before you, men of Uri!
  It will be placed upon a lofty column,
  I' th' midst of Altorf, in the highest place,
  And this is both the Governor's will and purpose:
  The hat should have like honor as himself,
  One should show reverence for him with bent knee
  And with uncovered head—Thus will the King
  Distinguish who are the obedient.
  His limb and goods are forfeit to the King,

Whoe'er distains to follow this command.

*(The people burst out loudly laughing, the drums are beat, they pass on.)*

FIRST JOURNEYMAN: What new outrageous thing the Governor
Hath now devised! We must revere a hat!
Say! Hath one ever heard of such a thing?

MASTER STONEMASON: We are to bend our knees before a hat!
He plays his game with earnest worthy people?

FIRST JOURNEYMAN: If it were but the imperial crown! So is't
The hat of Austria; I saw it hang
Above the throne, where one assigns the fiefs!

MASTER STONEMASON: The hat of Austria! Pay heed, it is
A trick, to sell us out to Austria!

JOURNEYMEN: No worthy man will yield to this disgrace.

MASTER STONEMASON: Come, let us reach agreement with the others. *(They go to the rear.)*

TELL *(to STAUFFACHER):*
You know now what occurs. Fare well, Lord Werner!

STAUFFACHER: Where will you go? O haste not so from hence.

TELL: My home's without its father. Fare ye well.

STAUFFACHER: My heart is now so full, to speak with you.

TELL: The heavy heart doth not grow light through words.

STAUFFACHER: However words could lead us unto deeds.

TELL: The only deed is now be still and patient.

STAUFFACHER: Should one endure, what's unendurable?

TELL: 'Tis hasty rulers, who but briefly rule.
—When out of its abyss the Föhn arises,
One puts the fires out, the ships make haste
To seek the harbor, and the mighty spirit

Walks harmless, without trace, across the earth.
Let every one live quietly at home,
The peaceful man is gladly granted peace.

STAUFFACHER: You think?

TELL:                    The snake bites not if unprovoked.
They'll finally grow weary of themselves,
If they see that the provinces stay calm.

STAUFFACHER: We could do much, if we but stood
   together.

TELL: In shipwreck one more eas'ly helps himself.

STAUFFACHER: So coldly do you quit the common
   cause?

TELL: A man counts safely only on himself.

STAUFFACHER: In unity the weak are mighty too.

TELL: The strong man is most mighty when *alone*.

STAUFFACHER: So can the fatherland not count on you,
   When desperately it acts in self-defense?

TELL (*gives him his hand*): Tell fetches a lost sheep
   from the abyss,
And would he then be one to quit his friends?
*Whate'er* you do, excuse me from your *counsel*,
I can't consider or select for long.
If you have need of me for certain *deeds*,
Then call on Tell, I shall not fail to act.
   (*Depart to different sides. A sudden riot ensues
   around the scaffolding.*)

MASTER STONEMASON (*runs in*):
   What is't?

FIRST JOURNEYMAN (*comes forward, shouting*):
                    The slater is now fallen from the roof.

   (BERTA *with retinue.*)

BERTA (*rushes in*): Hath he been shattered? Run now,
   save him, help—
If help is possible, save him, here is gold—
   (*Throws her jewelry among the people.*)

MASTER STONEMASON: Hence with your gold—You
   think all can be bought

With gold, when you have torn the father from
The children and the husband from his wife,
And have brought misery upon the world,
You think to make amends with gold—Be gone!
We were a happy people, ere you came,
With you hath desperation entered in.
BERTA (*to the* TASKMASTER, *who returns*):
    Is he alive?   (TASKMASTER *gives a sign to the*
      *contrary.*)
              O ill-begotten castle, built
With curses, curses shall inhabit thee! (*Exit.*)


## SCENE IV

*Walter Fürst's house.*

WALTER FÜRST *and* ARNOLD VON MELCHTAL *enter
simultaneously from different sides.*

MELCHTAL:  Lord Walter Fürst—
WALTER FÜRST:            If we should be surprised!
    Stay, where you are. We are beset by spies.
MELCHTAL:  You bring me naught from
      Unterwalden?  Naught
    From my dear father?  I can bear't no longer,
    To lie here idly like a prisoner.
    What have I done then that's so criminal,
    That I should hide just like a murderer?
    O' th' brazen rascal, who would drive away
    From me the oxen, my most excellent team,
    Before mine eyes on orders from the Governor,
    I have but with my staff the finger broken.
WALTER FÜRST:
    You are too rash. The rascal was the Gov'rnor's,
    He was dispatched by your superiors,
    You had received a penalty, you should,
    As harsh it was, have paid it silently.

MELCHTAL: Should I have countenanced the flippant
  talk
  Of one so unashamed: "If peasants want
  Their bread, then, let them pull the plow themselves!"
  It cut me to the soul, to see the knave
  Unyoke the oxen, beauteous creatures, from the plow,
  They bellowed low, as though they had the sense
  Of some abuse, and struck out with their horns,
  Here I was overwhelmed by righteous anger,
  And of myself not lord, I struck the mess'nger.
WALTER FÜRST: O scarcely do we master our own
  hearts,
  How should the hasty youth restrain himself!
MELCHTAL: I pity but the father—He demands
  So much attention, and his son's away.
  The gov'nor's hateful to him, since he e'er
  Hath striven honestly for right and freedom.
  So therefore they will harry the old man,
  And there is none, who shields him from affront.
  —Come what may come with me, I must go over.
WALTER FÜRST: Just wait and patiently compose
  yourself,
  Until reports come to us from yon forest.
  —I hear a knocking, go—Perhaps a message
  From th' Gov'nor—Go in there—You are not safe
  In Uri 'fore the Landenberger's arm,
  Since tyrants give a hand to one another.
MELCHTAL:
  They're teaching us, what we should do.
WALTER FÜRST:                                    Now go!
  I'll call you back, when it is safe out here.
  (MELCHTAL *goes therein.*)
  The wretched man, I may not now confess
  To him, what evil I suspect—Who knocks?
  So oft the door doth creak, I fear disaster.
  Mistrust and treason lurk in every corner,
  Into the house's inmost rooms the bearers

Of power penetrate, soon we shall need,
To place a lock and key upon our doors.

*(He opens and steps back astounded, as* WERNER
STAUFFACHER *enters.)*

What see I?  You, Lord Werner! Now, by God!
A worthy, cherished guest—No better man
Hath ever walked across this threshold yet.
You're highly welcome underneath my roof!
What brings you here?  What seek you here in Uri?
STAUFFACHER *(extending him his hand):*
The olden times and olden Switzerland.
WALTER FÜRST: You bring them with you—Look, how
    I rejoice,
My heart grows warm upon the sight of you,
—Sit down, Lord Werner—How did you depart
From Lady Gertrud, your most pleasant wife,
Sagacious Iberg's highly prudent daughter?
By all the wand'rers from the German lands,
Who cross the Meinrad's Cell to Italy,
Your hospitality is praised—But say,
Have you just come direct from Flüelen hence,
And did you look in any other place,
Before you placed your foot upon this threshold?
STAUFFACHER *(sits down):* Yes, an astonishing new
    work I've seen
In preparation, with which I'm not pleased.
WALTER FÜRST: O friend, you have it then with but
    *one* glance!
STAUFFACHER: A thing like that hath never been in
    Uri—
In human mem'ry was no prison here,
Nor dwelling fortified except the grave.
WALTER FÜRST: A grave of freedom is't. You name its
    name.
STAUFFACHER: Lord Walter Fürst, I won't hold back
    with you,
No idle curiosity conducts

Me here, I'm pressed by heavy cares—Oppression
I've left at home, oppression find I here.
For 'tis insufferable, what we endure,
And there's no end in sight to this distress.
Free hath the Schweizer been from ancient times,
We are accustomed, to be treated well,
The like of this was in the land ne'er known,
So long a herdsman drove upon these mountains.

WALTER FÜRST: Yes, 'tis unparalleled, how they are
    acting!
Even our noble Lord of Attinghausen,
Who hath the ancient times still seen himself,
Believes, it is no longer to be borne.

STAUFFACHER: Below yon forest goes it poorly too,
And bloody is the penance—Wolfenschiessen,
The Emp'ror's Governor, who dwelt at Rossberg,
He had a longing for forbidden fruit,
Baumgarten's wife, that keeps house in Alzellen,
He wished to misuse her to bold excess,
And with his axe the man hath struck him dead.

WALTER FÜRST: O righteous are the judgments of the
    Lord!
—Baumgarten, do you say? A modest man.
He's rescued surely and is well concealed?

STAUFFACHER: Your son-in-law took him across the
    lake,
I keep him hidden at my house in Steinen—
—Yet more atrocious things hath this same man
Conveyed to me, of what's been done in Sarnen.
The heart of every honest man must bleed.

WALTER FÜRST (attentively):
Say on, what is't?

STAUFFACHER:        In *Melchtal*, then, where one
Goes into *Kerns*, there lives an upright man,
They call him Heinrich von der Halden, and
His voice is of some weight in the Assembly.

WALTER FÜRST: Who knows him not! What is't with
    him?

Proceed!

STAUFFACHER:  The Landenberger penalized his son
  For some small misdeed, ordered his best pair
  Of oxen, be unharnessed from the plow,
  The boy then struck the knave and took to flight.

WALTER FÜRST (*in highest excitement*):
  And yet the father—say, how's it with him?

STAUFFACHER:  The Landenberger had the father
    summoned.
  He should produce his son upon the spot,
  And as the old man swore with truthfulness,
  That he knew nothing of the fugitive,
  The Gov'rnor ordered torturers to come—

WALTER FÜRST (*Springs up and wants to lead him to
    the other side.*):
  O hush, no more!

STAUFFACHER (*with climbing sound*):
              "E'en hath the son escaped me,
  Yet have I *thee!*"—Has him thrown to the ground,
  The pointed steel has plunged into his eyes—

WALTER FÜRST:  Merciful Heaven!

MELCHTAL (*rushes out*):              In his eyes, you say?

STAUFFACHER (*astonished, to* WALTER FÜRST):
  Who is the youth?

MELCHTAL (*grasps him with convulsive vehemence*):
              Into his eyes?  Speak on!

WALTER FÜRST:  O the lamentable old man!

STAUFFACHER:                          Who is't?
  (*As* WALTER FÜRST *gives him a sign.*)
  This is the son?  All righteous God!

MELCHTAL:                          And I
  Had to be hence!—Into both of his eyes?

WALTER FÜRST:  Restrain yourself, endure it like a man!

MELCHTAL:  Because of my *offense*, of *my* misdeed!
  —He's blind then! Really *blind* and *fully* blinded?

STAUFFACHER:  I say't. The fountain of his sight's run
    out,
  The sunlight he will ne'er behold again.

WALTER FÜRST:  O spare his anguish!
MELCHTAL:                              Never! Never more!
   *(He presses his hand upon his eyes and is silent a few
   moments, then he turns from the one to the other and
   speaks with a gentle voice, choked by tears.)*
   O, what a noble gift of heaven is
   The light o' th' eye—For every being lives
   From light, and each and every happy creature—
   The plants themselves turn joyously toward light.
   And *he* must sit there, feeling, in the night,
   In constant darkness—he's refreshed no more
   By meadows of warm green, the flower's glaze,
   The reddish glaciers he can see no more—
   To die is naught—to *live* and not to *see*,
   That's misery—Why do you look at me
   So grievously?  I have two lively eyes,
   And can give neither to my blinded father,
   Nor any shimmer from the sea of light,
   That splendid, dazzling, breaks upon mine eyes.
STAUFFACHER:  Alas, I must enlarge your sorrow
      further,
   Instead of healing it—He wants still more!
   The Governor hath stolen all from him,
   Naught hath he left to him except his staff,
   To wander bare and blind from door to door.
MELCHTAL:  Naught but his staff to th' sightless aged
      man!
   Everything robbed, and e'en the light o' th' sun,
   The common good o' th' poorest wretch—Now speak
   To me no more of staying or of hiding!
   What kind of wretched coward have I been,
   That of *mine* own security I thought,
   And not of thine—thy precious head left as
   Security within the tyrant's hands!
   Faint-hearted caution, travel hence—On naught
   But bloody retribution shall I think—
   I will go over there—No one shall stop me—
   And from the Governor claim my father's eyes—

I'll find him even in the midst of all
His mounted men—Life is but naught to me,
If I can only quench this feverish,
Enormous pain in his life's blood! *(He wants to leave.)*
WALTER FÜRST:                    Remain!
What could you do to him?  He sits in Sarnen
Upon his lofty lordly keep and scoffs
At unavailing wrath in his safe fortress.
MELCHTAL:  And lived he yonder in the icy palace
Of *Schreckhorn* or much higher, where the *Jungfrau*
Sits veiled eternally—I still would make
My way to him, with only twenty youths,
Disposed like I, then I would break his fortress.
And if none follows me, and if you all
So frightened for your huts and for your herds,
Bow down before the tyrant's yoke—I'll call
The herdsmen all together in the mountains,
There underneath the open roof of heaven,
Where still the mind is fresh and heart is sound,
Relate the story of this monstrous horror.
STAUFFACHER *(to* WALTER FÜRST*):*
It hath now reached its height—Are we to wait,
Until the last extreme—
MELCHTAL:                    What last extreme
Is to be feared yet, if the star o' th' eye
Is safe no longer in its cavity?
—Are we defenseless?  Wherefore did we learn
To bend the bow and swing the heavy weight
Of battle axes?  Every creature hath
Been granted a defense in its despair,
Th' exhausted stag will take a stand and show
His dreaded antlers to the pack of hounds,
The chamois drags the hunter in th' abyss—
The ox itself, the gentle fellow lodger
Of man, who bends th' enormous power of
His neck with patience underneath the yoke,
Springs up, provoked, whets his gigantic horns
And slings his enemy up to the clouds.

WALTER FÜRST:  If the three cantons thought as we
    three men,
  So then might we perhaps accomplish something.
STAUFFACHER:  If Uri calls, if Unterwalden helps,
  The Schweizer will revere the ancient bond.
MELCHTAL:  In Unterwalden I have many friends,
  And each would risk his life and limb with joy,
  If he hath back up from the others and
  A shield—O pious fathers of this land!
  I'm standing here now but a youth between you,
  The much experienced—my voice must be
  Discreetly silent in the land's Assembly.
  Because I'm young and know not much of life,
  Do not disdain my counsel and my speech,
  Not lustful youthful blood impels me, but
  The painful violence o' th' greatest woe,
  Which e'en the stone o' th' rock must move to pity.
  You both are fathers, heads of both your houses,
  And you desire to have a virtuous son,
  Who will revere your head's most sacred locks,
  And piously protect your eyesight's star.
  O since you both have suffered nothing yet
  In limb and property, your eyes still move
  Themselves alert and bright within their spheres,
  So therefore be not distant to our need.
  The tyrant's sword hangs over you as well,
  You've turned away the land of Austria,
  My father's crime was nothing more than that,
  You share an equal guilt and condemnation.
STAUFFACHER (to WALTER FÜRST):
  Do *you* decide, I am prepared to follow.
WALTER FÜRST:  We wish to hear, what do the noble
    lords
  Of Sillinen, and Attinghaus advise—
  Their names, I think, will win us over friends.
MELCHTAL:  Where's there a name within the forest
    mountains
  That's worthier than yours or that of yours?

The people do believe i' th' genuine worth
Of names like these, their ring is good i' th' country.
Rich was your heritage in father's virtue
And richly you've enlarged on it—What need
Of noblemen? Let's finish it alone.
Were we indeed alone i' th' land! I think,
We'd know already how to shield ourselves.

STAUFFACHER: The noble's plight is not the same as
    ours,
The stream, which rages in the lower grounds,
Til now hath not yet reached unto the heights—
But they will not refuse us their support,
When they once see the country up in arms.

WALTER FÜRST: Were there 'tween us and Austria an
    umpire,
So then would justice and the law decide,
But he who doth oppress us, is our Emp'ror
And highest judge—so therefore *God must help us
Through our own arm*—Now *you* seek out the men
Of Schwyz, and *I'll* win over friends in Uri.
But whom are we to send to Unterwalden—

MELCHTAL: Send me o'er there—whom should it more
    concern—

WALTER FÜRST: I won't allow it, you're my guest, I
    have
To guarantee your safety!

MELCHTAL:                    Let me go!
I know the byways and the rocky paths,
Friends too I find enough, who'll hide me from
The enemy and gladly give me shelter.

STAUFFACHER: Let him with God go over there. O'er
    there
There are no traitors—so detested is
This tyranny, that it can find no tool.
Below the forest too should the Alzellen
Recruit confederates and rouse the land.

MELCHTAL: How shall we safely then communicate,
That we deceive suspicions of the tyrants?

STAUFFACHER: We could perhaps arrange to meet at
    *Treib*
Or *Brunnen,* where the merchant vessels land.
WALTER FÜRST: So openly we may not go to work.
  Hear my idea. To th' left o' th' lake, on th' way
  To Brunnen, opposite the Mythenstein,
  A meadow lies concealed within the woods,
  It's called the Rütli by the shepherd folk,
  Because the timber there was all uprooted.
  That's where our canton's boundary and yours *(to*
    MELCHTAL*)*
  Adjoin each other, and a little trip *(to* STAUFFACHER*)*
  In your light boat bears you across from Schwyz.
  Upon deserted paths can we go thence
  At night and quietly deliberate.
  Let each bring there with him ten trusted men,
  Who are at one with us within their hearts,
  So then may we discuss the common cause
  In common and with God resolve afresh.
STAUFFACHER: So be't. Now give your staunch right
    hand to me,
  And give me yours as well and thus, as we
  *Three men* have now, among ourselves, entwined
  Our hands, in honesty, without deception,
  So too shall we *three cantons* stand together
  In defense and in offense, death and life.
WALTER FÜRST AND MELCHTAL:
  In death and life! *(They hold their hands clasped*
    *together for a few moments longer and are silent.)*
MELCHTAL:        O blinded, aged father!
  Thou can'st no longer *see* the day of freedom,
  But thou shalt *hear* it—When from Alp to Alp
  The fiery signals rise aloft in flame,
  The sturdy castles of the tyrants fall,
  Unto thy cottage shall the Schweizer travel,
  To carry to thine ear the joyous news,
  And in thy night shall it be day to thee.
*(They part from one another.)*

# ACT II

## SCENE I

*Manor of the* BARON VON ATTINGHAUSEN.

*A Gothic hall adorned with escutcheons and helmets. The* BARON, *an old man of eighty-five years, of tall and noble stature, on a staff, on which there is a chamois horn, and clothed in a pelisse.* KUONI *and another six farm hands stand around him with rakes and scythes.*—ULRICH VON RUDENZ *enters in knight's apparel.*

RUDENZ:  Here am I, Uncle—Now what is your will?
ATTINGHAUSEN:  Permit, that I by ancient fam'ly custom
First share the morning drink with these my workmen.
*(He drinks from a beaker, which then is passed around.)*
In former times I was with them in field and forest,
Directing all their work with mine own eye,
Just as my banner led them into battle,
Now I can not be more than but the steward,
And if the genial sun come not to me,
I can no longer seek it on the mountains.
And so in closer still and closer circles,
I move on slowly to the closest and
The last, where every life comes to a stop,
I'm but my shadow, soon I'm but my name.
KUONI *(to* RUDENZ *with the beaker):*
I bring it to you, squire.
*(Here* RUDENZ *hesitates, to take the beaker.)*
                    Drink up! It is
From out *one* beaker and from out *one* heart.
ATTINGHAUSEN:  Go, children, and when closing time is
    come,
Then we shall talk about the country's business.
*(Farm hands exit.)*

(ATTINGHAUSEN *and* RUDENZ.)

ATTINGHAUSEN:  I see that you are girded and prepared.
   Thou wilt to Altorf and the master's castle?
RUDENZ:  Yes, Uncle, and I may not tarry longer—
ATTINGHAUSEN *(sits down):*
   Art thou so hurried?  How?  Are th' hours of
   Thy youth so meanly measured, that thou must
   Be sparing of them to thine aged uncle?
RUDENZ:  I see, that you are not in need of me,
   I am now but a stranger in this house.
ATTINGHAUSEN *(Hath scrutinized him with his eyes for*
   *some time.):*
   Yes sadly art thou. Sadly hath this home
   To thee become so strange!—Oh, Uly! Uly!
   No longer know I thee. In silks thou struttest,
   The peacock feather thou displayest proudly,
   And fling'st the purple mantle round thy shoulders,
   Thou look'st with scorn upon the countryman,
   And art ashamed of his familiar greeting.
RUDENZ:  The honor, which is due him, give I gladly,
   The rights, that he usurps, I must deny him.
ATTINGHAUSEN:  Th' entire land lies 'neath the heavy
   wrath
   O' th' King—And every man of honor's heart
   Is deeply troubled by the tyrant's force,
   Which we must suffer—Thee alone moves not
   The universal pain—One sees thee stand
   Apostate from thine own upon the side
   O' th' country's enemies, defying our
   Distress to follow after easy joys,
   And court for princely favor, all the while
   Thy fatherland bleeds from the heavy scourge.
RUDENZ:  The land is sore oppressed—Wherefore,
   mine uncle?
   Who is't, who plunged it into this distress?
   It would cost but a single easy word,
   To instantly be free of this oppression,
   And win a favorable Emperor.
   Woe unto those, who seal the people's eyes,

That they resist what truly is the best.
For their own selfish gain they would prevent
The cantons taking oath to Austria,
As every country all around hath done.
It suits them well, to take their seats upon
The master's bench with noblemen—they wish
The *Emperor* lord, to have *no* lord at all.

ATTINGHAUSEN:  Must I hear *that* and from thy very
    mouth!

RUDENZ:  'Twas you who summoned me, now let me
    finish.
  —What person is it, Uncle, you yourself
Play here?  Have you no higher pride than to
Be canton magistrate or standard bearer
And govern here alongside of these herdsmen?
How?  Is it not a far more glorious choice,
To pay one's homage to our royal lord,
Attach oneself unto his splendid camp,
Than yours to be the peer of one's own servants,
And share the judgment seat with countrymen?

ATTINGHAUSEN:  Ah, Uly! Uly! I discern them now,
The voices of seduction! They have seized
Thine open ear, they've filled thine heart with poison.

RUDENZ:  Yes, I conceal it not—deep in my soul
I'm pained by scorn of strangers, who call us
The *peasant noblemen*—Nor can I bear't,
Whilst all the noble youth from everywhere
Are reaping honor under Hapsburg's banner,
To sit here idly on my heritage,
And see the springtime of my life depart
In ordinary daily labor—Elsewhere
Great deeds are happening, a world of fame
Is brilliantly astir beyond these mountains—
*My* helm and shield are rusting in the hall,
The martial trumpeting of valiant tones,
The herald's call, which summons to the tourney,
It doth not penetrate into these valleys,
Naught but the *cowherd dance* and cattle bells

Do I hear here in one unchanging peal.
ATTINGHAUSEN: Deluded man, seduced by idle glow!
Despise thy land of birth! Thou art ashamed
Of ancient pious customs of thy fathers!
With burning tears thou wilt some day be sick
With longing for your own paternal mountains,
And for that melody i' th' cowherd's dance,
Which now in proud disgust thou dost disdain,
With painful longing will it capture thee,
When it awakes thee in the foreign land.
Oh, mighty is the urge o' th' fatherland!
The false and alien world is not for thee,
There in the haughty Emperor's court thou wilt
Remain forever strange with thy true heart!
The world, it doth require other virtues,
Than those thou hast acquired in these valleys.
—Go hither then, dispose of thy free soul,
Take land in fief, become a prince's servant,
There thou canst be lord of thyself and prince
Of thine own heritage and thy free soil.
Ah, Uly! Uly! Stay among thine own!
Go not to Altorf—O, do not forsake,
The sacred cause of thine own fatherland!
—I am the last one of my line. My name
Will end with me. There hang my helm and shield,
These will they bury with me in the grave.
And must I think with my last dying breath,
That thou but wait'st the closing of mine eyes,
To take thyself 'fore this new feudal court,
And all my noble goods, which freely I
Received from God, receive from Austria!
RUDENZ: It is in vain that we resist the King,
The world belongs to him, wish we alone
To stiffen selfishly and to withdraw,
To interrupt the chain of territories,
Which he hath mightily drawn up around us?
*His* are the markets, and the courts, *his* are
The merchant roads, and e'en the horse of burden,

That passes on the Gotthard, pays him toll.
By his dominions, as within a net,
Are we enmeshed and circled round about.
—And will the Empire fend for us? Can it
Defend itself 'gainst Austria's growing power?
Helps God us not, no Emperor can help us.
What good can be assigned the Emperor's word,
When they to meet both war and money needs,
May pawn the cities, which have fled beneath
The eagle's shield, and sell them to the Empire?
—No, Uncle! 'Tis a blessing and wise caution,
In grievous times like these of party strife,
To join oneself unto some mighty chief.
The Emperor's crown proceeds from line to line,
*It* hath no memory for faithful service,
To serve hereditary masters well,
Means strewing seeds i'th' future.

ATTINGHAUSEN:                              Th'art so wise?
Wilt see more clearly, than thy noble father,
Who battled for the precious gem of freedom
With property and blood and hero's strength?
—Sail down unto *Lucerne*, inquire *there*,
How Austria's rule doth weigh upon the land!
Soon they will come up here to count our sheep
And cows, to measure off our Alpine lands,
To ban the fowl and large game animals
In our free forest lands, to set up tolls
At all our bridges, and at all our gates,
Out of our poverty to pay for lands
They purchase, with our blood to fund their wars—
—No, if we have to risk our blood thereon,
So be't *for us*—we purchase liberty
More cheaply than enslavement!

RUDENZ:                              What can we,
A shepherd folk, i' th' face of Albrecht's armies!

ATTINGHAUSEN:  O learn to know this shepherd people,
    boy!
I know them, I have led them into battle,

I have observed them fighting at Favenz.
Let them come here, to force a yoke on us,
That we are resolute, we shall not bear!
—O learn to feel, the stock from which thou art!
Cast not away the genuine pearl of thine
Own worth for idle show and hollow pomp—
To be known as the head of a *free* people,
That but from love devotes itself to thee,
That's loyal to thee both in strife and death—
*That* be thy pride, of *this* nobility
Make boast—the native bonds knit firmly to
The fatherland, to th' cherished, join thyself,
Hold fast to it with thine entire heart.
Here are the sturdy roots of all thy strength,
There in the alien world thou stand'st alone,
A slender weed, that every storm may snap.
O come, thou hast not seen us for some time,
Try it with us for but *one* day—today
Go not to Altorf—Hear'st thou?  Not today,
But this one day bestow thee on thine own!
(*He takes his hand.*)

RUDENZ:  I gave my word—Let go of me—I'm bound.

ATTINGHAUSEN (*Lets go of his hand, with earnestness.*):
Th'art bound—O yes indeed, unhappy one!
Thou art, though not by word and oath,
'Tis through the ropes of love that thou art bound!
(*Rudenz turns away.*)
—Conceal it, as thou wilt. It is the lady,
Berta von Bruneck, who draws thee unto
The castle, fetters thee to th' Emperor's service.
The knightly lady thou hast hopes to win
By thy defection from thy land—Be not deceived!
They show the bride to thee but as a lure,
Yet she's not granted to thine innocence.

RUDENZ:  Enough have I now heard. Fare well to you.
(*He exits.*)

ATTINGHAUSEN:  Deluded youth, stay here!—He's gone
away!

I can not hold him back, not rescue him—
So hath the Wolfenschiessen turned away
From his own country—so will others follow,
The alien magic tears the youth away,
By force aspiring far beyond our mountains.
—O ill-begotten hour, when what is strange
Came here into these tranquil blessed valleys,
To ruin the pious innocence of custom!
—The new is pressing on with might, the old,
The worthy is now leaving, other times are coming,
A different-thinking generation lives!
What do I here? All those are buried now,
With whom I shared my work and passed my life.
Beneath the earth *my* time already lies;
He's blest, who with the *new* no longer needs to live!
(*Exit.*)


## SCENE II

*A meadow surrounded by high rocks and woods.*

*Upon the rocks are tracks, with rails, also ladders, by which one later sees the countrymen descend. In the hinterground the lake shows itself, above which at first a lunar rainbow is to be seen. The prospect is closed by high mountains, behind which still higher glaciers tower. It is completely night upon the stage, only the lake and the white glacier shine in the moonlight.* MELCHTAL, BAUMGARTEN, WINKEL-RIED, MEIER VON SARNEN, BURKHARDT AM BÜHEL, AR-NOLD VON SEWA, KLAUS VON DER FLÜE *and yet four other countrymen, all armed.*


MELCHTAL (*still backstage*):
  The mountain pass is op'ning, follow *me*,
  I know the rock and little cross thereon,
  We're at our goal, here is the Rütli.
  (*Enter with storm-lanterns.*)

WINKELRIED:                             Hark!
SEWA:  Deserted.
MEIER:                 There's no countryman here yet.
  We are the first to come, we Unterwaldners.
MELCHTAL:
  How far is't in the night?
BAUMGARTEN:                 The fire watch
  In Selisberg hath only just called two.
  *(One hears ringing in the distance.)*
MEIER:  Hush! Hark!
AM BÜHEL:              The matin bell i' th' forest chapel
  Rings clearly over here from Schwyzerland.
VON DER FLÜE:  The air is pure and bears the sound so
    far.
MELCHTAL:  Go some of you and light some fire wood,
  That it burn brightly, when the men arrive.
  *(Two countrymen exit.)*
SEWA:  It is a beauteous lunar night. The lake
  Lies calmly here just like a level mirror.
AM BÜHEL:  They have an easy voyage.
WINKELRIED *(points toward the lake):*  Ha, behold!
  Look yonder! See you naught?
MEIER:                        What then?—Yes,
    truly!
  A rainbow in the middle of the night!
MELCHTAL:  It is the light o' th' moon, that causes it.
VON DER FLÜE:  That is a passing strange and wondrous
    sign!
  There live full many, who've not seen the like.
SEWA:  'Tis doubled, see, a paler one's above.
BAUMGARTEN:  A boat is passing underneath it now.
MELCHTAL:  That's Stauffacher who crosses in his boat,
  The worthy man would not delay for long.
  *(Goes with BAUMGARTEN toward the shore.)*
MEIER:  It is the Uri, who delay the longest.
AM BÜHEL:  They have to detour widely through the
    mountains,
  So that they may deceive the Governor's spies.

*(In the meantime the two countrymen have set a fire in
the middle of the place.)*

MELCHTAL *(on the shore):*
Who is it?  Give the word!

STAUFFACHER *(from below):*  Friends of the land.

*(All go to the rear, toward those arriving. Out of the
boat climbs* STAUFFACHER, ITEL REDING, HANS AUF
DER MAUER, JÖRG IM HOFE, KONRAD HUNN, ULRICH
DER SCHMIED, JOST VON WEILER *and yet three
other countrymen, likewise armed.)*

ALL *(shout):*  Be welcome!

*(Whilst the rest linger in the rear,* MELCHTAL *comes
forward with* STAUFFACHER.*)*

MELCHTAL:                    O Lord Stauffacher! I've him
Beheld, who never could see *me* again!
I've placed my hands upon his very eyes,
I've drawn the burning feeling of revenge
From the extinguished sunlight of his glance.

STAUFFACHER:  Speak not of vengeance. We desire to
        meet
The threatened evil, not avenge the past.
—Now say, what you in Unterwalden have
Achieved and 'listed for the common cause,
How think the countrymen, how you yourself
Have managed to escape the snares of treason.

MELCHTAL:  Through the Surenen's fearsome mountain
        range,
Upon the widespread empty fields of ice,
Where but the croaking lammergeyer caws,
I reached the Alpine meadow, where the herdsmen
From Uri and from Engelberg extend
Their greetings and in common tend their flocks,
My thirst relieving with the glacier's milk,
Which in the Runsen foams and gushes down.
I stayed in isolated Alpine huts,
Both mine own host and guest, until I came
Unto the homes of social living men.
—Already through these valleys word rang out

Of new atrocities, which had occurred,
And pious awe I found for my misfortune
'Fore every gate, where wandering I knocked.
Indignant did I find these upright souls
About the violence of the new regime,
For as their Alpine meadows ceaselessly
Give nourishment to the same plants, their springs
Flow uniformly, even clouds and winds
Pursue unchangeably the self-same course,
So hath the ancient customs here from grandsire
To grandson persevered just as before,
Nor do they bear audacious innovation
I' th' old accustomed even way of life.
—Their hardened hands to me they did extend,
From the walls they lifted down their rusty swords,
And from their eyes there flashed a joyous feeling
Of courage, as I spake the names to them,
Which to the mountain countryman are holy,
Your name and that of Walter Fürst—What you
Would deem is right, they swore an oath to do,
They swore to follow you e'en unto death.
—So sped I safely 'neath the holy shield
Of hospitality from farm to farm—
And as I came into my native vale,
Where widely scattered round my cousins dwell—
As I beheld my father, robbed and blind,
On stranger's straw, sustained by charity
Of tender-hearted people—
STAUFFACHER:                    Lord in Heaven!
MELCHTAL: Then wept I not! No—not in helpless tears
Did I pour out the force of my hot grief,
Deep in my bosom like a precious treasure
I locked it up and thought of action only.
I crept through every winding of the mountain,
No vale was so concealed, I spied it out,
Unto the glacier's ice-attired foot
Expected I and found inhabited huts,
And everywhere, my footsteps carried me,

Found I the self-same hate of tyranny,
For even at this final boundary
Of living nature, where the rigid earth
No longer gives, the governor's greed doth rob—
The very hearts of all those honest people
Aroused I with the goading of my words,
And all of them are ours with heart and mouth.

STAUFFACHER: Great things have you achieved in little
time.

MELCHTAL: I did still more. 'Tis those two fortresses,
*Rossberg* and *Sarnen,* the countryman doth fear,
For from behind their walls of stone the foe
Defends himself with ease and harms the land.
With mine own eyes I wished to study it,
I went to Sarnen and beheld the castle.

STAUFFACHER: You risked yourself e'en in the tiger's
den?

MELCHTAL: I was disguised there in a pilgrim's dress,
I saw the Governor feasting at the table—
Now judge, if I can master mine own heart,
I saw the enemy and slew him not.

STAUFFACHER: Forsooth, good fortune smiled upon
your boldness.
(*In the meantime the other countrymen are come
forward and are approaching both of them.*)
Yet tell me right away, who are the friends,
And upright men, who followed after you?
Make me acquainted with them, that we may
Draw near in trust and open up our hearts.

MEIER: Who knows not *you,* my Lord, in these three
lands?
My name is Meier von Sarnen, this one here
Is Struth von Winkelried, my sister's son.

STAUFFACHER: You do not name me any unknown
names.
A Winkelried it was, who slew the dragon
I' th' swamp at Weiler and his life relinquished
In this affray.

WINKELRIED:    That was my sire, Lord Werner.
MELCHTAL *(points to two countrymen)*:
  *These* dwell behind the woods, are cloister monks
  From Engelberg—You will not look upon
  Them with disdain, because they're *serfs,* and sit
  Not free like we upon our heritage—
  They love the land, are else of good repute.
STAUFFACHER *(to both of them)*:
  Give me your hand. He's fortunate, whose body
  Is duty-bound to no one on this earth,
  But honesty doth thrive in every class.
KONRAD HUNN:  This is Lord Reding, our old
    Magistrate.
MEIER:  I know him well. He is my adversary,
  Who o'er a piece of land disputes with me.
  —Lord Reding, we are enemies at court,
  Here we are one. *(Shakes his hand.)*
STAUFFACHER:      Now that is bravely spoken.
WINKELRIED:  You hear? They're coming. Hear the
    horn of Uri!
  *(To the right and left one sees armed men climb down
    from the rocks with storm lanterns.)*
AUF DER MAUER:  Look! Is that not God's pious servant
    there,
  The worthy pastor climbing down? Nor shuns
  He toils o' th' way and terrors of the night,
  A faithful shepherd caring for his people.
BAUMGARTEN:  The Sacrist trails him and Lord Walter
    Fürst,
  But Tell I do not see among the number.
  *(WALTER FÜRST, RÖSSELMANN the pastor, PETERMANN
    the Sacristan, KUONI the shepherd, WERNI the
    hunter, RUODI the fisherman and yet five other
    countrymen, all together, thirty-three in number,
    step forward and take their places around the fire.)*
WALTER FÜRST:  So must we now upon our native soil
  And our paternal lands in secrecy
  Creep forth to meet, like murderers must do,

And by the night, which lends its sable cloak
But to the crime and to conspiracies
That shun the sunlight, we must seize upon
Our goodly right, the which is pure and clear,
Just as the splendid open womb of day.

MELCHTAL: Leave it at that. What darksome night hath
    spun,
Is free and joyous in the light o' th' sun.

RÖSSELMANN: Confederates, hear what God bids my
    heart!
We're meeting here in place of an Assembly
And can be deemed to represent the people,
So let us meet by ancient usages
O' th' land, as we were wont in tranquil times,
Whatever is unlawful in this meeting,
Be pardoned by the need o' th' time. Yet God
Is everywhere, where justice is dispensed,
And underneath his Heaven do we stand.

STAUFFACHER: 'Tis well, let's meet in line with ancient
    custom,
Though it is night, so shines our justice forth.

MELCHTAL: Though not in number full, the *heart* is
    here
Of all the people, here the *best* attend.

KONRAD HUNN: Are not the ancient books as well at
    hand,
Yet they are written down within our hearts.

RÖSSELMANN: Now then, so let the ring be formed at
    once.
Set *up* the swords of power in the ground.

AUF DER MAUER: Now let the Magistrate assume his
    place,
And let his bailiffs stand at either side!

SACRISTAN: There are three peoples here, to which
    belongs
The right, to give a head to the Assembly?

MEIER: Schwyz may contest with Uri for this honor,
We Unterwaldners freely stand aside.

MELCHTAL: We stand aside, we are the suppliants,
Who ask assistance from their mighty friends.
STAUFFACHER: Let Uri then assume the sword, its flag
Takes precedence upon our march to Rome.
WALTER FÜRST: The honor of the sword should fall to
Schwyz,
For we all pride ourselves upon its stock.
RÖSSELMANN: Let me resolve this noble competition,
Schwyz leads in council, Uri in the field.
WALTER FÜRST (*hands* STAUFFACHER *the swords*):
So take!
STAUFFACHER: Not I, to th' eldest be the honor.
IM HOFE: Ulrich der Schmied is most advanced in
years.
AUF DER MAUER: The man is brave, but not of free
estate,
No bondman can become a judge in Schwyz.
STAUFFACHER: Is not Lord Reding here, the
Magistrate?
Why should we seek for one yet worthier?
WALTER FÜRST: Let him be Magistrate and chief o' th'
day!
Who doth agree thereto, lift up his hand.
(*All lift up their right hand.*)
REDING (*steps into the middle*):
I can not place my hand upon the books,
So swear I by th' eternal stars above,
That I will never deviate from justice.
(*The two swords are placed upright before him, the
ring is formed around him,* SCHWYZ *holds the
center,* URI *places itself to the right, and*
UNTERWALDEN *to the left. He stands leaning on his
battle sword.*)
What is it, that hath brought together here
Three mountain people at this ghostly hour
Upon the barren shoreline of this lake?
What should the content be of this new league,
Which we here found beneath the heaven's stars?

STAUFFACHER (*steps into the ring*):
　No new alliance do we found, it is
　An old alliance from our fathers' time,
　That we renew! Know well, confederates!
　Though lake, though mountain range may us divide,
　And every people govern for itself,
　So are we yet of but *one* stock and blood,
　And but *one* homeland is't, from which we come.
WINKELRIED: So is it true, as it is said in song,
　That we've come from afar into this land?
　O, tell us now, whatever's known to you,
　That this new league be strengthened by the old.
STAUFFACHER: Hear, what the aged herdsmen do
　　relate.
　—There was a mighty people, in the land
　Back to the north, that suffer'd from harsh famine.
　In this distress th' Assembly did resolve,
　That every tenth man as the lot might fall
　Should leave his fatherland—that did occur!
　And forth, lamenting, men and women went,
　A giant army, toward the midday sun,
　With sword in hand they struck through German
　　lands,
　Unto the highlands of these mountain forests.
　And never did the host become fatigued,
　Until they came upon the savage vale,
　Where now the Muotta runs between the meads—
　No trace of human beings was here seen,
　But one lone shelter stood upon the shore,
　Here sat a man and waited for the ferry—
　Yet violently the lake did rage and was
　Not passable; so they beheld the land
　More closely and perceived the beauteous wealth
　Of timber and discovered goodly springs,
　And thought, they were in their dear fatherland—
　Then they at once determined to remain,
　Erected there the ancient town of *Schwyz*,
　And many bitter days they had, to clear

The forest with its widely spreading roots—
Then later, as the soil no more sufficed
The people's number, they proceeded hither
To the black mountain, yes to Weissland hence,
Where, hidden by eternal walls of ice
Another people speak another tongue.
The village *Stanz* they built beside the Kernwald,
The village *Altorf* by the valley of the Reuss—
Yet stayed they ever mindful of their source,
From all the foreign races, that since then
Have settled in the middle of their land,
The men of Schwyz each other recognize,
There is the heart, the blood by which they're known.
*(Extends his hand to the right and left.)*
AUF DER MAUER: Yes, we are of one heart and of one
    blood!
ALL *(extending their hands):*
We are *one* people and will act as one.
STAUFFACHER: The other people bear a foreign yoke,
They have submitted to the conqueror.
Even within our country's bounds there live
Some settlers, who are bound by foreign duties,
And pass their servitude on to their children.
Yet *we*, the genuine race of ancient Schwyz,
We have forever kept our liberty.
Never to princes have we bowed the knee,
Freely we chose the Emperor's protection.
RÖSSELMANN: We freely chose the Empire's shield and
    refuge,
So doth it read in Emp'ror Friedrich's charter.
STAUFFACHER: For masterless is also not the freest.
There has to be a chief, a highest judge,
Where one may turn for justice in disputes.
Hence for the ground, which they have salvaged from
The ancient wilderness, our fathers granted
The honor to the Emperor, who's called
The Lord of German and Italian soil,
And like the other freemen of his realm

Pledged him the noble service of their arms,
For this alone is every freeman's duty,
To shield the Empire, which gives him protection.
MELCHTAL: What is beyond that, hath the mark of
    serfdom.
STAUFFACHER: Whene'er the call to arms went forth,
    they follow'd
The Empire's banner and they fought its battles.
To Italy they marched with arms in hand,
To place the Roman crown upon his head.
At home they ruled themselves most cheerfully
By ancient usages and their own law,
Blood sentences alone were th' Emp'ror's right.
And thereto was assigned a noble count,
Who had his domicile not in the land,
When blood guilt came to pass, they summon'd him,
And 'neath the open heavens, plain and clear,
Spake he the law and with no fear of men.
Where are the traces here, that we are slaves?
Is there one, who knows otherwise, speak out!
IM HOFE: No, everything stands thus, just as you state,
We've never tolerated despotism.
STAUFFACHER: E'en to th' Emperor we refused
    obedience,
When he once bent the law to favor parsons.
For as the clerics from the Abbey of
*Einsiedeln* laid a claim upon the Alp,
Which we have grazed on since our fathers' time,
The Abbot yielded up an ancient charter,
Which granted him the unowned wilderness—
For our existence there had been concealed—
And then we spake: "The charter is a fraud.
No Emperor can bestow, that which is ours.
And does the Realm deny our rights, we can
Amidst our mountains do without the Realm."
—In such a way our fathers spake! Should we
Endure the infamy of this new yoke,
And suffer from the foreign vassal, what

No Emp'ror in his might would do to us?
—This soil we have *created* for ourselves
By labor of our hands, the ancient wood,
Which else was but the savage home of bears,
We've changed into a domicile for men,
The brood of dragons have we extirpated,
Which poison-swollen climbed out of the swamps,
The misty cover have we torn away,
Which always grey hung o'er this wilderness,
The solid rocks blown up, o'er the abyss
The wanderer conducted on safe paths,
By the possession of a thousand years
The soil is ours—and now the foreign vassal
Should dare to come and forge his chains on us,
And bring disgrace upon our very soil?
Is there no help against such great distress?
*(A great motion among the countrymen.)*
No, there's a limit to the tyrant's power,
When the oppressed can find no justice, when
The burden grows unbearable—he reaches
With hopeful courage up unto the heavens
And seizes hither his eternal rights,
Which hang above, inalienable
And indestructible as stars themselves—
The primal state of nature reappears,
Where man stands opposite his fellow man—
As last resort, when not another means
Is of avail, the sword is given him—
The highest of all goods we may defend
From violence.—We stand before our country,
We stand before our wives, before our children!
ALL *(striking their swords):*
Thus stand we 'fore our wives and 'fore our children!
RÖSSELMANN *(steps into the ring):*
Before you seize the swords, bethink it well.
You could resolve it calmly with the Emperor.
It costs you but a word and those same tyrants,
Who now oppress you harshly, flatter you.

—Accept, what often hath been offered you,
Renounce the Empire, yield to Austria's power—

AUF DER MAUER:
What says the priest?  We swear to Austria!

AM BÜHEL:
Hark not to him!

WINKELRIED:          It is a traitor's counsel,
A foe o' th' country!

REDING:                    Calm, confederates!

SEWA:  We swear to Austria, after such disgrace!

VON DER FLÜE:  We let ourselves be cowed by force to
do,
What we refused to kindliness!

MEIER:                              Then were
We slaves and would deserve to be the same!

AUF DER MAUER:
Let him be stripped of all a Schweizer's rights,
Whoever speaks of giving up to Austria!
Magistrate, I insist thereon, this be
The first law of the land, that we here give.

MELCHTAL:  So be't. Who speaks of giving up to
Austria,
Shall be an outlaw and all honor lack,
No countryman receive him at his hearth.

ALL (*raise their right hands*):
We're all agreed, that this be law!

REDING (*after a pause*):              It is't.

RÖSSELMANN:  Now be you free, you are so through the
law,
Never shall Austria extort by force,
What it could not obtain by friendly suit—

JOST VON WEILER:
To the agenda, now.

REDING:                    Confederates!
Have all the gentle means as well been tried?
Perhaps the King is not aware, it is
Not by his will at all, that we must suffer.
This final means we should as well attempt,

First bring our grievances before his ear,
Before we seize the sword. For force is still
Atrocious, even in a righteous cause,
God only helps, when men no longer help.

STAUFFACHER (*to* KONRAD HUNN):
  Now is't for you, to give report. Speak forth.

KONRAD HUNN: I was at Rheinfeld at the Emperor's
    palace,
To plead against the Governor's harsh oppression,
To claim the charter of our ancient freedom,
Which each new King hath formerly confirmed.
I found the envoys there of many cities,
From Swabia and from the path o' th' Rhine,
Who each and all received their documents,
And joyously returned unto their lands.
*Your envoy*, I was shown to councillors,
And they sent me away with empty comfort:
"The Emperor at present had no time,
He would attend to us some other time."
—And as I tearfully passed through the halls
Of the King's castle, I beheld Duke Hansen
Stand weeping in a window bay, 'round him
The noble Lords of Wart and Tegerfeld.
They called to me and stated: "Help your selves,
And do not wait for justice from the King.
Did he not rob his very brother's child,
And keep from him his just inheritance?
The Duke implored him for his mother's land,
He had now fully come of age, it were
Now time, for him to rule both land and people.
How did he answer him? The Emperor placed
A wreath on him: that be the jewel of youth."

AUF DER MAUER: You have now heard it. Do not wait
    for right
And justice from the Emperor! Help your selves.

REDING: Naught else is left to us. Now give advice,
  How we shall guide it to a happy end.

WALTER FÜRST (*steps into the ring*):

We want to drive away the hated force,
The ancient rights, as we inherit them
From our own fathers, we want to preserve,
Not unrestrain'd to reach for what is new.
The Emperor retain, what is the Emperor's,
Who hath a master, serve him dutifully.

MEIER:  I hold my land in fief from Austria.

WALTER FÜRST:  Continue then, to give its due to
  Austria.

JOST VON WEILER:  The Lords of Rappersweil receive
  my tax.

WALTER FÜRST:  Continue then, to pay your rent and
  tax.

RÖSSELMANN:  To Zürich's noble Lady am I sworn.

WALTER FÜRST:  Give to the cloister, that which is the
  cloister's.

STAUFFACHER:  I hold no fief except those of the
  Empire.

WALTER FÜRST:  What needs be, that be done, but not
  beyond.
  The gov'rnors with their vassals would we drive
  Away and all their fortress castles raze,
  Yet, if it might be, bloodlessly. Thus let
  The Emperor see, that only under force
  We've shed the pious duties of respect.
  And sees he us remain within our bounds,
  Perhaps he'll statesmanlike o'ercome his wrath,
  For a just fear is wakened by a people,
  That *moderates* itself with sword in hand.

REDING:  Yet let us hear! *How* can it be achieved?
  The enemy hath weapons in his hands,
  And verily he will not yield in peace.

STAUFFACHER:  He will, when he beholds us under
  arms,
  We shall surprise him, ere he is prepared.

MEIER:  'Tis quickly said, but difficult to do.
  Two fortress castles tower in the land,
  Which shield the enemy and would be fearsome,

If e'er the King should fall upon our land.
Rossberg and Sarnen must be overcome,
Before a sword is raised in these three lands.
STAUFFACHER: Delay so long, so will the foe be
    warned.
There are too many, who now share the secret.
MEIER: There are no traitors in the forest states.
RÖSSELMANN: Zeal also, though 'tis good, can still
    betray.
WALTER FÜRST: Delay it longer, so the keep in Altorf
Is finished, and the Governor secured.
MEIER: You think but of *yourselves.*
SACRISTAN:                 And you're unjust.
MEIER *(jumping up):* Unjust! That Uri dares to say to us!
REDING: Upon your oath, be calm!
MEIER:                Indeed, if Schwyz
Be leagued with Uri, then must we be silent.
REDING: I must point out to you before th' Assembly,
That you disturb the peace with vehement mind!
Stand we not all of us for the same cause?
WINKELRIED: If we delay until it's Feast o' th' Lord,
Then custom brings with it, that all the serfs
Bring presents to the castle for the Governor,
And thus ten men or twelve are able to
Assemble unobserved inside the palace,
Who secretly bear sharpened blades with them,
Which one can swiftly mount upon a staff,
For none can come with weapons in the castle.
Close by i' th' woods the larger number waits,
And if the others have successfully
Secured the gate, so will a horn be blown,
And those will burst forth from their ambush place,
Thus is the castle ours with little work.
MELCHTAL: The Rossberg I will undertake to scale,
A wench i' th' castle is disposed to me,
And I'll delude her easily, to pass
A ladder to me for a nightly visit,
Am I once up, my friends will follow me.

REDING:  Are all agreed, that it shall be postponed?
*(The majority raise their hands.)*
STAUFFACHER *(counts the votes):*
It is a twenty to twelve majority!
WALTER FÜRST:  If on a certain day the castles fall,
So from one mountain to another we
Shall give the sign with smoke, th' militia will
Be summoned, quickly, in each capital,
Then when the governors see our armed resolve,
Believe me, they will soon give up the fight
And willingly accept a peaceful escort,
To flee beyond the borders of our land.
STAUFFACHER:  From Gessler only fear I fierce
    resistance,
Surrounded by his cavalry he's dreadful,
Not without blood quits he the field, yes though
Repelled he still is dreadful to the land,
Hard is't and almost dangerous to spare him.
BAUMGARTEN:  Where it is dang'rous to the neck, place
    me.
To Tell I owe the saving of my life.
With pleasure I shall stake it for the land,
My honor I've secured, my heart contented.
REDING:  Time brings advice. Await it patiently.
One must as well entrust some things to th' moment.
—Yet see, while we still meet here in the night,
Upon the highest mount the morn already
Displays her glowing beacon—Come, let's part,
Before the light of day surprises us.
WALTER FÜRST:  Fear not, the night yields slowly from
    the valleys.
*(All have involuntarily removed their hats and
    contemplate the sunrise with silent concentration.)*
RÖSSELMANN:  Upon this light, that gives us greeting
    first
Of all the people, who far under us
With heavy breathing dwell in smoke-filled cities,
Now let us take the oath of this new league.

—We will become a single land of brothers,
Nor shall we part in danger and distress.
*(All repeat the words with three fingers raised.)*
—We will be free, just as our fathers were,
And sooner die, than live in slavery. *(As above.)*
—We will rely upon the highest God
And we shall never fear the might of men.
*(As above. The countrymen embrace one another.)*
STAUFFACHER:  Now each one go in silence on his way
Unto his friendships and community,
Who's herdsman, winter up his herd in peace
And quietly 'list friends into the league,
—*What* still must be endured until that time,
Endure it! Let the tyrant's reckoning
Increase, until *one* day the universal
And th' individual debt at once are paid.
Let every one restrain his righteous rage,
And save his vengeance only for the whole,
For he despoils the universal good,
Who only helps himself in his own cause.
*(Whilst they exit in greatest calm to three different
sides, the orchestra breaks in with a magnificent
flourish, the empty stage remains open for a time
and displays the spectacle of the rising sun over the
ice-capped mountains.)*

# ACT III

## Scene I

*Court before* TELL's *house.*

*He is busy with the carpenter's axe,* HEDWIG *with some domestic work.* WALTER *and* WILHELM *play at the rear with a small crossbow.*

WALTER *(sings)*:
　With the shaft, the crossbow,
　　Over mounts and streams
　　Doth the archer follow
　　Soon as morning beams.

　As in realms of breezes
　　Kites soar regally,
　　Over mounts and gorges
　　Rules the archer free.

　He commands the yonder,
　　That his shaft achieves,
　　That is his own plunder,
　　What there creeps and flees.
　*(Comes springing.)*
　My string is snapped in two. Please mend it, Father.
TELL:  I not. A genuine archer helps himself.
　*(Boys move away.)*
HEDWIG:  The boys commence betimes to shoot the bow.
TELL:  'Tis only early practice, makes a master.
HEDWIG:  Ah would to God, they never learnt!
TELL:  They should learn everything. Whoever wants
　To pass through life alert, must be prepared
　For defense and for offense.
HEDWIG:　　　　　　　　Ah, he'll find
　No peace at home.
TELL:　　　　　　I can not either, Mother,
　I was not formed by nature for a herdsman,

Restless I must pursue a fleeting goal,
And only then do I enjoy my life,
If every day I seize anew some quarry.
HEDWIG: And think'st thou not about the fear o' th'
   housewife,
Who in the time, while thee awaiting, grieves,
For I am overwhelmed with dread, at what
The servants tell about your daring trips.
With each farewell my heart begins to quake,
That thou wilt never more return to me.
I see thee on the savage icy mountain,
Astray, from one cliff to the other make
A leap that's false, and see, how leaping back
The chamois drags thee with him in th' abyss,
How avalanches bury thee alive,
How underneath thy foot the treach'rous snow
Gives way and then thou sinkest down, into
A living tomb, within the gruesome vault—
Ah, in a hundred alternating forms
Doth death pursue the daring Alpine hunter,
That is an ill-begotten way of life,
That leads with breakneck speed to the abyss!
TELL: Who freshly looks around with healthy senses,
Who trusts in God and his own agile strength,
Will easily escape each need and danger,
The mountain frights not him, who's born thereon.
*(He hath finished his work, lays his tools aside.)*
And now, methinks, the door will hold for years.
The axe at home doth save the carpenter.
*(Takes his hat.)*
HEDWIG: Where art thou bound?
TELL:                   To Altorf, to thy father.
HEDWIG: Hast thou naught dangerous in mind?
   Confess.
TELL: What mak'st thou think so, wife?
HEDWIG:                 There is some plot
   Against the gov'rnors—On the Rütli they
   Conferred, I know, and thou art in the league.

TELL:  I was not there with them—however I
　　Will not foresake my country, when it calls.
HEDWIG:  They'll put thee in a place, where there is
　　danger,
　　The heaviest will be thy share, as always.
TELL:  Each man is taxed according to his means.
HEDWIG:  The Unterwaldner hast thou brought across
　　The lake i' th' storm—It was a miracle,
　　That you escaped—Didst thou think then at all
　　Of child and wife?
TELL:　　　　　　　Dear wife, I thought of you,
　　Therefore I saved the father for his children.
HEDWIG:  To sail upon that raging lake! That is
　　Not putting trust in God! That's tempting God.
TELL:  Who ponders far too much, will little do.
HEDWIG:  Yes, thou art good and helpful, servest all,
　　And when thou com'st in need, no one helps thee.
TELL:  Forbid it God, that ever I need help.
　　*(He takes the crossbow and arrows.)*
HEDWIG:  What wilt thou with the crossbow?  Leave it
　　here.
TELL:  I lack my arm, when I'm without my weapon.
　　*(The boys come back.)*
WALTER:  Father, where art thou bound?
TELL:　　　　　　　　　　　　To Altorf, boy,
　　To Grand-dad—Wilt thou come?
WALTER:　　　　　　　　　Yes sure I will.
HEDWIG:  The Gov'rnor is now there. Stay out of Altorf.
TELL:  He *leaves*, today.
HEDWIG:　　　　　　　Then let him first be gone.
　　Remind him not of thee, thou know'st, he hates us.
TELL:  His ill-will shall not greatly injure me,
　　I do what's right and shrink before no foe.
HEDWIG:  'Tis those who do what's right, he hates the
　　most.
TELL:  Because he cannot come at them—The knight,
　　Will probably leave me in peace, methinks.
HEDWIG:  So, know'st thou that?

TELL:                                    It was not long ago,
  That I went hunting through the wild ravines
  Of Schächental on a deserted trail,
  And there I did proceed alone upon
  A rocky trail, where 'twas no room to yield,
  For over me the wall of rock hung sheer,
  And under thundered frightfully the Schächen,
  *(The boys press toward him to the right and left and*
    *look at him with anxious curiosity.)*
  Then came the Governor in my direction,
  He was alone with me, I too alone,
  Just man to man, and next to us the chasm.
  And when the gentleman caught sight of me
  And knew 'twas me, whom he not long before
  Had punished harshly for some minor cause,
  And saw me with my stately arms in hand
  Come striding hitherward, then turned he pale,
  His knees began to fail, I saw it coming,
  That he would sink against the wall of rock.
  —Then feeling sorry for him, I advanced
  Respectfully and said: 'Tis I, Lord Governor.
  But he could not bring forth a sound
  Out of his mouth—He beckoned silently
  To me with but his hand, to go my way,
  Then went I forth and sent his train to him.
HEDWIG: He hath before thee trembled—Woe to thee!
  That thou hast seen him weak, he'll ne'er forgive.
TELL: Thus shun I him, and he'll not seek for me.
HEDWIG: Just stay away today. Go hunting rather.
TELL: What mean'st thou?
HEDWIG:                              I'm uneasy. Stay away.
TELL: How can'st thou worry so without a reason?
HEDWIG: *Because* there is no reason—Tell, stay here.
TELL: I gave my promise, my dear wife, to come.
HEDWIG: *Must* thou, then go—But leave the boy with
  me!
WALTER: No, Mother dear. I'm going with my father.
HEDWIG: Walty, dost thou intend to leave thy mother?

WALTER:  I'll bring thee something pretty back from
    Grand-dad.
    *(Leaves with his father.)*
WILHELM:  Mother, I'll stay with thee!
    HEDWIG *(embraces him):*            Oh yes, thou art
    Mine own dear child, th'art left alone to me.
    *(She goes to the courtyard gate and follows the
        departing ones with her eyes for some time.)*


### SCENE II

*An enclosed wild region of the forest, waterfalls plunge
in spray from the rocks.*

BERTA *in hunting dress. Directly thereafter* RUDENZ.


BERTA:  He follows me. At last I can explain.
RUDENZ *(enters rashly):*  My lady, now at last alone I
    find you,
    Abysses close us in on every side,
    I fear no witness in this wilderness,
    I throw this lengthy silence from my heart—
BERTA:  You're sure, the huntsmen do not follow us?
RUDENZ:  The huntsmen are out there—'Tis now or
    never!
    I have to seize upon this precious moment—
    I have to see my destiny decided,
    And should it sever me from you forever.
    —O, do not arm your gracious glances with
    This dark severity—For *who* am I,
    That I would raise this daring wish to you?
    Fame hath not named me yet, nor may I take
    My place along the side of all those knights,
    Who woo you with their glory and their glitter.
    Naught have I but my faithful loving heart—
BERTA *(solemnly and sternly):*
    How can you talk of love and faithfulness,
    Who is not faithful to his nearest duties?

(RUDENZ *steps back.*)
The slave of Austria, who sells himself
To th' stranger, to th' oppressor of his people?
RUDENZ: From you, my lady, hear I this reproach?
Whom seek I then, but you upon that side?
BERTA: You think to find me then upon the side
Of traitors? Rather would I give my hand
To Gessler himself, to th' oppressor, than
To th' nature-forgetting son of Schweiz,
Who can transform himself into his tool!
RUDENZ: O God, what must I hear?
BERTA:                     And how? What can
Lie nearer to a good man than his own?
Can any noble heart have fairer duties,
Than to defend those who are innocent,
And to protect the rights of the oppressed?
—My very soul bleeds for your countrymen,
I suffer *with* them, for I have to love them,
Who are so modest and yet full of strength,
They draw all of my heart unto them hence,
Each day I learn to honor them the more.
—But you, whom nature and your knightly duty
Have given them as natural protector,
And who *desert* them, faithlessly go over
To th' foe, and place his countrymen in chains,
You are the one, who hurts and injures me,
I must constrain my heart, that I not hate you.
RUDENZ: Do I not want the best then for my people?
Not peace for them beneath the mighty scepter
Of Austria—
BERTA:         You want to give them bondage!
You want to banish freedom from the last
Castle, that still remains to her on earth,
The people understand their fortune better,
Vain show will not seduce their certain feelings,
They have now cast the net about your head—
RUDENZ: Berta! You hate me, you have scorn for me!
BERTA: Did I, 'twere better for me—But to *see*

Him who's despised and is contemptible,
Whom one would rather love—
RUDENZ:                     O Berta! Berta!
You show to me the highest heav'nly bliss,
And hurl me down at *one and the same* moment.
BERTA:  No, no, the noble is not all suppressed
Within you! It but slumbers, I'll awake it,
You must use violence against yourself,
To deaden your hereditary virtue,
Yet well for you, 'tis mightier than you,
Despite yourself you are both good and noble!
RUDENZ:  You trust in me! O Berta, with your love
I can become and be all things!
BERTA:                     Then be,
That for which glorious nature fashioned you!
Fulfill the place, where she hath stationed you,
Stand by your people and your native land,
And battle for your holy right.
RUDENZ:                     Woe's me!
How can I hope to win you, to possess you,
If I resist the power of the Emperor?
And is it not your kinsmen's mighty will,
That like a tyrant dictates to your hand.
BERTA:  All my estates lie in the forest cantons,
And is the Schweizer free, so am I too.
RUDENZ:  Berta! O what a view you ope to me!
BERTA:  Hope not, to win my hand through Austria's
        favor,
They stretch their hand out for my heritage,
Which they would add to their great heritage.
This self-same greed for land, which would devour
Your liberty, endangers mine as well!
—O friend, I'm destined to be sacrificed,
Perhaps to be rewarded to some minion—
Yonder where falsehood and intrigue reside,
They'll drag me hence to the Imperial court,
'Tis there my hated chains of wedlock wait,
And love alone—your love can rescue me!

RUDENZ: You could resolve yourself, to living here,
  In mine own fatherland to be mine own?
  O Berta, all my yearning in the distance,
  What was it, but a striving after you?
  I sought you only on the path of fame,
  And all my greed for honor was my love.
  Could you enclose yourself with me in this
  Still valley and renounce all earthly show—
  O then I've found the goal of all my striving,
  Then may the stream of the ferocious world
  Strike on the certain shore of this great mountain—
  I have no further fugitive desires
  To cast forth yonder in life's distances—
  Then may these rocky heights around us here
  Spread an impenetrable solid wall,
  And this sequestered blessed vale alone
  Be open to the heavens and be lit!
BERTA: Now art thou fully, as my prescient heart
  Hath dreamt thee, my belief hath not deceived me!
RUDENZ: Be gone, thou vain illusion, that deludes me!
  I should find happiness in mine own home.
  Here where the boy grew up so merrily,
  Where traces of a thousand joys surround me,
  Where every spring and tree hath life for me,
  In mine own fatherland thou wilt be mine!
  Ah, I have always loved it well! I feel,
  Without it I lacked every earthy joy.
BERTA: Where were the blessed island to be found,
  If it's not here in th' land of innocence?
  Here, where the old fidelity's at home,
  Where falsehood hath not found a way in yet,
  No envy clouds the fountain of our bliss,
  And ever bright the hours escape from us.
  —There see I *thee* in genuine manly worth,
  The foremost of the free and of thy peers,
  Revered with homage that is pure and free,
  Great as a king would act within his realm.
RUDENZ: There see I thee, the crown of womanhood,

In charming womanly activity,
Erect the heaven for me in my house,
And, as the springtime scatters forth its flowers,
Adorn my path of life with beauteous grace
And all around bring life and happiness!
BERTA: See, my dear friend, the reason why I grieved,
As I saw thee this highest bliss of life
Destroy thyself—Woe's me! What were my fate,
If I were forced to follow the proud knight,
The land's oppressor to his gloomy castle!
—There is no castle here. No walls divide
Me from a people, whom I can make happy!
RUDENZ: Yet how to save myself—how 'scape the snare,
That I have placed around my head in folly?
BERTA: Tear it apart with manly resolution!
Whate'er therefrom occurs—Stand by thy people,
It is thy place by birth.
(*Hunting horns in the distance.*)
                     The hunting party
Comes nearer—Go, we must now part—Fight for
The fatherland, thou fightest for thy love!
It is *one* foe, before whom we all quake,
And 'tis *one* freedom that shall free us all!
(*Exeunt.*)


## Scene III

### *Meadow near Altorf.*

*In the foreground trees, to the rear the hat upon a pole.
The prospect is bound by the Bannberg, over which a snow-
covered mountain towers.*

FRIESSHART *and* LEUTHOLD *keep watch.*


FRIESSHART: We keep our watch in vain. There's no
    one who
Will pass this way and render his obeisance to

The hat. Yet here it was just like a fair,
Now is th' entire meadow as deserted,
E'er since the bugbear hung upon the pole.
LEUTHOLD: But common rabble show themselves and
    swing
Their scruffy caps at us in peevishness.
The decent people, all would rather make
The lengthy detour half way round the town,
Before they bent their backs before the hat.
FRIESSHART: They have to pass across this place, when
    they
Come from the town hall at the midday hour.
Then was I sure, to make a goodly catch,
For no one thought thereon, to greet the hat.
Then it is seen by Rösselmann, the priest—
Came just then from an invalid—and set
Forth with the Rev'rend, right there 'fore the pole—
The Sacrist had to tinkle with the bell,
Then all fell on their knees, myself with them,
And greeted thus the monstrance, not the hat.—
LEUTHOLD: Harken, companion, I begin to think,
We stand here in the pillory 'fore this hat,
'Tis after all an insult for a trooper,
To stand on guard before an empty hat—
And every honest fellow must despise us.
—Obeisance to perform unto a hat,
This is in confidence! a foolish order!
FRIESSHART: Why not unto an empty, hollow hat?
Bow'st thou indeed 'fore many hollow skulls.

(HILDEGARD, MECHTHILD *and* ELSBETH *enter with chil-
    dren and place themselves around the pole.*)

LEUTHOLD: And thou art also such an eager knave,
And gladly brak'st misfortune to brave people.
Let anyone that wants, pass by the hat,
I'll close mine eyes and look not over there.
MECHTHILD: There hangs the Governor—Have respect,
    you rogues.

ELSBETH: Would t' God, he went, and left his hat to us,
The country would not be the worse therefor!
FRIESSHART (*chases them away*):
Would you leave here? Accursed women folk!
Who asks for you? Dispatch your husbands here,
If they've the courage, to defy the order.
(*Wives go.*)

(*Tell enters with his crossbow, leading his boy by the hand.
They pass by the hat to the front of the stage, without taking
notice thereof.*)

WALTER (*points toward the Bannberg*):
Father, is't true, that on the mountain there
The trees will bleed, if anyone should strike
Upon them with his axe?
TELL:                                    Who says that, boy?
WALTER: The master herdsman says—The trees have
    been
Bewitched, he says, and he who injures them,
Will have his hand grow up from out the grave.
TELL: The trees have been bewitched, that is the truth.
—See'st thou the glaciers there, those icy horns,
Which high up in the heavens disappear?
WALTER: Those are the glaciers, which at night so
    thunder,
And send the avalanches down on us.
TELL: So is't, and long ago had avalanches
Submerged the town of Altorf underneath
Their weight, had not the forest over there
Stood up against it as a kind of bulwark.
WALTER (*after some reflection*):
Are there some countries, Father, with *no* mountains?
TELL: If one descends down under from our heights,
And always deeper climbs, along the streams,
Arrives one in a giant, level land,
Where forest waters no more roaring foam,
The rivers run in leisure and in peace,
There sees one freely all of heaven's spaces,

The grain grows there in lengthy, beauteous pastures,
And like a garden is the land to see.

WALTER: Oh, father, why then do we not descend
Below with speed into this beauteous land,
Instead of worrying and toiling here?

TELL: The land is fair and goodly as the Heaven,
Yet those who till it, *they* do not enjoy
The blessings, which they plant.

WALTER:                                   Live they not free
As thou upon their own inheritance?

TELL: The field belongs to th' Bishop and the King.

WALTER: So may they yet hunt freely in the woods?

TELL: To th' master doth belong the game and fowl.

WALTER: They may indeed fish freely in the streams?

TELL: The stream, the sea, the salt belong to th' King.

WALTER: Who *is* the King then, whom they all do fear?

TELL: He is the *one*, who fosters and protects them.

WALTER: They can't courageously defend themselves?

TELL: The neighbor there may not his neighbor trust.

WALTER: Father, for me 'tis cramp'd in that wide land,
I'd rather live here 'neath the avalanches.

TELL: 'Tis better, child, to have these glacier peaks
Behind one's back, than evil-minded men.
*(They want to pass by.)*

WALTER: Oh, Father, see the hat there on the pole.

TELL: What is this hat to us? Come, let us go.
*(Whilst he wants to leave, Friesshart steps toward him
with pike held out.)*

FRIESSHART: I' th' name o' th' Emperor! Halt there and
stand!

TELL *(seizes the pike):* What would ye? Wherefore do
ye hold me up?

FRIESSHART: You've broke the mandate, you must
follow us.

LEUTHOLD: You have not shown obeisance to the hat.

TELL: Friend, let me go.

FRIESSHART:                     Away, away to prison!

WALTER: My father into prison! Help! Oh help!

*(Calling into the stage.)*
This way, you men, you goodly people, help,
By force, by force, they take him prisoner.

(RÖSSELMANN *the priest and* PETERMANN *the sacristan
    come hither, with three other men.)*

SACRISTAN: What gives?
RÖSSELMANN:        Why layst thou hand upon this man?
FRIESSHART: He is a foe o' th' Emperor, a traitor!
TELL *(seizes him violently)*:
    A traitor, I!
RÖSSELMANN: Thou errest, friend, that's Tell,
    A man of honor and good citizen.
WALTER *(catches sight of Walter Fürst and hastens to
    him)*: Grandfather, help, violence is done to father.
FRIESSHART: To prison, away!
WALTER FÜRST *(rushing hither)*: I offer surety, halt!
    —For God's sake, Tell, what is occurring here?

(MELCHTAL *and* STAUFFACHER *come.)*

FRIESSHART: The Governor's sovereign authority
    He hath contemned, and will not recognize.
STAUFFACHER: That had been done by Tell?
MELCHTAL:                            Thou liest, rogue!
LEUTHOLD: He hath not shown obeisance to the hat.
WALTER FÜRST: And therefor he should go to
        prison? Friend,
    Accept my surety and let him free.
FRIESSHART: Stand surety for thyself and thine own life!
    We're doing, what we have to—Hence with him!
MELCHTAL *(to the country people)*:
    No, that is flagrant violence! Shall we endure,
    That one remove him, brashly, 'fore our eyes?
SACRISTAN: We are the stronger. Friends, allow it not,
    We have one back against the other here!
FRIESSHART: Who disobeys the order of the Governor?
THREE MORE COUNTRYMEN *(rushing hither)*:

We'll help. What's happ'ning? Strike them to the
   ground.

   (HILDEGARD, MECHTHILD *and* ELSBETH *return.*)

TELL: I help myself indeed. Go, goodly people,
   Think you, if I had wanted to use strength,
   That I would be afraid before their pikes?
MELCHTAL (*to* FRIESSHART):
   Try, if you dare, to take him from our midst!
WALTER FÜRST AND STAUFFACHER:
   Be calm! Be peaceful!
FRIESSHART (*shouts*): Riot and rebellion!
   (*One hears hunting horns.*)
WIVES: Here comes the Governor!
FRIESSHART (*raises his voice*): Mutiny! Rebellion!
STAUFFACHER: Shout, 'til thou burstest, knave!
RÖSSELMANN *and* MELCHTAL: Wilt thou be silent?
FRIESSHART (*calls still louder*):
   Come help, come help the servants of the law.
WALTER FÜRST: The Governor's here! Woe's us, what
   will occur!

(GESSLER *on horseback, the falcon on his fist,* RUDOLF DER
HARRAS, BERTA *and* RUDENZ, *a large retinue of armed
servants, who form a circle of pikes around the entire stage.*)

RUDOLF DER HARRAS: Room for the Governor!
GESSLER: Drive them from another!
   Why gather people here? Who calls for help?
   (*General silence.*)
   Who was't? I want to know it. (*To* FRIESSHART)
                                    *Thou* step forth!
   Who art thou and why holdest thou this man?
   (*He gives the falcon to a servant.*)
FRIESSHART: Severest Lord, I am thy man in arms
   And duly-appointed watchman of the hat.
   This man I seized while in the very act,
   As he refused obeisance to the hat.
   I wanted to arrest him, as thou bad'st,

And forcibly the people want to free him.

GESSLER *(after a pause):*
Despisest thou *so* much thine Emperor, Tell,
And *me,* who have here acted in his stead,
That thou denyst the honor to the hat,
Which I've hung up to test obedience?
Thine evil aims thou hast betrayed to me.

TELL:  Excuse me, gracious Lord! From thoughtlessness,
Not from contempt of you is it occurred,
Were I discreet, then would I not be Tell,
I beg for mercy, it shan't occur again.

GESSLER *(after some silence):*
Thou art a master of the crossbow, Tell,
One says, thou'd take it up with any archer?

WALTER TELL:  That must be true, my Lord—my father
    shot
An apple from a tree at a hundred strides.

GESSLER:  Is that thy boy there, Tell?

TELL:                            Yes, gracious Lord.

GESSLER:  Hast thou yet other children?

TELL:                            Two boys, Lord.

GESSLER:  And which one is't, whom thou dost love the
    most?

TELL:  Lord, both alike are children dear to me.

GESSLER:  Now, Tell! since at a hundred strides thou
    hitt'st
An apple from a tree, so thou wilt have
To prove thine art to me—Now take the crossbow—
Thou hast it there at hand—and make thee ready,
To shoot an apple from the young boy's head—
Yet I would counsel, aim it well, that thou
The apple hitt'st with the initial shot,
For miss't thou it, so is thine own head lost.
*(All give signs of terror.)*

TELL:  Lord—what monstrosity do you demand
Of me—I'm from the head of mine own child—
—No, no, my gracious Lord, that have you not
In mind—Forbid it merciful God—that you

Could not in earnest from a father ask!

GESSLER: Now thou shalt shoot the apple from the head
O' th' stripling—I desire and will it.

TELL:                              I
Should aim my crossbow at the darling head
Of mine own child—I'd rather perish first!

GESSLER: Thou shootest or thou die'st *with* thine own
    boy.

TELL: I should become the murd'rer of my child!
Lord, you do not have children—you know not,
What is bestirr'd within a father's heart.

GESSLER: Oh, Tell, thou art now suddenly discreet!
They said to me, that thou wouldst be a dreamer,
And wander'st from the ways of other men.
Thou lov'st unusual things—thus have I now
Picked out a special daring task for thee.
An other would consider well—*Thou* shut'st
Thine eyes and seizest on it heartily.

BERTA: O do not jest, my Lord! with these poor people!
You see them standing pale and trembling here—
They're little used to humor from your mouth.

GESSLER: Who tells you, that I jest?
*(Reaches toward a branch of the tree, which hangs*
    *down over him.)*            Here is the apple.
Make room for him—And let him take his distance,
As custom is—I give him eighty strides—
Not fewer, and not more—It was his boast,
That at a hundred he could hit his man—
Now, archer, hit, and do not miss the mark!

RUDOLF DER HARRAS: God, this grows earnest—Fall,
    boy, on your knees,
It counts, and beg the Governor for thy life.

WALTER FÜRST *(aside to* MELCHTAL, *who scarcely*
    *controls his impatience)*:
Constrain yourself, I beg of you, keep calm.

BERTA *(to the* GOVERNOR*)*:
Let this suffice, my Lord! It is inhuman,
To play thus with a father's anxious fears.

If this poor man as well hath forfeited
Both life and limb through his slight guilt, by God!
He had already suffered tenfold death.
Release him now uninjured to his hut,
He hath now come to know you, and this hour
He and his children's children will remember.

GESSLER: Open a lane there—Quick! Why waitest thou?
  Thy life is forfeit, thee I can destroy,
  And see, I mercifully place thy fate
  Upon the art of thine own practiced hand.
  He can't complain about the harsh decree,
  Whom one makes master of his destiny.
  Thou boastest of thy certain eye. Well then!
  'Tis time then, *Archer*, to display thine art,
  The aim is worthy and the prize is great!
  To hit the black within the target, *that*
  Can others do as well, to me *he's* master,
  Who's certain of his art at any time,
  Whose heart doth not disturb his hand nor eye.

WALTER FÜRST (*throws himself down before him*):
  Lord Governor, we recognize your highness,
  Yet now let mercy pass for justice, take
  The half of my possessions, take them all,
  But from this ghastly deed release a father!

WALTER TELL: Grandfather, do not kneel 'fore the false
  man!
  Say, where I am to stand, I'm not afraid,
  My father hits the bird in midst of flight,
  He will not miss the heart of his own child.

STAUFFACHER: Lord Governor, doth his innocence not
  move you?

RÖSSELMANN: Remember, that there is a God in
  Heaven,
  To whom you must account for all your deeds.

GESSLER (*points to the boy*):
  Bind him to yonder linden tree!

WALTER TELL:             Bind me!
  No, I will not be bound. I will keep still,

Just like a lamb, nor will I even breathe.
But if you bind me, no, then I can not,
Then I shall surely rage against my bonds.

RUDOLF DER HARRAS: Just let your eyes at least be
covered, boy.

WALTER TELL: And why the eyes? Do you think, I'm
afraid
O' th' shaft from father's hand? I will await
It firmly, nor so much as bat an eyelash.
—Quick, father, show them, that thou art an archer,
He doubts thou art, he thinks to ruin us—
To spite the ruthless tyrant, shoot and hit.
*(He goes to the linden, the apple is placed on his
head.)*

MELCHTAL *(to the country people):*
What? Shall this outrage be performed before
Our very eyes? Whereunto have we sworn?

STAUFFACHER: It is in vain. We have no weapons here,
You see the wood of lances that surrounds us.

MELCHTAL: O would that we had acted with quick
deeds,
God pardon those, who counseled to delay!

GESSLER *(to Tell):* To work! One carries weapons not in
vain.
'Tis dangerous, to bear a murder weapon,
And on the archer may the shaft rebound.
This haughty right, the peasant doth assume,
Offends the highest master of the land.
Let none be armed, except he who commands.
It pleases you, to bear the shaft and bow,
Well, then will I give you the mark thereto.

TELL *(bends the crossbow and inserts the shaft):*
Open the lane! Make room!

STAUFFACHER: What, Tell? You mean to—By no
means—You tremble,
Your hand is shaking, and your knees give way—

TELL *(lets the crossbow sink):*
It swims before mine eyes!

WIVES:                          Oh God in Heaven!
TELL *(to the* GOVERNOR*)*:  Excuse me from this shot.
    Here is my heart!
*(He tears open his breast.)*
Call forth your mounted men and strike me down.
GESSLER:  I do not want thy life, I want the shot.
    —Thou canst do all things, Tell, at naught despair'st
        thou,
The rudder thou directest as the bow,
No storm frights thee, when there is need of rescue,
Now, savior, help thy self—thou savest all!
*(*TELL *stands in fearful battle, with his hands moving
    convulsively and his rolling eyes directed now at the*
    GOVERNOR, *now at the heaven.—Suddenly he
    reaches into his quiver, takes out a second arrow
    and sticks it in his collar. The* GOVERNOR *observes
    all of these motions.)*
WALTER TELL *(beneath the linden)*:
    Father, take shot, I'm not afraid.
TELL:                            I must!
*(He gathers himself together and takes aim.)*
RUDENZ *(who the entire time stood in the most violent
    excitement and restrained himself with force, steps
    forward)*:
    Lord Governor, further you will not proceed,
    You will *not*—It was surely but a test—
    The end you have achieved—But too far driven
    Severity will miss its own wise end,
    And much too tightly stretched the bow will split.
GESSLER:  Be silent, till you're called on.
RUDENZ:                            I *will* speak,
    I may, the King's esteem is holy to me,
    But such a rule as this must hatred earn.
    That's not the purpose of the King—I may
    Maintain—Such cruelty my people don't
    Deserve, thereto are you not authorized.
GESSLER:  Ha, you are growing bold!
RUDENZ:                            I have been silent

At every grievous action, which I saw,
My seeing eyes have I kept tightly closed,
My overswelling and indignant heart
Have I pressed downwards deep within my bosom.
Yet to be silent further were now treason
Unto my fatherland and to the Emperor.

BERTA (*throws herself between him and the* GOVERNOR):
O God, you rouse this maniac still more.

RUDENZ: My people I abandoned, I renounced
The kindred of my blood, I broke all bonds
Of nature, to attach myself to you—
The best for all I hoped thus to promote,
When strengthened I the power of the Emperor—
The blind hath fallen from mine eyes—With dread
I see myself led up to the abyss—
My independent judgment you've misled,
My honest heart seduced—With best intent,
I had well-nigh achieved my people's ruin.

GESSLER: Audacious man, this language to thy Lord?

RUDENZ: The Emperor is my Lord, not you—I'm free
As you are born and I compare myself
With you in every virtue of a knight.
And stood you not here in the Emperor's name,
Which I esteem, e'en where it is disgraced,
My glove I would throw down 'fore you, you should
Give answer to me after knightly custom.
—Yes, beckon to your mounted men—I'm not
Defenseless here, as *they*—(*pointing to the people*)
                              I have a sword,
And who comes near to me—

STAUFFACHER (*calls*):          The apple's fallen!
(*Whilst everyone turned himself toward this side and*
    BERTA *threw herself between* RUDENZ *and the*
    GOVERNOR, TELL *hath discharged his arrow.*)

RÖSSELMANN: The boy's alive!

MANY VOICES:                 The apple hath been struck!
(WALTER FÜRST *reels and threatens to sink,* BERTA
    *holds him.*)

GESSLER (*astonished*):  He hath then shot the
   arrow? How? the madman!

BERTA:  The boy's alive! come to yourself, good father!

WALTER TELL (*comes running with the apple*):
   Father, here is the apple—Knew I well,
   That thou would'st never injure thine own boy.
     (TELL *stood with body bent forward, as though he*
     *wanted to follow the arrow—the crossbow drops*
     *from his hand—as he sees the boy come, he hastens*
     *to meet him with open arms and lifts him with*
     *intense ardor to his heart, in this position he*
     *collapses exhausted. All stand moved.*)

BERTA:  O gracious Heaven!

WALTER FÜRST (*to father and son*):
                 Children! my dear children!

STAUFFACHER:  Oh God be praised!

LEUTHOLD:               That was a shot! Thereof
   Will they still speak unto the end of time.

RUDOLF DER HARRAS:  They will relate the tale o' th'
   archer Tell,
   So long the mountains stand upon their ground.
   (*Hands the* GOVERNOR *the apple.*)

GESSLER:  By God, the apple's shot right through the
   middle!
   It was a master shot, I have to praise him.

RÖSSELMANN:  The shot was good, yet woe to him, who
   him
   Thereto hath driven, that he tempted God.

STAUFFACHER:  Come to yourself, Tell, rise, you've like
   a man
   Redeemed yourself, and can go freely home.

RÖSSELMANN:  Come, come and bring the son unto his
   mother.
   (*They want to lead him away.*)

GESSLER:  Tell, listen!

TELL (*comes back*):  What command you, Lord?

GESSLER:                   Thou stuck'st
   A second arrow on thyself—Yes, yes,

I saw it well—What meantest thou therewith?

TELL (*embarrassed*): Lord, that is but a custom with all
  archers.

GESSLER: No, Tell, I will not let that answer pass,
  There must have been some other purpose to it.
  Say to me truthfully and gladly, Tell,
  Whate'er it be, thy life I promise thee.
  Whereto the second shaft?

TELL:                            Well then, O Lord,
  Since you have promised to ensure my life,
  So will I thoroughly report the truth.
  (*He pulls the shaft from his collar and looks at the*
    GOVERNOR *with a frightful glance.*)
  This second arrow I had shot through—you,
  If with the first I'd struck my darling child,
  And you—in truth! I would not then have missed.

GESSLER: Well, Tell! I've promised to ensure thy life,
  I gave my knightly word, that I will keep—
  But since I have perceived thine evil mind,
  I'll have thee taken and put under guard,
  Where neither moon nor sun will shine on thee,
  Thereby I shall be safer 'fore thine arrows.
  Arrest him, servants! Bind him up!
  (TELL *is bound.*)

STAUFFACHER:                     What, Lord?
  How could you treat a man in such a way,
  In whom God's hand is visibly proclaimed?

GESSLER: Now let us see, if it will save him twice.
  —Bring him unto my ship, I'll follow straight
  Away, I'll pilot him myself to Küssnacht.

RÖSSELMANN: You will imprison him outside the land?

COUNTRY PEOPLE: That you may not, that may the
    Emperor not,
  That violates the charters of our freedom!

GESSLER: Where are *they*? Hath the Emperor
    confirmed them?
  He hath them not as yet confirmed—This favor
  Must needs be earned first through obedience.

You are all rebels 'gainst the Emperor's court
And foster here audacious mutiny.
I know you all—I see completely through you—
Him I am now removing from your midst,
Yet all of you are sharers in his guilt.
Who's smart, learn to be silent and obey.

(*He departs,* BERTA, RUDENZ, HARRAS *and servants follow,*
FRIESSHART *and* LEUTHOLD *remain behind.*)

WALTER FÜRST (*in violent pain*):
  It is foreby, he hath resolved, to bring
  Destruction on myself with all my house!
STAUFFACHER (*to* TELL): O why had you to rouse the
  tyrant's rage!
TELL: Restrain himself, who felt my pangs of pain!
STAUFFACHER: Now everything, oh everything is lost!
  With you are we all fettered and enchained!
COUNTRY PEOPLE (*ring around* TELL):
  With you our final comfort goes away!
LEUTHOLD (*approaches*): Tell, I have pity—yet I must
  obey.
TELL: Farewell!
WALTER TELL (*clinging to him with intense pain*):
          O Father! Father! Dearest Father!
TELL (*lifts his arms toward the heaven*):
  Up yonder is thy father! call on him!
STAUFFACHER: Tell, shall I say naught of you to your
  wife?
TELL (*lifts the boy with ardor to his breast*):
  The boy's uninjured, God will give me help.
  (*Tears himself away quickly and follows the armed
  servants.*)

# ACT IV

## SCENE I

*The eastern shore of the Vierwaldstättensee.*

*The unusually shaped rugged rocks in the West close the
prospect. The lake is agitated, violently roaring and raging,
between which lightning and peals of thunder.*

KUNZ VON GERSAU. FISHERMAN *and* FISHERBOY.

KUNZ: I saw it with mine eyes, you can believe me,
    It all hath happened, as I said to you.
FISHERMAN: Tell led away a prisoner to Küssnacht,
    The best man in the land, the bravest arm,
    If it should once be meant for liberty.
KUNZ: The Gov'rnor bears him up the lake himself,
    They were just now about to board the ship,
    When I set off from Flüelen, yet the storm,
    That even now is on its way, and which
    Compelled me also, suddenly to land here,
    May very well have hindered their departure.
FISHERMAN: Tell now in fetters, in the Gov'rnor's
        power!
    O surely, he'll entomb him deep enough,
    That he'll not see the light of day again!
    For he must fear the righteous vengeance of
    The free man, whom he's grievously provoked!
KUNZ: The Magistrate as well, the noble Lord
    Of Attinghaus, 'tis said, lies near to death.
FISHERMAN: So breaks the final anchor of our hope!
    He was the only one, who still might raise
    His voice in favor of the people's rights!
KUNZ: The storm is growing worse. So fare ye well,
    I'll take some quarters in the town, for none
    Will give more thought today to a departure. *(Exits.)*
FISHERMAN: Tell taken prisoner and the Baron dead!
    Lift up thy brazen forehead, tyranny,

Cast all your shame away, the mouth of truth
Is dumb, the seeing eye is blinded now,
The arm, that should have saved us, is in fetters!
BOY: It's hailing hard, come in the cottage, Father,
It is not good, to house here in the open.
FISHERMAN: Rage on, ye winds, descend in flames, ye
     lightning,
Ye clouds burst open, pour hereunder, streams
O' th' heav'n and drown the land! Annihilate
The unborn generations in their seed!
Ye savage elements become our lord,
Ye bears come back, ye ancient wolves return
To this great wilderness, the land is yours,
Who wants to live here without liberty!
BOY: Hark, how the chasm roars, the whirlpool howls,
So hath it never raged within this gorge!
FISHERMAN: To take aim at the head of his own child,
Such had before been ordered of no father!
And should not nature in ferocious wrath
Rise in revolt—O I'd not be surprised,
If th' rocks were now to bow into the lake,
If yonder jagged peaks, yon tow'rs of ice,
Which since creation's day have never thawed,
Were now to melt down from their lofty summits,
If th' mountains break, if ancient crevices
Collapse, that then a second flood would come
To swallow up all dwellings of the living!
*(One hears ringing.)*
BOY: Hark ye, they're ringing on the mountain yonder,
They've surely seen a vessel in distress,
And toll the bell, that we be called to prayer.
*(Climbs upon a high ground.)*
FISHERMAN: Woe to the vessel, that now underway,
Within this dreadful cradle is now rocked!
Here is the rudder useless and the helmsman,
The storm is master, wind and waves play ball
With human beings—There is near and far
No haven, which accords him friendly shelter!

Sheer and ascending jaggedly the rocks
Stare inhospitably across at him,
And show him but their stony jagged breast.
BOY *(points left):* Father, a ship, it comes from Flüelen
  hence.
FISHERMAN: God help the wretched people! If the
  storm
Is once entangled in this waterway,
Then it will rage with th' anguish of a beast,
That strikes against the cage's iron bars,
Howling it seeks to find a door in vain,
For it is on all sides confined by rocks,
Which high as Heaven wall the narrow pass.
*(He climbs upon the high ground.)*
BOY: It is the master's ship from Uri, Father,
I know't by its red roof and by its flag.
FISHERMAN: Judgments of God! Yes, he it is himself,
The Gov'rnor, who here sails—There ships he hence,
And carries in the ship his own offense!
Swift hath the arm of the avenger found him,
Now over him he knows the stronger Lord,
These waves will not pay heed unto his voice,
These rocky cliffs will not bow down their heads
Before his hat—My boy, now do not pray,
Do not attempt to stay the Judge's arm!
BOY: I pray not for the Governor—I pray
For Tell, who is upon the ship with him.
FISHERMAN: O mindlessness o' th' sightless elements!
Must thou, to catch a *single* guilty man,
Destroy the ship together with the helmsman!
BOY: Look, look, they were already safely by
The *Buggisgrat,* but now the force o' th' storm,
Which is rebounding from the *Teufelmünster,*
Hurls them back unto the great *Axenberg.*
—I see them no more.
FISHERMAN:                There is the *Hakmesser,*
Where many ship already hath been broken.
If they don't steer thereover prudently,

So will the ship be shattered on the rocks,
Which sink precipitously in the depths.
—They have a helmsman who is very good
On board, if *one* could save them, it were Tell,
Yet they have fettered both his arms and hands.

(WILHELM TELL *with his crossbow. He comes with rapid strides, glances around in amazement and displays the most violent movement. When he is in the middle of the stage, he throws himself down, his hands to the earth and then stretching out to the heaven.*)

BOY (*notices him*):  Look, Father, who's the man, who's
    kneeling there?
FISHERMAN:  He clutches at the earth with both his
    hands,
And doth appear to be beside himself.
BOY (*comes forward*):  What see I! Father! Father, come
    and see!
FISHERMAN (*approaches*):  Who is it?—God in Heaven!
    What! Is't Tell?
How come you hither?  Speak!
BOY:                            But were you not
In yonder ship imprisoned and bound up?
FISHERMAN:  Were they not taking you away to
    Küssnacht?
TELL (*stands up*):  I am set free.
FISHERMAN AND BOY:        Set free! O miracle of God!
BOY:  Whence come you here?
TELL:                        From yonder vessel.
FISHERMAN:                                        What?
BOY (*simultaneously*):
    Where is the Gov'rnor?
TELL:                        Drifting on the waves.
FISHERMAN:  Is't possible?  But *you*?  How are you
    here?
How 'scaped you from your bonds and from the storm?
TELL:  By God's most gracious providence—Attend!
FISHERMAN AND BOY:

O speak on, speak on!

TELL:                     Do you know, what's come
  To pass in Altorf?

FISHERMAN:        I know all, speak on!

TELL: Of how the Gov'rnor had me seized and bound,
  And would convey me to his fort in Küssnacht.

FISHERMAN: And that with you at Flüelen he embarked!
  All this we know, say, how have you escaped?

TELL: I lay there in the ship, fast bound with cords,
  Defenseless, an abandoned man—nor hope I,
  To see again the joyful light o' th' sun,
  The lovely countenance of wife and children,
  And cheerlessly I look i' th' waste of water—

FISHERMAN: O wretched man!

TELL:                 So then we disembark,
  The Governor, Rudolf der Harras and the servants.
  And yet my quiver and my crossbow lay
  Upon the bow beside the pilot's rudder.
  And just as we now come around the bend
  Near little Axen, God ordained it so,
  That such an awful murd'rous thunderstorm
  Burst forth abruptly from the Gotthard gorges,
  That every rower's heart within him sank,
  And all thought it their wretched fate to drown.
  Then heard I, how one of his servants turned
  To th' Governor and spake these words to him:
  You see your need and that of ours, my Lord,
  And that we all are near the edge of death—
  And yet the helmsmen know not what to do
  Because of their great fear and are not well
  Apprised o' th' course to take—But now here's Tell,
  A robust man and knows to steer a ship,
  What, if we were to use him in our need?
  Then spake the Governor to me: Tell, if
  Thou dar'st, to help us to escape this storm,
  So I've a mind to free thee from thy bonds.
  But I then spake: Yes, Lord, with help of God
  I'll venture it, and help us to escape.

So from my bonds I was released and stood
Up at the helm and steered uprightly forth.
Yet glance I sideways, where my weapons lay,
And on the shore I sharply look to see,
Where there might be a chance for my escape.
And when I did perceive a shelf of rocks,
That sprang forth flattened out into the lake—
FISHERMAN: I know't, 'tis at the foot of the great Axen,
Yet I can't deem it possible—it rises
So steep—to reach it springing from a boat—
TELL: I bade the men, to put forth handily,
Until we came before the rocky ledge,
There, cried I, shall the worst be overcome—
And as we briskly rowing soon arrived,
I pray that God be merciful, and force,
With all my body's power pressed together,
The vessel's bow hence to the rocky wall—
Now quickly snatching up mine arms, I swing
Myself upon the ledge by leaping high,
And with a forceful footkick to my rear,
I send the little craft i' th' gorge of water—
There let it, as God wills, drift on the waves!
So am I here, delivered from the might
O' th' storm and from the might far worse of man.
FISHERMAN: Tell, Tell, the Lord hath wrought a miracle
Through you, I scarce can trust it to my senses—
But say on! Whence intend you now to go,
For there's no safety for you, in so far
The Gov'rnor hath escaped this storm alive.
TELL: I hear him say, as I lay bound in chains
Upon the ship, he fain would land at Brunnen,
And crossing Schwyz bring me unto his castle.
FISHERMAN: Will he then make his way thence over
    land?
TELL: He plans to.
FISHERMAN:          O so hide yourself without
    Delay, not twice God helps you from his hands.
TELL: Name me the nearest way to Arth and Küssnacht.

FISHERMAN: The open highway leads by way of Steinen,
But yet a shorter way and more concealed
My boy can take you on by way of Lowerz.

TELL (*gives him his hand*):  May God reward your
kindness. Fare ye well.
(*Goes and comes back again.*)
—Have you not also sworn an oath at Rütli?
Methinks, I heard your name—

FISHERMAN:                         Yes, I was there,
And I have sworn the oath unto the League.

TELL:  So speed to Bürglen, do me this one favor,
My wife despairs of me, report to her,
That I've escaped and am now well concealed.

FISHERMAN:  Yet whither shall I tell her, that you've
fled?

TELL:  You'll find my father-in-law there by her side
And others, who have sworn the oath in Rütli—
They should be resolute and of good courage,
For Tell is *free* and master of his arm,
And soon shall they hear further news from me.

FISHERMAN:  What have you now in mind?  Reveal it
freely.

TELL:  Is it once done, 'twill also be discussed. (*Exits.*)

FISHERMAN:  Show him the way, Jenni—God be with
him!
He leads to th' goal, whate'er he's undertaken.
(*Exits.*)


## SCENE II

*The noble court at Attinghausen.*

*The* BARON, *in an armchair, dying.* WALTER FÜRST, STAUF-
FACHER, MELCHTAL *and* BAUMGARTEN *busy around him.*
WALTER TELL *kneeling before the dying man.*

WALTER FÜRST:  It is foreby with him, he's over there.

STAUFFACHER:  He lies not as one dead—Behold, the
feather

Doth move upon his lips! His sleep is now
At rest, and peacefully his features smile.
(BAUMGARTEN *goes to the door and speaks with
someone.*)
WALTER FÜRST (*to* BAUMGARTEN):
Who is't?
BAUMGARTEN (*comes back*):
It's Lady Hedwig, your own daughter,
She'd like to speak with you, would see the boy.
(WALTER TELL *stands up.*)
WALTER FÜRST: Can I console her now? Am I
consoled
Myself? Is every pain heaped on my head?
HEDWIG (*pushing her way in*):
Where is my child? Let me, I must see him—
STAUFFACHER: Be calm, bethink, you're in the house of
death—
HEDWIG (*falls upon her boy*):
My Walty! O he is alive.
WALTER TELL (*clings to her*): Poor Mother!
HEDWIG: Can it be truly so? Art thou unharmed?
(*Examines him with anxious care*)
Is't possible? Could he take aim at thee?
*How* could he? O he hath no heart—He could
Dispatch the arrow at his very child!
WALTER FÜRST: He did with dread, with pain-
dismembered soul,
Compelled he did it, since it meant his life.
HEDWIG: O if he had a father's heart, before
He'd done it, he'd have died a thousand times!
STAUFFACHER:
You should give praise to God's kind dispensation,
Which guided it so well—
HEDWIG: Can I forget,
What *could* have been the issue—God in Heaven!
And live I eighty years—I'll see the boy
Forever bound, his father aim at him
And ever flies the shaft into my heart.

MELCHTAL: If you knew, how the Gov'rnor taunted
　　him!
HEDWIG: O brutal heart of men! If once their pride
　　Hath been abused, then they heed nothing more,
　　In the blind frenzy of the game he'll stake
　　The child's existence and the mother's heart!
BAUMGARTEN: Is then your husband's lot not hard
　　enough,
　　That you insult him more with harsh rebuke?
　　Have you no feelings for *his* sufferings?
HEDWIG (*turns around toward him and looks upon him*
　　*with a large view*):
　　Hast *thou* tears only for thy friend's distress?
　　—Where were you, when they put that excellent man
　　In shackles? Where was your assistance then?
　　You just looked on, you let the horrible occur,
　　You bore it patiently, that they led off
　　Your friend from out your midst—Hath Tell e'er acted
　　In such a way to you? Did he stand there
　　Lamenting, when the Gov'rnor's troopers were
　　Pursuing thee, or when the raging lake
　　Roared out before thee? Not with idle tears
　　Bemoaned he thee, he sprang into the vessel, wife
　　And child forgot he and delivered thee—
WALTER FÜRST: What could we dare to do to rescue
　　him,
　　Since we were few in number and unarmed!
HEDWIG (*throws herself upon his breast*):
　　O Father! And as well hast thou lost him!
　　The country, we have all of us lost him!
　　He misses all of us, ah! we miss him!
　　God save his very soul before despair.
　　To him down in the solitary dungeon
　　Doth come no friendly comfort—Fell he ill!
　　Ah, in the prison's dank obscurity
　　He must fall ill—Just as the Alpine rose
　　Turns pale and withers in the swampy air,
　　So there's no life for him but in the light

O' th' sun, and in the balsam stream of air.
Imprisoned! He! His very breath is freedom,
He can not live in the rank breath o' th' grave.

STAUFFACHER: Becalm yourself. For we all want to act,
To open up his prison doors.

HEDWIG: What can *you* do without him?—Just so long
As Tell was free, yes, *then* there was still hope,
Then innocence could always find a friend,
Then did the persecuted have a helper,
Tell rescued all of you—But all of you
Together could not free him from *his* chains!
(*The* BARON *awakes.*)

BAUMGARTEN: He's stirring, still!

ATTINGHAUSEN (*sitting up*):        Where is he?

STAUFFACHER:                          Who?

ATTINGHAUSEN:                    I need him,
In my last moment he abandons me!

STAUFFACHER: He means the squire—Have they sent
after him?

WALTER FÜRST: They have sent after him—Be
comforted!
For he hath found his heart, he's one of ours.

ATTINGHAUSEN: Hath he then spoken for his fatherland?

STAUFFACHER: With hero's daring.

ATTINGHAUSEN:                Wherefore comes he not,
That he may now receive my final blessing?
I feel, that soon my life will swiftly end.

STAUFFACHER: Not so, my noble Lord! For this short
sleep
Hath quickened you, and now your look is bright.

ATTINGHAUSEN: The pain is life and even it hath left
me,
My suffering is, just like my hope, at end.
(*He notices the boy.*)
Who is the boy?

WALTER FÜRST: Give him your blessing, Lord!
He is my grandson and is fatherless.

(HEDWIG *sinks down with the boy before the dying man.*)

ATTINGHAUSEN: And fatherless I leave you all, yes all
Behind—And woe is me, that my last sight
Hath seen the ruin of the fatherland!
Must I attain the utmost height of life,
To perish utterly with all my hopes!

STAUFFACHER (*to* WALTER FÜRST):
Shall he depart amid this dark affliction?
Shall we not brighten up his final hours
With beauteous beams of hope?—O noble Baron!
Raise up your spirit! We are not entirely
Abandoned, are not lost beyond all rescue.

ATTINGHAUSEN: Who is to save you?

WALTER FÜRST:                       We ourselves. Now hear!
The Cantons three have to each other pledged
Their solemn word, to drive away the tyrants.
The League has now been formed, a holy oath
Binds us together. Action will be taken,
Before the year begins anew its cycle,
Your ashes shall repose in a free land.

ATTINGHAUSEN: O say to me! The League has now been
formed?

MELCHTAL: On the same day the Forest Cantons will
Rise up all three of one accord. All is
Prepared, and to this hour the secret is
Well kept, though many hundreds share in it.
The ground is hollow underneath the tyrants,
The days of their continued rule are numbered,
And soon no trace of them will e'er be found.

ATTINGHAUSEN: But what of all the fortresses i' th'
land?

MELCHTAL: On the same day they all shall fall to us.

ATTINGHAUSEN: And are the nobles party to this
League?

STAUFFACHER: We hope for their assistance, when it
counts,

But now the peasant on his own hath sworn.

ATTINGHAUSEN (*raises himself up slowly, with great
    astonishment*):

And hath the peasant ventured such a deed,
With his own means, with no help from the nobles,
Hath he relied so much on his own strength—
Yes, then there is no further need of ours,
We can descend in comfort to our graves,
For after *us*—the majesty of man
Will live and be maintained by others' strengths.

(*He lays his hand upon the head of the child, who lies
    before him on his knee.*)

Upon this head, whereon the apple lay,
Your new and better freedom shall grow green,
The old is falling down, the times are changing,
And from the ruins blossoms forth new life.

STAUFFACHER (*to* WALTER FÜRST):

See, what a splendor pours forth round his eye!
That is not the extinction of mere nature,
That is the beam of renovated life.

ATTINGHAUSEN: The noble climbs down from his
    ancient castle

And swears his civic oath unto the cities,
In *Üchtland*, and in *Thurgau* it's begun,
The noble *Bern* lifts up her ruling head,
And *Freiburg* is a stronghold of the free,
The busy *Zürich* arms its guilds to form
A host prepared for war—it breaks the might
Of kings against her everlasting walls—

(*He speaks the following in the tone of a seer—his
    speech rises to inspiration.*)

The princes see I and the noble lords
Equipped in suits of armor coming forth,
To war upon a harmless folk of herdsmen.
'Twill be a fight unto the death, and glorious
Will many pass become by bloody decision.
The peasant hurls himself with naked breast,
A willing sacrifice, i' th' troop of lances,
He breaks them, and the blood o' th' noble falls,

And freedom lifts its winning banner high.
(*grasping* WALTER FÜRST'*s and* STAUFFACHER'*s hands*)
Therefore hold fast together—fast and always—
No place of freedom be strange to another—
Set watches high upon your mountain tops,
That League with League can quickly be assembled—
Be one—be one—be one—
(*He falls back on the cushion—his hands now soulless*
*still hold the others clasped.* FÜRST *and*
STAUFFACHER *regard him for some time still in*
*silence, then they step away, each one given over to*
*his own grief. Meanwhile the servants have quickly*
*forced themselves in, they approach with signs of a*
*more silent or more agitated grief, some kneel down*
*by him and shed tears on his hand, during this*
*silent scene the castle bell tolls.*)

(RUDENZ *to former.*)

RUDENZ (*entering hastily*): Lives he? O tell me, can he
hear me still?
WALTER FÜRST (*points hence with averted face*):
*You* are our feudal lord and our protector,
And now this castle hath another name.
RUDENZ (*beholds the corpse and stands seized by intense*
*pain*): O gracious God!—Comes my remorse too
late?
Could he not live a few more pulses longer,
That he might see my altered heart?
Oh, I have held his faithful voice in scorn,
While he still wandered in the light—He is
Now gone, is gone eternally and leaves
Me with this heavy unpaid debt!—O speak!
Did he depart this life displeased with me?
STAUFFACHER: He heard while he was dying, what
you've done,
And blessed the courage, with which you have spoken!
RUDENZ (*kneels down before the dead man*):
Yes, sacred vestige of a precious man!
Thou soulless body! Here I pledge to thee

Upon thy hand of death now cold—I have
Forever broken all my foreign bonds,
I am restored once more unto my people,
I am a Schweizer and I wish to be—
With my entire soul—*(Standing up.)*
                          Mourn for our friend,
The father of us all, yet don't despair!
'Tis not his lands alone that fall to me,
His heart—his spirit hath devolved on me,
And my fresh youth shall execute for you,
Whate'er his great old age still owed to you.
—O venerable father, give your hand to me!
And give me yours as well! Melchtal, you too!
Bethink you not! O do not turn away!
Receive my promise and my solemn oath.

WALTER FÜRST:  Give him your hand. For his repentent
    heart
Deserves our trust.

MELCHTAL:  You've held the countryman in disregard.
Now speak, what is one to expect from you?

RUDENZ:  O think not of the errors of my youth!

STAUFFACHER *(to* MELCHTAL*):*
Be one! That was our father's final word,
Be mindful now thereof!

MELCHTAL:                 Here is my hand!
The farmer's handshake, noble Lord, is also
A good man's word! What is the knight without us?
And our estate is older far than yours.

RUDENZ:  I honor it, and with my sword shall guard it.

MELCHTAL:  *The* arm, Lord Baron, which subjects the
    hard
Earth to itself and fructifies her womb,
Can just as well protect the breast of man.

RUDENZ:  You shall defend *my* breast, and I will *yours*,
So are we each one through the other strong.
—Yet whereto talk we, while our fatherland
Is still a prey of foreign tyranny?
If first the soil is swept clean of the foe,

Then we'll no doubt be reconciled in peace.
*(After that, he pauses for a moment.)*
You're silent? Have you naught to tell me? How?
So must I force myself against your will
Into the secret bus'ness of your League.
—You have convened—you've sworn an oath at
    Rütli—
I know—know all, that you transacted there,
And what was not confided me by you,
I've kept as if it were a sacred pledge.
I never was my country's foe, trust me,
And never had I acted there against you.
—Yet wrongly did you act, to put it off,
The hour is pressing, and swift action's needed—
Tell was the sacrifice of your delay—
STAUFFACHER: We swore an oath to wait 'til Christmas
    Day.
RUDENZ: I was not there, I have not sworn thereto.
    Wait if you will, I'm acting.
MELCHTAL:                     What? You would—
RUDENZ: I count me now among the country's fathers,
    And it is my first duty, to protect you.
WALTER FÜRST: To give this precious dust unto the
    earth,
Is now your nearest duty and most sacred.
RUDENZ: When we have freed the land, then we can lay
    The fresh-cut wreath of victory on his bier.
—O friends! I do not have your cause alone,
I also have mine own which I must fight
Out with these tyrants—Hear and know! My Berta
Hath disappeared, abducted secretly,
With brazen crime from out our very midst!
STAUFFACHER: And hath the tyrant dared commit an act
    So violent 'gainst a free and noble woman?
RUDENZ: Alas my friends! I promised help to you,
    And now must I implore it first from you.
My loved one's stolen, torn away from me,
Who knows, where the berserker's hidden her,

What violence they may make bold to use,
To force her heart into the hated bond!
Forsake me not, O help me to her rescue—
She loves you, she deserves it of the land,
That all should take up arms in her behalf—

WALTER FÜRST:  What would you do?

RUDENZ:                                    How can I
   know? Alas!
In this dark night, which veils her destiny,
In monstrous dread of this uncertainty,
Where I know nothing firm to seize upon,
There's only this that's clear within my soul:
. Beneath the ruins of the tyrant's might
Alone can she be brought forth from the grave,
The fortresses must all we overcome,
If we perhaps can penetrate her prison.

MELCHTAL:  Come, lead us forth. We follow you. Why
   leave
Until tomorrow, what we can today?
Tell was still free, when we at Rütli swore,
The monstrous thing had not yet taken place.
The times now bring about another law,
Who is so cowardly, to waver now!

RUDENZ:  Meanwhile well-armed and ready for the task
Await the fiery signals on the hills,
For swifter than an herald's canvas flies,
Shall you have tidings of our victory,
And you shall see the welcome flames shine forth,
Then strike upon the foe, as lightning bolts,
And smash the edifice of tyranny. (*Exits.*)


## SCENE III

*The hollow lane near Küssnacht.*

*One climbs hereunder from behind between rocks, and the
travellers are seen already on the high ground, before they*

*appear upon the stage. Rocks surround the entire stage, on
one of the foremost there is a projection overgrown with
bushes.*

TELL *(enters with his crossbow):*
  He needs must come along this hollow lane,
  There is no other way to Küssnacht—Here
  I'll do't—The opportunity is good.
  I'm hidden from him by yon elder bush,
  And down from there my shaft can reach to him,
  The narrowness o' th' way prevents pursuit.
  Now settle thine account with Heaven, Gov'rnor,
  Thou must be gone, thy time hath run its course.

  I lived a quiet, harmless life—My shaft
  Was only aimed at forest animals,
  My thoughts were absolutely free of murder—
  *Thou* hast aroused me from my peaceful state,
  Into a seething dragon's poison hast
  Thou turned the milk of my good disposition,
  Thou hast accustomed me to monstrous things—
  Who took aim at the head of his own child,
  Can just as well strike at the heart o' th' foe.

  My wretched children, in their innocence,
  My faithful wife must I protect before
  Thy fury, Gov'rnor—Since, when I last drew
  My bowstring—when my hand was quivering—
  When thou with gruesome devilish delight
  Mad'st me, take aim at th' head of mine own child—
  When I writhed begging helplessly before thee,
  'Twas then I took within my inner self
  A fearful solemn oath, which only God
  Did hear, that my *next* arrow's *foremost* target
  Would be thine heart—That which I pledged myself
  Amid the hellish torment of that moment,
  Is a most sacred debt, which I will pay.

Thou art my lord, my Emp'ror's Governor,
And yet the Emp'ror would have ne'er allowed,
What *thou*—He sent thee here unto this land,
To render justice—sternly, for he's wroth—
Yet not, to practice each atrocity
With murd'rous joy and with impunity,
There lives a God, to punish and avenge.

Come thou here forth, thou bringer of bitter pain,
My precious jewel now, my highest treasure—
A target I will give thee, that 'til now
Hath been impenetrable to pious prayers—
And yet to *thee* it shall not give resistance—
And thou, my trusted bowstring, that so oft
Hath served me faithfully i' th' joys of play,
Desert me not in this dread earnestness.
Only be firm this once, my faithful cord,
Which hath so oft bewinged my bitter shaft—
Escaped it just now feebly from my hand,
I do not have a second one to send.
(*Travelers pass over the stage.*)

Upon this bench of stone I'll sit me down,
Afforded for the traveller's brief repose—
For here there is no home—Each presses past
The other hastily and distantly,
And questions not about his pain—Here goes
The apprehensive merchant and the lightly
Attired pilgrim—the attentive monk,
The somber robber and the cheerful player,
The driver with his heavy laden horse,
Who comes here from the distant lands of men,
For every road leads to the end o' th' world.
Each one of them goes forth upon his way
Concerned with his affairs—and mine is murder!
(*Sits down.*)

Before when father travelled forth, dear children,

There was a joy, when he came back again,
For ne'er returned he, 'less he brought you
   something,
Was it a beauteous Alpine flower, was
It an unusual bird or ammonite,
Such as the traveller finds upon the hills—
Now he pursues another venery,
By th' savage path he sits with thoughts of murder,
The life o' th' foe it is, for which he waits.
—And yet he thinks alone of *you*, dear children,
E'en now—to fend for you, your lovely innocence
To shield before the vengeance of the tyrant,
He now intends to bend his bow to murder!
*(Stands up.)*

I wait upon a noble beast—Let not
The hunter be discouraged, days on end
To roam about amid the winter's harshness,
To make the daring leap from rock to rock,
To climb the jagged slippery mountain walls,
To which his limbs are glued by his own blood,
—In order to hunt down the wretched chamois.
A far more precious prize is here at stake,
The heart o' th' deadly foe, who would destroy me.
*(One hears cheerful music from a distance, which*
   *comes nearer.)*

Through my entire life have I employed
The bow—been practiced in the rules of archery,
I've often hit the target in the black
And many beauteous prizes I've brought home
From joyous shooting—But today I mean
To make the *master shot* and win the best
Within the whole circumference of the mountains.

*(A wedding procession passes over the stage and up the*
*hollow lane.* TELL *observes it, leaning on his bow.* STÜSSI
   *the game keeper joins him.)*

STÜSSI:  That is the cloister stew'rd of Mörlischachen,
   Who holds the wedding here—A wealthy man,
   He hath ten herd of cattle on the Alps.
   He goes to get his bride at Imisee,
   Tonight there will be revelry in Küssnacht.
   Come with us! every honest man's invited.
TELL:  An earnest guest fits not the wedding house.
STÜSSI:  If grief oppress you, cast it from thine heart,
   Bear with, what comes, the times are heavy now.
   Therefore the man must lightly seize his joy.
   Be married here and somewhere else be buried.
TELL:  And oft the one comes close upon the other.
STÜSSI:  So goes the world now. Everywhere there is
   Enough distress—A landslide hath occurred
   In Canton Glarn and one entire side
   O' th' Glarnish hath caved in.
TELL:                  Do even hills
   Now totter too? There stands naught firm on earth.
STÜSSI:  And somewhere else one hears of wondrous
      things.
   Here spake I to one man, who came from Baden.
   A knight would go by horse unto the King,
   And as he rode along a swarm of hornets
   Encountered him, they fell upon his horse,
   That it for martyr's death sinks to the ground,
   And he proceeds unto the King on foot.
TELL:  His sting is also given to the weak.

(ARMGARD *enters with several children and places herself*
      *at the entrance to the hollow way.*)

STÜSSI:  'Tis said it bodes a great disaster to
   The land, a heavy deed opposed to nature.
TELL:  Yet every day brings forth such deeds as this,
   No portent is required to make them known.
STÜSSI:  Yes, happy's he, who tills his field in peace
   And unimpaired sits by his own at home.
TELL:  The very meekest cannot rest in peace,
   If some malicious neighbor likes it not.

(TELL *looks often with uneasy expectation toward the
    crest of the pass.*)

STÜSSI:  So fare you well—You wait for someone here?

TELL:  I do.

STÜSSI:     A pleasant journey home to you!
  —You are from Uri?  Our most gracious lord
  The Gov'rnor we await today from there.

TRAVELER *(comes):*  The Gov'rnor don't expect today.
    The waters
  Have overflowed their banks from heavy rains,
  And all the bridges hath the stream ripped up.
  (TELL *stands up.*)

ARMGARD *(comes forward.):*  The Governor comes not!

STÜSSI:                 Do you seek him?

ARMGARD:  Indeed I do!

STÜSSI:              Why are you standing then
  Upon this hollow alley in his way?

ARMGARD:  He can't avoid me here, he must hear me.

FRIESSHART *(Comes hastily down the hollow path and
    calls upon the stage.):*
  Now move out of the way—My gracious lord
  The Governor comes riding close behind me.
  (TELL *exits.*)

ARMGARD *(full of life):*  The Gov'rnor comes!
  (ARMGARD *goes with her children to the front of the
    stage.* GESSLER *and* RUDOLF DER HARRAS *appear on
    horseback on the crest of the way.*)

STÜSSI *(to* FRIESSHART*):*  How came you through the
    waters,
  Now that the stream hath swept away the bridges?

FRIESSHART:  We've been in battle with the lake, my
    friend,
  And we fear not before the Alpine water.

STÜSSI:  You were upon the ship in that ferocious storm?

FRIESSHART: Yes, that we were. I shall not soon forget
    it—

STÜSSI:  O stay, and speak!

FRIESSHART:             Let me, I must away,

I must announce the Gov'rnor in the castle. (*Away.*)
STÜSSI:  Had virtuous people been upon the ship,
To th' bottom had it sunk with man and mouse,
*This* crew can neither water kill nor fire. (*He looks
   around.*)
Where hath the huntsman gone, with whom I spake?
(*Exits.*)


(GESSLER *and* RUDOLF DER HARRAS *on horseback.*)


GESSLER:  Say, what you will, I am the Emp'ror's
   servant
And must give thought, to how I best can please him.
He hath not sent me to this land, to flatter
The people and be soft to them—He wants
Obedience, the issue is, shall farmers
Be master in the land or shall the Emp'ror.
ARMGARD:  Now is the moment! Now I'll bring it up!
(*Approaches timidly.*)
GESSLER:  I have not had the hat put up as jest
In Altorf, nor was it to test the hearts
O' th' people, these I've known for quite some time.
I have had it put up, that they might learn
To bend their necks to me, which they hold high—
I had the *inconvenient* thing set up
Upon their path, where they would have to pass,
That they would meet it with their eyes, and it
Would bring to mind their lord, whom they forget.
RUDOLF DER HARRAS:  And yet the people do have
   certain rights—
GESSLER:  To ponder these, there is just now no time!
—Far reaching projects are at work and growing,
The Imperial house would grow, and what the father
Hath gloriously begun, the son will end.
This little people is to us a stone
I' th' way—this way or that, they must submit.
(*They want to pass on. The woman throws herself
   down before the* GOVERNOR.)

ARMGARD: Kind-heartedness, Lord Governor! Mercy!
Mercy!

GESSLER: Why stand you on the public highway in
My way—Stand back!

ARMGARD: My husband lies in prison,
The wretched orphans cry for bread—Have pity,
Severest Lord, on our great misery.

RUDOLF DER HARRAS: Who are you? And who is your
man?

ARMGARD: A poor
Wild hay man, gracious Lord, from Rigiberg,
Who over the abyss mows down the grass
Which freely grows from jagged rocky walls,
To which the cattle do not dare to climb—

RUDOLF DER HARRAS (*to the* GOVERNOR):
By God, a miserable and wretched life!
I beg you, set him free, the wretched man,
However heavy his offense may be,
His ghastly trade is punishment enough.
(*To the woman.*)
You shall have justice—Yonder in the castle
Bring your petition—Here is not the place.

ARMGARD: No, no I will not budge from out this place,
Until the Gov'rnor hath returned my husband!
Six months already lies he in the tower
And waits the sentence of the judge in vain.

GESSLER: Woman, would you use force with me, away.

ARMGARD: I ask for justice, Gov'rnor! Thou art judge
I' th' country in the Emp'ror's stead and God's.
Perform thy duty! As thou hop'st for justice
Yourself from Heaven, so show it to us.

GESSLER: Hence, drive this brazen people from mine
eyes.

ARMGARD (*Seizes the reins of his horse.*):
No, no, there's nothing more for me to lose.
—Thou com'st not, Gov'rnor from this place, 'til thou
Hast rendered justice to me—Knit thy brows,
And roll thine eyes, just as thou wilt—We are

In such unbounded misery, that we
Care not about thine anger—
GESSLER:                          Woman, hence,
Or else my horse will trample over thee.
ARMGARD:  So let it trample over me—there—
(*She pulls her children to the ground and throws
    herself with them in his way.*)          Here I lie
With all my children—Let the wretched orphans
Be trodden under by thy horses' hooves,
It will not be the worst, that thou hast done—
RUDOLF DER HARRAS:
Woman, are you mad?
ARMGARD (*vehemently continuing*):
                          Thou hast for some time
Trampled the Emperor's land beneath thy feet!
—O I am but a woman! Were I man,
I would know something better, than to lie
Here in the dust—
(*He hears the previous music again upon the crest of
    the way, but muffled.*)
GESSLER:                  Where are my servants?  Have
Them carry her away from here, or I'll
Forget myself and do what I will rue.
RUDOLF DER HARRAS:  The servants can not pass
    therethrough, O Lord,
The hollow way is blocked up by a marriage.
GESSLER:  An all too gentle ruler am I to
This people still—their tongues are still too free,
They have not yet been tamed, as they should
    be—
Yet this shall all be changed, I promise it,
I will yet break this stubborn mood of theirs,
The brazen spirit of freedom I will bend.
Throughout these canton lands I'll promulgate
A new decree—I will—
(*An arrow pierces through him, he puts his hand on
    his heart and starts to fall. With feeble voice.*)
                          God grant me mercy!

RUDOLF DER HARRAS:  Lord Gov'rnor—God what is
  this?  Whither came it?

ARMGARD (*starting up*):
  Murder! Murder! He totters, sinks! He's hit!
  The arrow's hit the center of his heart!

RUDOLF DER HARRAS (*springs from his horse*):
  What horrible occurrence—God—Lord knight—
  Call on the mercy of your God—For you
  Are now a man of death—

GESSLER:                      That is Tell's shot
  (*Is slid down from his horse into the arms of* RUDOLF
    DER HARRAS *and is laid upon the bench.*)

TELL (*appears above on the top of the rocks*):
  Thou ken'st the archer, seek not for another!
  Free are our huts, the innocent are safe
  'Fore thee, thou wilt no longer harm the land.
  (*Disappears from the heights.*)

(*People rush in.*)

STÜSSI (*in front*):  What is the matter?  What hath
  happened here?

ARMGARD:  The Gov'rnor hath been shot through by an
  arrow.

PEOPLE (*rushing in*):  Who hath been shot?
  (*Meanwhile the foremost of the wedding train come on
    the stage, the hindmost are still on the heights, and
    the music continues.*)

RUDOLF DER HARRAS:  He's bleeding fast to death.
  Go forth, get help! Pursue the murderer!
  —Unhappy man, so must it end with thee,
  And yet thou would'st not listen to my warning!

STÜSSI:  By God! here lies he pale and without life!

MANY VOICES:  Who's done the deed?

RUDOLF DER HARRAS:  Hath madness seized these
  people,
  That they make music for a murder?  Silence.
  (*Music suddenly breaks off, still more people come in.*)
  Lord Gov'rnor, speak now, if you can—Have you

No more to trust to me?
(*Gessler gives a sign with his hand, which he repeats
   with vehemence, when it is not understood at once.*)
                    Where shall I go?
—To Küssnacht?—I can't understand you—O
Be not impatient—Leave all thought of earth,
Think now, to reconcile yourself with Heaven.
(*The whole marriage party stands around the dying
   man with an unfeeling horror.*)
STÜSSI:  Behold, how pale he grows—Now enters death
Into his heart—his eyes have now grown dim.
ARMGARD (*lifts up a child*):
See, children, how a maniac expires!
RUDOLF DER HARRAS:  O insane women, have you then
      no feeling,
That you must feast your eyes upon his horror?
—Help—Lend your hand—Will no one stand by me,
To draw the painful arrow from his breast?
WOMEN (*step back*):  We touch the man, whom God
      himself hath struck!
RUDOLF DER HARRAS:
Curse on you and damnation!  (*Draws his sword.*)
STÜSSI (*seizes him by the arm*):  Dare it, Lord!
Your rule is at an end. The tyrant of
The country is now fallen. We'll endure
No further violence. We are free men.
ALL (*tumultuously*):  The land is free.
RUDOLF DER HARRAS:                   And is it come to this?
Fear and obedience so quickly end?
(*To the men in arms, who are thronging in.*)
You see the horrifying act of murder,
The which hath happened here—Help is in vain—
'Tis useless, to pursue the murderer.
We're pressed by other worries—On, to Küssnacht,
That we may save the Emp'ror's fortresses!
For in this moment are dissolved alike
All bonds of order and all ties of duty,
And no man's loyalty is to be trusted.

*(Whilst he exits with the men in arms, six* BROTHERS
OF MERCY *appear.)*
ARMGARD:  Make room! Make room! Here come the
Brothers o' Mercy.
STÜSSI:  The victim lies—The ravens now descend.
BROTHERS OF MERCY *(form a half-circle around the
dead man and sing in deep tones):*
With hasty step death comes to man,
It hath no respite to him given,
It strikes him midway in his span,
Forth from life's fullness is he driven,
If he's prepared or not, to die,
He must stand 'fore his Judge on high!

*(Whilst the last lines are repeated, the curtain falls.)*


# ACT V

## SCENE I

*Public square near Altorf.*

*In the hinterground to the right the Fortress Keep of Uri
with the scaffold still standing as in the third scene of the
first act; to the left a view out into many mountains, upon
all of which signal fires burn. It is just the break of day,
bells resound from various distances.*

RUODI, KUONI, WERNI, MASTER STONEMASON *and many
other countrymen, also women and children.*

RUODI:  See you the fire signals on the mountains?
STONEMASON:  Hear you the bells above the forest
there?
RUODI:  The foe is put to flight.
STONEMASON:                    The fortresses are captured.
RUODI:  And we in Canton Uri still endure

The tyrant's castle on our native soil?
Are we the last, who do declare we're free?

STONEMASON: This *yoke* shall stand, which was to force
    us down?
Up, tear it down!

ALL:                Tear't down! Tear't down! Tear't
    down!

RUODI: Where is the Steer of Uri?

STEER OF URI:                  Here. What shall I?

RUODI: Climb up the tower, blow into your horn,
    That it resound afar among the mountains,
    And every echo in the rocky clefts
    Awakening, call all the mountain men
    Together quickly.

(STEER OF URI *exits.*)

(WALTER FÜRST *enters.*)

WALTER FÜRST: Hold! Friends! Hold! We still
    Lack information, as to what hath happened
    In Unterwald and Schwyz. Let's first await
    The messengers.

RUODI:            Why should we wait? The tyrant
    Is dead, the day of freedom hath appeared.

STONEMASON: Are not these flaming messengers
    enough,
Which burn on every mountain top around?

RUODI: Come all, come all, take hold, ye men and
    women!
Break up the scaffold! Pull the arches down!
Tear down the walls! No stone stand on another.

STONEMASON: Companions come! We have constructed
    it,
We know how to destroy it.

ALL:              Come! tear't down.

(*They fall upon the structure from all sides.*)

WALTER FÜRST: It's underway. I cannot stop them
    now.

(MELCHTAL *and* BAUMGARTEN *enter.*)

MELCHTAL: What? Stands the fortress still and Sarnen
    lies
  In ashes and the Rossberg's broken down?
WALTER FÜRST:
  Is that you, Melchtal? Do you bring us freedom?
  Speak! Have the Cantons all been cleansed o' th' foe?
MELCHTAL (*embraces him*):
  We've swept them from the soil. Rejoice, old father!
  Now at this very moment, as we talk,
  There is no tyrant left in Switzerland.
WALTER FÜRST: O speak, how came the forts into your
    power?
MELCHTAL: Rudenz it was, who took the fort at Sarnen
  With manly and courageous acts of daring,
  The Rossberg had I climbed the night before.
  —But hear, what then occurred. As we the fort
  O' th' foe devoid, with joy now set on fire,
  The crackling flames already rose to th' heaven,
  When Diethelm, Gessler's boy, rushed out toward us
  And cried, the Bruneck woman burns to death.
WALTER FÜRST:
  O righteous God!
  (*One hears the beams of the scaffold fall.*)
MELCHTAL:        'Twas she herself, was locked
  Up here in secret on the Gov'rnor's bidding.
  In frenzy Rudenz rose—for we already
  Had heard the beams, the stout supports collapse,
  And from the midst of smoke the piteous cry
  —Of the unhappy woman.
WALTER FÜRST:        She's been rescued?
MELCHTAL: What counted then was swiftness and
    resolve!
  —Had he been *nothing but* our nobleman,
  We would indeed have cherished our own lives,
  But he was our confederate, and Berta
  Esteemed the people—So we staked our lives
  In confidence, and rushed into the fire.
WALTER FÜRST: Hath she been rescued?

MELCHTAL:                          She hath. Rudenz and I,
We carried her we two from out the flames,
And timber fell behind us with a crash.
—And now, when she discerned that she'd been
     rescued,
Her eyes rose up unto the heaven's light,
The Baron threw himself upon my heart,
And silently a compact was now sworn,
That firmly hardened in the fire's glow
Will persevere through every test of fate—

WALTER FÜRST:
Where is the Landenberg?

MELCHTAL:                          Across the Brünig.
No fault of mine it was, that he who blinded
My father should escape with his own sight.
Pursued I him, o'ertook him in his flight,
And dragged him then unto my father's feet.
The sword was brandished over him already,
From the compassion of the blind old man
He won the gift of life for which he begged.
An *oath of truce* he swore, to ne'er return,
And he will keep it, he hath felt our arm.

WALTER FÜRST: 'Tis well, you have not put the stain of
     blood
On this unsullied triumph!

CHILDREN (*hasten across the stage with the wreckage
     of the scaffold*):          Freedom! Freedom!
(*The horn of Uri is blown with might.*)

WALTER FÜRST: See, what a festival! The children will
     Recall this day as late as in old age.

(*Girls bring the hat carried on a pole, the whole stage is
               filled with people.*)

RUODI: Here is the hat, to which we had to bow.

BAUMGARTEN: Instruct us, what we ought to do with it.

WALTER FÜRST: God! Underneath this hat my grandson
     stood!

SEVERAL VOICES: Destroy the emblem of the tyrant's
    power!
  Into the fire with it.
WALTER FÜRST:      No, let it be preserved!
  It had to serve as tool of tyranny,
  'Twill be the lasting symbol of our freedom!
  *(The country people, men, women and children stand*
    *and sit upon the beams of the shattered scaffold*
    *grouped around picturesquely in a large half-circle.)*
MELCHTAL: So stand we happ'ly now upon the
    wreckage
  Of tyranny, and grandly is't fulfilled,
  What we at Rütli swore, confederates.
WALTER FÜRST: The work hath been begun, but not
    completed.
  We now need courage and firm unity,
  For be assured, the King will not delay,
  In taking vengeance for his Gov'rnor's death,
  And bringing back by force the one expelled.
MELCHTAL: Let him march up with all his army's
    might,
  If from within the enemy's dispelled,
  We will engage the enemy outside.
RUODI: There are but few approaches to the land,
  These we will cover with our very bodies.
BAUMGARTEN: We are united by eternal bonds,
  And never shall his armies frighten us!

      (RÖSSELMANN *and* STAUFFACHER *come.*)

RÖSSELMANN *(entering):* These are the fearful
    judgments of the Heaven.
COUNTRYMEN:
  What is the matter?
RÖSSELMANN:      In what times we live!
WALTER FÜRST: Say on, what is it?—Ha, is't you, Lord
    Werner?
  What bring you us?
COUNTRYMEN:      What is it?

RÖSSELMANN:                              Hear and marvel!
STAUFFACHER:  From one great cause of fear are we set
    free—
RÖSSELMANN:  The Emp'ror hath been murdered.
WALTER FÜRST:                              Gracious God!
  (*Countrymen become riotous and throng around*
   STAUFFACHER.)
ALL:  He's murdered! What! The Emp'ror! Hark! The
    Emp'ror!
MELCHTAL:  Not possible! Whence came this news to
    you?
STAUFFACHER:  'Tis true indeed. Near Bruck King
    Albrecht fell
  By an assassin's hand—a trusted man,
  Johannes Müller, brought it from Schaffhausen.
WALTER FÜRST:  Who would have dared so horrible a
    deed?
STAUFFACHER:  'Tis made more horrible by him who did
    it.
  It was his nephew, his own brother's child,
  'Twas Duke Johann of Schwabia, who did it.
MELCHTAL:  What drove him to this deed of patricide?
STAUFFACHER:  The Emp'ror kept his patrimony back
  Despite impatient importunities,
  'Tis said, he never meant to grant it him,
  But with a bishop's hat to pay him off.
  However this may be—the youth gave ear
  To th' evil counsel of his friends in arms,
  And with the noble Lord von Eschenbach,
  Von Tegernfelden, von der Wart and Palm
  He did resolve, since he could find no justice,
  To take revenge on him with his own hands.
WALTER FÜRST:  O speak, how was this monstrous deed
    achieved?
STAUFFACHER:  The King was riding down from Stein to
    Baden,
  Toward Rheinfeld, where the court was held, to join,

With him the princes, Hans and Leopold,
And a large retinue of high-born lords.
And when they came unto the *Reuss*, where one
Can only cross upon a ferry boat,
There the assassins forced themselves on board,
That they detach the Emp'ror from his train.
Thereafter, as the prince rode hence across
A cultivated field—'neath which, 'tis said,
An old large city stood in heathen times—
The ancient Hapsburg fortress now in sight,
From whence the grandeur of his line proceeded—
Duke Hans then thrusts a dagger in his throat,
Rudolf von Palm runs through him with his spear,
And Eschenbach then splits his head in two,
So that he sinks thereunder in his blood,
He's slain by his own kin, *on* his own land.
Upon the other shore they saw the deed,
Yet cut off by the stream they could do naught
But raise an unavailing cry of woe;
Yet by the wayside a poor woman sat,
And in her lap the Emp'ror bled to death.
MELCHTAL:  So hath he only dug his early grave,
  Who would insatiably have everything!
STAUFFACHER:  A monstrous horror is abroad i' th'
    land,
  All passes of the mountains are blockaded,
  And each estate doth fortify its borders,
  E'en ancient Zürich closes up its gates,
  The which stood open thirty years, in fear
  O' th' murderers and even more—th' avengers.
  For armed now with the imperial ban, the Queen
  Of Hungary doth come, the stringent Agnes,
  Who doth not know the gentleness of her
  Frail sex, to venge her father's royal blood
  Upon the murderers' entire line,
  Upon their servants, children, children's children,
  Yes even on the stones of their great castles.

She's sworn an oath, that she'll dispatch below
Whole generations to her father's grave,
To bathe herself in blood as in May dew.

MELCHTAL:  Knows one, whereto the murderers have
    fled?

STAUFFACHER:  They fled no sooner had the deed been
    done
Their separate ways upon five different routes
And parted, ne'er to see each other more—
'Tis said Duke Johann wanders in the mountains.

WALTER FÜRST:  And thus the crime hath yielded them
    no fruit!
For vengeance yields no fruit! It is itself
The dreadful food it feeds on, its delight
Is murder, and its satisfaction horror.

STAUFFACHER:  The murd'rers gain no profit from their
    crime,
But *we* shall pluck with unpolluted hands
The blessed fruit o' th' bloody wickedness.
For we are now relieved of a great fear,
The greatest foe of liberty is fallen,
And as it's rumored, that the crown will pass
From Hapsburg's house unto another line,
The Empire will assert electoral freedom.

WALTER FÜRST AND SEVERAL OTHERS:
What have you heard?

STAUFFACHER:        The Count of Luxemburg
Already hath been chosen by most votes.

WALTER FÜRST:  'Tis well, that we kept loyal to the
    Empire,
For there is cause of hope for justice now!

STAUFFACHER:  The new lord will have need of valiant
    friends,
He'll be our shield 'gainst Austria's revenge.
(*The countrymen embrace one another.*)


(SACRISTAN *with an imperial messenger.*)

SACRISTAN: Here are the worthy leaders of the land.

RÖSSELMANN AND MANY OTHERS:
Sacrist, what is't?

SACRISTAN: A courier brings this letter.

ALL (to WALTER FÜRST):
Open and read it.

WALTER FÜRST: "To the honest men
Of Uri, Schwyz and Unterwalden, Queen
Elizabeth bids grace and all good wishes."

MANY VOICES: What would the Queen? Her reign is
over now.

WALTER FÜRST (reads): "In her great sorrow and her
widowed grief,
Wherein the bloody passing of her lord
Hath left the Queen, she still remembers well
The ancient faith and love of Switzerland."

MELCHTAL: In her prosperity she's ne'er done that.

RÖESSELMAN: Be still! Let's listen!

WALTER FÜRST (reads): "And she doth look unto this
loyal people,
Assured that they will righteously abhor
The cursed perpetrators of this deed.
Therefore she doth expect from the three Cantons,
That they will never help the murderers,
But rather that they'll loyally assist,
To give them up to the avenger's hand,
Remembering the love and ancient favor,
Which they received from Rudolf's princely house."
(Signs of resentment among the countrymen.)

MANY VOICES: The love and favor!

STAUFFACHER: We have received the favor of the
father,
But what have we to boast of from the son?
Hath he confirmed the charter of our freedom,
As 'fore him every Emperor had done?
Hath he passed judgments based on righteous
judgment,

And lent to hard pressed innocence protection?
Had he but listened to the messenger,
That we had sent to him in our distress?
Not one of all these things had e'er the King
Performed for us, and had we not ourselves
Obtained our rights with our own valiant hand,
Our need would not have moved him—Give him
    thanks?
No thanks hath he sown here within these vales.
He stood upon an eminence, he could
Have been a father to his people, yet
It pleased him, to provide but for his own,
Those whom he hath enriched, may cry for him!

WALTER FÜRST: We will not shout for joy o'er his
    demise,
Nor *now* recall to mind the suffered evil,
Far be't from us! Yet, that we shall *avenge*
The death o' th' King, who never did us good,
And those pursue, who never made us grieve,
That fits us not, and it will never suit us,
As love's a freely given offering,
So death absolves from all enforced duties,
—To him we have no further debt to pay.

MELCHTAL: And if the Queen laments within her
    chamber,
And blames the Heaven for her savage pain,
So see you here a people freed of fear,
To this same Heaven send their thankful prayers—
He who will harvest tears, must first sow love.
(IMPERIAL MESSENGER *exits.*)

STAUFFACHER (*to the people*):
But where is Tell? Shall *he* alone be absent,
Who is the founder of our freedom? *He*
Hath done the most, endured the most severe.
Come all, now come, let's go unto his house,
And there acclaim the savior of us all.
(*All exit.*)

## SCENE II

*Entrance to* TELL'*s house.*

*A fire burns on the hearth. The door standing open shows into the outside.*

HEDWIG. WALTER *and* WILHELM.

HEDWIG: Today your father comes. Dear children,
    children!
  He lives, is free and we are free and all!
  And it's your father, who hath saved the land.
WALTER: And I have also been there with him, Mother!
  One must name me as well. My father's shaft
  Went closely by my life, and I have not
  So much as trembled.
HEDWIG *(embraces him):* Yes, thou art restored
  To me! Twice have I given birth to thee!
  It is foreby—I have you both now, both!
  Twice suffered I the mother's grief for thee!
  And your dear father comes again today!

    *(A monk appears at the entrance to the house.)*

WILHELM: Look, Mother, look—There stands a pious
    brother,
  He surely will be asking us for alms.
HEDWIG: Lead him inside, that he may be refreshed,
  And feel, that he is come to th' house of joy!
  *(Goes inside and comes back soon with a beaker.)*
WILHELM *(to the monk):* Come in, good man. My
  mother will refresh you.
WALTER: Come in, rest up and go from here the
  stronger.
MONK *(timorously looking around, with shattered
  features):*
  Where am I now? Pray tell me, in which land?
WALTER: Are you then lost, that you do not know that?

You are at Bürglen, Lord, i' th' land of Uri,
Just where one enters in the Schächental.

MONK (*to* HEDWIG, *who returns*):
Are you alone? Or is your Lord at home?

HEDWIG: Soon I expect him—what's it to you, man?
You do not look, as if you've brought aught good.
—Whoe'er you are, you are in want, take that!
(*Hands him the beaker.*)

MONK: E'en as my yearning heart pines for
refreshment,
I'll touch naught here, 'til you have promised me—

HEDWIG: Touch not my garment, step not near to me,
Stand far away, if I should listen to you.

MONK: Now by this fire, that flames hospitably,
And by your children's precious head, which I
Embrace—(*Seizes the boy.*)

HEDWIG: Man, what is your intent? Stand back
From my dear children!—You're no monk! You are
Not one! For peace should dwell within this habit,
But in your features peace doth not reside.

MONK: I am the most unfortunate of men.

HEDWIG: Unhappiness speaks forcefully to th' heart,
And yet your look ties up my inner soul.

WALTER (*springing up*):
Mother, here's father! (*Rushes out.*)

HEDWIG: O my God! (*Wants to follow,
trembles and stops.*)

WILHELM (*rushes after him*): Here's Father!

WALTER (*outside*):
Th'art here once more!

WILHELM (*outside*): O Father, my dear Father!

TELL (*outside*): Here am I once again—Where is your
Mother?
(*Enters.*)

WALTER: There at the door she stands and can no
further,
So trembles she with terror and with joy.

TELL: O Hedwig, Hedwig! Mother of my children!

God's helped—No tyrant shall divide us more.

HEDWIG *(on his neck):* O Tell! My Tell! For thee what
    fear I've suffered!

*(*MONK *becomes attentive.)*

TELL: Forget it now and live with joy alone!
    I am at home once more! This is my cottage!
    I stand again on that which is mine own!

WILHELM: And yet where hast thou left thy crossbow,
    Father?
    I see it not.

TELL:        Thou wilt see it no more,
    It is preserved now in a sacred place,
    'Twill henceforth never serve the hunt again.

HEDWIG: O Tell! Tell! *(Steps back, releases his hand.)*

TELL:        What hath frightened thee, dear wife?

HEDWIG: How—*how* com'st thou to me again?—This
    hand
    —May I take hold of it?—This hand—O God!

TELL *(heartily and courageously):*
    Hath you defended and the land delivered,
    And I may raise it freely up to Heaven.
    *(Monk makes an hasty movement, he looks at him.)*
    Who is this brother here?

HEDWIG:           Ah, I forgot him!
    Speak *thou* with him, I shudder in his presence.

MONK *(steps nearer):* Are you the Tell, by whom the
    Gov'rnor fell?

TELL: Yes I am he, I hide it from no man.

MONK: You are the Tell! Ah, it's the hand of God,
    The which hath led me underneath your roof.

TELL *(measures him with his eyes):*
    You are no monk! Who are you?

MONK:           You have slain
    The Gov'rnor, who did you wrong—I too
    Have slain an enemy, who had denied
    My rights—He was your foe as well as mine—
    And I have freed the land of him.

TELL *(starting back):*        You are—

Oh horror!—Children! Children, go inside.
Go in, dear wife! Go! Go!—Unhappy man,
You would be—
HEDWIG:          God, who is it?
TELL:                              Do not ask!
Away! Away! The children must not hear.
Go from the house—Go far away—Thou must
Not dwell beneath a *single* roof with him.
HEDWIG: Woe's me, what is this? Come!
*(Goes with the children.)*
TELL *(to the monk):* You are the Duke
Of Austria—You are! And you have slain
The Emperor, your uncle and your lord.
JOHANNES PARRICIDA: He was the robber of my
      heritage.
TELL: Your uncle slain, your Emperor! And you
The earth still bears! The sun still shines on you!
PARRICIDA: Tell, listen to me, ere you—
TELL:                              Dripping with
The blood of patricide and Emp'ror's murder,
Dar'st thou to step into my stainless house,
Thou dar'st, to show thy face to a good man
And want the rights of hospitality?
PARRICIDA: From you I hoped that I would find
      compassion,
You too took vengeance on your foe.
TELL:                              Unhappy man!
Must thou confound ambition's bloody guilt
With what a father did in self defense?
Didst thou defend beloved heads of children?
Protect the sanctity o' th' hearth? Ward off
The most dreadful, the utmost from thine own?
—To th' Heaven lift I mine unsullied hands,
And curse thee and thine act—I have avenged
The holiness of nature, which thou hast
Disgraced—I have no part with thee—For *thou*
Hast murdered, *I've* defended those most dear.
PARRICIDA: You cast me off, unsolaced, in despair?

TELL: A horror grips me, when I speak with thee.
Away! Pursue thy dreadful course, and leave
My cottage pure, where innocence resides.
PARRICIDA *(turns to go):* So *can* I, and so *will* I live no
more!
TELL: And yet I've pity for thee—God i' th' Heavens!
So young, of such a noble family,
Grandson of Rudolf, of my Lord and Emp'ror,
As fugitive from murder, at my threshold,
O' th' wretched man, imploring and despairing—
PARRICIDA: O, if you could but weep, then let my fate
Move you, it is an hideous one—I am
A prince—I *was*—and I could have been happy,
If I had mastered my desires' impatience.
But envy gnawed upon my heart—I saw
The youth of mine own cousin Leopold
Becrowned with honors and with land rewarded,
And me, who was of equal age with him,
Held down i' th' slavish status of a minor—
TELL: Unhappy man, well knew thine uncle thee,
When he refused to give thee lands and people!
Thou with thine hasty, savage insane acts
Hast horribly confirmed his wise resolve.
—Where are the bloody helpers in thy murder?
PARRICIDA: Wherever the avenging spirits led them,
I have not seen them since the hapless deed.
TELL: Know'st thou, that thou art banned by law, that
thou
To friends forbidden and to foes allowed?
PARRICIDA: Therefore avoid I every public road,
I venture not to knock at any cottage—
I turn my footsteps to the wilderness,
A terror to myself, I roam the mountains,
And shrink back shuddering before my self,
A brook shows me mine own unhappy image.
O felt you pity and humanity—*(Falls down before
him.)*
TELL *(turning away):* Stand up! Stand up!

PARRICIDA:  Not, 'til you give the hand to me in help.
TELL:  Can I help you?  Can any man of sin?
  Yet stand up now—Whatever horror you've
  Committed—You're a man—I am one too—
  From Tell no man should part uncomforted—
  What I can do, that will I do.
PARRICIDA (*springing up and grasping his hand with
     vehemence*):                    O Tell!
  You rescue my poor soul from desperation.
TELL:  Let go my hand—You must away. You could
  Not stay here undiscovered, could discovered
  Not count on refuge—Whither will you go?
  Where hope you to find quiet?
PARRICIDA:                    Know I?  Ah!
TELL:  Hear, what God grants my heart—You must away
  To Italy and to Saint Peter's city,
  There cast yourself at the Pope's feet, confess
  To him your guilt and thus redeem your soul.
PARRICIDA:  Will he not give me up to the avengers?
TELL:  What he may do, accept it as from God.
PARRICIDA:  How shall I come into that unknown land?
  I'm unfamiliar with the way, dare not
  To join my steps to those of travellers.
TELL:  The way I will describe to you, mark well!
  You must ascend, upstream along the *Reuss*,
  Which from the mountain plunges wildly down—
PARRICIDA (*terrified*):  See I the Reuss?  It flows beside
     my deed.
TELL:  The road goes through the gorge, and many
     crosses
  Mark it, erected to the memory
  O' th' trav'lers, buried by the avalanche.
PARRICIDA:  I have no fear of nature's terrors, if
  I tame the savage torments of my heart.
TELL:  Before each cross fall down and expiate
  Your guilt with ardent tears of penitence—
  And are you safely through the frightful pass,
  And if the mountain doth not send its snowdrifts,

Down here upon you from the frozen ridge,
So come you to the *bridge*, which hangs in *spray*.
If it doth not cave in beneath your guilt,
If you have left it safely to your rear,
So will a gloomy *rocky gate* burst open,
No day hath shone on it—proceed therethrough,
It leads you to a cheerful *vale* of joy—
Yet must you hurry on with rapid steps,
You may not tarry, where'er peace resides.
PARRICIDA:  O Rudolf! Rudolf! Royal ancestor!
So comes thy grandson on thine Empire's soil!
TELL:  So climbing always, come you to the heights
O' th' *Gotthards*, where th' eternal *lakes* are found,
Which from the streams of heaven fill themselves.
There take departure from the German earth,
Another stream with cheerful course leads you
Down into Italy, your promised land—
*(One hears the cowherd's dance song blown from
    many Alpine horns.)*
But I hear voices. Hence!
HEDWIG *(hurries in)*:        Where art thou, Tell?
My father comes! All the confederates
Approach in gay procession—
PARRICIDA *(covers himself)*:    Woe is me!
I may not tarry midst this happiness.
TELL:  Go now, dear wife. And freshen up this man,
Load presents richly on him, for his way
Is far and he will not find any quarters.
Hurry! They near.
HEDWIG:          Who is it?
TELL:                    Ask me not!
And when he leaves, so turn thine eyes away,
That they see not, upon which road he travels!

*(PARRICIDA goes toward TELL with an hasty movement, but
the latter beckons him with the hand and goes. When both
have left to different sides, the scene changes and one sees
    in*

## THE FINAL SCENE

*the whole valley bottom in front of* TELL'*s dwelling, along
with the hills, which enclose it, occupied by countrymen,
who are grouped as a whole. Others are coming over a high
bridge, which leads over the Schächen.* WALTER FÜRST *with
both boys,* MELCHTAL *and* STAUFFACHER *come forward,
others press after them; as* TELL *steps out, all receive him
with loud jubilation.*)

ALL:  May Tell live long! the archer and the savior!

(*Whilst the foremost press around* TELL *and embrace him,*
RUDENZ *and* BERTA *also appear, the former embracing
the countrymen, the latter* HEDWIG. *The music from the
mountain accompanies this mute scene. When it ends,*
BERTA *steps into the midst of the people.*)

BERTA:  My countrymen! Confederates! Take me
    Into your league, as the first happy woman,
    Who found protection in this land of freedom.
    Into your valiant hands I lay my rights,
    Will you protect me as your citizen?
COUNTRYMEN:  That we will do with life and property.
BERTA:  'Tis well, so to this youth I give my hand,
    A free Swiss woman to this free Swiss man!
RUDENZ:  And I proclaim that all my serfs are free.

(*Whilst the music strikes up anew, the curtain falls.*)

*End.*

# THE PARASITE

## OR, THE ART
## OF SELF-ADVANCEMENT

*A Comedy in five acts
adapted from the French of Picard*

## CAST OF CHARACTERS

NARBONNE,
  *the Minister*
MADAME BELMONT,
  *his Mother*
CHARLOTTE,
  *his Daughter*
*Members of the
  Minister's staff:*
SELICOUR
LAROCHE
FIRMIN

KARL FIRMIN, *the former's
  son, lieutenant*
MICHAEL, *valet of the
  Minister*
ROBINEAU, *a young
  farmer, cousin of
  Selicour*

*The scene is in Paris, in an antechamber of the ministry.*

---

This work by the French playwright Louis Benoit Picard (1769–1828) was translated by Schiller in March 1803, together with Picard's *The Nephew as Uncle*, within a few weeks after completing *The Bride of Messina*. Schiller translated from the French with much liberty, to craft an hilarious and poignant critique of evil in government. It was first performed on October 12, 1803 in the city of Weimar.

# ACT I

## SCENE 1

FIRMIN *the father and* KARL FIRMIN.

KARL: What a marvelous coincidence—just imagine, Father!—

FIRMIN: What is it?

KARL: I have found her again!

FIRMIN: Whom?

KARL: Charlotte. Since being in Paris, I searched in every public place in vain—and the first time, I come with you to the office, my lucky star guides me to her!

FIRMIN: But how then?—

KARL: Just think! The wonderful young lady, on whom I called in the home of her aunt in Kolmar—this Charlotte, whom I love and will always love—she is the daughter—

FIRMIN: Of whom?

KARL: Of your superior, the new Minister.—I always knew her only as Charlotte.

FIRMIN: She is the daughter?

KARL: Of Lord Narbonne.

FIRMIN: And you love her *still*?

KARL: More than ever, my father!—I don't believe, she recognized me; I was about to bow to her, as she entered.—And it's best, that you disturbed me! for what could I have said to her! My confusion would have been obvious and thus have betrayed my feelings!—I simply cannot control myself any longer. In the six months, I have been separated from her, she has been my only thought—she is the sole content, the soul of my poetry— any acclaim I have received is due only to her; for my love is the divinity, that inspires me.

FIRMIN: A poet in love can talk himself into virtually anything at age twenty.—When I was your age, I too squandered my time on verses.—It is a pity, that the better part of our lives is given over to such pretty delusions.—

And if there were any hope for this love at all.—But to strive after something, which can never be attained!—Charlotte Narbonne is the daughter of a rich and distinguished man—Our entire fortune consists in my position and your lieutenant's salary.

KARL: And isn't that something for which you are yourself partly responsible, my father? Forgive me! With your abilities, to what could you not aspire! If you were to assert your worth, you could perhaps be a minister yourself, rather than a mere secretary, and your son could make his feelings known to Charlotte without hesitation.

FIRMIN: Your father is a great genius, if one listens to *you*! Leave well enough alone, my son, I know better, what I am worth! I have some ability and can be of some service—but how many other men, as qualified as I, remain in obscurity and see themselves pushed aside by insolent upstarts?—No, my son! Let us not attempt to reach too high!

KARL: But likewise we should not sell ourselves short. What? Aren't you of infinitely more worth than this Selicour, your supervisor—this inflated bubble brain, who would do anything, no matter how vile, to ingratiate himself with the former Minister, who sold positions, embezzled pensions, and who is now, I hear, very high in the favor of the new Minister?

FIRMIN: What do you have against Selicour? Doesn't his work get done, just as it should?

KARL: Certainly, but only because *you* help him.—You cannot deny, that you really take care of three-fourths of his job.

FIRMIN: One must exchange favors with others. I look after his duties, so he often looks after mine.

KARL: Precisely, and therefore you should be in his position, and he in yours.

FIRMIN: I will force no one from his position, and I am glad, to remain where I am, in obscurity.

KARL: You should strive to reach as high, as you possibly can. The fact that you held yourself at a distance from the previous minister does your character honor, and I admire you all the more for that.—You were too honorable, to attempt to achieve through currying favor that which should be the reward of merit. But Narbonne, they say, is an excellent man, who seeks out men of merit, who desire the good. Why do you insist, out of this exaggerated modesty, on leaving the field to mere intrigue and mediocrity?

FIRMIN: Your passion misleads you into exaggerating Selicour's faults and my merits. Even granting, that Selicour aims too high for his somewhat mediocre talents, he is honest and means well. Whether he does his own work or has it done through others—the work gets done!— And granted, he is not very able—does that mean that *I* am more so because of that? Do *I* gain merit through his lack of worth? Up to now, my anonymity has suited me very well, and I have sought no higher goal. Should I change my way of thinking at my age?—My current position be not enough for me! All right. But far better, than if I were not enough for it!

KARL: And thus I must renounce my love for Charlotte!


## SCENE 2

### LAROCHE. *Both* FIRMIN.


FIRMIN: Isn't that LaRoche?

LAROCHE (*dejected*): He himself.

FIRMIN: So dejected? What has happened to you?

LAROCHE: You are on your way to your office! How fortunate for you!—I—I will simply enjoy a pleasant morning and take a walk along the dike.

FIRMIN: LaRoche! What's this! You mean you are no longer—

LAROCHE (*shrugs his shoulders*): No longer—My position is lost. Yesterday evening, I received notice of my termination.

KARL: For God's sake!

LaRoche: My wife knows nothing of this. You mustn't tell her. She is ill, it would be the death of her.

KARL: Don't worry. She will learn nothing from us.

FIRMIN: But tell me, LaRoche, how—

LaRoche: Has anyone the slightest reason for reprimanding me? I do not wish to praise myself, but my paperwork is as good as anyone's and my correspondence is certainly well managed. I have no debts, there is nothing to say against my morals.—I am the first to arrive at the office in the morning and the last to leave, and yet I have been terminated!

FIRMIN: Anyone who knows you, will certainly vouch for you—

KARL: But who could have done you this evil service?

LaRoche: Who? It was an act of friendship done by Selicour.

KARL: Is that possible?

LaRoche: I have it from a good source.

KARL: But why?—

LaRoche: Selicour and I are from the same home town, as you know. We are both the same age. His minimal clerical skills he learned through me, for my father was the schoolmaster in our town. I introduced him into the civil service. As thanks, for that, he now shoves me out of my job, to make room for I know not which cousin of our new Minister's valet.

KARL: A neat little scheme!

FIRMIN: But were there not still something to do?

LaRoche: That is exactly what I would expect from you, Mister Firmin!—I had wanted to turn to you.—You think like a decent man.—Listen! There is nothing that can be done for my position, but I shall have my revenge. This arrogant scoundrel, who to his superiors is so fawning, so grovelling, thinks he can get away with shoving aside a poor wretch like me. But watch out, Selicour, my old friend!—Your contemptible opponent may create some serious problems for you! And should it cost me my position, my livelihood for ever—I must have my revenge! I will plunge into the fire for my friend—but let my enemies take heed.

FIRMIN: Dear LaRoche, no more of that!—To forgive and forget is the revenge of an honorable man.

LAROCHE: No forgiveness, Sir, for such a rascal! To unmask such wicked fellows is a worthy, a noble thing to do!— His position, as you well know, belongs by God and in justice to *you*—and for more than one reason. You work, you sweat, you drive yourself, and you are merely wasting your time and efforts! Who asks about your merits? Who is concerned with that? Creep, flatter—make ingratiating bows, stroke the cat's tail—then you are noticed! That is the way to fame and honor!—That is how Selicour has worked, and you can see, what he has accomplished!

FIRMIN: But are you not doing a good man an injustice, dear LaRoche?

LAROCHE: I, him, an injustice! Well, well—I do not pretend to any deep knowledge of humanity, but this Selicour, I see through him!—Him I have—I know myself not so well as I know *him*.—Already in school one saw what fruit he would bear! He fawned over the teacher and obeyed and flattered and knew how to take credit for others' works and lay his eggs in others' nests. He was capable of anything despicable in order to worm his way into favor, to ingratiate himself. And as he grew older, it simply got worse. Here he played the hypocrite, there the buffoon, whatever was timely; he could always tell which way the wind was blowing. Don't think I am slandering him! It is well known, how things were under the former Minister.—Now, he is dead—I have nothing to say against him.—But how well this Selicour knew how to flatter his weaknesses, his vices through the most shameful pandering!—And hardly does the Minister fall, so he is the first, who abandons him, who disowns him.

KARL: But how can he establish himself with the new Minister, who is such a worthy man?

LaRoche: How? With hypocrisy! He knows how to judge his people and to adapt his character to fit the circumstances.—He will even resort to decency, if there is something to be gained by it, just as he will pull some rotten trick, if that leads to his goal.

Karl: But Lord Narbonne has a penetrating intelligence, and will soon see through his man.

LaRoche: And that is just, what he fears.—But as empty is his head of any useful knowledge, just that full is it of sly and dirty tricks.—Right now, for example, he is pretending to be overloaded and extremely pressed with work, and so is able to avoid any real discussions, which would, of course, expose his ignorance.—Also, he is working on no small projects; I know exactly what he is up to, though he thinks he has concealed them well.

Karl: What do you mean? What sort of projects?

LaRoche: Narbonne, who has such influence with the government now, is seeking a talented individual for an important ambassadorial position. *He* has the responsibility, whomever he recommends will get the appointment. Further, this Narbonne has an only daughter, seventeen years old, beautiful, charming, and of enormous wealth.—If Selicour succeeds in getting such a high post out of the country, away from any close scrutiny from his perceptive Minister, he can, with the help of an able and discreet secretary, conceal his emptyheadedness for a long time.—Then, when the day finally comes, as it can not fail to come—how will that affect the son-in-law of the Minister? So, first of all, the minister must be won over, and for that one assumes the manner of the skilled and experienced diplomat.—The Minister's mother is a gossipy older woman, who fancies herself a connoisseur, and is extremely concerned about music.—He has ingratiated himself with this dear old lady, has recited poems and performed charades for her, yes and this bungler has even had the presumption, to strum out a few pieces on the guitar and sing for her evenings.—The young lady

herself reads novels, with her he plays the part of the
sensitive critic, of the admirer, and thus he is the favorite
of the entire household, coddled by the mother, esteemed by the daughter. The ambassadorship is to him
as good as certain, and soon he will snatch the hand of
the daughter.

KARL: What am I hearing! He has the presumption to court
Charlotte?

LaRoche: That he has, you can believe me.

KARL: Charlotte, whom I love! whom I worship!

LaRoche: You love her? You!

FIRMIN: He is a fool! He is quite out of his mind! Don't
listen to him!

LaRoche: What's this I hear! Is this possible?—No, no,
Mister Firmin! This love is not foolishness in the least—
Wait—wait—this could lead to something for us.—I wel-
come this love—it fits perfectly into my project!

KARL: What has he dreamed up?

LaRoche: This Selicour is to be blown into the air. Into
the air, I say—completely destroyed! The father will un-
seat him in his ambitions and the son in his love!

FIRMIN: But I ask you—

LaRoche: Let *me* take care of it! Let me take care of it, I
say. And in a short time, you will be the ambassador, and
Karl will marry Charlotte!

KARL: I, marry Charlotte!

FIRMIN: I, the ambassador!

LaRoche: Well! Well! Why not? You deserve it better,
certainly, than this Selicour.

FIRMIN: Dear LaRoche! Before you work on such glorious
positions for the two of us, I would think, you should be
more concerned, about getting back your own.

KARL: Isn't this just like our friend! Always enterprising,
always hatching plans! But that is not enough! It takes
skill and ingenuity to actually follow through—and because our friend thinks it will be so easy, he always gets
into a lot of trouble!

LaRoche: It may be, that I promise a bit more than I can deliver. But everything, that I see, inspires my hopes, and the attempt can do no harm.—Nothing can induce me to spin out an intrigue for its own sake—but to blow Selicour into the air and also do a service for my friends—that is admirable, that is delightful, and will give me a heavenly pleasure—and success is not to be doubted.

Firmin: Not to be doubted? Then you already have your plan in order—

LaRoche: In order?—How?—I haven't even thought about it, but I'll come up with something, I'll think of something.

Firmin: Oh! Oh! This dangerous plan hasn't been developed very far as yet, as I see.

LaRoche: Don't worry—I'll come out of this with honor; this Selicour will not win out over me, he will not, I assure you.—Who needs the indirect approach? I shall go straight ahead, I shall announce myself to the Minister, it is not difficult to approach him; he loves justice, he can stand the truth.

Firmin: How? What? You would dare—

LaRoche: So what! I am not fearful.—I fear no one.—All right now—I—speak to the minister—I open his eyes—He sees how shamelessly he has been deceived—all that is the work of a half hour.—Selicour is out—out in disgrace and dishonor. And I enjoy the most complete triumph.—And I shall not take pity on the poor devil, when he is driven from the house in shame.

Karl: Whatever you do, dear LaRoche—In any case leave me and my love out of your game! I have no hope.—I cannot allow my desire to soar so high! But for my father you can never do too much.

Firmin: Allow me to answer for myself, my friend!—You mean well, dear LaRoche, but you are allowing your good intentions to run away with your judgment. What kind of amusing project is this, which you have contrived! Sheer empty fantasy!—And were success so certain, as it is not, I would not consent to it. Such grand positions are not for me, nor I for them; inclination and fate have assigned me a more modest sphere. Why should I seek to change myself, if I am satisfied where I am? I hope, the state will not seek me out, and I am too proud, to beg for an appointment—and far more so, to let someone else beg for me.—Concern yourself therefore only with yourself! You have friends enough, someone will gladly intercede for you.

LaRoche: Then neither of you wants my services?—That is of no importance! I will make your fortune, whether you want it or not.

Firmin: He is a fool. But he is a good fellow, and his misfortune pains me deeply.

Karl: Pity me as well, my father! I am unhappier than he! I will lose my Charlotte!

Firmin: I hear someone coming—It is the Minister with his mother—Let us go!—I wish to avoid the impression, that I have placed myself here to meet him. (*Both exit.*)


## SCENE 3

### NARBONNE. MADAME BELMONT.

Madame Belmont: Was Mister Selicour already with you?

Narbonne: I have not yet seen him today!

Madame Belmont: You really must admit, my son, what a veritable treasure you possess in this man.

Narbonne: He does seem quite capable in his special area! And since I have been transferred from my country residence into this great city, into such a demanding position, where things are not at all done according to mere book learning, I must consider it a great fortune, to have met such a man as Selicour.

Madame Belmont: Who understands everything—to whom nothing is alien! Taste and knowledge—the most intelligent conversation, the most pleasant talents. Mu-

sic, painting, poetry—ask, whatever you please, he is
familiar with everything!

NARBONNE: Well, and my daughter?

MADAME BELMONT: Good, that you remind me of her. She
is seventeen now, she has eyes, this Selicour has so many
qualities.—And he is so gallant! His face lights up in her
presence—Oh, I haven't missed that! This delicacy, this
tender attentiveness, that he shows her, these are only a
short step from love!

NARBONNE: Well, that were not a bad match for our child!
The accidental privileges of birth do not matter to me—
haven't I myself worked my way up from below? And this
Selicour can, with his intelligence, his knowledge, and
his honesty, go a long way. I have already considered him
for an outstanding position for which an able and worthy
individual is being sought! Well! I shall test his ability.—
If he shows himself worthy of such a post, as no doubt he
will, and if he knows how to win over my daughter, I will
gladly accept him as my son.

MADAME BELMONT: That is my single wish! He is so correct,
so pleasing, the dearest of men!


## SCENE 4

*The same.* CHARLOTTE.


CHARLOTTE: Good morning, dear Father!

NARBONNE: There you are, my maiden!—Now, how are
you enjoying this great city?

CHARLOTTE: Ah, I wish we were back in the country—For
here I must watch for a chance to see my own father!

NARBONNE: Yes, I too miss my honest country folk. With
them I joked and was happy.—Yet I hope to remain that
here as well—my post should not change my disposition:
it is possible to be a statesman and retain one's good sense
of humor.

MADAME BELMONT: This residence delights me. I—I am
as though in Heaven here. I already know everyone here,

everything is open to me—and Mister Selicour wants me to subscribe to the symphony.

CHARLOTTE: Grandmama, just imagine, whom I think I saw this morning!

MADAME BELMONT: Whom then?

CHARLOTTE: That young officer—

MADAME BELMONT: Which officer?

CHARLOTTE: Young Karl Firmin—

MADAME BELMONT: The one who called on your aunt in Kolmar every evening—

CHARLOTTE: Who always talked to you.

MADAME BELMONT: A very correct young man.

CHARLOTTE: Isn't he, Grandmama?

MADAME BELMONT: Who also composed such pretty verses?

CHARLOTTE: Yes, yes, he!

MADAME BELMONT: Well, since he is here, he will call on us.

NARBONNE: Where can Selicour be? For once, he keeps me waiting!

MADAME BELMONT: Here he comes now!


## SCENE 5

SELICOUR *to the same.*


SELICOUR (*gracious and charming to all*): How utterly enchanting that I should find you all together!

NARBONNE: Good morning, dear Selicour!

SELICOUR (*to Narbonne, handing him some papers*): Here is the memorandum you referred to earlier—I deemed it a good service, to add a few lines of clarification.

NARBONNE: Excellent!

SELICOUR (*giving the ticket to the Madame*): I have reserved a seat for you at the premiere.

MADAME BELMONT: How lovely!

SELICOUR: And for the gracious young lady, I bring this didactic novel.

CHARLOTTE: Have you read it, Mister Selicour?

SELICOUR: The first section, yes, I have leafed through quickly.

CHARLOTTE: Well, and—

SELICOUR: You will find a touching scene there.—An unfortunate father—a degenerate daughter!—The parents helpless, thrown into adversity by their thankless children!—An outrage I cannot grasp—of which I can form no conception!—For isn't it true, only the total gratitude of our lives can make up for the care, that they bestowed upon our helpless childhood?

MADAME BELMONT: In everything he says this worthy man shows such delicacy!

SELICOUR *(to Narbonne):* We need a supervisor in our Department.—The position is important, and there are many interested who wish to apply.

NARBONNE: I will rely on you! You will know how to handle the applications—the years of service, industriousness, ability, and, above all, honesty are to be taken into consideration.—But I was forgetting, there are some papers which I need to sign. I must go!

SELICOUR: And I too must be about my affairs as well!

NARBONNE: I request, that you wait here for me, we must speak together!

SELICOUR: But I had so much to finish before dinner.

NARBONNE: Stay here or at least, come back immediately! I have need of your presence. A man of your knowledge, of your honesty is just what I need right now! Come back soon!—I have a plan which will be of some interest to you. *(He exits.)*

## SCENE 6

*The same without* NARBONNE.

MADAME BELMONT: You cannot imagine, Mister Selicour, how highly my son thinks of you!—But I had something to do, I should think.—Our relatives, our friends are dining here this evening.—Shall we also see you, Mister Selicour?

SELICOUR: If my other pressing business—

MADAME BELMONT: If you were to stay away, our banquet would lack its crown. You are the very soul of our society! And Charlotte, I would wager, would take it badly, if you were not to come.

CHARLOTTE: I, mama? Well yes! Any friend of yours and Papa's is always welcome to me!

MADAME BELMONT: Good! Good!—And now you must go dress! It is high time!—You must know, Mister Selicour, that I designed her ensemble for this evening.

SELICOUR: And thus lovely Art comes to the aid of already lovely Nature—who could resist that?

MADAME BELMONT: He is charming! charming is he! He cannot open his mouth without having something utterly delightful and gallant to say. (*Exits with Charlotte.*)


## SCENE 7

### SELICOUR. MICHAEL.


MICHAEL (*as he enters*): At last, she is gone!—Now I can have a word with him!—Have I the honor of addressing Mister Selicour—

SELICOUR (*rude and irritable*): That is my name!

MICHAEL: Permit me, Sir!

SELICOUR: Must I be bothered even here? What do you want?

MICHAEL: Sir!—

SELICOUR: To be sure more begging—a petition.—I cannot help you.

MICHAEL: Permit me, Sir!

SELICOUR: No! This is not the place—make an appointment to see me at my office!

MICHAEL: I hardly expected such a rude reception—

SELICOUR: I beg your pardon.

MICHAEL: I come, not to ask you for anything—I come, Mister Selicour, to express my gratitude!

SELICOUR: Gratitude? What for?

MICHAEL: That you arranged a position for my nephew.

SELICOUR: What? How?

MICHAEL: I only arrived here yesterday, since my Master left me behind in the country. As I wrote you, I have not had the honor, to meet you in person.

SELICOUR: What are you saying, my most worthy friend! That you were in the service of the Minister?

MICHAEL: His valet, at your service!

SELICOUR: My God, what a misunderstanding! Monsieur Michael, personal servant, valet, confidant of the Minister.—A thousand times I beg your pardon, Monsieur Michael! I am truly ashamed—I am inconsolable, that I received you so rudely. On my honor, Monsieur Michael!—I took you for a mere clerk.

MICHAEL: And if I had been one?

SELICOUR: One is beleaguered by so many pressing people! One cannot always tell who people are by their dress.

MICHAEL: But one can at least be polite to everyone, I would think!

SELICOUR: Of course! Of course! It was an unfortunate distraction!

MICHAEL: Very unpleasant for me, Mister Selicour!

SELICOUR: I am sorry, so sorry—In all eternity, I cannot forgive myself.

MICHAEL: Then shall we forget it!

SELICOUR: Well! Well!—I have already demonstrated my zeal to you—Your dear, dear nephew! were well cared for now!

MICHAEL: I have just come from him! He is a very clever young man.

SELICOUR: That young man will make his way. Count on me.

MICHAEL: Isn't his handwriting excellent?

SELICOUR: He doesn't write badly at all!

MICHAEL: And his spelling—

SELICOUR: Yes! That is the essence!

MICHAEL: One thing, Mister Selicour! Concerning my letter, please do not let my gracious master find out. He told us quite strictly, as he left for the city, that we were not to make any solicitations. He is rather peculiar about some things, my Master!

SELICOUR: Is he? So! So!—You know him rather well, the Lord Minister?

MICHAEL: Since he stands on intimate relations with his servants, I know him inside and out—and can, if you wish, fully inform you about him.

SELICOUR: I believe you! I believe you! But I am not curious, not in the least! You see, Monsieur, my fundamental principle is this: Do right and fear no man.

MICHAEL: Well said!

SELICOUR: But go on! Continue, Monsieur Michael!—You say your good master is a bit peculiar?

MICHAEL: He is a bit strange, but good. His heart is pure, as gold!

SELICOUR: He is wealthy, he is a widower, a pleasant man, still in his best years.—Only confess—he doesn't hate women, this dear, worthy man.

MICHAEL: He is capable of tender feelings.

SELICOUR (*smiling delicately*): Ha! Ha! So some little romantic affairs, perhaps?

MICHAEL: That may well be! But on such matters he is—

SELICOUR: I understand, I understand, Monsieur Michael! You are discreet and know when to be silent.—I ask with the best intentions in the world, for I am certain, that whatever I learn, will do him honor.

MICHAEL: Yes! Listen! He is seeking an apartment in one of the suburbs.

SELICOUR: An apartment, and for whom?

MICHAEL: I will soon discover the answer to that.—But you must not say anything about this, do you hear?

SELICOUR: God forbid!

MICHAEL: He was quite the gallant in his youth.

SELICOUR: And so you believe, that he now still has his little love—

MICHAEL: Not in the least! But—

SELICOUR: Let it be, whatever! As a loyal servant of a worthy master, you must cast a Christian cloak over his weakness. And why might it not be a secret act of benevolence? Why not, Mr. Michael?—I hate vicious interpretations— I have a deadly hatred of anything that even resembles gossip.—One must always think the best of one's benefactors. Well! Well! Well, we must see one another again, Monsieur Michael!—You have forgiven me the unfortunate reception I gave you? Have you? On my honor! I blush with shame over that. *(Offers his hand.)*

MICHAEL *(refuses the hand):* On no, no, Mister Selicour! I know my place and what is fitting for me.

SELICOUR: No formalities! Count me among your friends!— I ask that of you, Monsieur Michael.

MICHAEL: I should never presume to that—I am only a servant.

SELICOUR: My friend! my friend! No distinction between us. I insist on that, Monsieur Michael!—*(They exit, amid mutual compliments.)*

# ACT II

## SCENE 1

### NARBONNE *and* SELICOUR *sit.*

NARBONNE: Are we finally alone?

SELICOUR *(uncomfortable):*—Yes!

NARBONNE: This discussion concerns me very much. I already have an excellent opinion of you, Mister Selicour, and I am sure, it will be improved considerably, before we are done today. But to the matter at hand, and, please, all false modesty aside. It is said, that you are well-versed in diplomacy and statecraft?

SELICOUR: I have worked diligently in those areas, and perhaps not entirely without fruit. But I would hardly call myself an expert—

NARBONNE: Good! Good! And now, let's hear what you have to say.—What do you take to be the first requirement of a good ambassador?

SELICOUR (*hesitantly*): Above all, he must have great versatility in affairs of state.

NARBONNE: Great versatility, yes, but always combined with the greatest honesty.

SELICOUR: Exactly what I meant.

NARBONNE: Continue.

SELICOUR: In the foreign court, where he is stationed, he must seek to make himself popular.

NARBONNE: Yes! But without compromising his dignity in any way. He maintains the honor of the state, which he represents, and establishes the reputation of his nation through his behavior.

SELICOUR: That is exactly, what I intended to say. He is to be firm in all matters, and will know how to acquire a reputation.

NARBONNE: A reputation, yes, but one quite without arrogance.

SELICOUR: That is what I meant.

NARBONNE: He is to have a watchful eye on all, that—

SELICOUR (*interrupts him*): He is to be watchful in general, and will know how to ferret out the most hidden things—

NARBONNE: Without becoming a spy.

SELICOUR: Just what I meant.—Without betraying an anxious curiosity.

NARBONNE: Without *having* it.—He will know when to remain silent, and will possess a certain modest reserve—

SELICOUR (*quickly*): His face will be a closed book.

NARBONNE: But he will not be a mystery monger.

SELICOUR: That's what I meant.

NARBONNE: He will possess a spirit of peace, and will seek, each dangerous dissension—

SELICOUR: To preempt as quickly as possible.

NARBONNE: Quite right. He is to have an exact knowledge of the peoples of different lands—

SELICOUR: Of their condition—their products, their exports and imports, their balance of trade—

NARBONNE: Quite right.

SELICOUR *(carried away):* Of their constitution—their treaties—their allies—their military strength—

NARBONNE *(interrupts):* For example: Let's assume you were sent to Sweden or Russia—would you possess the necessary knowledge of these states?

SELICOUR *(embarrassed):* I—I must confess, that—I have concerned myself more with Italy. Of the North, I know very little.

NARBONNE: So! Hm!

SELICOUR: But I have just now begun, to study it.

NARBONNE: So your specialty is Italy!

SELICOUR: Understandably, the Land of the Caesars was the first to attract my attention. Here was the cradle of the arts, the fatherland of heroes, the seat of loftiest virtue! What moving memories to a heart, that feels!

NARBONNE: Indeed! Indeed! But to return to our theme—

SELICOUR: As you order! Ah, the beautiful arts are so attractive! They are so stimulating to the imagination!

NARBONNE: It is Venice, which first occurs to me.

SELICOUR: Venice!—Excellent! I have recently done an essay on Venice, in which I treat many relevant topics in great detail.—I will go and get it—*(stands up)*

NARBONNE: Not at all! not at all! A little patience!


## SCENE 2

*The same.* MICHAEL.

MICHAEL: There is someone outside, who has requested a confidential conference on a matter of some urgency.

SELICOUR *(very quickly):* I will not disturb you.

NARBONNE: No! Stay, Selicour! This someone can certainly be patient a few moments.

SELICOUR: But—if it is an urgent matter—

NARBONNE: The most urgent matter to me now is our discussion.

SELICOUR: Permit me, but—

MICHAEL: The gentleman says, it will only take a few minutes, and he is in a great hurry. (*Selicour hurries away.*)

NARBONNE: Please return here, when the visitor has left.

SELICOUR: I will be entirely at your command.

NARBONNE (*to Michael*): Let him enter.


## SCENE 3

### NARBONNE. LAROCHE.

LAROCHE (*with much bowing*): I *am* happy—I assume—it is his Excellency the Minister, before whom I—

NARBONNE: I am the Minister. Please come closer!

LAROCHE: Please forgive me—I—I come—It is—I wanted—I am in truly great confusion—the great respect—

NARBONNE: Oh, then please dispense with the respect and come to the point. What brings you here?

LAROCHE: My duty, my conscience, my love of my country!—I have come, to bring you some important confidential information.

NARBONNE: Then speak at once!

LAROCHE: You have placed your trust in a man, who lacks both conscience and ability.

NARBONNE: And who is this man?

LAROCHE: His name is Selicour.

NARBONNE: What! Sel—

LAROCHE: To put it bluntly, this Selicour is as incompetent as he is contemptible. Allow me to sketch a little portrait of him for you.

NARBONNE: A little patience! (*Rings a bell.—Michael enters.*) Call Mister Selicour!

LaRoche: Your Excellency, please!—He is in no way needed for this conversation.

Narbonne: Not by you, I can well imagine, but it is my practice, never to accept a complaint against people, who cannot defend themselves.—When you are face to face with him, then you can begin your portrait.

LaRoche: But it is difficult, face to face—

Narbonne: Most certainly, if you have no proof.—Is that the case with *you*—

LaRoche: I simply had not counted on saying this to him face to face. He is such a cunning devil, a cool and collected scoundrel.—Oh well! Face to face is fine with me.—Hang it, I have nothing to fear from him. Let him come! You will see, that I have absolutely nothing to fear from him.

Narbonne: Indeed! Indeed! We shall soon see. Here he comes!


# SCENE 4

*The same.* SELICOUR.


Narbonne: Do you know this individual?

Selicour *(very embarrassed):* He is Mister LaRoche.

Narbonne: I have had you summoned here, to defend yourself against him. He has come, to make a complaint against you. All right, you may speak!

LaRoche *(after clearing his throat):* I should tell you first, that we were in school together, that he perhaps owes me a debt of gratitude. We began our careers together—it is now fifteen years ago—and we entered the same office as clerks. Mister Selicour has made a brilliant success, I—still sit, where I began. That he has forgotten the poor devil who was his school friend after all these years, that may be! I have nothing against that. But after so long a period of forgetfulness, to think again of his old childhood friend only to unjustly deprive him of his livelihood, as he has done, that is cruel, that can only outrage me! He cannot say the least evil against me; but I can against him and I assert boldly, that this Mister Selicour, who is now playing the honest man with your Excellency, has been quite a rogue, when the times allowed it. Now he helps you accomplish your good works; but your predecessor, I know for certain, he helped just as much with his dirty business. Like any unscrupulous lackey, this hypocrite knows how to change with the times and assume the manner of his new master. He is a flatterer, a liar, a swaggering braggart, a supercilious bully! Insidious, when he is out to get something, haughty and insolent against all those, who are so unfortunate as to need his help. As a child, there was actually something decent about him, but he has now overcome that single human weakness.—And now he has wormed himself into a really important position, and I am convinced, that he is simply not competent for it. He has always called attention of his superior only to himself, and he has kept people of real ability, of genius and style, such as Mister Firmin, from receiving the credit they deserve.

NARBONNE: Firmin! What's this?—Is Firmin in our Department?

LAROCHE: He is an excellent man, I can assure you.

NARBONNE: I know of him.—A truly distinguished statesman!

LAROCHE: And the father of a family! His son made the acquaintance of your daughter in Kolmar.

NARBONNE: Karl Firmin! Yes! Yes, that's right!

LAROCHE: An extremely talented young man!

NARBONNE:—Please continue!

LAROCHE: Well, that would be it! I have said enough, I should think!

NARBONNE (*to Selicour*): You may answer the charges!

SELICOUR: I am accused of ingratitude.—Me of ingratitude! I would think, that my friend LaRoche would know me better!—It is my lack of influence and not my lack of good intentions, that has kept him in obscurity so long.—What harsh accusations against a man, who has remained loyal to him for twenty years! To be carried away with his suspicion, to interpret my actions in the worst light, and to attack me with such intensity, such bitterness!—To show how much I am his friend—

LaRoche: My friend! Does he take me for utterly stupid!—What a demonstration of friendship he has given me!

Narbonne: He allowed you to speak!

LaRoche: So I will be proven wrong!

Selicour: His position was given to another, that is true, and no one deserves this setback less than he. But I would have hoped, that my friend LaRoche, rather than attacking me as an enemy, would have come to my office as a friend and demanded an explanation from me. I will confess I expected him to do that, and was looking forward to the pleasant surprise I had prepared for him. What a sweet pleasure for me, to make him happy beyond all his expectations! It was for that executive position, of which I spoke to Your Excellency this morning, that I had selected my old friend LaRoche!

LaRoche: Me, a supervisor! Many thanks, Mister Selicour!—But I am a clerk and not a statesman! My clerical skills and not my intelligence recommend me, and I am not one of those, who takes on a burden beyond his capacity, in order to then secretly load someone else with the work and take the credit for himself.

Selicour: The position is made for you, comrade, believe *me*, I know you better than you know yourself. *(to Narbonne)* He is an excellent worker, precise, untiring, full of good sense; he has earned the respect of all his fellow workers. He accuses me of holding down individuals of talent and gives Mister Firmin as an example.—That is not a good choice, as excellent as the individual in question actually is.—First of all, his present position is not bad—but, certainly he deserves a better one, and it has already been found—for Mister Firmin is just the individual I intended to recommend to Your Excellency as my replacement, if I were to be transferred to that post which you, as my sponsor, are considering me.—It is further claimed that I am not capable enough for my present position.—I know very well, I possess only moderate talents.—But one should remember, this charge concerns my sponsor as much as myself.—If I am not able enough for my responsibilities, then my supervisor is to blame for entrusting the position to me and for being satisfied so often with my weak abilities.—Finally, I am said to have been the accomplice of the former Minister! To the voice of truth I have made him listen; the language of the honest man I have spoken at a time, when my accusers perhaps grovelled before him in the dust.— Twenty times I wanted to renounce my service to this incompetent Minister; nothing but the hope of being of some service to my country prevented me. What a gratifying reward for my heart if *here* I could prevent some evil, *there* effect some good! I defied his power; fought against him for decency, while he was still in power! He fell, and I paid my heartfelt pity to his misfortune. If all that is a crime, then I am proud of it and I glory in it! It is hard, very hard for me, dear LaRoche, to see you as one of my enemies—that I should find it necessary, to defend myself against a man, whom I value and love! But come! Let us make peace, give me again your friendship, and let all be forgotten!

LAROCHE: What a rogue!—He's almost convinced me!

NARBONNE: Well, what do you have to say to all that?

LAROCHE: I?—Nothing!—That cursed rascal has me completely rattled.

NARBONNE: Mister LaRoche! It is courageous and praiseworthy to fearlessly attack an evildoer, no matter what his position, and to pitilessly pursue him—but to stubbornly persist in unjust hatred suggests a depraved heart.

SELICOUR: He doesn't hate me! Certainly not! My friend LaRoche has the best heart in the world! I know him— he is enraged—he lives for his work—that fully excuses him! He believed he had lost his livelihood! I was at

fault—I confess it—Come! come, let us embrace, let all
be forgotten!

LaRoche: I embrace him! Never in all eternity.—Of
course, the way he puts it all, I don't know, in order to
deceive even me—to deceive your Excellency—but No!
I stand by my complaint.—No peace between us until
I unmask him, until I've exposed him in his complete
nakedness!

Narbonne: I am convinced of his innocence.—It will take
facts and strong evidence to convince me otherwise.

LaRoche: Facts! Evidence! I have a multitude!

Narbonne: Then out with them!

LaRoche: Proof enough that—the mass of—But that is it—
I can prove nothing with it! Such cunning rascals allow
nothing to be proved.—Earlier he was as poor as I; now
he sits in the lap of luxury! I told you, that he has turned
his former influence into money, that his whole fortune
stems from that—so I cannot bring you proof that is as
they say, signed, sealed, and delivered—but God knows,
it is the truth, and I will stake my life on it.

Selicour: This charge is too contemptible to be dignified
by an answer.—I will submit to the strictest investigation!—What I possess, is the fruit of fifteen years of labor;
I have earned it with bitter sweat and long hours, and I
do not think I spent it ignobly. It supports my poor
relatives, it lengthened the life of my poor mother!

LaRoche: Lies! Lies! Of course, I cannot prove it! But lies,
insidious lies!

Narbonne: Temper yourself!

Selicour: My God! What I have to go through! It is my
friend LaRoche, who persecutes me in this way.—What
sort of madness has gripped you? I don't know, whether
I should laugh or become angry over this mad rage.—
But to laugh at the expense of a friend, who deems himself
offended—No, I cannot do it! that is too serious!—To so
drastically mistake your old friend!—Come to yourself,
dear LaRoche, and at least do not, out of this ill-timed

defiance, deny yourself the excellent position I intended for you!

NARBONNE: To tell the truth, Mister LaRoche, this stubbornness does not help my opinion of you.—Must I too ask, that you show justice to your friend? Upon my honor! my heart goes out to the poor Mister Selicour.

LAROCHE: I can well believe that, Gracious Sir! He had almost taken me in for a moment, despite my perfectly justified outrage.—But no, no! I know him *too* well—I am *too* certain of what I have charged.—War, war between us and no reconciliation! For now, I see, that all further discussion would be in vain! But however far this trickster pushes me, I would rather die of a thousand hungers, than depend on him for my livelihood. With your approval, Your Excellency, I will leave. (*Exits.*)

## SCENE 5

### NARBONNE. SELICOUR.

NARBONNE: Can you comprehend such dogged obstinacy—

SELICOUR: There's nothing to it! He is a good fool! I will soon pacify him again.

NARBONNE: He is rash and unreflective, but it may be that basically he is a good man.

SELICOUR: A good-hearted man, I vouch for it—however, at present his thoughts are a bit rattled.—It may be, that someone has provoked him against me.

NARBONNE: What do you mean?

SELICOUR: There may be something hidden going on.— Who knows? Perhaps a secret enemy, someone envious of me—for this poor devil is only an instrument.

NARBONNE: But who—

SELICOUR: There are many, who wish my downfall!

NARBONNE: You have, perhaps, a suspicion?

SELICOUR: I suppress it! for that I should think such a thing of Mister Firmin.—Nonsense! utter nonsense! that would be shameful! that is not possible!

NARBONNE: I quite agree! That man seems to me to be far too honest and too modest for such a thing.

SELICOUR: Modest, ah yes, that he is.

NARBONNE: Then you know him.

SELICOUR: We are friends.

NARBONNE: Well, what is your opinion of the man.

SELICOUR: Mister Firmin, I must say, is the sort of man, that one wishes to have in this Department—though of no great intelligence, he is a skilled worker—I don't mean to imply that he lacks judgment and knowledge.—Not at all! He may know much, but he hardly displays it at all.

NARBONNE: You make me quite curious, to get to know him.

SELICOUR: I have suggested to him for quite some time, that he introduce himself to you—but perhaps he feels he should keep to a mere subordinate role and that he was born for obscurity. However, I will—

NARBONNE: Don't trouble yourself.—Toward a man of service, without regard to his rank, it is appropriate for one in our position to make the first step.—I will seek Mister Firmin out.—But now to return to our prior subject, that this LaRoche interrupted—

SELICOUR (*embarrassed*): It is already somewhat late—

NARBONNE: That's not important.

SELICOUR: It is almost time for your audience to begin.

NARBONNE (*looks at the clock*): Yes, that's true.

SELICOUR: We can certainly continue in the morning—

NARBONNE: All right! we'll do just that!

SELICOUR: And now I will—

NARBONNE: One further word—

SELICOUR: At your service.

NARBONNE: I can at least assign you one project that requires both industry and courage.

SELICOUR: I am at your disposal!

NARBONNE: Through his misadministration my predecessor permitted a large number of abuses to prevail, that are still not all rectified despite our best efforts. We need, therefore, a memorandum drafted, in which all his flaws are exposed and the truth about his administration is told without reservation.

SELICOUR: If you will permit me, Your Excellency—such a document could have dangerous consequences for its author, as well as for yourself.

NARBONNE: That does not concern us.—Neither danger nor personal considerations are of significance, when it is a matter of duty.

SELICOUR: A noble thought!

NARBONNE: You are the man for this job.—I need say nothing further on the matter to you.—You know the problems better still than even I.

SELICOUR: And I am, I hope, of one mind with you on this subject.

NARBONNE: No doubt of it. There is some urgency in this matter, so I suggest, that you lose no time, since now is precisely the right moment—I would send such a document to the authorities today if possible.—Keep it short and to the point—much can be said in a few words! I will see you later! Start to work immediately. *(He exits.)*


## SCENE 6

### SELICOUR. MADAME BELMONT.


MADAME BELMONT: Are you alone, Selicour? I wanted to wait, until he had left—he is to know nothing of this.

SELICOUR: Of what are you speaking, Madame?

MADAME BELMONT: We want to have a small concert this evening, and my Charlotte is to sing.

SELICOUR: She sings so beautifully!

MADAME BELMONT: You have devoted yourself to poetry on occasion? Have you?

SELICOUR: Who has not written verse at some time or other in his life?

MADAME BELMONT: Well, then you are to make us a song or something of the sort for this evening!

SELICOUR: Perhaps you mean a romanza?

MADAME BELMONT: Excellent, we especially love romanzas!

SELICOUR: If enthusiasm can compensate for the lack of genius then—

MADAME BELMONT: Of course! of course! I understand.

SELICOUR: And I certainly need such a light task as my recreation!—I was up the entire night, going through documents and correcting calculations—

MADAME BELMONT: A loathsome job!

SELICOUR: That I really feel a bit exhausted.—Who knows! Perhaps the flower of poetic art with its lovely fragrance will revive me, and you, balm of all hearts, divine friendship.


## SCENE 7

*The same.* ROBINEAU.


ROBINEAU (*from off stage*): Well! Well now! If he is in there, then surely I will be permitted in—

MADAME BELMONT: What is that?

ROBINEAU (*enters*): This pack of servants is more conceited than their masters.—I want to speak to Lord Selicour.

SELICOUR: I am he.

ROBINEAU: That I will soon see for myself.—Yes, by my soul, that's he!—in the flesh—I can see him now, as he chased around our village with the other young fellows.— Now look at me.—Consider me well. I am indeed a little changed—Do you know me?

SELICOUR: No!

ROBINEAU: Oh, oh, I am Christoph Robineau, son of the grape grower, who married fat Madelon, your grandfather's aunt, Lord Selicour.

SELICOUR: Ah so!

ROBINEAU: Well—it is the custom of cousins to embrace, I think.

SELICOUR: With pleasure—I bid you welcome, cousin!

ROBINEAU: Gracious thanks, cousin!

SELICOUR: But let us go to my office—I am not at home here.

MADAME BELMONT: Please go ahead, Selicour! Continue just as though I were not here.

SELICOUR: With your permission, Madame, you are too gracious! One must forgive him his common manner; he is a good honest farmer and a cousin, whom I hold very dear.

MADAME BELMONT: That is just like you, Mister Selicour!

ROBINEAU: I have just arrived, Lord Cousin!

SELICOUR: So—where have you come from?

ROBINEAU: Oh, where else but from our village.—But this Paris is like twenty villages.—For over two hours, after getting off the stagecoach, I wandered about, looking for you and LaRoche. You know, your neighbor and school friend.—Well, now that I've found you at last, and all will be well.

SELICOUR: You come to Paris on business, Cousin?

ROBINEAU: On business! That I have! By all means on business—

SELICOUR: And what business is that?—

ROBINEAU: Why, to make my fortune here, cousin!

SELICOUR: Ha! Ha!

ROBINEAU: Well now, that business is important enough, I should think.

SELICOUR (*to Madame Belmont*): Please excuse him!

MADAME BELMONT: He amuses me.

SELICOUR: He is very entertaining.

ROBINEAU: Peter, the teamster, said, that my cousin had really done well by himself in Paris.—When he was small, my cousin, he was a rascal, so it was said: he will *not* spoil—he'll make his way!—We heard a lot about him, but the news was too good to be believed. But when we couldn't doubt it any longer, my father said to me, Christoph, go there, find your cousin Selicour in Paris, it's a trip you won't regret—and perhaps you'll make your fortune with a good marriage.—I, on my way at once, and here I am!—Don't take it badly of me, Madame! The Robineaus are straightforward; what the heart thinks, the tongue must say—and when I saw my dear Lord Cousin here before me, you see, my heart opened up.

MADAME BELMONT: Well, that is only natural.

ROBINEAU: Do you hear, cousin, I would really and truly like to make my fortune! You know the secret, how one gets started; share it with me!

SELICOUR: Be ever honest, true, and modest! That is my whole secret, Cousin—beyond that I have none.—Is all well at home?

ROBINEAU: God be praised, yes! The family prospers. Bertrand has married Susanna; and she will soon have a child and hopes, the Lord Cousin will be the godfather. It is going well, except with your poor mother. She says, it's hard that she has to be so poor and have such a fabulously wealthy son in the city.

SELICOUR (softly): Shut your trap, idiot!

MADAME BELMONT: What did he say about your mother?

SELICOUR (aloud): Is it possible? The thousand talers, which I sent her, have not yet arrived?—That concerns me deeply. What sort of wretched service is this from the postal service—My poor good mother! What must she have gone through!

MADAME BELMONT: Yes, indeed! One must help her.

SELICOUR: Very true! I will immediately ask the Minister for a leave—it is a legitimate request. I will insist on it.—The duty of Nature precedes all others.—I will hurry to my place—I can take care of it all in eight days!—She has refused to come to Paris, no matter how I insisted! The dear old mother clings too much to her place of birth.

ROBINEAU: You'd never know it to hear her tell it, for she says to us, she would gladly come to Paris, but the cousin will simply not have it!

SELICOUR: The good woman never knows, what she wants. But to think of her in real need—dear God! that troubles me and pains me deeply.

MADAME BELMONT: I can well believe you, Lord Selicour!—But you will soon find a way. I will go now and
leave you alone with your cousin. Happy is the wife, that
will possess you. Such a dutiful son will certainly become
a tender husband! (*Exits.*)


## SCENE 8

### SELICOUR *and* ROBINEAU.

ROBINEAU: In truth, Lord Cousin, I am very surprised by
you—such a heartfelt reception I had hardly expected
from you. They said, he is so hard and haughty, that he
will not even recognize you!
SELICOUR (*after he has made certain Madame Belmont has
gone*): Tell me, you jackass! What could you have been
thinking of, coming in on me like this at such a time!
ROBINEAU: Well, well! As I already told you, I come, to
make my fortune!
SELICOUR: To make your fortune! You dunce!
ROBINEAU: Well now, cousin! How you treat me.—I won't
be treated in this way.
SELICOUR: How sensitive you are. Too bad about your
anger.—To come all the way from your village to Paris!
You loafer!
ROBINEAU: But what kind of treatment is this all of a sudden,
Lord Cousin!—First a friendly reception and now this
nasty tone with me.—It is not an honest and straightfor-
ward way to act, you shouldn't take this badly of me, that
is false and if I told people, how you are treating me—it
would disgrace you! Yes it would!
SELICOUR (*shocked*): Told people! What?
ROBINEAU: Yes, yes, Cousin.
SELICOUR: Calm down, my boy!—I'll provide a place for
you.—I will take care of my mother. Be calm, I will find
a place for you, you can rely on it.
ROBINEAU: And now if you will—

SELICOUR: But we cannot discuss it here any further! Away!
   To my rooms!
ROBINEAU: Well, listen Cousin! Right now I would like a
   peaceful and comfortable job. If you can arrange a job in
   the customs department.
SELICOUR: Rely on it, I will find you an excellent position—
   Back to the village with this idiot as soon as possible.
   (*Exit.*)

# ACT III

## SCENE 1

LAROCHE *and* KARL FIRMIN *meet one another.*

LAROCHE: I have been looking for you everywhere.—Listen!—Well, I kept my word—I have exposed this Selicour to the Minister.
KARL: Really? And is he finished off? Quite finished off?
LAROCHE: Not just yet!—not entirely—for I must admit to
   you, that he lied his way out of it, that I just stood there,
   like an idiot.—The fraud pretended to be touched, he
   played the sensitive friend, the magnanimous one with
   me, he overloaded me with assurances of friendship and
   said he wants to appoint me as an executive in the office.
KARL: What! What! That is really marvelous! I wish you
   luck in it.
LAROCHE: I always took him to be an unscrupulous career-
   ist, I believed, that he was after only position and
   money—but to be this false, this traitorous I would never
   have thought possible, even for him. This fraud with his
   sweet talk! But I was not his fool and flatly refused his
   offer!
KARL: And so we are still, where we started from? And my
   father no better off than before?

LaRoche: Perhaps that is true—but leave it to me! Leave it to me!

Karl: I too have accomplished nothing. I slipped into the garden, in the hope that I might perhaps meet my beloved.—But in vain! A few stanzas of verse, which I thought up while alone, are all that I can show for my time.

LaRoche: Excellent! Just the thing! You make verses for your beloved! Meanwhile, I stalk my prey: the faker is seriously deceiving himself, if he believes, that I have abandoned my plans!

Karl: Dear LaRoche! This is beneath our dignity. Let the wretch do his dirty work, and let us accomplish through our merit, what he must do through his contemptible vileness.

LaRoche: None of this pride! It is mere weakness, it is prejudice!—What? Are we to wait until honesty rules the world—then we would have to wait a long time. Everyone plots and schemes! All right, then we return like for like. But that doesn't concern you.—Write your verses, develop your talent, I will bring it off, I—it is my affair!

Karl: All right, but remember, be clever.—You let yourself get badly caught today.

LaRoche: And it won't be the last time.—But that doesn't matter in the least! I march forward, I will not allow myself to be frightened off. I will so persistently and so frequently attack that I will finally land a decisive blow. I have been his fool for so long, but now I will turn the tables on him. If we allow him to continue, as he has begun, then I will be taken to be the villain, and your father the fool!

Karl: Someone is coming!

LaRoche: It's he himself!

Karl: I cannot tolerate the sight of him. I will go back into the garden and complete my poem. (*Exits.*)

LaRoche: I will leave as well! I will immediately get on with my business. But no—it is better, that I remain. Otherwise, this fop will think I am afraid of him!

## SCENE 2

SELICOUR *and* LAROCHE.

SELICOUR: Well, see here! Do I find Mister LaRoche here?

LAROCHE: Himself, Mister Selicour.

SELICOUR: Quite ashamed, I see.

LAROCHE: Not particularly.

SELICOUR: Your insane sortie against me has produced nothing—My friend has fired his salvo in vain!

LAROCHE: It is not important in the least.

SELICOUR: Honestly, old friend LaRoche! To be so hard on me—You have made me sad, with your foolish ideas.

LAROCHE: Lord Narbonne is not here. There is not need to force yourself!

SELICOUR: I beg your pardon.

LAROCHE: Be arrogant to your heart's content.

SELICOUR: Now see here!

LAROCHE: Celebrate your triumph! You have won out over me!

SELICOUR: Certainly, victory over such a terrifying opponent is enough to make one proud.

LAROCHE: If I did not do it right today, I shall soon learn better in your school.

SELICOUR: What, Mister LaRoche? You have not given up trying to harm me?

LAROCHE: One bad move does not end the game!

SELICOUR: A devoted sword bearer of the honorable Firmin!—Look, look!

LAROCHE: He has often had to help you in difficult situations, this honorable Firmin.

SELICOUR: What is he giving you for your devoted service?

LAROCHE: What do you pay him for all the problems, which he solves for you?

SELICOUR: Be careful, friend LaRoche!—I can make things extremely difficult for you.

LAROCHE: Don't become angry, friend Selicour!—Wrath betrays a bad conscience.

SELICOUR: Of course I should but laugh over your foolishness.

LaROCHE: You have contempt for an enemy, who appears
to be weak. But I shall soon have a way, to earn your
respect! (*Exits.*)


## SCENE 3

SELICOUR *alone*.

They want to make Firmin ambassador.—Gently, comrade!—We have not yet succeeded.—But Firmin always
behaves so properly with me.—Perhaps it is the son—
this young man, who devotes himself to verses, yes, of
course—and this LaRoche is the one, who incites them!—
This Firmin has merit, that I will acknowledge, and if
they ever rouse his ambition, I can think of no one, who
were more dangerous to me.—That must in all events be
prevented!—But what a spot I am in myself!—These two
Firmins were to have been most useful to me, the father
with his judgment, and the son with his poetry.—First
let's get some use out of them, and then contrive some
way of getting rid of them as the occasion arises.


## SCENE 4

FIRMIN *the father and* SELICOUR.

SELICOUR: Is that you, Mister Firmin? Just as I was about
to go see you.

FIRMIN: To see me?

SELICOUR: To offer you an explanation—

FIRMIN: Concerning what?

SELICOUR: Concerning something rather pitiable.—Dear
Firmin, it is a real consolation for me, to see you. Someone has attempted to set us at odds with one another.

FIRMIN: At odds with one another!

SELICOUR: Most certainly. But I hope, the attempt will not succeed. I am your true and honest friend, as I proved today, I should think, when that foolish LaRoche attempted to denounce me to the the Minister.

FIRMIN: What? Did LaRoche—

SELICOUR: He exposed me to the most hideous accusations.

FIRMIN: He has lost his position.—Put yourself in his place.

SELICOUR: He is an ingrate! After all that I have done for him—And it all happened, he said, to do you a service.— But he serves you badly, if he seeks to hurt me.—What do I want other than your success?—But I know what will serve your interest far better than that hothead. Therefore, I have an excellent little plan for you.—The strident activities at the Department are hateful to you, I know; and you are not fond of living in this noisy city.— Everything is to be provided for you, Mister Firmin!— You can find for yourself an isolated, quiet place, draw a good salary, I will send the work out to you, you may enjoy the work, and there shall be nothing lacking for you in that regard.

FIRMIN: But how—

SELICOUR: This is all still in the planning stage, it will take some time.—Happy he who lives his day in the peaceful countryside! Ah, Mister Firmin! It can never be so for *me*! I am caught in the city, a beast of burden of circumstances, exposed to the evil arrows of resentment.—Thus, I took it as a matter of duty to send a dear relation, who wanted to settle here, back to the country as quickly as possible.—My good cousin! Naturally I was happy to pay for his travel expenses—for, as you say yourself, is it not far, far better to live a private life freely in the country, than a public life here in the city, in drudgery and torment?

FIRMIN: My opinion exactly.—But what do you really want of me?

SELICOUR: Well, as I said, I want above all to prove my friendship to a dear fellow brother.—And then—You have helped me so many times out of embarrassment, I confess, I am very—I am very much obliged to you!— My position is destroying me—It piles so many burdens on my back.—Truly, it takes my entire intelligence, merely to survive here.—Are you satisfied with our Minister?

FIRMIN: I admire him.

SELICOUR: Indeed, he is what I call an able administrator! And truly, it was most necessary, that someone like that came into this position, if everything were not to be destroyed.—Everything is still not, as it should be here, as I was telling him today.—If you wish, to finally rectify the situation, then you must have a report prepared, in which all, that still needs improvement, would be analyzed in the most truthful detail.—He accepted my idea with great enthusiasm and wants such a report done immediately.—He assigned it to me.— But with the endless work I have—I tremble at the thought of any additional—

FIRMIN: And so you thought of me.—Isn't that so!

SELICOUR: Well yes! I confess that I did!

FIRMIN: Well, you couldn't have come to a better man this time!

SELICOUR: Oh, that I know! How well I know!

FIRMIN: I was a witness of the abuses of the former administration for a considerable time—not wishing to merely sigh over the wrongs as an idle observer, I wrote down all my complaints and my plans for improvement—and so, the work, which is required of *you*, has already been done by *me*!—I had not intended to make any particular use of the material.—I merely wrote it down, to relieve my own heart.

SELICOUR: Is it possible? You have—

FIRMIN: It is all prepared, if you wish to make use of it.

SELICOUR: I shall! With the greatest pleasure!—This is an entirely opportune coincidence!

FIRMIN: However, the papers are not in the best order!

SELICOUR: Oh, I will gladly take care of that. The Minister is to have the report this evening.—I will name you as the author, and you shall have all the credit.

FIRMIN: You know, that that is not important to me in the least! If I but bring about something good, no matter under which name.

SELICOUR: Worthy, charming man! No one does more justice to your unpretentious merit than I!—And now as to the report—

FIRMIN: I can get it immediately, if you wish to wait.

SELICOUR: Yes, go immediately! I will wait here.

FIRMIN: Here comes my son—He can keep you company while you wait.—But say nothing to him of this.—I insist!

SELICOUR: So! Why not then?

FIRMIN: I have my reasons.

SELICOUR: Well, if you wish it so!—But it is unpleasant to me, to remain silent about your kindness.—(*When Firmin is gone.*) The poor fool! he fears, quite rightly, his son will berate him for it.


## SCENE 5

### KARL. SELICOUR.


KARL (*enters, reading from a piece of paper, which he quickly hides when he sees Selicour*): Once again this Selicour—(*turns to leave*)

SELICOUR: But wait, my young friend!—Why do you always avoid company so?

KARL: Please pardon me, Mister Selicour!—(*to himself*) That I would run into this blabbermouth!

SELICOUR: I have wanted to see you for quite some time, my good man!—How are the Muses? How are the verses flowing? The good Mister Firmin is opposed to your work; but I know, he is wrong.—You have such a genuine talent!—If only the world knew about you—but that will come. Just this morning I spoke of you—

KARL: Of me?

SELICOUR: With the mother of our Lord Minister—and the
way I referred to you created an excellent impression for
you.

KARL: So! On what occasion was that?

SELICOUR: She fancies herself a connoisseur—I don't know
where she gets the idea.—People flatter her, because of
her son.—Well! If you can court her in a particularly
clever way—which is just what I wanted to talk to you
about.—She asked me for a few couplets for this evening.—Now, I have written poetry in my time, like anyone, but my wit is somewhat rusty from a life spent in
tiresome business! How would it be, if you, rather than
I, wrote the verses—You then turn them over to me—
I read them—everyone is charmed—they compliment
me—I—I *name* you! I will take the opportunity, to deliver a tribute to you.—Everyone will be full of your
praise, and before long, a new poet will be established,
as famous for his wit as for his sword!

KARL: You offer me a glorious prospect!

SELICOUR: It is within your power, to make it happen!

KARL (*to himself*): He is going to talk me into it! It is all
treachery, I know perfectly well, that he is a liar—but,
how vulnerable I am to praise! He can talk me into it
against my will.—(*to Selicour*) Then you need for this
evening—

SELICOUR: A mere trifle! A nothing! A mere song—in which
the Minister is paid tribute, in a natural way of course.

KARL: I do not write tributes! The dignity of poetry will not
be desecrated through me. Any such praise of those in
power, even if deserved, is mere flattery.

SELICOUR: The true pride of a genuine son of the Muses!
All right, forget the tribute—but something that treats of
love—something delicate—sensitive—

KARL (*looks at the piece of paper*): Could I have thought,
when I wrote this down, that I would have an opportunity
so soon?—

SELICOUR: What's this? That is not a poem—

KARL: Oh, pardon me! A very weak little work—

SELICOUR: Aha! My God! Here we have exactly, what we
need!—Quickly, give it to me—You will soon see how
effective it is.—It does not need to be a romance—these
small things—these pleasing trifles often accomplish far
more, than one imagines—through them one wins over
the ladies, and the ladies rule everything!—Give it to me!
Give it to me! What! You hesitate! Well, as you wish! I
only wanted to be useful to you.—To make you known—
You don't want to be known—Keep your verses! It is your
advantage I had in mind, not mine.

KARL: If only—

SELICOUR: If you don't like—

KARL: I don't know—

SELICOUR (*snatches the paper from Karl's hand*): Don't be
a child! Give it to me! I will serve your interests against
your will.—Then your father himself will soon recognize
your talents. Here he comes now! (*He sticks the paper
into his right pocket.*)

## SCENE 6

### Both FIRMIN. SELICOUR.

FIRMIN: Here, my friend!—but remember, say nothing of
this to anyone! (*Gives him the paper secretly.*)

SELICOUR: I know how to keep silent. (*Puts the paper into
his left pocket.*)

KARL (*to himself*): Was I wrong, to give it to him?—But
what can he do with my poetry?

SELICOUR: My worthy friends! You have given me a valuable quarter of an hour.—But one tends to forget oneself
in your company.—The Minister awaits me—I must tear
myself unwillingly away from you, for there is always so
much to be gained from such excellent company. (*Exits,
seizing his pockets with both hands.*)

## SCENE 7

*Both* FIRMIN.

FIRMIN: Now that is the man, whom you call a weaver of intrigues and cabals—and yet no one here takes more of an interest in me than he!

KARL: You can take me as a mere dreamer—But the more good he does to you, the less I trust him.—This sweet manner, which he adopts with you—Either he needs you, or else he will destroy you.

FIRMIN: Your mistrust is ridiculous!—No, my son! And even if I am to be the victim of malice—I will put off as long as possible believing something evil of anyone.

## SCENE 8

*The same.* LAROCHE.

LAROCHE: There you are, Mister Firmin!—I am glad to find you—The Minister wants to see you.

KARL: My father—

FIRMIN: Me?

LAROCHE: Yes, you!—I noticed, when I made a reference to you, that you had already roused his interest.—Selicour is hardly pleased by this.—So the step I took today has done some good.

KARL: And so you see that, against your own will, you are brought into prominence!—What a happy turn of events!

FIRMIN: Yes! yes! You imagine me already as ambassador and minister—Lord Narbonne will probably give me some small assignment, that is all there is to it!

LAROCHE: No, no, I assure you—he wants to get to know you better—And that is not all! No! No! His eyes have finally been opened! This Selicour's fall is near, I know it! Even today—It is shameful and horrible—but I can say no more.—The Minister sent for you at your home;

he was told, that you were at the office—Quite certainly
he will seek you here! Didn't I tell you?—See, here he
is now! *(He retires into the background.)*


## SCENE 9

NARBONNE *to the same.*

NARBONNE: I have seen some of your work, Mister Firmin,
which has given me a high idea of your abilities, and I
hear from all sides of your honesty and modesty.—I am
in the greatest need of men of your sort—I come to you,
to enlist your support, your advice, and your cooperation
in the difficult task, that has been entrusted to me.—Will
you give me your friendship, Mister Firmin?
FIRMIN: Such trust both puts me to shame and makes me
proud.—I accept your kind offer with joy and thankful-
ness—but I fear, that you may have been given a too high
opinion of me.
KARL: You have only been told what is true, Lord Narbonne!—I ask you, do not believe my father on this point.
FIRMIN: Do not glorify too much, my son, what is only a
quite ordinary merit.
NARBONNE: That is your son, Mister Firmin?
FIRMIN: Yes.
NARBONNE: The Karl Firmin, of whom my mother and
daughter only this morning spoke?
KARL: Your mother and the lovely Charlotte remembered
Karl Firmin!
NARBONNE: They have told me many flattering things about
you.
KARL: May I be worthy of so much kindness!
NARBONNE: It will please me to become more closely
acquainted with you, excellent young man, and with
your worthy father.—Mister Firmin! If it is my duty,
to seek you out, then surely it is no less yours, to let
yourself be found. Let those without ability surrender

to contemptible leisure!—The man of talent, who loves his fatherland, will himself seek the attention of his superiors and seek to attain the position, for which he knows he is capable.—Simpletons and incompetents are always at hand, priding themselves on their presumed abilities—but how is one to distinguish true merit, if it is not even placed in competition with its contemptible rivals? Consider, Mister Firmin, that one is as responsible for the good one does *not* do as for the evil one *tolerates*!

KARL: Listen to this, my father!

FIRMIN: If you give me the opportunity, to serve my fatherland, I will accept it gladly!

NARBONNE: And I ask no more—So that we can become better acquainted with one another, please dine with me this evening. You will find congenial company—a few good friends, some relatives—It won't be formal, and my mother, who couldn't be more proud of my new position, will receive you both in the most friendly fashion, I can promise you.

FIRMIN: We gladly accept your kind invitation.

KARL (*to himself*): I will see Charlotte!

LaROCHE (*aside*): Matters are on a good course—the moment is propitious—Quickly now, another attack on this Selicour! (*Comes forward.*) So, finally, merit receives its just reward! Excellent! And now it remains, to unmask depravity!—It is fortunate that I find you here and can continue, where I left off this morning.—This Selicour silenced me today—I behaved stupidly, I confess, since I blundered in without thinking, but the truth *remains* the truth! And I am right *nonetheless*! You demanded facts—I am ready to produce them!

NARBONNE: What? How?

LaROCHE: This man, who would give the impression, that he supports his mother and his entire family, gave a fine welcome to his poor devil of a cousin, who just today in his simplicity, in confidence came to him in the city, to obtain assistance from him. The hypocrite drove him away as though he were a tramp! That is how he treats his relatives—and how cruel his heart is, thereof can his poverty stricken mother—

FIRMIN: You do him an injustice, dear LaRoche! This cousin, whom he sent away, goes back to his village, overloaded with his favors and relieved of false hopes!

NARBONNE: He behaved quite properly with this cousin.

LaRoche: How? What?

NARBONNE: My mother was present at their conversation.

FIRMIN: Dear LaRoche! Do not follow the dictates of blind revenge.

LaRoche: Beautiful, Mister Firmin! Now *you* speak up for him!

FIRMIN: He is not present, it is my duty, to defend him.

NARBONNE: This conviction does you honor, Mister Firmin; also Mister Selicour behaved in exactly the same way with regard to you earlier today.—How it pleases me, to be surrounded by such worthy individuals.—*(to La-Roche)* But you, who so ruthlessly persecute poor Selicour, you hardly seem to me to be the decent man, that people take you for!—What I have seen from you so far hardly does honor to your reputation!

LaRoche *(to himself):* I feel like exploding—But patience!

NARBONNE: I am inclined, to think always better of good Selicour, the more bad things are said of him, and I intend to bind myself ever closer to him.

KARL *(shocked):* How so?

NARBONNE: My mother has certain plans, with which I am in full sympathy.—And I have plans for you, Mister Firmin!—but more on those this evening.—Do not fail to appear. *(to Karl)* You, my young friend, devote yourself to poetry, I hear; my mother was praising your talents just today.—Let us soon hear something of your work.— I too love the Muses, even though I am not able to devote my life to their service—Your servant, my gentlemen. Please excuse me. *(He exits.)*

## SCENE 10

### *The same without* NARBONNE.

KARL: I shall see her! I shall speak to her!—But these certain
plans of her grandmother—God! I shudder—There can
be no doubt, it has to do with Selicour.

FIRMIN: Well, my son! Isn't it a happy day today!

LAROCHE: For you, perhaps, Mister Firmin—but, for me?

FIRMIN: Don't be concerned. I hope to smooth everything
out once again.—*(to Karl)* Don't do anything foolish, my
son! at the very least, do not forget yourself in front of
the minister.

KARL: Don't worry! But you too, my father, for once you
will have to take action!

FIRMIN: Fine! I receive my lecture too.

KARL: And am I not right, Mister LaRoche?

FIRMIN: You should let *his* example at least serve as a
warning to you!—Take courage, LaRoche! If my support
means anything, your case is not yet lost. *(He exits.)*

## SCENE 11

### KARL FIRMIN *and* LAROCHE.

LAROCHE: Well, what do you have to say? Is it tolerable,
that your father himself discredits me as a liar and protects
that rogue?

KARL: Dear friend, earlier today I scorned your assistance,
now I implore your help. There is no longer any doubt,
that Selicour is intended as her husband. I may not be
worthy, to possess her, but how much less is that contemptible villain!

LAROCHE: Does it take a spur, to bring me into action? You
are a witness of how I have been mistreated because of
him! Listen to me! I have learned, that the Minister has
just today given him some very important and delicate
work, that must be finished this evening. Either he will

not be able to do it at all, or will produce something quite mediocre. And thus his incompetence will come to light! In spite of his sweet manners everyone detests him and wants to see him fall. No one will help him, I can assure you, he is that hated!

KARL: I will make sure my father doesn't help.—I can see now, why he talked me out of my poem. Will he have the gall, in my presence, to pretend to be the author?

LaRoche: Come with me into the garden, he must not see us together. You take yourself to be my master, friend Selicour! Beware—Your student is marshalling his forces, and this evening, perhaps he will teach you a lesson! (*Exit.*)

# ACT IV

## SCENE 1

### MADAME BELMONT. CHARLOTTE.

MADAME BELMONT: Stay here, Charlotte! We need to have a little word with one another, before the company arrives.—Tell me, my child! What do you think of Mister Selicour?

CHARLOTTE: I, Mama?

MADAME BELMONT: Yes, you!

CHARLOTTE: Well, he seems to me to be a pleasant, deserving, dignified man.

MADAME BELMONT: I am glad to hear that! I am happy, dear child, that you have such a good opinion of him— for, if your father and I have any influence over you, then Mister Selicour will soon be your husband.

CHARLOTTE (*shocked*): My husband!—

MADAME BELMONT: Does that shock you?

CHARLOTTE: Mister Selicour?

MADAME BELMONT: We believe there is no better way to provide for your happiness—

CHARLOTTE: I will gladly accept a husband under your and my father's guidance—But, you are going to think of me as capricious, dear Grandmama!—I don't know—this Mister Selicour, whom I otherwise respect so highly,— against whom I have nothing to say—I don't know, how is it that—if I think of him as my husband, that—that I feel in the depth of my heart a sort of—

MADAME BELMONT: Surely not a dislike?

CHARLOTTE: *Horror*, I would say rather! I am sure that I am doing him an injustice, but I can't overcome it.—I feel far more fear of him than love.

MADAME BELMONT: That is fine! This fear is well known, my daughter.

CHARLOTTE: No! Please listen!

MADAME BELMONT: A pleasant, maidenly shyness! I know all about that, believe me.—Wasn't I young once?—After all, this individual suits the family well.—A man, who knows everything—a man of taste—a sensitive connoisseur—and such a pleasing, trusted friend.—He is also in much demand everywhere.—Were he not too troubled now because of his mother, he has promised me to compose a love song for you this evening—for he can do anything, and would be attentive to you down to the smallest detail.—But I hear him coming now! He is always so prompt! Truly, there is no one who is his equal!

## SCENE 2

### SELICOUR *to the same.*

SELICOUR: You demanded from me today a delicate song, full of feeling! I have done my very best, Madame!—and lay it now at your feet.

MADAME BELMONT: What, Mister Selicour! You have really done it?—I had feared, as a matter of fact, that because of the terrible news—

SELICOUR: What news is that?

MADAME BELMONT: About your mother—

SELICOUR: About my mother!—Yes—I—I have just received a letter from her—a letter, in which she reports to me, that she finally—

MADAME BELMONT: That she finally received the thousand talers.—Ah, that makes me happy—

SELICOUR: Otherwise, would I have had the presence of mind for composition?—But, thank Heavens!—Now that stone is removed from my heart, and in my first joy of relief, I wrote these little verses, that I now have the honor, of presenting to you.

MADAME BELMONT (to Charlotte): It would have pained you, had you seen him!—It was then, that I became acquainted with his truly excellent heart. Mister Selicour, I love your little song, even before reading it.

## SCENE 3

### The same. NARBONNE.

NARBONNE: Selicour here with you! Oh, oh, dear Mother, you draw him away from matters of importance.—He has such pressing duties, and you load him down with these useless tasks.

MADAME BELMONT: Look, look, my son!—There is no need to be so ill-natured about it.

NARBONNE: But what will become of that report, which really is quite urgent and important?

SELICOUR: The report is done. Here it is!

NARBONNE: What, finished already?

SELICOUR: And I assure you, that I have spared neither time nor effort on it.

NARBONNE: But how is it possible?

SELICOUR: The abuses of the former administration often weighed heavily on my heart—I could not rest satisfied, to merely idly complain—I entrusted my disapproval, my criticism, and my plans for improvements to paper, and

so it was, that the assignment, which you gave me had
already been done some time ago by me privately.—I
would not have lacked the courage, to make it public
myself, if the government had not finally come on its own
to recognize the situation and to appoint, in your person,
a man, who will put everything back into order.—Now
is the time, to make public use of these papers—It took
only a bit of straightening out, and that could be done in
a moment!

MADAME BELMONT: Now, my son! You can be satisfied, I
should think—Mister Selicour has fulfilled your wish,
before he ever knew of it, has worked for you in advance,
and now you come together through the happiest of circumstances—

NARBONNE: With great pleasure, I see, that we are in agreement.—Give it to me, Mister Selicour, I will send it to
the authorities this very evening.

SELICOUR (*to himself*): Everything goes well—Now to get
rid of this Firmin, who is in my way. (*aloud*) Will you
pardon me, Lord Narbonne?—I am sorry, to say this—
but I must fear, that the charges of Mister LaRoche this
morning may have made some impression after all.

NARBONNE: Not in the least.

SELICOUR: I was apprehensive.—After all, according to
everything I see, LaRoche has already picked a successor
for me.

NARBONNE: How?

SELICOUR: I have always thought very well of Mister Firmin, but, I confess—I finally begin, to become confused
about him.

NARBONNE: How? You were just this morning praising him
for his good disposition.

SELICOUR: Is even the best disposed of men to be trusted
only up to a certain point?—I see myself surrounded by
enemies. Traps are set for me everywhere.

NARBONNE: You are doing Mister Firmin an injustice, I
know him better, and will vouch for him.

SELICOUR: I only wish, that I could think that way about him.

NARBONNE: The shameful ingratitude of this LaRoche has naturally made you distrustful. But if you have the shadow of a doubt about Mister Firmin, you will have the opportunity immediately, to reverse your error.

SELICOUR: How is that?

NARBONNE: He will be here in a moment himself.

SELICOUR: Mister Firmin—here?

NARBONNE: Here—I could not resist. I have seen him!

SELICOUR: Seen! Excellent!

NARBONNE: He and his son will dine with us this evening.

SELICOUR: Dine—His son! Excellent!

MADAME BELMONT AND CHARLOTTE: Karl Firmin?

NARBONNE: The young officer, whose merits you have extolled so often to me.—I invited the father and son to dine here this evening.

MADAME BELMONT: I will welcome them with greatest pleasure.

NARBONNE (to Selicour): You have nothing against that, I trust?

SELICOUR: Why no—Quite the contrary!

MADAME BELMONT: I am pleasantly disposed toward the father in advance because of the son. And what does Charlotte have to say on the matter?

CHARLOTTE: I, Mama—I am entirely of your opinion!

NARBONNE: You will be able to frankly discuss these matters, face to face.

SELICOUR: Oh, that isn't necessary—not in the least. To tell the truth, I have always considered Mister Firmin to be the most honest of men—and if for a moment I did him an injustice, then I will gladly acknowledge my error.—For my part I am convinced, that he is my friend!

NARBONNE: He has proved it! He speaks with the greatest respect of you—Indeed I only just this morning met him, but he certainly deserves—

SELICOUR *(interrupting)*: All the praise, which, as you
know, I paid to him a short while ago.—That is how I am!
My heart knows nothing of envy!

NARBONNE: He combines a sound mind with an excellent heart, and no man is more free of ambition
than he. He is the sort of man that would let someone
else take the entire credit, for what he himself has
done!

SELICOUR: Do you think so?

NARBONNE: He would be the man to do it!

MADAME BELMONT: In such a case, his son might think
differently.

CHARLOTTE: Yes indeed, he is a young, fiery artistic spirit,
who will stand for no nonsense.

SELICOUR: Would he perhaps give the glory of his work to
another?

CHARLOTTE: Oh, I doubt that very much!

NARBONNE: I admire such fire in a young soldier.

SELICOUR: Oh, above all, that is most appropriate.

NARBONNE: If each of them occupies the proper position,
both will be of excellent service.

SELICOUR: It is so wonderful, how you seek out able
people!

NARBONNE: That is my duty! *(He speaks to his daughter.)*

SELICOUR: Indeed! *(to Madame Belmont, taking her aside)*
A word, Madame!—It might still be thought, that you
have been distracting me from my real work—Therefore,
if my poem is sung this evening, then—do not ascribe it
to me!

MADAME BELMONT: If you do not wish it, then I won't.

SELICOUR: Yes—that will please me.—What? If I should,
out of a desire for greater safety, acknowledge someone
in the company as the author—

MADAME BELMONT: What? You could give the glory to
someone else?

SELICOUR: It is a small thing! *(Both Firmins enter.)*

CHARLOTTE *(sees them, excitedly)*: Here they are!

## SCENE 4

*The same. Both* FIRMIN.

NARBONNE *(going to meet them):* I have been expecting you, my gentlemen!—Come in! Come closer! You are truly welcome!—Here, Mister Firmin, my mother and here my daughter—You are no stranger to my family.

MADAME BELMONT *(to Karl Firmin):* I had not expected, to see you here in Paris; it is extremely pleasant, to meet dear friends unexpectedly.

KARL: This name has a high value for me. *(to Charlotte)* I trust you left your aunt well.

CHARLOTTE: Yes, Mister Firmin!

KARL: Those were unforgettable days, which I spent in your house. There it was, my young Lady—

NARBONNE *(to Firmin the father):* Let's allow the young people to renew their acquaintance.—Well, Mister Firmin! Here is Selicour!

SELICOUR *(to Firmin):* Indeed—I am—I cannot say enough, how glad I am—To see you introduced to Lord Narbonne.

NARBONNE: The two of you are men enough, to do justice to one another. *(to Firmin)* He has something on his mind, I wish, you could clarify among yourselves, my gentlemen.

SELICOUR: Oh, not at all! not at all! Mister Firmin knows me as his friend.

NARBONNE: And be assured, he is the same to you. I wish, you could have heard, with what warmth he took your side today. Quite certainly this LaRoche has again—

SELICOUR: But what in the world might it be that has so incensed LaRoche against me?

NARBONNE: This LaRoche is not the man for me at all—at least, I now have a poor opinion of his character.

FIRMIN: You are doing him an injustice. Today I spoke *against* him, but now I must defend him.

SELICOUR: It is completely unnecessary. I value him, I think highly of his good heart and also know all his little quirks—And he can slander me ultimately to the whole world, just as long as you do not believe him!—You see, we are done—Our strife is gone, there is no need for further discussion.

MADAME BELMONT: Well, won't you take your places, my Lords?

SELICOUR (*to Karl Firmin*): Your poem has been delivered.

KARL: Really?

SELICOUR: The grandmother has it, and I have not kept the author's name from her. (*Taking Madame Belmont to one side.*) Do you know, what I have done?

MADAME BELMONT: Well?

SELICOUR: The young Firmin—You know, he devotes himself to writing verse.

MADAME BELMONT: Yes!—Well!

SELICOUR: I have urged him, to take credit as the author of the song—He has consented.

MADAME BELMONT: Consented? I can believe that!

SELICOUR: You mustn't reveal my deception!

NARBONNE: Until our other guests arrive, dear Mother, perhaps you can think of a little entertainment for us.— But not some game—Certainly we can better occupy ourselves.

FIRMIN: We are at your service.

KARL: It is up to you, Madame.

CHARLOTTE: Are you fond of music, Mister Firmin?

NARBONNE: It is indeed true, that you sing rather well— Let's hear.—Don't you have something new to perform for us?

KARL: If it is not too much trouble for Charlotte—

CHARLOTTE: Some verses have just been given me.

NARBONNE: Good!—I will, with your permission, meanwhile look through this report done by our friend.

SELICOUR: But we will disturb you, Lord Narbonne!

NARBONNE: Not at all! I am used to working in extremely distracting situations—and here it is just a matter of reading! (*He goes to the far side of the stage, where he sits down.*)

SELICOUR: But if you had rather—

NARBONNE: Please excuse me! but the situation allows no delay. Duty before all!

MADAME BELMONT: We leave him then, if that is what he wants, and we shall have our song. (*All sit, Charlotte at the end of the table, Madame Belmont next to Charlotte, Selicour between Madame Belmont and Karl, who in turn is seated next to his father.*)

CHARLOTTE: I can see, that the melody is excellent.

MADAME BELMONT: The author is not far away—I can see him from here without my glasses.

SELICOUR (*to Madame Belmont, softly*): Do not betray me—(*to Karl Firmin*) That concerns you, my dear friend!

CHARLOTTE: Him? How?

FIRMIN: Is that true, Karl? Were you the one—

SELICOUR: He is the author.

CHARLOTTE (*to her grandmother*): What? Karl Firmin were the author!

MADAME BELMONT (*aloud*): Yes. (*privately*) Do not mention the real author.

CHARLOTTE: Why not?

MADAME BELMONT: There are reasons. (*to Selicour*) Won't you accompany Charlotte?

SELICOUR: With pleasure.

FIRMIN (*angrily to his son*): Certainly a hasty piece of work—but you must have just written—

KARL: But dear Father, please hear it first, before you judge it!

CHARLOTTE (*sings*):

By the fountain sat the stripling,
Flowers wove he in a wreath,
And he saw them ripped asunder,
Driven by the waves beneath:—
And my days are so escaping
As the fountain flows away!
And so pales my youth before me,
As the wreath doth fast decay.

MADAME BELMONT (*looking at Selicour*): The opening has
much promise!

SELICOUR (*pointing at Karl*): To this gentleman belong all
compliments.

MADAME BELMONT: Good! Good!—I understand!

FIRMIN: The thought is everyday, common.

KARL: Yes, but it is true.

NARBONNE (*occupied on the other side of the stage with the
report*): This introduction is quite good and immediately
awakens one's attention.

CHARLOTTE (*sings again*):

Question not, wherefore I sorrow
In the bloomtime of my life!
All is hopeful and rejoicing,
When the spring renews itself.
But these thousand sounds of nature,
Which awaken on the plain,
Rouse within my deepest bosom
Only heavy cries of pain.

MADAME BELMONT: Enchanting!

FIRMIN: Not bad.

SELICOUR (*To Karl Firmin*): You see, how they all admire
you.

NARBONNE (*reading*): Excellently developed and impres-
sive presentation.—Read this with me, Mister Firmin!
(*Firmin goes over to the Minister and reads over his left
shoulder.*)

MADAME BELMONT: Utterly divine!

SELICOUR (*walking over to Narbonne*): I naturally have
Mister Firmin to thank much, very, very much concerning this. (*Goes back to his place between Karl Firmin and
Madame Belmont without taking his eyes off the other
group.*)

CHARLOTTE (*sings again*):

What to me are all the pleasures,
Which the lovely spring awards?
One there is, for whom I'm searching,
She is near and ever far.

Stretch I wide my arms with longing
For the precious silhouette,
Ah, I cannot yet attain it
And my heart's unstill'd as yet!
Come below, thou beauteous darling,
And thy castle proud depart!
Flowers, born of springtime's bounty,
Will I on thy lap impart.
Hark, the woods resound with singing,
And the fountain ripples fair!
Room is in the smallest shelter
For a happy loving pair.

MADAME BELMONT: How touching the conclusion is!—The dear child has been quite moved by it.

CHARLOTTE: Yes—whoever may have written it, it flows from a heart, that knows love.

SELICOUR (*bends toward Charlotte*): That is praise that is too flattering.

KARL: What? He takes credit—

SELICOUR (*turns quickly to Karl Firmin*): Isn't that true, dear friend?

MADAME BELMONT: I am quite carried away by it—

SELICOUR (*bends toward Madame Belmont*): Far too gracious, Madame!

KARL: How do I understand this?

SELICOUR (*just as quickly, again to Karl*): Well! didn't I tell you! You have made a complete conquest.

KARL: Does he take me for a fool?

NARBONNE: This work is excellent! Totally excellent!

SELICOUR (*to Firmin the father*): You see, I have completely subscribed to your ideas.

FIRMIN (*smiles*): I'll confess, that I noticed as much.

CHARLOTTE: I know not, which of the two gentlemen—

SELICOUR (*to Charlotte, while pointing at Karl Firmin*): A sweet triumph for the author.

NARBONNE (*laying the report aside*): This is a true masterwork. Indeed!

SELICOUR (*bows to Narbonne*): Far too much honor!

MADAME BELMONT (*repeats the last strophe*):
 Hark, the woods resound with singing,
 And the fountain ripples fair!
 Room is in the smallest shelter
 For a happy loving pair.
 Beautiful! Heavenly! Who could resist it!—Selicour, it is
determined! You shall marry my Charlotte!

KARL: O Heavens!

CHARLOTTE: What do I hear?

NARBONNE (*stands up*): I know few pieces of work, which
were so excellent—Selicour, you are the ambassador!

KARL: My God!

NARBONNE: You are chosen! I will recommend your appointment! Whoever can write like that, must not only be
a man of great integrity, but also of considerable genius!

SELICOUR: But permit me—I don't know, if I can accept—
Content as I am with my present position—

NARBONNE: You must be prepared to break loose from
anything, if the state has other needs of you.

SELICOUR: May I at least invite Mister Firmin to come as
my secretary?

FIRMIN: What are you thinking of! Me? Me? As your secretary?

SELICOUR: Indeed, Mister Firmin. I have great need of
you.

KARL: That I can believe!

NARBONNE: We will see about that! And now! How did the
music go?

SELICOUR: Young Lady Charlotte has sung quite divinely.


## SCENE 5

MICHAEL *to the same.*


MICHAEL: The company has gathered in the Hall.—

NARBONNE: Be so good, dear Mother, as to receive them.—
I intend to send this away immediately.—(*softly to Seli-*

*cour):* Win the consent of my daughter, and I will gladly accept you as my son—Again! This work is excellent, and I would give much to have done it myself! *(Exits.)*

SELICOUR *(to Charlotte):* Our young friend knows how to take compliments well.

CHARLOTTE: After the wonderful things, which I have seen from him, I would never have believed, that he would find it necessary, to decorate himself with the laurels of others.

SELICOUR: Mere kindness, my young Lady!—But the company awaits—

FIRMIN *(to his son):* Well, you have indeed earned yourself some wonderful praise! *(Selicour gives his arm to Charlotte.)*

KARL: Yes, I have every reason, to be honored.

MADAME BELMONT *(to Selicour):* Yes, quite right! You take Charlotte's arm.—Just everything suits him well. He is such a charming man! *(She takes Firmin's arm.)*

SELICOUR *(pointing to Firmin):* To this gentleman, not to me, the praise is due.—In fact, I don't know, if I am permitted to accept it!—Everything, that I am, is his merit! *(Exit.)*

## SCENE 6
### KARL *alone remains.*

My agitation will betray me.—I must control myself before I can follow them. Do I really have the patience to endure all of this?—A beautiful triumph, that I've won.—They mock me with their compliments—It is obvious, that they take *him,* not *me,* to be the author. I am their fool and that rogue gets the honor!

## SCENE 7
### KARL. LAROCHE.

LAROCHE: Look here, Mister Firmin!—So all alone—Everything is going according to wish, I suppose?

KARL: Oh quite wonderfully!

LaRoche: I also have high hopes.

Karl: Selicour now stands higher in everyone's favor than ever.

LaRoche: What! What are you saying!

Karl: There is no more clever person, no more honest citizen.

LaRoche: Is it possible? What of this important report, which the Minister assigned him and for which he was incompetent?

Karl: The report is complete.

LaRoche: You must be joking!

Karl: It is complete, I tell you.

LaRoche: You are mocking me! It isn't possible!

Karl: A masterpiece in style and content!

LaRoche: I tell you, it isn't possible!

Karl: And I tell you, it *is*! The report has been read, admired, and is now being sent forward.

LaRoche: Then he must have a devil in his pay, who did the work for him.

Karl: And this ambassadorship!

LaRoche: What about the ambassador—

Karl: He has it! And he has the hand of the young lady!

LaRoche: But she can't stand him.

Karl: She will be obedient.

LaRoche: The ambassadorship as well as the young lady! No, by the devil!—It can't be! That must not be!— How?—What? That this hypocrite, this insidious little man should carry off such a prize, that is only the reward of merit.—No, as truly as I live! We cannot go along with this, we, we who know him. That violates our conscience, we would become his accomplices, if we tolerate that!

Karl: Then I will go immediately to the grandmother.—I will open her eyes about the poem—

LaRoche: About the poem—We aren't talking about the poem—The old mama can perhaps be charmed by such a thing, but the Minister would never let his opinion be determined by such a trifle.—No, Lord! This *report* is the thing and that was so excellent, that he must have conjured up from somewhere by magic—for he could never have done it, now nor ever, I swear that—but his magic consists in mere cheap tricks! And so we must trap him with his own weapons. If the goal cannot be reached by a straight path—then we shall look for an indirect approach. Wait, something occurs to me—Yes, that will work—quickly away—away, we must not be seen together.

KARL: But nothing rash, Mister LaRoche! Remember, how much there is at stake here!

LaROCHE: My honor is at stake, young sir, and that is no less important to me than your love to you—Quick! Inside!—You will hear from me later.


## SCENE 8

### LAROCHE *alone.*

Let's see now—He always tries to find some weakness in his superior, to make himself necessary. Only this morning he was with the valet—That fellow is such a gossip. He was trying to find out something about any possible romantic adventures the Minister might have—He spoke of an apartment in the suburbs.—I don't believe a word of it, but it can be looked into.—Hold on! Here he comes!


## SCENE 9

### LAROCHE *and* SELICOUR.

SELICOUR (*without noticing him*): Everything is going according to plan, and yet I am not entirely without concern—I still have neither the position nor the bride, and then there is that father and son, lurking for the chance at any moment to snatch both prizes away from me.—If I could get them out of the way—But how? There is no way to get to the Minister—These people, who travel their straight path, need no one! It's so hard to get at them! Yes, if only he had something to hide—if I could only unearth some weakness, to make me indispensible to him!

LaROCHE *(aside):* Marvelous! He is falling into my hands!

SELICOUR: Ah, look here! Mister LaRoche!

LaROCHE: It is I, and I come, Mister Selicour—

SELICOUR: What do you want?

LaROCHE: To confess that I have been unjust!

SELICOUR: Aha!

LaROCHE: And it did not help me in any way!

SELICOUR: This is really excellent! It was not from the lack of your evil tongue, that I was not destroyed!

LaROCHE: That is unfortunately true, but perhaps I am able to hope, that you can forgive me.

SELICOUR: Aha! Is that the way it stands? Are we to become more flexible!

LaROCHE: I can have no hope for the beautiful position which you had in mind for me—but for the sake of our old friendship, please, at least, do not harm me!

SELICOUR: I harm you!

LaROCHE: Please do not! Have pity on a poor devil!

SELICOUR: But—

LaROCHE: Especially since there is someone who will take my case to the Minister—

SELICOUR: So! You have found someone?—And who is that?

LaROCHE: A lady, that Michael, the valet, pointed out to me.

SELICOUR: The valet Michael! So! You know this Michael?

LaROCHE: Not well! But, because it is his nephew, who forced *me* out of my position, he is happy to show me a favor—

SELICOUR: The lady is perhaps a relative of the Minister?

LaROCHE: She is said to be a beautiful woman—he is said to be seeking an apartment for her in the suburbs—

SELICOUR: Enough, I don't want to know about all that.—And what is the woman's name?

LaROCHE: I don't know.

SELICOUR: Good! Good!

LAROCHE: Michael can give you complete information on that point.

SELICOUR: To me? Do you think, this matter is important to me?

LAROCHE: I didn't say that.

SELICOUR: I ask nothing about the matter—I am not concerned in the least.—You are going to speak to this woman tomorrow?

LAROCHE: Tomorrow.

SELICOUR: There seems to be a great mystery—

LAROCHE (*quickly*): Indeed! Indeed! Therefore I ask, that you not let anyone know—

SELICOUR: Good! Good! No more about it—I will not ruin you, Mister LaRoche!—It has always been my fate, to be subjected to the sting of ingratitude—In spite of the wretched things, which you would have done to me, I am still fond of you—and to show you, how far my feelings go, I will make common cause with your protectress.— Yes, that I will—Count on it!

LAROCHE: Ah, you are so generous!

SELICOUR: But I hope you have learned a lesson—

LAROCHE: Oh, certainly, as you shall soon see—

SELICOUR: Enough. So be it between us!

LAROCHE (*aside*): He has taken the bait. He is as good as trapped! How much quicker success comes through deceit than through honesty! (*Exits.*)

SELICOUR: Now to find this valet Michael as quickly as possible! Certainly a love affair is involved here. Most certainly—Excellent! I have you, Narbonne!—You are just a man—You too have weaknesses—and I am your master! (*Exits.*)

# ACT V

## SCENE 1

### LAROCHE *enters.*

They are still sitting at the table—the Minister will be coming out soon—I have completely run out of breath— But, thank Heavens, I am on the right track, I know everything—Do I have you at last, friend Selicour!— There was nothing for you to do with the Minister, as long as he was virtuous—but God bless me, if he were to have a vice! Then there are secrets to keep! Then there are services to provide! And then the confidant, the pro- curer has won the game—He believes to have found a weakness in the Minister—which gives a glorious field of action for his viciousness!—Well, go to it! Well, go to it! We are better prepared friend Selicour!—and you have no idea, that we are setting an evil, very evil trap for you.—Here comes the Minister—Take courage! Now is the time, to deliver the decisive blow.—

## SCENE 2

### NARBONNE. LAROCHE.

NARBONNE: What do I see? Is it really you again, who wanted to see me?

LAROCHE: Let this be the last audience, that you grant me, Lord Narbonne, if I cannot convince you this time.— Your own honor, however, and mine as well, demand, that I insist on it—everything, that I have attempted to use, to undercut your good opinion of Selicour has backfired to his honor and my humiliation.—But I have not given up hope of eventually unmasking him.

NARBONNE: This is too much! My patience is at an end!

LaRoche: A single word, Lord Minister!—You are presently looking for an apartment in the suburbs? Is that not so?

Narbonne: What? What's that?

LaRoche: It is planned for a woman, who finds herself alone with her entire family in the greatest distress. Isn't that true?

Narbonne: How? What? You dared to have me followed?

LaRoche: Don't be angry—I merely followed the lead of your friend Selicour. It was he, who first enticed that information out of your valet just this morning—He then gave the whole matter a most obscene interpretation—I, on the contrary, had grounds for thinking otherwise. For I will confess, I undertook a more precise investigation—I was there—I saw the woman, of whom we are speaking—*(he laughs)* she is quite a striking *older* woman.—Selicour takes her to be a young beauty—Oh, don't be outraged—please—let him continue to do so! Hear him out to the end, and if you do not come to see what a complete rogue he is, then let me spend my entire life in disgrace.—Here he comes—I will leave, so that you may get to the bottom of this situation. *(Exits.)*

Narbonne: That madman! How terribly his passion has blinded him! How? That Selicour could—No, no, no, no, it's not possible! not possible.


## SCENE 3

### NARBONNE. SELICOUR.


Selicour *(aside):* He is alone! Now I can trap him!—If I don't hurry now, to make myself indispensible to him, then this Firmin may gain in his favor.—But once I know his secret, then he is entirely in my hands.

Narbonne: I was just thinking, dear Selicour, about what they'll say of your report in the Cabinet—Since I sent it off so quickly, it should be in their hands by now, and I have no doubt, that it will receive the most enthusiastic approval.

SELICOUR: If it has yours, then I am fully satisfied. *(to himself)* How shall I bring this up?—I am risking nothing, since I am sure of my ground. I will go right ahead—

NARBONNE: You seem deep in thought, dear Selicour!

SELICOUR: Yes—I—I was reflecting, on how the rumor mongers can put a vicious interpretation on the most innocent of things!

NARBONNE: What do you mean?

SELICOUR: It must come out—I cannot keep this to myself any longer—malicious tongues have dared to attack you—it is going around—please—answer a few questions for me, and forgive the concerned friendship, if I seem somewhat presumptuous.

NARBONNE: Then ask! I will answer everything.

SELICOUR: If I may believe your valet, then you are seeking an apartment in the suburbs.

NARBONNE: Since you already know—yes.

SELICOUR: And quite secretly, I hear.

NARBONNE: I have kept it a secret, at least up to now.

SELICOUR: For an unmarried woman?

NARBONNE: Yes!

SELICOUR: She is of much—*(hesitates)* of much worth to you?

NARBONNE: I confess, that I take great interest in her.

SELICOUR *(to himself):* He makes no secret of it—This thing is a certainty—*(aloud)* And you would like to avoid public attention on the matter, isn't that so?

NARBONNE: If it were possible, yes!

SELICOUR: Ah, good! Good! I understand!—The matter is of a delicate nature, and the world judges so harshly.— But I can serve you.

NARBONNE: You?

SELICOUR: I can serve you! You may rely on me.

NARBONNE: But in what way?

SELICOUR: I will get you, whatever you need.

NARBONNE: How then? What then?

SELICOUR: I have ways! I can procure it for you—a quiet little house, isolated—simple from the outside and quite innocent! But most delicately laid out within—the furniture, the decor in the latest mode—an intimate little room—charming and heavenly—in short—the most beautiful little boudoir, that can be found anywhere.

NARBONNE *(to himself):* Can LaRoche be right—*(aloud)* And what secret cause could I have, to seek such a house?

SELICOUR *(smiling):* In matters, which are to be secret from me, I know how to restrain any presumptuous curiosity— You should see in me a friend ready for service in all things—There is nothing, I would not be prepared to do, to be pleasing to you. Order, what you want, I will obey, without questioning. You understand me?

NARBONNE: Perfectly.

SELICOUR: One must have an indulgent attitude.—I—I take morality seriously myself—But in a matter like this— If one can simply avoid public offense—Perhaps I am going too far into it—but my tender heart carries me away—and it is my highest wish, to see you happy—

## SCENE 4

*The same.* MICHAEL.

MICHAEL: The mail has just been delivered.

NARBONNE *(to Selicour):* These are for you.

SELICOUR: With your permission! They are business letters, which must be attended to immediately.—Ready for business, and ready for pleasure! That is always my way! *(Exits.)*

## SCENE 5

NARBONNE alone.

I am utterly astounded—This Selicour—yes, there can be no doubt now, this Selicour was certainly the accomplice of my predecessor. I do not consider myself better than others, everyone has faults—But to volunteer oneself

with such shamelessness—And I wanted to sacrifice my
child to this contemptible man—I wanted to defraud the
nation with this traitor?—So he will do anything for me,
out of friendship, he says? Are those our friends, who
cater to our vices?

## SCENE 6

### NARBONNE *and* LAROCHE.

LAROCHE: Now, he has left you—may I ask what happened?

NARBONNE: I have misjudged both *you* and *him.*—You have
shown me an essential service, Mister LaRoche, and I
will do justice to you at last.

LAROCHE *(with great joy):* Am I finally to be recognized as
an honest man? May I hold my head up again?

NARBONNE: You have succeeded!—You have unmasked the
hypocrite.—But how am I to give up my long cherished
belief, that talent and intellect are incompatible with a
degenerate heart?—This man, whose viciousness I have
just seen, gave me a manuscript today, which would do
honor to the greatest statesman and author—Is it possible? I cannot comprehend it—Such sound judgment, so
much intellect in such a despicable character! I have sent
the report to the government, and I will wager, that the
letter, which I have just received, is full of praise for it.
*(He opens the letter and reads.)* Quite right! It is, just as
I said.

LAROCHE: I can't make any sense of this—You say the work
is really good?

NARBONNE: Excellent!

LAROCHE: Then I would wager, he's not the author!

NARBONNE: Who would be then!

LAROCHE: It's not he, I'll stake my soul on that—for in the
end, I would sooner attribute a heart to him than a
mind.—If one were to try—Yes!—Right—I have it! That
will work—Lord Narbonne! If you will go along with me,
then he will betray himself.

NARBONNE: But how?

LAROCHE: Let me take care of it—He comes! Give me your support!


## SCENE 7

*The same.* SELICOUR.

LAROCHE *(with passion):* My God! What hideous misfortune!

SELICOUR: What's going on, Mister LaRoche?

LAROCHE: How much can happen in a single moment!

SELICOUR: What is it? What could cause this distress . . . this outcry of terror?

LAROCHE: It is as though I had been struck by lightning!

SELICOUR: But what is it?

LAROCHE: This unhappy letter—The Minister has just received it—*(to Narbonne):* May I? Shall I?

NARBONNE: Tell everything!

LAROCHE: He is destroyed!

SELICOUR: For God's sake!

LAROCHE: He has been relieved of his duties!

SELICOUR: It isn't possible!

LAROCHE: But only too true! There was talk of it around, but I did not want to believe it, so I hurried here, to find out for myself—and the Minister has confirmed it himself!

SELICOUR: So it is true, this horrible news? *(Narbonne confirms with a silent nod.)*


## LAST SCENE

*The same.* MADAME BELMONT. CHARLOTTE. *Both* FIRMIN.

LAROCHE: Come in, Madame! Come in, Mister Firmin!—

MADAME BELMONT: What is going on here?

LAROCHE: Comfort our Lord.—Give him courage in his misfortune!

MADAME BELMONT: His misfortune!

CHARLOTTE: My God! What is it?

LAROCHE: He has lost his position.

CHARLOTTE: Great God!

SELICOUR: I am as astounded, as you!

MADAME BELMONT: Who could have foreseen such a disaster!

KARL (*passionately*): Such is the contemptuous treatment meted out to talent—even honesty is now a crime in this degenerate nation! An honest man is hardly able to maintain himself for a single day, and only the unscrupulous prosper.

NARBONNE (*very seriously*): Don't be too rash, young man!—Heaven is just, and sooner or later the guilty will receive their due.

SELICOUR: But tell me! Does anyone have the least idea of the reason for this terrible disaster?

LaROCHE: Unfortunately, we know only too well. A certain report is responsible for the entire misfortune!

FIRMIN (*agitated*): A report! (*to the Minister*) The same one perhaps, that I saw you reading earlier today?

SELICOUR: The government saw itself treated with a freedom, a boldness—

LaROCHE: Quite right! That's exactly right!

SELICOUR: Well, there we have it! Well, was I wrong, to say, that it is not always advisable, to speak the truth?

NARBONNE: When duty speaks, I do not stop to consider. And whatever the result, I will never regret having done my duty.

SELICOUR: Well said! Most certainly! But it has cost you a fine position!

LaROCHE: And that is not all! It could also have an effect on others on your staff.—It is well known, that a Minister is seldom the author of the writings, which come out of his office.

SELICOUR: How so? How's that?

LaROCHE (*to himself*): He never misses a trick!

FIRMIN: Explain yourself more clearly!

LaROCHE: Whoever put together this vehement report will most certainly be exposed.

SELICOUR: He will? And will he be involved in the fall of
the Minister?

LaRoche: Certainly! That is very much to be feared.

SELICOUR: Well, it's not I!

FIRMIN: I am the author!

NARBONNE: What do I hear?

MADAME BELMONT: What? You, Mister Firmin?

FIRMIN: I am the author and I am proud of it.

LaRoche (to Narbonne): Well, what did I tell you?

FIRMIN: I could willingly allow the credit for this work to go
to Mister Selicour, but not the danger or the responsibility—I have been silent until now, but now I must name
myself.

KARL: Rightly so, my father! That is how a man of honor
speaks. Be proud in your misfortune, Lord Narbonne! My
father can have written nothing that is punishable—Oh,
my heart tells me, this misfortune can be a source of happiness—Charlotte's hand will now not be sacrificed to circumstances.—Greatness falls and fearful love takes
courage!

MADAME BELMONT: What do I hear? Mister Firmin?

FIRMIN: Forgive him the warmth of his sympathy, his passion leads to confusion in the expression of his emotion!

NARBONNE: So each of you has betrayed a secret.—Mister
Firmin! *You* are the author of this report, so it is fitting,
that you should earn the credit and reward.—The government appoints you as ambassador—(all are astonished)
Yes, I am still Minister, and I am happy, to be so, since
it is within my power, to reward true merit.

MADAME BELMONT: What is this?

SELICOUR (in utter dismay): What have I done?

NARBONNE (to Selicour): You have betrayed your game—
We recognize you now, hypocrite of talent and virtue—
Contemptible man, how could you have taken me to be
as vile as you?

LaRoche: How shamefully did he twist a noble action! I
know everything from the mouth of the lady herself. This

woman, for whom he imputed to you a culpable interest—
is an ill, an elderly matron, the widow of a much-decor-
ated officer, who lost his life in the service of the fatherland and for whom you have assumed the responsibility
of the government in compensation.

NARBONNE: No more about that, please!—*(to Selicour)* You
can see, your presence is quite superfluous here. *(Selicour exits silently.)*

LaROCHE: I am sorry for the poor wretch—Indeed I knew
in advance, that my hatred would abate, the moment he
was removed from his position of excellence.

FIRMIN *(softly presses his hand):* Let's be decent about it.
We will try to console him later.

LaROCHE: Enough, I agree!

NARBONNE *(to Karl):* Our lively young friend is suddenly
quite silent—I have seen into your heart, dear Firmin!—
In your surprise, you revealed your secret and I will never
forget, that your interest was hidden during our good
fortune and only to be revealed during our misfortune.—
Charlotte! *(She throws herself into her father's arms without a word.)* Good, we understand one another! You may
count on your father's love.

LaROCHE: And I will swear, that Karl Firmin is the true
author of the poem!

MADAME BELMONT: Is it possible?

CHARLOTTE *(with a delicate look at Karl):* I never doubted
it! *(Karl kisses her hand with great passion.)*

MADAME BELMONT: Such a modest young man! Certainly,
he will make our daughter happy!

NARBONNE: Become like your father, and I will accept
you with joy as my son!—*(half to the actors, half to the
audience)* This time, merit has gained the victory.—But
it is not always so. The web of deception entangles the
good, the honest are unable to succeed, servile mediocrity advances further than true talent: Appearance rules
the world—and justice is found only on the stage.

*End.*

# HISTORY

# What Is, and to What End Do We Study,

# UNIVERSAL HISTORY?

TRANSLATED BY
CAROLINE STEPHAN AND ROBERT TROUT

Gentlemen, it is a delightful and honorable commission for me to wander into the future at your sides, through a field which reveals so many objects of study to the thinking observer, such magnificent examples for the emulation of the active, worldly man, such important explanations for the philosopher, and such rich sources of most noble joy for everyone without exception—the grand and broad field of universal history. The sight of so many splendid young men gathered about me by their noble thirst for knowledge, and in whose midst some genius flourishes who will make himself felt in future ages, transforms my obligation into pleasure, but also makes me feel the weight and importance of this enterprise in its full force. The greater the gift I must bequeath upon you,—and what greater gift than truth has any man to give to man?—the more I must take caution,

---

On May 26–27, 1789, Schiller delivered this lecture on Universal History at Jena University. It was his first lecture in his new position as Professor of History, a post which Goethe had arranged for him (though without compensation), in January of that year. The young Schiller's reputation was already such, that, for his first lecture, the classroom was filled to overflowing. A virtual march of hundreds of students occurred in the street, much to Schiller's amusement, to secure a larger classroom, before Schiller could begin.

that its value is not debased in my hands. The more lively and pure your spirit conceives in this happiest epoch of its activity, and the quicker your youthful passions glow, the greater the demand upon me to prevent this enthusiasm, which only truth has the right to awaken, from being wasted unworthily by fraud and deception.

The field of history is fecund and vastly encompassing; in its sphere lies the entire moral world. It accompanies us through all the conditions mankind has experienced, through all the shifting forms of opinion, through his folly and his wisdom, his deterioration and his ennoblement; history must give account of everything man has *taken* and *given*. There is none among you to whom history had nothing important to convey; however different the paths toward your future destinies, it somewhere binds them together; but one destiny you all share in the same way with one another, that which you brought with you into this world— to educate yourself as a human being—and history addresses itself to this human being.

But, gentlemen, before I can undertake to determine more exactly your expectations of this object of your diligence, and to explain its connection with the real purpose of your diverse studies, it were not superfluous for me to first reach agreement with you on that purpose of your studies. A preliminary clarification of this question, which seems appropriate and worthwhile enough to me, at the beginning of our future academic relationship, will enable me directly to draw your attention to the most dignified side of world history.

The course of studies which the scholar who feeds on bread alone sets himself, is very different from that of the philosophical mind. The former, who, for all his diligence, is interested merely in fulfilling the conditions under which he can perform a vocation and enjoy its advantages, who activates the powers of his mind only thereby to improve his material conditions and to satisfy a narrow-minded thirst for fame, such a person has no concern upon entering his academic career, more important than distinguishing most carefully those sciences which he calls 'studies for bread,' from all the rest, which delight the mind for their own sake. Such a scholar believes, that all the time he devoted to these latter, he would have to divert from his future vocation, and this thievery he could never forgive himself. He will direct all of his diligence to the demands made upon him by the future master of his fate, and he will believe he has achieved everything once he has made himself capable of not fearing this authority. Once he has run his course and attained the goal of his desires, he dismisses the sciences which guided him, for why should he bother with them any longer? His greatest concern now is to display these accumulated treasures of his memory, and to take care, that their value not depreciate. Every extension of his bread-science upsets him, because it portends only more work, or it makes the past useless; every important innovation frightens him, because it shatters the old school form which he so laboriously adopted, it places him in danger of losing the entire effort of his preceding life.

Who rants more against reformers than the gaggle of bread-fed scholars? Who more holds up the progress of useful revolutions in the kingdom of knowledge than these very men? Every light radiated by a happy genius, in whichever science it be, makes their poverty apparent; their foils are bitterness, insidiousness, and desperation, for, in the school system they defend, they do battle at the same time for their entire existence. On that score, there is no more irreconcilable enemy, no more jealous official, no one more eager to denounce heresy than the bread-fed scholar. The less his knowledge rewards him *on its own account*, the more he devours acclaim thrown at him from the outside; he has but *one* standard for the work of the craftsman, as well as for the work of the mind—effort. Thus, one hears no one complain more about ingratitude than the bread-fed scholar; he seeks his rewards not in the treasures of his mind—his recompense he expects from the recognition of others, from positions of honor, from personal security. If he miscarries in this, who is more unhappy than the bread-

fed scholar? He has lived, worried, and worked in vain; he
has sought in vain for truth, if for him this truth not transfer
itself into gold, published praise, and princely favor.

Pitiful man, who, with the noblest of all tools, with
science and art, desires and obtains nothing higher than the
day-laborer with the worst of tools, who, in the kingdom of
complete freedom, drags an enslaved soul around with him.
Still more pitiful, however, is the young man of genius,
whose natural, beautiful stride is led astray by harmful
theories and models upon this sad detour, who was persuaded to collect ephemeral details for his future vocation,
so wretchedly meticulous. His vocational science of patch-
work will soon disgust him, desires will awaken in him
which it cannot satisfy, his genius will revolt against his
destiny. Everything he does appears to him but fragments,
he sees no purpose to his work, but purposelessness he
cannot bear. The tribulation, the triviality in his professional
business presses him to the ground, because he cannot
counter it with the joyful courage which acompanies only
the enlightened understanding, only expected perfection.
He feels secluded, torn away from the connectedness of
things, since he has neglected to connect his activity to the
grand whole of the world. Jurisprudence disrobes the jurist
as soon as the glimmer of a better culture casts its light upon
its nakedness, instead of his now striving to become a new
creator of law, and to improve deficiencies now discovered
out of his own inner wealth. The physician is estranged
from his profession as soon as grave errors demonstrate to
him the unreliability of his system; the theologian loses
respect for his calling as soon as his faith in the infallibility
of his system begins to totter.

How entirely differently the philosophical mind com-
ports itself! As meticulously as the bread-fed scholar distinguishes his science from all others, the latter strives to
extend the reach of his own, and to reestablish its bond with
the others—*reestablish*, I say, for only the abstracting mind
has set these boundaries, has sundered these sciences from
one another. Where the bread-fed scholar severs, the philo-

sophical mind unites. He early convinced himself, that everything is intertwined in the field of understanding as well as in the material world, and his zealous drive for harmony cannot be satisfied with fragments of the whole. All his efforts are directed toward the perfection of his knowledge; his noble impatience cannot rest until all of his conceptions have ordered themselves into an organic whole, until he stands at the center of his art, his science, and until from this position outward he surveys its expanse with a contented look. New discoveries in the sphere of his activities, which cast the bread-fed scholar down, delight the philosophical mind. Perhaps they fill a gap which had still disfigured the growing whole of his conceptions, or they set the stone still missing in the edifice of his ideas, which then completes it. Even should these new discoveries leave it in ruins, a new chain of thoughts, a new natural phenomenon, a newly discovered law in the material world overthrow the entire edifice of his science, no matter: *He has always loved truth more than his system,* and he will gladly exchange the old, insufficient form for a new one, more beautiful. Indeed, if no blow from the outside shatters his edifice of ideas, he himself will be the first to tear it apart, discontented, to reestablish it more perfected. Through always new and more beautiful forms of thought, the philosophical mind strides forth to higher excellence, while the bread-fed scholar, in eternal stagnation of mind, guards over the barren monotony of his school-conceptions.

There is no fairer judge of the merits of others than the philosophical mind. Shrewd and imaginative enough to make use of every activity, he is also equitable enough to honor the creation of even the smallest contribution. All minds work for him—all minds work against the bread-fed scholar. The former knows how to transform everything around him, everything which happens and is thought, into his own possession—among thinking minds an intimate community of all goods of the mind is in effect; what is obtained in the kingdom of truth by one is won for all. The bread-fed scholar fences himself in against all his neighbors, whom he jealously begrudges light and sun, and keeps worried watch over the dilapidated barrier which but weakly defends him against victorious reason. For everything the bread-fed scholar undertakes, he must borrow incentive and encouragement from others; the philosophical mind, in his diligence, finds in his subject matter itself his incentive and reward. How much more enthusiastically can he set about his work, how much more lively will his eagerness be, how much more tenacious his courage and his activity, because for him work rejuvenates itself through work. Even small things become grand under his creative hand, because he always has the grand objective, which they may serve, in view, while the bread-fed scholar sees even in great things only that which is petty. It is not *what* he does, but how he treats what he does, which distinguishes the philosophical mind. Wherever he may stand and work, he always stands at the center of the whole; and however far the object of his labors may draw him away from his other brothers, he is allied with them, and *near* them through a harmonically working understanding; he meets them where all enlightened minds find one another.

Should I now carry on further in this description, or may I hope, that you have already decided which of these two portraits I have held up to you here you will want to take as your model? Whether the study of universal history can be recommended to you, or whether you should leave it alone, depends upon the choice you have made between these two. My only concern is with the second portrait, for by endeavoring to make oneself useful to the first, science might depart too far from its higher, ultimate aim, and might purchase a small profit with a sacrifice too great.

If we are agreed upon the point of view from which the value of science should be determined, I can now draw closer to the conception of universal history itself, the topic of today's lecture.

The discoveries which our European mariners have made in distant oceans and on remote coastlines, present us a spectacle as constructive as it is entertaining. They show us tribes which surround us at the most diverse levels of culture, like children of different ages gathered around an adult, reminding him by their example of what he used to be, and where he started from. A wise hand seems to have preserved these raw tribes for us down to our times, where we would be advanced enough in our own culture to make fruitful application of this discovery upon ourselves, and to restore out of this mirror the forgotten origin of our species. But how shaming and sad is the picture these people give us of our childhood! And yet the level at which we see them is not even the first. Mankind began even more contemptuously. Those we study today we already find as nations, as political bodies: But mankind first had to elevate itself by an extraordinary effort, to political society.

Now what do these travellers tell us about these savages? They found some without any knowledge of the most indispensable skills, without iron, without the plow, some even without the possession of fire. Some still wrestled with wild beasts for food and dwelling, among many language had been scarcely elevated from animal sounds to understandable signs. In some places, there was not even the simple bond of *marriage*, as yet no knowledge of property, and in others the flaccid soul was not even able to retain an experience which repeats itself every day; one saw the savage carelessly relinquish the bed on which he slept, because it did not occur to him, that he would sleep again tomorrow. War, however, was with them all, and the flesh of the vanquished enemy was not seldom the prize of victory. Among others, acquainted with various leisures of life, who had already achieved a higher level of culture, slavery and despotism presented us a dreadful picture of them. Once we find a tyrant in Africa trading his subjects for a gulp of brandy; another time they would be slaughtered on his grave to serve him in the underworld. Where once pious simplicity prostrates itself to a ridiculous fetish, another time it is to a terrible monster; mankind portrays himself in his gods. Where over there we see denigrating slavery, stupidity, and superstition bow him down, yet another time we see him utterly miserable on the other extreme of lawless freedom. Always armed for attack and defense, startled by every noise, the savage strains his cautious ear into the desert; everything new is the *enemy*, and woe to the stranger whom a storm has cast upon the coast! No hospitable hearth will smoke for him, no sweet hospitality comfort him. But even where mankind has elevated itself from hostile solitude to community, from privation to luxury, from fear to joy—how bizarre and atrocious he seems to our eyes! His crude taste seeks joy in stupor, beauty in distortion, glory in exaggeration; even his virtue awakens horror in us, and what he calls his bliss can only arouse our disgust and pity. So were *we*. Caesar and Tacitus found us not much better eighteen hundred years ago. What are we now?— Let me linger for a moment at this epoch in which we are now living, at this present shape of the world we inhabit.

Human diligence has cultivated it and subdued the resisting land through persistence and skill. In one part of the world we see, that mankind redeemed the land from the sea, somewhere else he opened rivers into the arid land. Mankind has intermingled the regions and the seasons, and has toughened the weak plants of the Orient to his own harsh climate. As he brought Europe to the West Indies and the South Seas, so he also let Asia arise in Europe. A merrier sky now laughs above Germany's forests, which the powerful hand of man tore open to the rays of sunshine, and in the waves of the Rhine are mirrored Asia's grapevines. Populous towns arise on its banks, which swarm with vigorous life of pleasure and work. Here we find a man secure in peaceful possession of his acquisitions among millions of others, whom previously a single neighbor had robbed of his slumbers. The equality he lost upon entering the community, he regained through wise laws. He escaped from the blind constraint of pure chance and poverty under the more gentle constraint of treaties, and surrendered the liberty of the beast of prey to redeem the more noble freedom of the human being. Prevailing need compels him no longer to the plowshare, no enemy any longer demands of him, that he leave his plow to defend home and fatherland on the battlefield. With the arm of the husbandman he fills his barns, with the weapons of a warrior he protects his territory. The law keeps watch over his property—and that invaluable right remains for him to decide for himself what his duty is.

How many creations of art, how many wonders of diligence, what light in all fields of knowledge, since man no longer consumes his energies in pitiful self-defense, since it has been placed at his discretion to reconcile himself with need, which he ought never fully to escape; since he has obtained the valuable privilege to command freely over his capabilities, and to follow the call of his genius! What lively activity everywhere, since desires multiplied lent new wings to inventive genius and opened new spheres to his diligence.—The boundaries are breached which isolated states and nations in hostile egoism. All thinking minds are now bound together by the bond of world-citizenry, and all the light of the century can now illuminate the spirit of a new Galileo and Erasmus.

Since the time when the laws descended to the weakness of man, man, too, accommodated to the laws. With them he has become gentle, just as he ran wild when they were wild; barbaric crimes follow their barbaric punishment gradually into oblivion. A great step toward ennoblement has taken place, so that the laws are virtuous, although mankind still is not. Where duties enforced upon mankind are relaxed, morality takes command of him. Whom no punishment terrifies and no conscience curbs, is now held within bounds by laws of decency and honor.

It is true, that some barbaric remnants of the former age have penetrated into our own, the progeny of accident and violence, which the Age of Reason should not perpetuate. But how much which is useful has the understanding of mankind also given to this barbaric legacy of the ancient and Middle Ages. How harmless, yes—how useful—it has often made that which it could not yet dare to overturn! Upon the rough terrain of feudal anarchy, Germany established the system of its political and clerical freedom. The silhouette of the Roman Emperor presented on this side of the Apennines serves the world infinitely better than its dreadful archetype in ancient Rome, for it holds together a useful system of states through concord: The former had suppressed the most active forces of mankind in slavish uniformity. Even our religion, so much distorted at the hands of the faithless, from which it has been handed down to us—who can deny the ennobling influence of a better philosophy in it? From Leibnizes and Lockes, the *dogma* and *morality* of Christianity gained in the same way the brush of a Raphael and Correggio bequeathed to sacred history.

Finally, our nations: With what intensity, with what art they are intertwined with each other! How much more durably fraternal through the charitable force of need, than in earlier times through the most ceremonious treaties! The peace is now guarded by a permanently bridled war, and the self-love of one nation makes it the guardian over the prosperity of the other. The European community of states appears to be transformed into a great family. The family members may treat each other with hostility, but hopefully no longer tear each other limb from limb.

What very different pictures! Who would suspect in the refined European of the eighteenth century only an advanced brother of the modern Canadian, or the ancient Celt? All these skills, artistic impulses, experiences, and all these creations of reason, were implanted and developed in mankind during the span of a few thousand years, all these wonders of art, these grand achievements of diligence evoked from mankind. What awakened them to life, what enticed them forth? Through which conditions did man wander until he ascended from *one* extreme, from the unsociable troglodyte, to the ingenious thinker, the cultured man of the world? Universal world history gives the answer to this question.

These same people present themselves on this same tract of land so immeasurably different when we view them in different periods of time. No less striking is the difference offered us by the contemporary generation in different countries. What a multitude of customs, constitutions, and manners! What a rapid alternation between darkness and light, between anarchy and order, bliss and misery, even when we meet people only in this small part of the world, Europe! Free at the Thames, and for this freedom his own debtor; here, unconquerable between the Alps, somewhere else invincible between his artificial rivers and swamps. At the River Vistula, without energy and miserable in his discord; on the other side of the Pyrenees, without energy and miserable in his calmness. Wealthy and blessed in Amsterdam without harvest; poor and unhappy in the unused paradise of the Ebro. Here two distant nations, separated by an ocean, transformed into neighbors by force of necessity, diligence of arts, and political bonds; there are adjacent residents of *one* river immeasurably distant in their different liturgies! What led Spain's power across the Atlantic Ocean into the heart of America, and not even across the Tajo and Guadiana? What preserved so many thrones in Italy and Germany, and in France let all, except *one*, disappear? Universal history solves this question.

Even that *we* found ourselves together here at this moment, found ourselves together with this degree of national culture, with this language, these manners, these civil benefits, this degree of freedom of conscience, is the result perhaps of all previous events in the world: The *entirety* of world history, at least, were necessary to explain this single moment. For us to have met here as Christians, this religion had to be prepared by countless revolutions, had to go forth from Judaism, had to have found the Roman state exactly as it found it, to spread in a rapid and victorious course over the world, and to ascend finally even the throne of the Caesars. Our raw forefathers in the Thuringian forests had to have been defeated by the superior strength of the Franks in order to adopt their religion. Through its own increasing wealth, through the ignorance of the people, and through the weakness of their rulers, the clergy had to have been

tempted and favored to misuse its reputation, and to transform its silent *power over the conscience* into a secular
sword. For us to have assembled here as Protestant Christians, the hierarchy had to have poured out all its atrocities
upon the human species in a Gregory and Innocent, so that
the rampant depravity of moral standards and the crying
scandal of spiritual despotism could embolden an intrepid
Augustinian monk to give the signal for the revolt, and to
snatch half of Europe away from the Roman hierarchy. For
this to have happened, the weapons of our princes had to
wrest a religious peace from Charles V; a Gustavus Adolphus
had to have avenged the breach of this peace, and establish
a new, universal peace for centuries. Cities in Italy and
Germany had to have risen up to open their gates to industry, break the chains of serfdom, wrest the scepter out of the
hands of ignorant tyrants, and gain respect for themselves
through a militant Hanseatic League, in order that trade
and commerce should flourish, and superfluity to have
called forth the arts of joy, so that the nation should have
honored the useful husbandman, and a long-lasting happiness for mankind should have ripened in the beneficent
middle class, the creator of our entire culture. Germany's
emperors had to have debilitated themselves in centuries
of battles with the popes, with their vassals, with jealous
neighbors; Europe had to have unloaded its dangerous
abundance in the graves of Asia, and the defiant feudal
aristocracy had to have bled its indignant rebellious spirit
to death in a murderous law of the fist, Roman campaigns
and crusades, so that confused chaos could sort itself out,
and the contending powers of the state rest in a blessed
equilibrium, and from thence is our present leisure the
reward. For our mind to have wrested itself free of the
ignorance in which spiritual and secular compulsion held it
enchained, the long-suppressed germ of scholarship had to
have burst forth again among its most enraged persecutors,
and an Al Mamun had to have paid the spoils to the sciences,
which an Omar had extorted from them. The unbearable
misery of barbarism had to have driven our ancestors forth

from the bloody *judgments of God* and into human courts
of law, devastating plagues had to have called medicine run
astray back to the study of nature, the idleness of the monks
had to have prepared from a distance a substitute for the
evil which their works had created, and profane industry in
the monasteries had to have preserved the ruined remains
of the Augustinian age until the time of the art of printing
had arrived. The depressed spirit of the Nordic barbarian
had to have uplifted itself to Greek and Roman models, and
erudition had to have concluded an alliance with the Muses
and Graces, should it ever find a way to the heart and
deserve the name of sculptor of man.—But, had Greece
given birth to a Thucydides, a Plato, an Aristotle, had Rome
given birth to a Horace, a Cicero, a Virgil and Livy, were
these two nations not to have ascended to those heights of
political wealth to which they indeed attained? In a word,
if their *entire history* had not preceded them? How many
inventions, discoveries, state and church revolutions had to
*conspire* to lend growth and dissemination to these new,
still tender sprouts of science and art! How many wars had
to be waged, how many alliances concluded, sundered, and
become newly concluded to finally bring Europe to the
principle of peace, which alone grants nations, as well as
their citizens, to direct their attention to themselves, and
to join their energies to a reasonable purpose!

Even in the most everyday activities of civil life, we
cannot avoid becoming indebted to centuries past; the most
diverse periods of mankind contribute to our culture in the
same way as the most remote regions of the world contribute
to our luxury. The clothes we wear, the spices in our food,
and the price for which we buy them, many of our strongest
medicines, and also many new tools of our destruction—do
they not presuppose a Columbus who discovered America,
a Vasco da Gama who circumnavigated the tip of Africa?

There is thus a long chain of events pulling us from the
present moment aloft toward the beginning of the human
species, the which intertwine as cause and effect. Only the
infinite understanding can survey these events wholly and

completely; for man, narrower limitations are set. *I*. Countless of these events have either found no human witness or
observer, or they have been preserved by no signs. Among
these are all those which have preceded the human species
itself, and the invention of letters. The source of all history
is tradition, and the organ of tradition is speech. The entire
epoch *prior to speech,* however momentous it may have
been for the world, is lost to world history. *II*. But after
speech was invented, through it the possibility existed to
express things which occurred, and to communicate further,
so in the beginning, this reporting occurred over the inse-
cure and changeable way of myths. From mouth to mouth,
such an event was transmitted over a long succession of
generations, and since it passed through media which are
changed, and do change, it too necessarily suffered these
changes. Living tradition, or the myth by word of mouth,
is thus a highly unreliable source for history; all events prior
to the use of the written word, therefore, are as good as lost
to world history. *III*. But the written word itself is not
eternal, either; countless monuments of ancient ages have
been destroyed by time and accidents, and only a few ruins
have been preserved from the ancient world into the time
of the art of printing. Most of them, by and large, are lost
to world history, together with the information they should
have provided us. *IV*. Among the few monuments, finally,
which time has spared, the larger number has been disfigured by *passion,* by *lack of judgment,* and often even by
the *genius* of those who describe them, and have been
rendered unrecognizable. Our mistrust awakens at the oldest of historic monuments, and it does not leave us even at
the chronicles of the present day. If we hear the testimonies
of an event which happened only today, and among people
with whom we live, and in the town we inhabit, and we
have difficulty making the truth out of their contradictory
reports, what courage can we summon up for nations and
times more distant from us on account of the strangeness of
their customs than the distance in time of thousands of
years? The small sum of events remaining after all these

deductions have been made is the substance of history in its broadest understanding. Now, what, and how much, of this substance of history belongs to Universal History?

Out of the entire sum of these events, the universal historian selects those which have had an essential, irrefutable, and easily ascertainable influence upon the contemporary form of the world, and on the conditions of the generations now living. It is the relationship of an historical fact to the *present* constitution of the world, therefore, which must be seen in order to assemble material for world history. World history thus proceeds from a principle, which is exactly contrary to the beginning of the world. The real succession of events descends from the origin of objects down to their most recent ordering; the universal historian ascends from the most recent world situation, upwards toward the origin of things. When he ascends from the current year and century in thoughts to the next preceding, and takes note of those among the events presented to him containing the explanation for the succeeding years and centuries, when he has continued this process stepwise up to the beginning—not of the world, for to that place there is no guide—but to the beginning of the monuments, then he decides to retrace his steps on the path thus prepared, and to descend, unhindered and with light steps, with the guide of those noted facts, from the beginning of the monuments down to the most recent age. That is the world history we have, and which will be presented to you.

Because world history depends on the wealth and poverty of sources, there must arise as many gaps in world history as there exist empty passages in written tradition. However uniformly, necessarily, and certainly the changes in the world develop out of each other, they will appear disconnected and accidentally connected to each other in history. Therefore, between the course of the world and the course of world history, a remarkable disparity is evident. One might compare the former with an uninterrupted, continually flowing stream, from which, however, only here and there will a wave be illuminated in world history. Since

it can also easily happen, that the relationship of a distant
world event to the circumstances of the present year appears
to us sooner than its connection with events which preceded
it, or were contemporary, it is thus also unavoidable, that
the events which are most precisely connected with the
most recent age not infrequently seem to be isolated in the
age to which they originally belong. A fact of this kind, for
example, would be the origin of Christianity, and particularly of Christian ethics. The Christian religion made such
diverse contributions to the form of our present world, that
its appearance becomes the most important fact for world
history: But neither in the time in which it appeared, nor
in the population in which it arose, does there lie a satisfac-
tory basis for explaining its appearance—beause we lack the
sources.

As such, our world history would never become anything but an aggregation of fragments, and would never
deserve the name of a science. But now the philosophical
understanding comes to its aid, and while it binds these
fragments together with artificial connections, it elevates
the aggregate to a system, to a reasonably connected whole.
Its authority for this lies in the uniformity and invariant
unity of the laws of nature and of the human soul, which
unity is the reason, that the events of most distant antiquity
return in the most recent times under the coincidence of
similar circumstances from the outside, as also the reason,
that, therefore, from events most recent, lying within the
field of our observation, a conclusion can be drawn and
some light shed, in hindsight, on events which faded away
in prehistoric times. The method of drawing conclusions by
analogies is as powerful an aid in history, as everywhere
else, but it must be justified by an important purpose,
and must be exercised with as much circumspection as
judgment.

The philosophical mind cannot dwell on the material of
world history long, until a new impulse striving for harmony
becomes active in him, one which irresistibly stimulates

him to assimilate everything around him into his rational nature, and to raise every phenomenon he sees to its highest recognizable effect, to *thought*. The more often, and the more successfully he thus repeats this attempt to connect the past to the present, the more he is inspired to connect that, as *means* and *intent*, which he sees to be interlocked as *cause* and *effect*. One phenomenon after the other begins to shed blind caprice, lawless freedom, and to add itself as a well-fitting link to an harmonious whole (which, admittedly, exists only in his imagination). Soon he finds it difficult to persuade himself, that the succession of phenomena, which achieved so much regularity and the quality of being intended in his imagination, does not have these qualities in reality; he finds it difficult to surrender that to the blind rule of necessity, which had begun to take on such vivid form under the borrowed light of the understanding. He thus takes this harmony from out of himself, and plants it outside of himself into the order of things, i.e., he brings a reasonable purpose into the course of the world, and a teleological principle into *world history*. With this principle he wanders once more through world history, and holds it up, testing it against each phenomenon which this grand theater presents him. He sees it *confirmed* by a thousand concurring facts, and disproved by just as many others; but as long as important links are missing in the course of changes in the world, as long as destiny withholds the final explanations about so many events, he declares this question to be undecided, and that opinion will triumph, which is able to offer the greater satisfaction to the mind, and to the heart, the greater bliss.

There is probably no need to recall, that a world history according to the latter plan can be expected only in the most recent times. A precipitous application of this grand standard could easily lead the historian into the temptation to do violence to events, and thus to move more and more away from this bright epoch of world history, in the desire to accelerate it. But attention cannot be called too early to this illuminated, and yet so neglected side of world history, that through which it attaches itself to the highest object of all human endeavors. Already the cursory glance in this regard, even if the goal is merely possible, must lend the diligence of the researcher an invigorating incentive, and sweet recreation. Even the smallest of efforts will be important for him when he sees himelf on the way, or when he guides a successor on the way toward solving the problem of the ordering of the world, and to meet the Supreme Mind in His most beautiful effect.

And, treated this way, gentlemen, the study of world history will give you an attractive as well as useful occupation. It will enkindle light in your mind, and a charitable enthusiasm in your heart. It will cure your mind of the common and narrow view of moral matters, and while it displays the grand picture of the times and nations before your eyes, it will improve upon the rash decisions of the moment, and the limited judgments of egoism. While it accustoms a person to connect himself with the entirety of what is past, and to rush on with his conclusions into the far future, so it veils the boundary between birth and death which circumscribes human life so narrowly and so oppressively, and it thus extends his brief existence, by optical illusion, into an infinite space, and, unnoticed, leads the individual over into the species.

Man changes himself, and flees the stage; his opinions change and flee with him: History alone remains incessantly on the scene, an immortal citizen of all nations and all times. Like the Homeric Zeus, it looks with an equally bright view down upon the bloody work of war, and upon peaceful nations which innocently feed themselves from the milk of their herds. However lawlessly the freedom of man may seem to deal with the contest, it calmly gazes upon the confused play, for its far-reaching view already discovered in the distant future the way where this lawlessly roaming freedom will be guided by the reins of necessity. What history keeps secret from the reproachful conscience of a Gregory and a Cromwell, it rushes to proclaim to mankind:

"The egoistic man may indeed pursue baser ends, but he unconsciously promotes splendid ones."

No false gleam will blind history, no prejudice of the times will seduce it, because it experiences the final destiny of all things. In the eyes of history, everything has endured an equally long time; it holds the rewarded olive garland fresh, and destroys the obelisk erected by vanity. By dissecting the fine mechanism by which the silent hand of nature methodically develops the powers of mankind from the very beginning of the world, and while it precisely indicates in each period of time what has been achieved on behalf of this great plan of nature, at the same time it restores the true standard of happiness and merit which prevailing delusion distorted in a different way in every century. History cures us of exaggerated admiration for antiquity and childish longing for times past; and while it draws our attention to our own possession, it does not let us wish back the praised golden ages of Alexander and Augustus.

All preceding ages, without knowing it or aiming at it, have striven to bring about our human century. Ours are all the treasures which diligence and genius, reason and experience, have finally brought home in the long age of the world. Only from history will you learn to set a value on the goods from which habit and unchallenged possession so easily deprive our gratitude; priceless, precious goods, upon which the blood of the best and the most noble clings, goods which had to be won by the hard work of so many generations! And who among you, in whom a bright spirit is conjugated with a feeling heart, could bear this high obligation in mind, without a silent wish being aroused in him to pay that debt to coming generations which he can no longer discharge to those past? A noble desire must glow in us to also make a contribution out of *our means* to this rich bequest of truth, morality, and freedom which we received from the world past, and which we must surrender once more, richly enlarged, to the world to come, and, in this eternal chain which winds itself through all human generations, to make firm our ephemeral existence. However different the destinies may be which await you in society, all of you can contribute something to this! A path toward immortality has been opened up to every achievement, to the true immortality, I mean, where the deed lives and rushes onward, even if the name of the author should remain behind.

*The Legislation of*

# LYCURGUS AND SOLON

### TRANSLATED BY GEORGE GREGORY

To properly appreciate the Lycurgian plan, we must look back to the political situation in Sparta of that time, and come to know the condition in which he found Lacadaemon when he came forth with his new design. Two kings, both furnished with the same authority, stood at the head of the state; each jealous of the other, each busy to secure himself a following, thus to set limits to the authority of his counter-part on the throne. This jealousy had been passed from the first two kings, Procles and Eurysthes, and their mutual lineages, down to Lycurgus, so that Sparta was incessantly troubled by factions over this long span of time. By bestow-ing greater freedoms, each king attempted to corrupt the people to incline to him, and these concessions led the people to become insolent and, ultimately, to insurrection. The state wavered to and fro, between monarchy and de-

---

Schiller delivered his essay on Lycurgus and Solon in the context of his lectures on Universal History, at Jena Univeristy, in August 1789. The essay puts forth two alternative conceptions of govern-ment—a republican and an oligarchic form—which have existed since the time of the Greeks. The oligarchic, associated with Lycurgus, reduces man to a beast, denying individual human creativity. Solon's republican government is premised on a con-ception of man raised to the level of participation in the divine. The essay was originally published in the 11th edition of *Thalia*, in 1790.

mocracy, and swung in rapid succession from one extreme
to the other. No line was drawn between the rights of the
people and the authority of the kings, and wealth flowed
into the hands of a few families. The rich citizens tyrannized
the poor, and the desperation of the latter expressed itself
in revolt.

Torn asunder by internal discord, the weak state had
inevitably fallen prey to hostile neighbors, or fallen completely apart into a number of smaller tyrannies. And that
is the condition in which Lycurgus found Sparta: No clear
distinction between the authority of the kings and the people, unequal distribution of earthly goods among the citizens, lack of public spirit and concord, and complete political destitution, were the maladies confronting the legislator,
of which, therefore, he had to take account in his legislation.

As the day arrived, when Lycurgus wanted to announce
his laws, he had thirty of the most prominent citizens, whom
he had previously won over to his plan, appear armed in
the marketplace, thus to instill fear in anyone who might
resist. King Charilaus, terrified by these measures, fled into
the Temple of Minerva, because he believed it all directed
against him. But he was dissuaded of this fear, and in the end
became so persuaded, that he actively supported Lycurgus's
plan himself.

The first decrees concerned the government. To prevent the republic from ever again being tossed to and fro
between royal tyranny and anarchic democracy, Lycurgus
established a third power, as a counterweight, between the
two; he founded a *senate*. The senators, 28 in number, or
30 together with the two kings, were to side with the people,
should the *kings* abuse their authority, and if, on the other
hand, the power of the people became too great, the senate
would protect the kings against the people. An excellent
arrangement, whereby Sparta was forever spared the violent domestic turmoil, which had previously so shaken it.
It was thus made impossible for either party to tread the
other under foot: Against the people and the senate, the
kings could do nothing, and it was impossible for the people

to gain the upper hand if the senate made common cause with the kings.

But there was a third case, which Lycurgus left unconsidered—that of the senate itself abusing its power. The senate, as intermediary, could as easily join with the kings, as with the people, without danger to the public order, but without danger to the public order, the kings could not join with the people against the *senate*. The senate, therefore, soon began to exploit this advantageous situation, and made excessive use of its authority, in which it was the more successful, since the small number of senators made it easy for them to reach agreement among themselves. Lycurgus's successors filled this gap, therefore, and introduced the ephors, who were to rein in the power of the senate.

More dangerous and bold was the second change Lycurgus instituted: To do away forever with the distinction between rich and poor, he distributed the entire land of the country in equal parts among the citizens. All Laconia was divided into 30,000 fields, the area around the city of Sparta itself into 9,000 fields, each sufficiently large, that a family could easily sustain itself. Now Sparta was beautiful to behold, and Lycurgus himself delighted in the sight of it, as he travelled through the country. "All Laconia," he proclaimed, "is a farm brotherly divided among its brothers."

Lycurgus would gladly have distributed the other earthly goods, as he had the farmland, but there were insuperable obstacles to this plan. He thus attempted to reach this goal by other means, and what he could not change by decree, he took into his own hands.

He began by outlawing all gold and silver coins, introducing iron ones in their stead. He likewise assigned a very low value to the large and heavy pieces of iron, so that a large space were needed to store even a small amount of money, and many horses to carry it away. Lo and behold, to assure, that no one might be tempted to place any great value on this money, and to horde it, on account of the *iron* in it, he had the glowing-hot iron, which was used for the coins, quenched and tempered in vinegar, which made it unfit for any other use.

Who would now steal, or allow himself to be corrupted, or even consider hoarding wealth, for the meagre gains could neither be *kept secret* nor employed?

Not enough, that Lycurgus thereby deprived his fellow citizens of the *means* of luxury—he removed the very objects of the same from their sight, the which might have excited their desire for luxury. Sparta's iron coins were of no use to a foreign merchant, and the Spartans had no others to give him. Artists who worked for luxury, now disappeared from Laconia, no foreign ships appeared any longer in its ports; no adventurer sought his fortune there, no merchants came to prey upon vanities and lusts, for they could carry nothing but iron coins away with them, and in all other countries these were despised. Luxury ceased to exist, for there was no one to sustain it.

In other fields, too, Lycurgus set to work against luxury. He decreed, that all citizens eat together in a public place, and that they all eat the *same* prescribed meals. It was not allowed to indulge in delicacies at home, nor to eat luxurious foods prepared by one's own cooks. Everyone was required to contribute a certain sum of money, once each month, for the food at the common meals, and he received his meals from the state in return. Fifteen persons usually ate together at one table, and each guest had to be accepted by his companions to be permitted to eat at the common meal. No one was permitted to remain absent without a valid excuse; this part of the decree was upheld so strictly, that Aegis himself, one of the later kings, upon returning from a war gloriously waged, was denied permission by the ephors, when he asked to eat with his wife alone at home. Among the Spartan meals, the black soup became famous—a meal in praise of which it is said, that the Spartans had to be courageous, for dying was hardly a worse fate than eating their black soup. They spiced their meals with merriment and humor, and Lycurgus himself was so great a friend of social humor, that he placed an altar to the god of laughter in his house.

Lycurgus gained much for his purpose by introducing these social meals. All luxurious delicacies at the dinner table ceased, because there was no use for them at a public meal. Gluttony was halted completely, healthy and strong bodies were the result of this moderation and order, and healthy fathers were fit to produce strong progeny for the state. The social meals accustomed the citizens to live with each other, and to look upon themselves as members of the same state institution, not to speak of the fact, that such *equality* in the manner of life necessarily exerted influence upon the same emotions.

Another law decreed, that no house be permitted to have a roof other than such as had been produced with an axe, and no doors other than such as produced only with aid of a saw. In such a bad house, no one was even capable of conceiving of purchases of expensive furniture, everything had to form an harmonic whole.

Lycurgus understood quite well, that it was not enough to fashion laws for his fellow citizens, he would also need to fashion citizens for these laws. It was in the souls of his Spartans, that he would have to anchor his constitution for eternity, in *these* he would have to kill the susceptibility to foreign influences.

The most important part of his legislation, therefore, was the provisions made for education, and with these he closed the circle, within which the Spartan state was intended to revolve. Education was an important work of the state, and the state a lasting work of this education.

His concern for children reached as far as their very reproduction. The bodies of virgins were hardened by exercise, to enable them to bear strong and healthy children. They even went naked, in order to withstand all inclement weather conditions. The groom had to kidnap his wife, and was allowed to visit her only at night, and only if he had kidnapped her. That meant, that for the first years of marriage, the two remained strangers to one another, and their love remained new and vital.

All jealousy was banned from the institution of marriage itself. Everything, even modesty, the legislator subordinated to his chief aims. He sacrificed the loyalty of the wife to gain healthy children for the state.

As soon as the child was born, it belonged to the state. It was examined by the eldest; if it were strong and well formed, it was given over to a nurse; if it were weak and malformed, it was thrown into an abyss at the Taygetus mountain.

Spartan nurses were famous throughout Greece for the hard education they gave the children, and were even called into foreign countries. As soon as a boy had reached his seventh year, he was taken from his nurse, and educated, fed, and cared for in common with other children of his age. He was trained to spite all hardships, and to achieve mastery of his limbs through physical training. Once they had reached the age of young men, the oldest among them had hopes of finding *friends* among the adults, who were bound to them through love. The elders were present at their games, observed their blossoming genius, and encouraged their thirst for glory by praise or criticism. If they wanted to eat themselves full, the children had to steal food, and hard punishment and shame awaited whomever was caught. Lycurgus chose this means to accustom them, from an early age, to deceits and intrigues, qualities he believed as important for the warlike purpose to which he trained them, as bodily strength and courage. We have already seen above, how unscrupulous Lycurgus was as concerns morality, when the achievement of his political purpose was at issue. And one must consider, that neither the profanation of marriage, nor this command to steal, could cause the same *political* damage in Sparta, which was the consequence of such practices in every other state. Since the state took over the education of the children, it was independent of happiness and purity in marriage; since in Sparta so little value was placed upon property, and nearly all earthly goods were possessed in common, so the security of property was not a very important point, and an attack upon it—particularly when the state itself controlled it and attained its own intentions thereby—did not constitute a civil offense.

It was forbidden to young Spartans to adorn themselves, except when they went into battle or some other great danger. Then they were allowed to do up their hair, adorn their clothes, and carry decorations on their weapons. Hair, said Lycurgus, made beautiful people more beautiful, and ugly people fearsome. It was certainly a fine trick of the legislator to connect something humorous and festive with matters of danger, to take from the people the sense of fear. He went yet further. In war, he relaxed the strict discipline somewhat, the lifestyle became freer, and offenses were less severely punished. Thus it was, that war alone was a form of recreation to the Spartans, and they took joy in war as if in a festive occasion. As the enemy approached, the Spartan king ordered the Catorian chant sung, soldiers formed in closed ranks, accompanied by flutes, and marched joyfully and fearlessly into danger to the sound of the music.

Lycurgus's plan also entailed, that attachment to property was supplanted by attachment to the fatherland, and that emotions, undiverted by any private concerns, only lived for the state. Thus, he thought it good and necessary, to also spare his fellow citizens the business of normal life, and to let these affairs be attended to by foreigners, so that not even concerns of work, nor the joy of domestic matters, would divert their attentions from the affairs of the fatherland. The farmland and the homes were, therefore, cared for by slaves, who were respected in Sparta as much as cattle. They were called helots, because the first of the Spartans' slaves had been inhabitants of the island of Helos in Laconia, whom the Spartans had subdued in war, and made their prisoners. It was from these helots, that all later Spartan slaves, whom the Spartans exploited in their wars, took their names.

The use the Spartans made of these unfortunates was an abomination. They were looked upon as tools, of which one might make use to accomplish one's own political aims, and humanity in them was derided in outrageous ways. To provide Spartan youth deterrent examples of intemperance in drinking, the helots were forced to become drunk, and they were displayed in this condition publicly. They were ordered to sing obscene songs, and to dance ludicrous dances; they were forbidden to dance the dances of the free-born. They were used to even more inhuman ends. The state was intent upon putting the courage of its youth to severe tests, thus preparing them for war through these bloody games. Thus, at certain times, the senate sent a number of these youth into the country; they were permitted to take nothing but a knife and some food with them on their travels. They were required to remain hidden in the daytime; but, at night, they took to the streets, and beat to death any helots who fell into their hands. This procedure was called the cryptia, or ambush, but whether Lycurgus was its originator still lies in doubt. At least, it was consistent with his principles. As the republic of Sparta was successful in war, the number of helots also increased, so that they became dangerous to the republic itself, and, indeed, brought to desperation by such barbaric treatment, incited insurrection. The senate passed an inhuman resolution, which it believed pardoned by necessity. Once, during the Peloponnesian War, under the pretext of granting their freedom, two thousand of the most valiant helots were as-sembled, and, adorned with wreaths, led into the temple in ceremonious procession. But here they suddenly disap-peared, and no one ever learned what had happened to them. So much is certain, that the *Spartan slaves* were the most unfortunate among all other slaves, just as the free Spartan citizen was the most free of all citizens.

Since they were relieved of all their work by the helots, Spartans spent their lives in indolence; the youth trained in war games and skills, and the adults were the audience and judges of these exercises. It was shameful for an older Spartan man to stay away from the place where the youth were trained. And thus, each Spartan lived with the state, and all deeds became *public* deeds. The youth matured under the eyes of the nation, and blossomed into old age. Sparta was constantly in the mind's eye of each Spartan, and Sparta had him, too, constantly in its view. He was witness to everything, and everyone was witness to his life. The lust for glory became an incessant spur, ceaselessly feeding the national spirit; the *idea of fatherland* and *national interests* became intertwined with the innermost life of all of its citizens. Other occasions to unleash these lusts were the public festivals, and these were quite numerous in indolent Sparta. Warlike folksongs were sung, which usually told of those fallen in battle to the glory of the fatherland, or were encouragements to be courageous. They were sung by three choruses during such festivals, the choruses divided by age. The elders' chorus began to sing: "Before time began, we were heroes." The adult men sang: "We are heros now! Let him come, who would test us!" The third chorus of the boys then chimed in: "Heros we shall become, and our deeds shall cast yours into the shadows."

If we cast a fleeting glace at Lycurgus's legislation, we are indeed beset with a pleasant amazement. Among all similar institutions of antiquity, his legislation is incontestably the most accomplished, excepting Mosaic legislation, which it resembles in many features, and particularly in the principles upon which it is founded. Lycurgus's legislation is really complete in itself, everything is encompassed by it, every single thing is bound to every other, and everything is bound together by each single feature. Lycurgus could not have chosen better instruments to accomplish the purpose he had in mind, to create a state, isolated from all others, self-sufficient, and capable of sustaining itself through its internal metabolism and its own vital power. No legislator had ever given a state this unity, this national interest, this community spirit, which Lycurgus gave his state. And how did Lycurgus achieve this? By knowing how to direct the activity of his citizens in the state, and depriving them of all other paths, which might have distracted them from that end.

Everything which captivates the human soul and en-
flames passions, everything except political interests, he
banned by law. Wealth and desires, science and art, had no
access to the emotions of the Spartans. Comparisons of
fortunes, which enkindle in most people the desire for gain,
fell to the side, displaced by the equality of common poverty; the desire for property dropped away with the opportunity for displaying and employing it. By virtue of the lack
of knowledge in science and art, which clouded all minds in
Sparta in the same way, he spared Sparta the intervention,
which an enlightened mind had made in the constitution;
just this impoverishment of knowledge, combined with raw
national pride, characteristic of every Spartan, always stood
in the way of the Spartan's intercourse with other Greek
people. They were stamped as Spartans from the cradle,
and the more they came up against other nations, the more
they had to hold firm to their own. The fatherland was the
first theater presented to the view of a Spartan boy, from
the moment when he began to think. He awoke in the
womb of the state, and all that surrounded him was nation,
state, and fatherland. This was the first impression in his
mind, and his entire life was a perpetual renewal of this
impression.

At home, the Spartan found nothing which might fasci-
nate him; the legislator had deprived his eyes of all entice-
ments. Only in the womb of the state did he find employment, amusement, honor, reward; all his desires and
passions were directed to this central point. The state took
possession of all the energy, the powers of each of its individual citizens, and it was upon the spirit of community that
the community spirit of each individual enkindled itself.
Thus, it is no wonder, that Spartan national virtue ultimately
attained a degree of strength, which must seem inconceivable to us. And thus it was, that there could be no doubts
among the citizens concerning this republic, when the
choice was posed between self-preservation and saving the
fatherland.

And so we may understand, how the Spartan king Leonidas, with his 300 heroes, could merit the inscription on his tombstone, the most beautiful of its kind, and the most sublime monument to political virtue. "Tell, you travellers, when you are come to Sparta, that we obeyed its laws, and here are fallen."

Thus, one must concede, that nothing could be more purposeful, nothing more thought-out, than this state constitution, and that it represents an accomplished work of art of its own kind, and, followed through in its full rigor, one which necessarily rested upon itself alone. But were I to end my description here, I had committed a very serious mistake. This most remarkable constitution is contemptible to the highest degree, and nothing more sad could befall humanity, than that all states be founded on this model. It will not be difficult to convince ourselves of this assertion.

In respect of the purpose set for it, Lycurgus' legislation is a masterpiece, of statecraft and human-craft. He wanted a powerful state, founded upon itself, and indestructible; political strength and longevity were the aims for which he strove, and he achieved these aims, to the extent possible under the conditions he confronted. But if one compares the aims Lycurgus set himself with the aims of mankind, then profound disapproval must take the place of the admiration, which our first fleeting glance enticed from us. Everything may be sacrificed for the best of the state, but not that, which serves the state itself only as an instrument. The state itself is never the purpose, it is important only as the condition under which the purpose of mankind may be fulfilled, and this purpose of mankind is none other than the development of all the powers of people, i.e., progress. If the constitution of a state hinders the progress of the mind, it is contemptible and harmful, however well thought-out it may otherwise be, and however accomplished a work of its kind. Its longevity then serves the more to reproach it than to celebrate its glory—it is then merely a prolonged evil; the longer it exists, the more harmful it is.

In general, we can establish a rule for judging political institutions, that they are only good and laudable, to the extent, that they bring all forces inherent in persons to flourish, to the extent, that they promote the progress of culture, or at least not hinder it. This rule applies to religious laws as well as to political ones: both are contemptible if they constrain a power of the human mind, if they impose upon the mind any sort of stagnation. A law, for example, by which a nation were forced to persist in a certain scheme of belief, which at a particular time appeared to it most fitting, such a law were an assault against mankind, and laudable intents of whatever kind were then incapable of justifying it. It were immediately directed against the highest Good, against the highest purpose of society.

Armed with this standard, we shall not long be in a quandary about how we shall judge Lycurgus's state. One single virtue, displacing all others, was exercised in Sparta: love of fatherland.

It was to this artificial impulse, that the most natural and the most beautiful emotions of mankind were sacrificed.

Political merit was sought at the expense of all moral emotions, and the capacity to attain this political merit was the only capability inculcated. In Sparta there was no marital love, no mother's love, no child's love, no friendship—there were nothing but citizens, and nothing but the virtue of citizens. Spartan mothers were admired, who, in annoyance, shunned their sons returning from battle, mothers who then hurried into the temple to thank the gods for those fallen in battle. One would hardly wish such unnatural strength of mind upon mankind. A tender mother is a far more beautiful phenomenon in the moral world than an heroic, hermaphroditic creature, which spurns natural emotions to fulfill an artificial duty.

What more beautiful theater is there, than that of the rough warrior Gaius Marius in his encampment at the gates of Rome, who sacrifices vengeance and victory because he cannot bear to see his mother's tears flow!

Since the state became the father of children, the natural father ceased to be it. The child never learned to love its mother, its father, because it was torn from them at the most tender age, and never knew its parents by their care for him, but only by hearsay.

Universal human emotions were smothered in Sparta in a way yet more outrageous, and the soul of all duties, respect for the species, was irrevocably lost. A law made it a duty of the Spartans to treat their slaves inhumanly, and in these unfortunate victims of butchery, humanity was cursed and abused. The Spartan Book of Laws itself preached the dangerous principle, that people be considered as means, not as ends—the foundations of natural law and morality were thereby torn asunder, by law. Morality was utterly sacrificed to obtain something, which can only be valuable as a means to this morality.

Can anything be more contradictory, and can any contradiction have more grievous consequences than this? Not enough, that Lycurgus founded his state on the ruin of morality; in an entirely different way, too, he worked against the highest purpose of humanity, in that, through his well thought-out system of state, he held the minds of the Spartans fast at the level where he had found them, and hemmed in all progress for eternity.

All industry was banned, all science neglected, all trade with foreign peoples forbidden, everything foreign was excluded. All channels were thereby closed, through which his nation might have obtained more enlightened ideas, for the Spartan state was intended to revolve solely around itself, in perpetual uniformity, in a sad egoism.

The business of all its citizens together, was to maintain what they possessed, and to remain as they were, not to obtain anything new, not to rise to a higher level. Unrelenting laws were to stand watch, that no innovation take grip upon the clockwork of the state, that the very progress of time change nothing in the form of the laws. To make this condition perpetual, it was necessary to hold the mind of the people at the level where they stood when the state was founded.

But we have seen, that progress of mind should be the purpose of the state.

Lycurgus's state could persist under but one condition, that the mind of the people stagnate, and he was thus only able to sustain his state by trespassing against the highest and only purpose of the state. Thus, what is cited in praise of Lycurgus, that Sparta would only flourish as long as it followed the letter of its laws, is the worst one might say about it. For the very reason, that it was not permitted to relinquish the old form of state which Lycurgus had given it, without exposing itself to its own destruction, that it had to remain what it was, that it had to stand where one single man had cast it, for that reason Sparta was an unhappy state—and its legislator could not have given it a sadder gift, than this renowned eternal longevity of a constitution, which so stood in the way of its true greatness and happiness.

If we take this together, the false glitter disappears, whereby a single outstanding feature of the Spartan state blinds an inexperienced eye: We see nothing more than a callow, imperfect attempt, the first exercise of the world at a young age, which still lacked experience and brighter insights to recognize the true relationship of things. As defective as this first attempt turned out, it will, and must, remain something noteworthy for a philosophical investigator of the history of man. It was ever a giant step of the human mind, to treat of a subject as a work of art, which up to now had been left to fortuitous consideration and passion. The first attempt in the most difficult of all arts was necessarily imperfect, but we treasure it still, because it was an attempt in the most important of all arts. Sculptors began to carve the pillars of Hermes before they rose up to the perfected form of an Antinuous, a Vatican Apollo; law-givers will exercise their attempts for yet a long time, until the happy balance of social forces ultimately comes forth to meet them of their own.

Stone suffers the work of the chisel patiently, and the strings struck by the musician answer him without resisting his finger.

It is only the legislator who works upon a material which is active and resistant of its own accord—human freedom. He can accomplish the ideal only imperfectly, however pure he may have designed it in his mind, but here the attempt alone is worthy of all praise, if it is undertaken in disinterested benevolence, and purposively accomplished.

## Solon

Solon's legislation in Athens was nearly the complete opposite of Lycurgus' in Sparta—and, since the two republics of Sparta and Athens play the major roles in Greek history, it is an attractive enterprise to compare their two state constitutions, and to weigh their defects and advantages against one another.

After the death of Codrus, the office of king was abolished in Athens, and its power transferred to an authority who bore the name of *archon,* who held the office *for life.* In a span of time of more than 300 years, *thirteen* such archons ruled in Athens, but history has preserved to us nothing noteworthy about the new republic over this span of time.

But the spirit of democracy, characteristic of the Athenians even in Homer's time, stirred once more at the close of this period. The lifelong duration of the archonate was an all too vivid image of the royal authority, and previous archons had perhaps abused this great and long-lasting power. The archon's time in office was thus reduced to *ten years*—an important step toward future freeom, since, by electing a new ruler every ten years, the people renewed

its act of sovereignty; every ten years it took back its bequeathed authority, then to relinquish it anew as it saw fit.
That served to keep fresh in memory, what the subjects of
hereditary monarchies ultimately forget entirely, that the
people are the source of supreme authority, that the prince
is but a creature of the nation.

For 300 years, the Athenian people had tolerated a
lifelong archon over itself, but it became tired of the ten-
year archons in only 70 years. This was quite natural, for
during this time, it had seven times elected an archon, thus
seven times had it been reminded of its sovereignty. The
spirit of *freedom*, therefore, stirred more lively, developed
more quickly, in the second period than in the first.

The seventh of the ten-year archons was also the last
of this kind. The people wanted to enjoy their supreme
authority every year, for they had experienced, that an
authority conferred for ten years, endured long enough to
be a temptation to abuse that authority. In the future, the
office of archon was to be held for one single year, at the
end of which new elections were held. Since even such a
brief duration of authority in the hands of one single person
comes quite close to a monarchy, the people attenuated this
authority, distributing it among nine archons, who governed simultaneously.

Three of these nine archons had privileges over the
other six. The first, called *archon eponymos*, chaired the
assembly, his name was entered in the public documents,
and the year was named after him. The second, called
*basileus* or *king*, was to watch over religious matters, and
to hold religious services; this was held over from earlier
times, when supervision of religious services had been an
essential prerogative of the office of the king. The third,
*polemarch*, was the commander in war. The six others bore
the name *thesmothes*, because they were to uphold the
constitution and the laws, and to interpret them.

The archons were elected from the most prominent
families, and it was only in later times, that persons from the
common people came into these offices. The constitution,

therefore, was closer to an *aristocracy* than to a people's
government, and so the people themselves ultimately
gained little from the changes.

The arrangement, that nine archons were elected anew
each year, had, in addition to its good side, preventing the
abuse of supreme authority, also a very bad side, and this
was, that it brought forth *factions* in the state. For now
there were *many citizens* in the state, who had exercised
supreme authority and relinquished it. Having given up
their office, they would not so easily lay aside their taste for
this office, nor for their initial enjoyment in ruling. So they
decided to again become what they had once been, secured
a following, and incited domestic storms in the republic.
The quick alteration and the large number of archons, *furthermore*, encouraged every reputable and rich Athenian
to seek to become archons, a hope which he had hardly
entertained, if at all, had only *one* person assumed this
office, one who would not be replaced so soon. So both,
those who had already been archons, as well as those who
yearned to become archon, became equally dangerous to
the public order.

The worst of it all was, that the authoritative power had
been broken by its distribution among many persons, and
being of such short duration. So, a strong hand was lacking
to restrain the factions, and to rein in the insurrectionary
heads. Powerful and audacious citizens threw the state into
confusion and strove for independence.

Eyes ultimately fell upon an irreproachable and generally feared citizen to bring this disorder under control, one
to whom powers were granted to improve the laws, which
up to that time consisted but in defective traditions. Draco
was this feared citizen—a man bereft of human sentiments,
who believed human nature capable of nothing good, who
saw all deeds but in the dark mirror of his own cheerless
soul, and was utterly lacking in indulgence for the weaknesses of humanity; a bad philosopher, and an even worse
judge of man, with a cold heart, a narrow mind, and unwa-
vering in his prejudices. Such a man was excellently suited

to *implement* laws, but to *give* laws, a worse choice were hardly possible.

Little of Draco's laws has been left to us, but this little describes to us the man, and the spirit of his legislation. All crimes, without distinction, he punished with death, indolence as well as murder, theft of charcoal or a sheep, high treason and arson. When he was asked, why he punished the lesser offenses as severely as the most grievous crimes, he answered: "The smallest of crimes are deserving of death; for the greater crimes, I know of no other punishment than death—so I treat both equally."

Draco's laws are the attempt of a novice in the art of governing men. *Fear* is the only instrument, through which they take effect. He only punishes an offense committed, he does not prevent it; he takes no care to close off the sources of offense, and to improve people. To snuff out the life of a man because he has committed an evil act, is as much as to cut down a tree because its fruit is foul.

His laws are doubly contemptible, because they have not only the sacred sentiments and rights of man against them, but also because they were not framed for the people *to whom* they were given. Were any people in the world unlikely to flourish under such laws, the Athenian people certainly were. The slaves of the pharaohs or of the king of kings might eventually have settled with them—but how could Athenians bow under such a yoke?

And they remained in force hardly a half century, although he had given them the immodest title of *immutable laws*.

Draco thus fulfilled his mission very badly, and instead of being useful, his laws only caused *damage*. Since they could not be obeyed, and there were as yet no others to put in their stead, it was as if Athens had no laws at all, and anarchy most sad tore in upon them.

The condition of the Athenian people at that time was lamentable in the extreme. *One* class of people possessed everything, the *other*, on the other hand, nothing at all; the rich mercilessly repressed and exploited the poor. An impenetrable wall grew between them. Distress forced the poor citizens to flee to the rich for relief, to the very leeches who had drained them; at their hands, they found but gruesome relief. For the sums they borrowed, they had to pay immense interest, and if they did not pay on time, they were forced to sell even their lands to their creditors. When they had nothing more to give, and yet had to live, they were forced to sell their own children as slaves, and finally, when this recourse, too, was exhausted, they took credit, secured on their own persons, and had to accept being sold by their creditors as slaves. There was as yet no law in Attica against this abominable slave-trade, and nothing held the gruesome greed of the rich citizens in check. So horrible were conditions in Athens. Were the state not to be destroyed, this disrupted balance of goods would have to be reestablished by violent means.

To this end, three factions had emerged among the people. The one, which the poor citizens particularly joined, demanded a *democracy*, an equal distribution of farmland, as Lycurgus had introduced in Sparta; the other faction, consisting of the rich citizens, argued for aristocracy.

The *third* faction wanted to see the two forms of state combined, and opposed the other two factions, so that no one faction won out.

There was no hope of settling this strife calmly, as long as no one was found to whom all three parties would submit, and whose mediation over them they would acknowledge.

Fortunately, such a man was found, and his services on behalf of the republic, his gentle and reasonable character, and the renown of his wisdom, had for a long time drawn the eyes of the nation to him. This man was Solon, of royal lineage as Lycurgus, for he counted Codrus among his forebears. Solon's father had been a very rich man, but had reduced his wealth through charity, and the young Solon had to become a merchant in his younger years. His spirit was enriched by the travels which this kind of life made necessary, and by intercourse with foreign peoples, and his genius developed in acquaintance with the wise men of foreign countries. Very early he devoted himself to the poet's art, and the skill he achieved in it served him well in later life, in cloaking moral truths and political rules in these pleasing robes. His heart was sensitive to joy and love; certain weaknesses in his youth made him the more considerate toward mankind, and lent his laws the character of gentleness and tenderness, which so beautifully distinguish them from the laws of Draco and Lycurgus. He had also been a valiant commander, had captured the island of Salamis for the republic, and performed other important deeds of war. At that time, the study of wisdom was not yet separated from its political and military effects, as it now is; the wise man was the best statesman, the most experienced soldier, his wisdom flowed into all business of public life. Solon's reputation resounded throughout Greece, and he enjoyed great influence in the general affairs of the Peloponnese.

Solon was the man who was equally esteemed by all the parties in Athens. The rich placed great hopes in him, for he was himself a man of wealth. The poor trusted him, because he was a righteous man. The judicious among the Athenians wanted him to be their *ruler*, because monarchy seemed the best means to suppress the factions; his relatives wished this also, but for selfish reasons, to share the rule with him. Solon rejected this advice: *Monarchy*, he said, *was a beautiful house to live in, but there was no exit from it.*

He contented himself with being named *archon* and law-giver, and assumed this office *reluctantly*, and only out of concern for the welfare of the citizens.

The first act, with which he began his work, was the famous edict, called *seisachtheia* or *the release*, whereby all debts were annulled, and it was forbidden at the same time, that in the future anyone be permitted to borrow on his own person. This edict was naturally a violent assault upon property, but the most urgent need of the state made a violent step necessary. It was the lesser of two evils, for the class of people which suffered from it was far smaller than those whom it made happy.

By this beneficent edict, he did away at once with the heavy burdens which had pressed down the poor class for centuries; but the rich did not become poor as a consequence, for he left them everything they had, and only took from them the means to be unjust. Nevertheless, from the poor he harvested as little gratitude as from the rich. The poor had expected a fully equal distribution of the land, for which Sparta was the example, and therefore grumbled against him, that he had betrayed their hopes. They forgot, that the law-giver owed *justice* to the rich, as to the poor, and that the arrangement of Lycurgus was unworthy of imitation, just for the reason that it was founded upon an injustice, which had been avoidable.

The ingratitude of the people forced a modest complaint from the law-giver: "Formerly," he said, "praise welled at me from all sides; now everyone looks upon me with hostile glances." Soon, however, the salutary effects of his edict began to manifest themselves. The land, previously worked by slaves, was now free, the citizen worked the land as his own property, which he had previously worked for his creditor. Many Athenians, sold into foreign countries, who had already begun to forget their mother tongue, saw their fatherland once again as free men.

Confidence was reestablished in the law-giver. He was commissioned with the entire reform of the state, and had unlimited authority to dispose of the property and rights of the citizens. The first use which he made of his powers was to abolish all of Draco's laws—except those against murder and the breach of marriage.

Now he undertook the great work of giving the republic a new constitution.

All Athenians had to submit to a census of their fortunes, and after the census they were divided into four classes, or guilds.

The first was comprised of those who had an annual income of 500 measures of dry and fluid goods.

The second consisted of those who had an income of 300 measures of these goods, and a horse.

The third were those who only had half as much, and where two fortunes had to be combined to make up this sum. They were therefore called the two-teamed.

In the fourth class were those, who owned no land and lived only from their craftwork: craftsmen, wage-earners, and artists.

The first three classes could assume public offices; those from the last class were excluded from public office, but had one vote in the *national assembly* as all the others, and, for that reason alone, had a large share in the government. All major issues were brought before the *national assembly,* called the *ecclesia,* and also decided by this assembly: the election of magistrates, assignments to offices, important affairs in law, financial affairs, war, and peace. Since, furthermore, Solon's laws were afflicted with a certain obscurity, in each case where a judge was in doubt about the interpretation of the law, appeal had to be made to the ecclesia, which made the final decision about how the law was to be understood. The appeal to the people could be made from all tribunals. No one was allowed into the national assembly before the age of thirty years, but as soon as someone had reached the required age, he could not absent himself from the assembly without incurring punishment, for Solon hated and fought against nothing more than indifference to the commonweal.

In this way, the constitution of Athens was transformed into a complete democracy; in the strict sense, the people was *sovereign,* and it ruled not merely through representatives, but in its *own* person and by *itself.*

But soon the disadvantageous consequences of this arrangement became evident. The people had become powerful too soon to wield this privilege with moderation, passion mingled in the public assembly, and the tumult, which such a large number of people excited, did not always permit mature deliberation and wise decision. To obviate this defect, Solon created a senate, into which were taken 100 members from each of the four guilds. This senate had to deliberate previously on the issues, which were to be laid before the ecclesia. Nothing, which had not previously been taken into consideration by the senate, was permitted to be taken before the people, but the people alone decided. Once an issue had been *presented* to the people by the senate, then the *speakers* rose to influence their decision. This class of people attained to great importance in Athens, and did as much damage to the republic by the abuse they made of their art, and of the easily swayed minds of the Athenians, as they might have contributed, if, free of private ambitions, they had had the *true* interests of the state always in mind. The speakers summoned up all the contrivances of eloquence to make the side of an issue appear best to the people, which they most favored themselves; and, if a speaker were a master of his art, all hearts were in his hands. The people were laid in gentle and permitted chains by these speakers, and their rule was no less, by virtue of their leaving something to the decision of a free vote. The people retained the full freedom to elect or reject, but, by the art employed to present issues to the people, its freedom was controlled. A most excellent arrangement, if the *function* of the speakers had always remained in pure and loyal hands. But soon these speakers became sophists, who staked their fame on making the bad appear good, and the good, bad. In the center of Athens, there was a large public square, surrounded by statues of the gods and heroes, called the *prytaneum*. The senate met on this square, and for that reason the senators were called *prytanes*. The prytanes were required to lead irreproachable lives. No spendthrift, no one who had treated his father irreverently, no one who had become *drunk* even once, might even conceive of seeking this office.

As the population of Athens increased, and instead of the four guilds, which Solon had introduced, ten were established, the number of prytanes was increased from 400 to 1,000. But of these 1,000 prytanes, only 500 were active in a given year, and even these 500, never all at once. Fifty of them governed for five weeks, such that, in any given week, only ten were in office. Thus, it was entirely impossible to

make decisions arbitrarily, for each of the prytanes had as
many witnesses and custodians of his actions as he had fellow
officials, and the successor was always able to criticize the
administration of his predecessor. Every five weeks, four
popular assemblies were held, not counting the extraordinary sessions, an arrangement; which made it entirely impossible, that an issue remained long undecided, and the
process of business delayed.

In addition to the senate of prytanes, which he newly
created, Solon also reestablished the authority of the *areopagus*, which Draco had degraded. He made it the supreme
keeper and guardian spirit of the laws, and tied the republic
to these two courts, as Plutarch says, the *senate* and the
areopagus, as to two anchors.

The two courts were established to guard over the *pres-
ervation* of the state and its laws. Ten other tribunals took
care of the application of the laws, the execution of justice.
There were four courts dealing with murder cases, the
palladium, the delphinium, the phreattys, and the heliá.
The existence of the first two, Solon only *confirmed*, for
they had already been established under the kings. Unpremeditated murders were judged before the palladium. The
phreattys court was called upon to speak judgment over
those accused of *premeditated* murder, after they had already fled the country on account of an *unpremeditated*
murder. The defendant appeared on a ship, and his judges
stood on the shore. If the defendant was innocent, he returned to his place of exile, in the joyous hope of returning
home one day. If he was found guilty, he returned into exile
unharmed, but he had lost his fatherland forever.

The fourth criminal court was the heliá, which took its
name from the sun, because it usually convened just after
sunrise, and at a place where the sun shone. The heliá was
an extraordinary tribunal of the other great tribunals; its
members were at once judges and magistrates. It existed
not only to apply and execute laws, but also to improve
them and interpret them. Its assembly was ceremonious,

and a gruesome oath bound its members to uphold the truth.

As soon as a death sentence was spoken, and the defendant had not chosen to escape it by voluntarily going into exile, he was handed over to the *eleven men*; this was the name of the commission, to which each of the ten guilds delegated one man; these ten, together with the executioner, made eleven. These eleven men were the guardians of the prison, and carried out the death sentence. The forms of death conceived for criminals in Athens were of three kinds: either the criminal was thrown into a gorge, or into the sea, or he was executed with a sword, or he was given hemlock to drink.

Before the death penalty, there came banishment. This punishment is horrible in happy countries; there are states, where it is no misfortune to be banished. That *banishment* came before the death penalty, and, if it were forever, it was equivalent to death, is a beautiful testimony to the self-conception of the Athenian people. The Athenian who lost his country, was unable to find another Athens anywhere the world over.

Banishment also entailed the confiscation of all property, except in the case of ostracism.

Citizens who, either on account of particular merit or of fortune, had attained to greater influence and reputation than compatible with republican equality, were temporarily banished—*before they had deserved it*. To save the state, one was unjust toward individual citizens. The idea behind this custom, is laudable in itself, but the means chosen manifests a childish policy. This form of banishment was called *ostracism*, because the vote was made on shards of pottery. Six thousand votes were necessary to impose this punishment upon a citizen. Ostracism, by its nature, necessarily affected the meritorious citizen, and therefore *honored* him more than it shamed him—but it was no less unjust on that account, and gruesome, for it deprived him, who was most worthy, of what was dearest to him, his homeland. A fourth kind of punishment of criminal offenses was the punishment of the pillars. The criminal's guilt was written upon a pillar, and this dishonored him and his entire family.

Six tribunals existed to decide lesser civil offenses, but they never became important, because those convicted could always appeal to the higher courts and to the ecclesia. Everyone represented his own case (women, children, and slaves excepted). A water-clock determined the length of his and his accuser's arguments. The most important of these civil offenses had to be decided within twenty-four hours.

So much for the civil and political institutions of Solon, but the legislator did not limit himself to these alone. The advantage the ancient legislators had over more recent ones, is that they framed their laws for the people who would be governed by them, that they also took account of the character of social relationships, and never severed the citizen from the human being, as we do. Among us, it is not seldom, that the laws are in direct contradiction to morality. Among the ancients, laws and morality stood in a more beautiful harmony. *Their* body politic, therefore, had a warmth of vitality, which ours lacks; the state was inscribed in the souls of its citizens with indestructible strokes.

One must, however, be very cautious in praise of antiquity. One may generally say, that the *intentions* of the ancient legislators were wise and laudable, but that they were *in want* of means. The means applied often manifested wrong ideas, and a biased form of conception. Where we remain too far *behind*, they hastened too far *forward*. If our legislators have been wrong to entirely neglect moral duties and morality, the Greek legislators were wrong, in that they enjoined moral duties with the force of law. The first condition for the moral beauty of deeds is freedom of will, and this freedom is gone, as soon as one wants to enforce moral virtue by punishment under law. The most noble privilege of human nature is to decide for itself, and do what is good for the sake of the good. No civil law may *command*

loyalty toward friends, generosity toward the enemy, gratitude to *father and mother*, for as soon as it does so, a free
moral sentiment becomes a work of fear, a slavish impulse.

But, once more we return to our Solon.

One of Solon's laws decrees, that every citizen consider
an insult against another person to be directed at himself,
and that he shall not rest until the insult has been avenged.
The law is an excellent one, considering Solon's intent. His
intent was to imbue the citizen with a warm sympathy for
all others, and to accustom all together to look upon each
other as members of a cohesive whole. How pleasantly
surprised we would be, if we came into a country, where
every passerby, uncalled for, stood to protect us against
someone who had insulted us. But much of our pleasure
were lost, were we told at the same time, that our protector
had been *compelled* to act so beautifully.

Another law which Solon enacted, declared anyone
*without honor*, if he remained neutral in an insurrection.
This law, too, was based upon an unmistakably *good* intention. The legislator's concern was to instill in the citizens
the most ardent interest in the state. To him, indifference
toward the fatherland was the most hateful quality of his
citizens. Neutrality can often be the consequence of this
indifference; but he forgot, that the most fervent interest in
the fatherland often compels one to *neutrality—for example,* when both sides are in the wrong, and the fatherland
would lose as much by either side. Another of Solon's laws
forbids speaking ill of the dead; another prohibits speaking
ill of a living person in public places, in court, in a temple,
or in the theater. Solon releases a bastard from filial responsibilities, for the father, he says, has been paid enough by
the sensuous lust he enjoyed; he likewise frees the son of
the responsibility for feeding his father, if the latter had not
permitted the son to learn an art. He permitted testaments
to be made, and properties given away as the person *chose,*
since friends whom one chooses, he said, are worth more
than mere relatives. He abolished *dowries,* because he
wanted love, and not selfishness, to be the reason for mar-

riages. Yet another fine touch of tenderness in his character, is that he gave milder names to hated things. Taxes were called contributions, military garrisons were guardians of the city, prisons were chambers, and the cancellation of debts was the release. Luxury, which the Athenian enjoyed so much, he moderated by wise decrees: Strict laws guarded over the morality of women, over the relations between the two sexes, and the sanctity of marriage.

These laws, he decreed, should be in force only for 100 years—how much further he saw than Lycurgus! He understood, that laws are but servants of education, that nations in their adulthood require a different guide than in their *childhood*. Lycurgus perpetuated the childhood of the minds of the Spartans, thereby to perpetuate his laws among them, but his state disappeared with its laws. Solon, on the other hand, expected his laws to last only 100 years, and many of them are still in force to this day in Roman Law books. Time is a just judge of merit.

Solon has been accused of having given the people too much authority, and the accusation is not unfounded. By steering too far wide of one reef, oligarchy, he ran too close to another, *anarchy*—but yet, only too *close*, for the senate of prytanes and the court of areopagus were strong reins upon democratic authority. The evils, which are inseparable from a democracy, tumultuous and impassioned decisions, and the spirit of faction, were obviously unavoidable in Athens—but these evils are to be attributed more to the form which he chose, than to the essence of democracy. It was a severe mistake, that he let the people decide in person, rather than through *representatives*, which could not proceed without tumult and confusion, on account of the large number of people without wealth. Ostracism, for which at least 6,000 votes were required, allows us to glean how stormy such popular assemblies may have been. On the other hand, if one considers, how familiar even the most common Athenian was with the affairs of the commonweal, how powerfully patriotism worked in him, how much the legislator had taken care, that the fatherland was the most important thing to every citizen, one will obtain a better idea of the political understanding of the Athenian populace, and also beware of premature conclusions about *their* common people, judging by *our own*. All large assemblies always have a certain lawlessness in the consequence—but all *smaller* assemblies have trouble keeping themselves pure of *aristocratic despotism*. To hit a happy mean between the *two*, is the most difficult problem, which coming centuries shall have to solve. To me, the spirit remains admirable, with which Solon was inspired in his legislation, the spirit of *healthy* and *genuine* statecraft, which never lost sight of the fundamental principles, upon which all states must rest: to give unto oneself the laws which are to be obeyed, and to fulfill the responsibilities of the citizen out of insight, and out of love of the fatherland, not out of slavish fear of punishment, not out of blind and feeble submission to the will of a higher authority.

Beautiful and fitting it was of Solon, that he had respect for human nature, and *never sacrificed people to the state, never the end to the means*, rather let the state serve the people. His laws were loose bonds, in which the minds of the citizens moved freely and easily in all directions, and never perceived, that the bonds were directing them; the laws of Lycurgus were iron chains, in which bold courage chafed itself bloody, which pulled down the mind by their pressing weight. All possible paths were opened by the Athenian legislator to the genius and diligence of his citizens; the Spartan legislator walled off all of his citizens' potentials, except one: political service. Lycurgus decreed indolence by law, Solon punished it severely. In Athens, therefore, all virtues matured, industry and art flourished, the blessings of diligence abounded, all fields of knowledge were cultivated. Where in Sparta does one find a Socrates, a Thucydides, a Sophocles, and Plato? Sparta was capable of producing only rulers and warriors—no artists, no poets, no thinkers, no world-citizens. Both, Solon and Lycurgus, were great men, both were righteous men, but how different were their effects, since they proceeded from principles

diametrically opposed. The Athenian legislator is surrounded by freedom and joy, diligence and superfluity—
surrounded by all the arts and virtues, all the graces and
muses, who look up to him in gratitude, and call him father
and creator. About Lycurgus, one sees nothing but tyranny
and its horrible partner, slavery, which shakes its chains,
and flees the cause of its misery.

The character of an entire people is the most faithful
impression of its laws, and thus also the surest judge of its
value, or lack thereof. *Limited* was the mind of the Spartan,
and insensitive his heart. He was proud and haughty toward
his fellows, severe toward the vanquished, inhuman toward
his slaves, and slavish toward his superiors; in his transac-
tions, he was unscrupulous and faithless, despotic in his
decisions, and his greatness, even his virtue, lacked the
pleasing grace, which alone wins hearts. The Athenian,
quite the contrary, was gentle and tender of behavior, po-
litely intelligent in discussion, kind to inferiors, hospitable
and helpful to foreigners. He loved delicacies and finery,
but that did not prevent him from fighting like a lion in
battle. Clothed in purple, in scented oils, he brought
Xerxes' millions and the raw Spartans, alike, to tremble. He
loved the pleasures of the table, and only with difficulty
resisted the lures of lust, but gluttony and shameless behavior brought *dishonor* in Athens. Delicacy and decorum were
more practiced by no other people in antiquity than the
Athenians; in a war with Philip of Macedon, the Athenians
had captured a number of the king's letters, among them
also one to his wife: all others were opened, this one was
returned unopened. The Athenian was generous in fortune,
and steadfast in misfortune; it cost him nothing to dare
everything for the fatherland. He treated his slaves hu-
manely, and a mistreated slave was permitted to accuse the
tyrant in court. Even animals experienced the generosity of
this people: After the construction of the temple of Heca-
tonpedon was completed, it was decreed, that all beasts of
burden employed in the construction were to be freed, to
feed themselves at no cost for the rest of their lives upon

the best meadows. Later, one of these animals came to work of his own, and ran mechanically around the other animals. This sight so touched the Athenians, that they decreed special treatment in the future for this animal at the cost of the state.

I owe it to justice, however, not to remain silent about the defects of the Athenians, for history should not be a eulogy. This people, whom we admire for its fine morality, its gentleness, and its wisdom, not seldom sullied itself with the most shameless ingratitude toward its greatest men, and with cruelty toward its vanquished enemy. Corrupted by the flattery of its speakers, haughty in its freedom, and in vanity of so many brilliant advantages, it repressed its allies and neighbors often with unbearable pride, and let itself be guided in public deliberations by frivolous swindlers, who often destroyed the efforts of the wisest statesmen, and tore the state to the abyss of ruin. Every individual Athenian was tractable and impressible; but in public assembly, he was no longer the same person. Thus, Aristophanes describes his countrymen to us as reasonable old men at home, and as fools in the assemblies. Love of fame and thirst for novelty took hold of them to the point of excess; for fame, the Athenian would often risk all his earthly goods, his life, and not seldom . . . his virtue. A crown of olive branches, an inscription of a pillar proclaiming his merit, were to him more a spur to fiery deeds than all the treasures of the great king were to the Persian. As much as the Athenian people exaggerated its ingratitude, it was as excessive, in turn, in its gratitude. To be accompanied home in triumph from the assembly by such a people, to entertain it only for *one* day, was a higher pleasure to the Athenian thirst for fame, and a *truer* pleasure, too, than his most beloved slave can give to a monarch, for it is something quite different indeed to stir an utterly proud and tender people, than to please one *single* person. The Athenian had to be in incessant movement; ceaselessly, his mind snatched for new impressions, new pleasures. This addiction to novelty had to be fed each day anew, should it not turn against the state itself.

Thus, a theater play often salvaged public order threatened by riot—and by the same token, a usurper often had easy game of it, if he but sacrificed a series of amusements to this bent of the people. But, just for that reason, woe to the most meritorious of citizens, if he did not understand the art of being something new every day, to rejuvenate his merits.

The *evening* of Solon's life was not as cheerful as his life had deserved. To escape the obtrusiveness of the Athenians, who haunted him daily with questions and proposals, as soon as his laws came into effect, he travelled through Asia Minor, to the islands, and to Egypt, where he discussed with the wisest men of his time, and visited the royal court of Croesus in Lydia, and the court at Saïs in Egypt. The stories told of his meetings with Thales of Miletus and with Croesus, are too well known to repeat here. Upon his return to Athens, he found the state thrown into confusion by three factions, led by two dangerous men, Megacles and Pisistratus; Megacles made himself powerful and feared by his wealth, Pisistratus by his political shrewdness and genius. This Pisistratus, Solon's former favorite and the Julius Caesar of Athens, once appeared before the popular assembly, pale and stretched out on his wagon, covered with blood from a wound he had inflicted upon his own arm. "Thus," he said, "have my enemies mistreated me on your account. My life is in perpetual danger, if you do not take measures to protect it." Thereupon his friends proposed, as he had instructed them, that he should receive a bodyguard, who should accompany him whenever he went out in public. Solon surmised the fraudulent intent of this proposal, and set himself energetically, but in vain, against it. The proposal was accepted, Pisistratus received a bodyguard, and soon thereafter he was at its head, when the guard seized the citadel of Athens. Now the veil fell from the Athenians' eyes; but too late. Terror took hold of Athens; Megacles and his followers escaped from the city, and left it to the usurper. Solon, who alone had not been deceived, was now the only one who did not lose courage; as much trouble as he had taken to hold his citizens from their rashness when there was still time, as much he now took to revive their sinking courage. When no door opened to him, he went home, placed his weapons in front of his door, and called out: "Now I have done what I could for the best of the country." When his friends asked him, what made him so courageous to spite those more powerful, he answered: *"My old age gives me the courage."* He died, and his last glimpses saw his country not free.

But Athens had not fallen into the hands of a barbarian. Pisistratus was a noble person, and honored Solon's laws. Subsequently banished twice by his opponents, and twice again become master of the city, until he finally maintained his rule in calm, by his services on behalf of the city and his brilliant virtues, it was soon forgotten, that he was a usurper. Under him, no one noticed, that Athens was no longer free, so mild and gentle was his government, and it was not *he*, but Solon's laws, which ruled—Pisistratus opened the Golden Age of Athens; under him, the beautiful morning of Greek arts dawned. He died, mourned as a father.

His work begun was carried forward by his sons, Hipparch and Hippias. Both brothers governed in harmony, and the same love of science inspired both. Simonides and Anacreon flourished under him, and the Academy was founded. Everything hastened toward the magnificent age of Pericles.

*The*

# MISSION OF MOSES

## TRANSLATED BY GEORGE GREGORY

The founding of the Jewish nation by Moses is one of the most notable events preserved by history, important for the strength of understanding whereby it was accomplished, more important still for its consequences upon the world, which last up to this moment. Two religions which rule the largest part of the inhabitants of the Earth, Christianity and Islam, both depend upon the religion of the Hebrews, and without the latter there would never have been either a Christianity or a Koran.

Indeed, in a certain sense it is irrefutably true, that we owe to Mosaic religion a large part of the enlightenment, which we enjoy today. For through it, a precious truth, the which Reason, left unto itself, had only found after a long development—the teaching of the one God—was temporarily spread among the people, and sustained among them as the object of blind faith, until it had finally matured in brighter minds into a concept of Reason. Thus was a large part of humanity spared the sad and errant ways toward which belief in pantheism must ultimately lead, and the

This essay belongs in Schiller's series of lectures on Universal History from the summer of 1789 at Jena University. It was first published in *Thalia*, Schiller's journal of original poetry and philosophical writings, in 1790. One of Schiller's major sources for this essay was Br. Decius's work, *The Hebrew Mysteries, or, The Oldest Religious Freemasonry* (Leipzig: 1788).

Hebrew constitution obtained the exclusive advantage, that the religion of the wise men did not stand in direct contradiction to the popular religion, as still was the case among the enlightened heathens. Considered from this point of view, the nation of the Hebrews must appear to us as an important, universal historical people, and everything evil, which one is accustomed to impute to this people, all the efforts of facetious minds to belittle this achievement, shall not prevent us from doing it justice. The disgrace and depravity of a nation cannot efface the sublime merits of its legislators, and just as little annul the great influence to which this nation makes just claim in world history.

Like an impure and base vessel, yet within which something very precious is preserved, we must treasure it; we must do homage to that channel in it, which, as impure as it was, elected the prescience to guide us toward the most noble of all goods, the truth; the which truth, however, also destroyed, as soon as it had accomplished, what it had to do. In this way, we shall also not impose upon the Hebrew people a merit which it never had, nor deprive it of a merit to which its rightful claims cannot be contested.

The Hebrews came, as we know, as a single nomadic family of not over 70 souls, to Egypt, and first became a people in Egypt. During a span of time of approximately 400 years during which they resided in this land, they increased to nearly two million, among which were counted some 600,000 warlike men when they left this kingdom. During this long sojourn, they lived segregated from the Egyptians, segregated as well by their own place of residence, which they adopted, and by their nomadic condition, which made of them the abomination of the native people of the country, and excluded them from partaking of the civil rights of the Egyptians. They continued to govern themselves in the nomadic manner, the father of the house ruling over the family, the prince of the tribe ruling over the tribes, and thus constituted a kind of state within the state, which, on acount of its immense increase, ultimately aroused the concern of the kings.

Such a segregated mass of people in the heart of the kingdom, indolent by their lifestyle, who banded together quite closely, but who had no interest whatever in common with the state, might become dangerous if there were a hostile invasion, and might easily be tempted to exploit the weakness of the state, whose indolent spectators they were. The wisdom of the state thus counseled to guard them closely, to keep them occupied with activity, and to take thought to the reduction of their numbers. They were set to heavy labor, and as it was learned to make them useful to the state in this way, self-interest joined hands with policy, to increase their burdens. Inhumanly, they were compelled to slave, and special taskmasters were assigned to goad and mistreat them at their work. This barbaric treatment, however, did not prevent them from multiplying more rapidly. A healthy policy had naturally led to dispersing them among other inhabitants, and giving them equal rights with these; but the general abhorrence the Egyptians felt toward them stood in the way. This abhorrence was enhanced still more by the consequences it inevitably had. When the king of the Egyptians bestowed the province of Goshen (on the East side of the lower Nile) upon Jacob's family for them to inhabit, he hardly expected a progeny of two million then to house there; the province was thus probably of no considerable extent, and the gift was generous enough, although conceived for but a one-hundredth part of the future generation. Since the living space of the Hebrews did not increase at the same pace as their population, with each successive generation they were compelled to live ever more closely together, until they ultimately pressed together in the most narrow spaces in a way most disadvantageous to health. What was more natural than that just those consequences transpired which are inevitable in such cases?—the greatest squalor and infectious pestilence. This first set the stage for that misfortune which has been this nation's down to the present time; but back then, it ravaged to a frightful extent. The most horrible epidemic in this latitude, leprosy, tore in upon them, and became the heritage of generations to come. The sources of life and procreation were gradually poisoned by it, and from a fortuitous ill finally arose an hereditary tribal constitution. How general this disease was, can be gleaned from the number of precautions the legislator took against it; and the unanimous testimony of the chronicles of the Egyptian Manetho, of Diodorus of Sicily, of Tacitus, or Lysimachus, Strabo, and many others, who know nearly nothing else of the Jewish nation than this plague of leprosy, demonstrates how general and how deep was the Egyptians' impression of it.

Thus, leprosy, a natural consequence of their close quarters, poor and scanty nutrition, and the mistreatment to which they were subjected, became in turn a new cause of the same. They, who were at first despised as nomads and shunned as foreigners, were now avoided and cursed for their pollution. In addition to the fear and repugnance ever harbored against them in Egypt, there was joined a loathing and a deeply repulsive contempt. Against people so fearsomely branded with the wrath of the gods, everything was permitted, and there were no reservations against depriving them of the most sacred human rights.

No wonder, that the barbarism against them increased in just the degree, as the consequences of this barbarous treatment became more evident, and as they were punished more severely for the misery, which the Egyptians themselves had inflicted upon them.

The bad policy of the Egyptians knew of no other means to improve upon the errors they had made than to commit new and more heinous errors. Since, despite all the pressures they applied, they did not succeed in quelling the growth of the population, they fell upon a solution as inhuman as it was wretched, that of having newborn sons at once smothered by the midwives. But thanks be to the better nature of Man! Despots are not always well followed, when their commands are the commission of abominations. The midwives in Egypt knew well to scoff at this unnatural decree, and the government was left no other recourse than to implement its violent expedients by violent means. Hired assassins roamed by royal order through the homes of the Hebrews, and killed every male child in its cradle. In this way, the Egyptian government had surely accomplished its purpose, and were no savior to intervene, it had seen the nation of the Jews eradicated in a few generations.

But whence should this savior come to the Hebrews? Hardly from among the Egyptians themselves, for how should one of them intercede on behalf of a nation foreign to him, whose language was incomprehensible to him, which he would certainly take no trouble to learn, a nation which must seem to him as unworthy as incapable of a better fate? Even less from their own midst, for what had the inhumanity of the Egyptian in the course of some centuries finally made of the Hebrew people? The coarsest, the most malicious, the most despised people of the Earth, turned savage by three hundred years of neglect, made despondent and embittered by such long pressure of slavery, degraded in their own eyes by a congenital infamy, too unnerved and paralyzed for heroic resolutions, by such long-enduring stupidity cast down to be hardly more than animals. How, out of such a depraved race of people, should a free man rise forth, an enlightened mind, a hero, or a statesman? Where should there be found among them a man to bequeath respect to such a deeply despised and enslaved mob, a feeling of itself—to a people so long repressed, to such an ignorant, raw rabble of shepherds, superiority over its more refined repressor? From among the Hebrews of that time, it was as impossible for a bold and courageous mind to emerge, as from among the outcast pariahs among the Hindus.

Here the great hand of Providence, which looses the most intricate of knots with the simplest of means, overwhelms us with wonder—but not that providence, which intervenes in the forceful way of a miracle in the economy of nature; rather, that which has prescribed such economy to nature herself, effecting things most extraordinary in the calmest of ways. A born Egyptian lacked the challenge necessary to become a redeemer on behalf of the national interests of the Hebrews. A mere Hebrew had necessarily foundered upon such an enterprise, for lack of the force and mind required. Thus, what solution did fortune elect? It took a Hebrew, but prematurely tore him forth from his own coarse people, and let him partake of the enjoyment of Egyptian wisdom; and thus did a Hebrew, Egyptian-educated, become the instrument through which this nation escaped from slavery.

A Hebrew mother of the Levite tribe hid her newborn son three long months from its assassins, who did away with all the male fruit of the womb among her people; finally, she gave up hope of providing him sanctuary any longer. Need breathed into her a deception, whereby she hoped possibly to keep him. She laid her infant into a small basket of papyrus, which she had sealed from the water with pitch, and awaited the time when the Pharaoh's daughters usually bathed. Shortly before, the child's sisters laid the basket in which the child lay into the reeds, where the royal daughters would pass by and must notice the child. She herself, however, remained nearby, to await the further fate of the child. Indeed, the Pharaoh's daughter soon caught sight of the child, and, since the child pleased her, she decided to save him. Then did his sister dare approach, and offered to bring him a Hebrew nurse, to which the princess conceded. Thus for the second time did the mother receive her son, and was now permitted to educate him without danger. And it was thus that he learned the language of his nation, became familiar with its customs, and it is likely that his mother failed not to implant a moving impression of general misery in his tender soul. As he had reached the years when he no longer needed his mother's care, and as it became necessary to remove him from the general fate of his people, his mother brought him once again to the royal daughter, and now surrendered to *her* the boy's further fate. The Pharaoh's daughter adopted him and gave him the name Moses, for he had been saved from the water. Thus of a slave-child and sacrificial victim became the son of a daugh-ter of the king, and as such, partaking in all the advantages enjoyed by the children of kings. The priests, to whose order he belonged from just that moment when he was adopted into the royal family, now took over his education, and instructed him in all matters of Egyptian wisdom, which were the exclusive prerogative of their caste. It is likely indeed, that they withheld none of their secrets from him, for a passage from the Egyptian historian Manetho, in which he portrays Moses as an apostate of the Egyptian religion, and as a priest fled from Heliopolis, leads us to suspect, that he was appointed to the priestly caste.

In order to determine what Moses may have learned in this school, and what part the education he received among the Egyptian priests had in his later legislation, we must enter into a close investigation of this institution, and hear the testimony of ancient writers on that which was taught and practiced there. The Apostle Stephen himself tells us, that he was instructed in all the wisdom of the Egyptians. The historian Philo says, that Moses was initiated by the Egyptian priests in the philosophy of symbols and hieroglyphics, as well as in the mysteries of the sacred animals. This testimony is confirmed by numerous others, and if one once looks upon what were called the Egyptian mysteries, a remarkable similarity appears between these mysteries and what Moses later did and legislated.

The worship of the most ancient peoples, as we know, soon degenerated into polytheism and superstition, and even among those whom the Bible describes to us as worshippers of the true God, the ideas they had of the Supreme Being were neither pure nor noble, and based upon nothing more than an enlightened, reasonable insight. But as soon as the social classes were set apart by a better institution of civil society and by the foundation of an orderly state, and concern for sacred things having become the province of a special class; as soon as the human spirit was freed of concerns diverting its attentions, and obtained leisure to devote itself solely to considerations of itself and nature; and, finally, as soon as a clearer look had been cast into the physical economy of nature, then was Reason's victory over those

coarser errors assured, and the ideas about the Supreme
Being necessarily ennobled. The idea of a universal connection among things must lead necessarily to the conception
of a single, Supreme Understanding, and where else should
that idea have taken seed than in the mind of a priest? Since
Egypt was the first cultured state known to history, and the
most ancient mysteries originally come from Egypt, here
too it was, in all probability, that the idea of the unity of the
Supreme Being was first thought in a human mind. The
happy discoverer of this idea, which so elevates the soul,
now sought capable subjects among those around him, to
whom he imparted this idea as a sacred treasure, and so it
was passed down through the generations from one thinker
to another, through who knows how many generations, until
it finally became the possession of a very small community
capable of comprehending it, and further developing it.

But since a certain measure of knowledge and a certain
development of the mind is required to correctly comprehend the idea of one single God, and to employ it, since
belief in the Divine Unity necessarily carried with it a
contempt for polytheism, which was still the prevailing
religion, one soon understood, that it were imprudent, even
dangerous, to propagate this idea in public and generally.
Without having previously overthrown the traditional gods
of the state, and exhibiting them in their ludicrous destitution, one could not promise the new teaching acceptance.
But one could neither foresee, nor hope, that those to whom
one made the old superstitions ludicrous, would also at once
be capable of elevating themselves to the pure and difficult
idea of the True. Besides, the entirety of the civil constitution was founded upon that superstition; were this caused
to collapse, all the pillars supporting the entire edifice of
the state had collapsed at the same time, and it was still
quite uncertain, whether the new religion, conceived to
take its place, would also stand at once firm enough to carry
that edifice.

On the other hand, were the attempt to overthrow the
old gods to end in failure, one had but armed blind fanati-

cism against oneself, and abandoned oneself into the hands
of mad masses to be their sacrificial victim. It was therefore
thought far better to make this new and dangerous truth
the exclusive possession of a small, closed community, to
draw those who demonstrated the requisite measure of
power of comprehension out of the multitude, and to take
them up into the covenant, to cloak the truth itself, which
it was deemed desirable to withhold from impure eyes, in
a veil of secrecy, a veil only those might draw aside who
had been made so capable.

To that purpose were the hieroglyphics chosen, a speaking language of images, holding a general conception hidden
in a composition of sensuous symbols, and based upon some
arbitrary rules, which had been agreed upon. As these
enlightened men of idolatry knew well how strong the effects of imagination and the senses can be upon young
hearts, they had no reservations against the use of this
artifice of deception to the advantage of the truth. They
thus implanted the new ideas into the soul with a certain
sensuous ceremony, and by all sorts of contrivances suited
to this purpose, they set the emotions of their apprentice
into a state of passionate motion, intended to make the
apprentice receptive for the new truth. Of this kind were
the purifications the initiates had to undergo, the washing
and sprinkling, wrapping in linen clothing, abstinence from
all enjoyments of the senses, tension and elevation of the
emotions through song, a meaningful silence, alternations
between darkness and light, and other such practices.

These ceremonies, in connection with such mysterious
images and hieroglyphics and the hidden truths, which lay
enshrouded within these hieroglyphics, and prepared by
such uses, were known collectively under the name of the
mysteries. Their seat was the temple of Isis and Serapis,
and they were the model, according to which the mysteries
in Eleusis and Samothracia, and, in more recent times, of
the Order of the Freemasons, were formed.

It seems beyond any doubt, that the content of the
most ancient mysteries in Heliopolis and Memphis, in their

uncorrupted condition, was the oneness of God and the refutation of paganism, and that the immortality of the soul was also taught in them. Those who partook of these important elucidations called themselves onlookers, or *epopts*, because the recognition of a formerly hidden truth is comparable to stepping from darkness into the light, and possibly also for that reason, that they really and truly looked upon the newly recognized truths in the form of sensuous images.

But they could not attain to this vision all at once, because the mind first had to be purified of many errors, had to have gone first through many preparations, before it could bear to look upon the full light of truth. There were, thus, levels or degrees, and the shadows first fell fully from the eyes only in the innermost sanctuary.

The *epopts* knew one simple, Supreme Cause of all things, a first power of nature, the Being of all beings, which was identical to the *demiourgos* of the Greek wise men. Nothing is more sublime than the simple grandeur with which they spoke of the Creator of the world. In order to distinguish Him in a clearer way, they gave Him no name at all. "A name," they said, "is merely a requirement of differentiation; he who is alone has need of no name, for there is no other existence with which he might be confused." Under an old statue of Isis, one read the words: *"I am, what there is,"* and upon a pyramid in Saïs, one found the ancient and most remarkable inscription: "I am all, that is, that was, and that will be; no mortal hath lifted my veil." No one was permitted to step into the temple of Serapis, who did not bear the name Jao—or J-ha-ho, a name which sounds nearly the same as the Hebrew Jehovah—upon his breast or forehead; and no name was pronounced with more reverence in Egypt than this name Jao. In the hymn which the *hierophant*, or master priest of the temple, sang to those undergoing initiation, this was the first elucidation given of the nature of the divinity: "He is unique and becomes of himself, and to this uniqueness do all things owe their existence."

A preparatory, necessary ceremony prior to every initiation was circumcision, to which Pythagoras, too, had to submit before his acceptance into the Egyptian mysteries. This distinction from others who were not circumcised, was supposed to demonstrate a close brotherhood, a closer relationship to the divinity, and this is how Moses, also, used it later among the Hebrews.

Inside the temple, various sacred instruments were demonstrated to the initiates, instruments expressing a secret meaning. Among these were a sacred chest, called the coffin of Serapis, and which originally was probably supposed to be an expression of hidden wisdom; but later, when the institution was corrupted, it served the mystery-mongering and games of the wretched priests. It was a prerogative of the priests, or one of their own class of servants of the temple, who were called *kistophors,* to carry this chest around. No one except the *hierophants* was permitted to open this chest, or even to touch it. Of one, who was so presumptuous as to open the chest, it is told, that he suddenly became insane.

In the Egyptian mysteries, furthermore, certain hieroglyphic sacred images are found, consisting of composites of several animal forms. The well-known sphinx is of this kind; one intended in this way to denote the characteristics unified in the Supreme Being, or also to throw together the most powerful creatures among all living things into one body. Something was taken from the most powerful bird, the eagle, something from the most powerful of wild animals, the lion, from the most powerful of domesticated animals, the steer, and, finally, something from the most powerful of all animals, Man. The image of the steer or of Apis was particularly used as a symbol of strength, to denote the omnipotence of the Supreme Being; but in the original language the steer was called *cherub.*

These mystical forms, to which none but the *epopts* had the key, gave the mysteries themselves a sensuous outside, which deceived the people, and indeed, had much in common with idolatry. Thus, superstition received an everlasting nourishment through the external garment of the mysteries, whereas in the sanctuary itself one mocked it.

Yet it is perfectly understandable, how this pure deism could cohabitate with idolatry, for it overthrew idolatry from within, while promoting it from without. The excuse offered by the founders of this system for the contradiction between the religion of the priests and the people's religion, was necessity; it seemed the lesser of two evils, because there was more hope to constrain the evil consequences of the concealed truth, than the damaging effects of the untimely discovery of this truth. As with the passage of time, unworthy members penetrated the circles of the initiated, and as the institution lost its original purity, recourse was taken to what had at first been only expediency, the mysteries became the purpose of the institution, and instead of gradually cleansing superstition, and skillfully preparing the people to receive the truth, advantage was sought in ever greater deception of the people, casting it ever deeper into superstition. Priestly crafts now took the place of those innocent and more open intents, and just that institution which was supposed to receive, maintain, and cautiously spread knowledge of the true and one God, began to become the most powerful instrument for the promotion of the contrary, and to devolve into a true school of idolatry. *Hierophants,* in order not to lose their command over the emotions of their subjects, and to sustain expectations ever-tensed, thought it most fit to postpone the final elucidation of the mysteries ever longer, the which must disappoint all false expectations forever, and to make access to the sanctuary the more difficult, by all kinds of theatrical tricks. Ultimately, the key to the hieroglyphics and the mysterious figures was utterly lost, and these were now taken to be the truth itself, the which they had originally been designed merely to cloak.

It is difficult to ascertain, whether Moses' years of education fell in the time when the institution was flourishing, or at the beginning of its corruption; it is probable, however, that it was already approaching its decline, as a number

of playful tricks lead us to conclude, which the Hebrew
legislator borrowed, and also a number of notorious decep-
tions which he brought into practice. But the spirit of the
founders had not yet disappeared from the institution, and
the teaching of the unity of the Creator of the world still
rewarded the expectations of the initiated.

This teaching, which inevitably resulted in the most
thorough contempt for polytheism, and connected to the
teaching of immortality, hardly separable from it, was the
rich treasure the young Hebrew brought forth from the
mysteries of Isis. At the same time, he became better
acquainted with the forces of nature, which at that time
were also the object of secret sciences, and this knowledge
later enabled him to work miracles, and to challenge his
own teachers and magicians, whom he surpassed in some
exercises, even in the presence of the Pharaoh. His
subsequent course of life proves, that he had been an
astute and adept student, and had reached the last and
highest degrees.

In this school he also assembled a treasure store of
hieroglyphics, mystical images, and ceremonies, of which
his inventive mind subsequently made use. He had traversed the entire expanse of Egyptian wisdom, thought
through the entire system of the priests, weighed its defects
and advantages, its strengths and weaknesses, and also
gained important insights into the statecraft of this people.

It is not known how long he stayed in the school of the
priests, but his later steps upon the political stage, taken
only as he approached his eightieth year, make it likely,
that he devoted himself to the study of the mysteries and
the state for twenty years and more. His stay among the
priests, however, seems not to have kept him from intercourse with his people, and he had opportunity enough to
witness the inhumanity under which they suffered.

Egyptian education had not supplanted his national feelings. The mistreatment of his people reminded him, that
he, too, was a Hebrew, and a just bitterness dug itself
deeply into his breast as often as he saw his people suffer.

The more he began to feel himself, the more did the injustice against his own people outrage him.

Once he saw a Hebrew abused by the whip of an Egyptian taskmaster; this sight overwhelmed him; he killed the Egyptian. The deed soon becomes renowned, his life is in danger, he must leave Egypt and flee into the Arab desert. Many put this flight in his fortieth year, but without any proof. It is enough for us to know, that Moses could no longer have been very young when it occurred.

With this exile, a new epoch of his life begins, and if we are to correctly judge his later political emergence in Egypt, we must also accompany him through his solitude in Arabia. A bloody hate against the repressors of his nation, and all the knowledge he had gathered from the mysteries, he carried with him into the Arabian desert. His mind was full of ideas and plans, his heart full of bitterness, and nothing distracted him in this deserted wasteland.

The chronicles tell of his herding the sheep of an Arab Bedouin Jethro.—Such a descent from all his prospects and hopes in Egypt to sheepherding in Arabia! From a future ruler of men to the slave of a nomad! How deeply this must have wounded his soul!

In the robes of a shepherd, he carries along the fiery spirit of a regent, a restless ambition. Here in this romantic desert, where the present has nothing to offer him, he seeks recourse in the past and future, and confers with his silent thoughts. All the scenes of repression he had witnessed back then, now pass over him in memories, and nothing now prevents them from pressing their sharp barbs deeply into his soul. Nothing is more unbearable to his great soul than to tolerate injustice; moreover, it is his own people which is suffering. A noble pride awakens in his breast, and a powerful impulse, to act and put himself forward, accompanies this offended pride.

Everything he has gathered over long years, everything beautiful and great which he has thought and planned, all of this should die with him in this desert, everything thought and planned in vain? This thought his fiery soul cannot withstand. He raises himself above his fate; this wasteland shall not become the limit of his activity; for the supreme being he learned of in the mysteries has directed him toward something grand. His imagination, enflamed by solitude and stillness, grasps at what lies closest, takes party with the repressed. Like emotions seek their like, and he who is unfortunate must incline to the side of the unfortunate. In Egypt, he had become an Egyptian, an *hierophant*, a military leader; in Arabia, he becomes Hebrew. Grand and magnificent, it arises before his mind—the idea: "I will redeem this people."

But what possiblity is there to execute this plan? Unfathomable are the obstacles which impress themselves upon him, and those he must needs take on among his people themselves are by far the most horrible. He cannot take for granted concord or confidence, neither sense of self nor courage, neither a common spirit, nor an enthusiasm calling to bold deeds; long years of slavery, a 400 years' misery, have smothered all these emotions.—The people, at whose head he shall step, are as little capable as worthy of this hazardous venture. From this people itself he can expect nothing, and yet without this people he can accomplish nothing. What recourse remains to him? Before he undertakes the liberation of his people, he must begin to make it capable of this beneficent act. He must reinstate it in those human rights which it has cast off. He must reinstill all the qualities which long savagery has smothered; he must enflame it with hope, confidence, heroism, and enthusiasm.

But these emotions among his people can only base themselves upon a (true or deceptive) feeling of their own power, and whence shall slaves of the Egyptians take this feeling? Were he even successful for a moment in sweeping them away with his eloquence—will this artificial enthusiasm not leave them at the first sight of danger? Will they not become more despondent than ever, fall back into their feeling of slavery?

Here is where the Egyptian priest and statesman comes to the help of the Hebrew. From his mysteries, from his

priestly school at Heliopolis, he now recalls the effective
instruments, by which a small order of priests controlled
millions of cruder men according to its will. This instrument
is none other than the confidence in a supraterrestrial protection, belief in supranatural forces. Since in the visible
world, in the natural course of things, he finds nothing with
which he can give his repressed nation courage, since he
can bind his people's confidence to nothing earthly, he
binds it to heaven. Since he gives up hope of being able to
give his people a feeling of its own power, there is nothing
for him to do, but to proclaim to his people a God who has
these powers. If he succeeds in instilling his people with
confidence in this God, he will have made his people strong
and bold, and confidence in this higher arm is the flame,
which must make him succeed in enkindling all other virtues and powers. If, to his brothers, he can become the
legitimate organ and emissary of this God, they will become
a ball in his hands, he can lead them as he will. But now
the question: Which God shall he proclaim to them, and
whereby can he procure their faith in Him?

Shall he proclaim to them the true God, the Demiurge,
or Jao, in whom he himself believes, whom he has come to
know in the mysteries?

How could he entrust to an ignorant, enslaved rabble,
which his nation is, even the slightest comprehension of a
truth, which is the heritage of a few Egyptian wise men,
and which presumes a high degree of enlightenment, to be
comprehended? How could he flatter himself with hope,
that the outcasts of Egypt might understand something
grasped by only few among the best of this country?

But even if he succeeded in bringing knowledge of the
true God to the Hebrews—in their situation, they had no
need of this God, and knowledge of this God would rather
undermine his design than promote it. The true God concerns himself for the Hebrew people no more than any
other people.—The true God could not fight for them,
throw over the laws of Nature for their sake.—He let them

fight out their cause with the Egyptians, and interceded with no miracles in their conflict, and why should He?

Shall he proclaim to them a false and mythical god, against which his own Reason takes outrage, one such as the mysteries have caused him to hate? His mind is too enlightened for that, his heart too sincere and too noble. Upon a lie he will not found his beneficent undertaking. The enthusiasm, which now fills his soul, would not lend her beneficent fire to a fraud, and to such a contemptuous role, which so contradicts his innermost convictions, and thus had he been bereft of his courage, joy, and determination. He wants the benefaction he bestows upon his people to be perfect: He wants his people not merely independent and free. He wants to make his people happy, too, and enlightened. He wants to found his work for eternity.

Thus, not upon a fraud, but upon truth must his work be founded. But how shall he make these contradictions accord? The true God he cannot proclaim to the Hebrews, because they cannot grasp Him: a mythical god he does not want to proclaim, for this he despises. The only recourse remaining is to proclaim to them *his true God in a mythical way*.

Now he examines his religion of Reason, and investigates what he must add and take away from it, to assure it a favorable reception among the Hebrews. He descends into their situation, into their limitations, into their souls, and espies there the latent threads to which he will be able to bind his truth.

He bestows upon his God those qualities, which the powers of comprehension of the Hebrews and their present needs require of Him. He thus accommodates his Jao to the people to whom he will proclaim Him; he accomodates Him to the circumstances under which he will proclaim Him, and thus arises his Jehovah.

In the hearts of the people, he indeed finds belief in sacred things, but this belief has devolved into the crudest of superstition. He must extirpate this superstition, but he must maintain the belief. He must merely dissolve it from its present unworthy subject, and direct it toward his new divinity. Superstition itself provides him the instruments to accomplish this. According to the general delusion of the time, every people stood under the protection of a special national divinity, and it flattered the national pride to set this divinity above all other gods among the other peoples. The latter, however, were not denied their divinity; they were recognized to be gods, but they were not allowed to rise above the particular national god of one's own nation. To this error Moses tied his truth. He made the Demiurge of the mysteries into the national God of the Hebrews, but he went one step further.

He was not satisfied to make this national God the most powerful of all gods; rather, he made Him the only God, and cast all other gods around back into their nothingness. He gave his God to the Hebrews as their property, in order to comfort their imaginations, but he designed Him at once for all other peoples and all forces of nature. In the image in which he presented Him to the Hebrews, he salvaged the two most important characteristics of his own true God, unity and omnipotence, and made them the more effective in this human guise.

The vain and childish pride, that of wanting to exclusively possess the divinity, now had to do its work to the advantage of truth, and to assure the reception of his teaching of the one God. Clearly, it is only a new folly, that he overthrows the old one; but this new folly is much closer to the truth than that which it replaces; and it is alone this small addition of folly, which makes his truth become joyous, and everything he gains thereby, he owes to this foreseen misunderstanding of his teaching. What had his Hebrews been able to do with a philosophical God? With this national God, on the other hand, he must inevitably accomplish miraculous things among them.—Just consider the situation of the Hebrews. Ignorant, as they are, they measure the strength of the gods according to the happiness of the peoples under their protection. Forsaken and repressed by men, they believe themselves forsaken by all gods; just that relationship they themselves have toward the Egyptians, must their God, according to their conception, have toward the god of the Egyptians; the former is thus but a small light in comparison to the latter, or the Hebrews even begin to doubt, that they have a God at all. Then at once it is proclaimed to them, that they, too, have a protector in the firmament, and that this protector is awoken from his rest, that he is girding and arming himself, to accomplish great deeds against their enemies.

This revelation of God is now tantamount to the call of a general to march under his victorious flag. If this general also provides demonstrations of his strength, or if they still know him from times past, the deception of enthusiasm will incite even the most fearful; and of this, too, Moses took account in his design.

The discussion which he holds with the apparition in the burning thornbush, presents us the doubts which he has cast upon himself, and the way and means he has answered them. "Will my unhappy nation gain confidence in a God who so long neglected it, who now appears, all of a sudden, as if fallen out of heaven, whose name they never heard called—who was an idle contemplator for centuries of the mistreatment which it suffered? Will it not, on the contrary, consider the God of its happy enemy more powerful?" This was the next thought, which necessarily rose up in the new prophet. How shall he now alleviate these doubts? He makes his Jao into the God of their fathers, he connects Him to their old folk legends, and thus transforms Him into a domestic God, into an ancient and well-known God. But, in order to demonstrate, that the God he means is the true and only God among them, in order to avoid any confusion with any creature whatsoever of superstition, in order to leave no room for any misunderstanding, he gives Him the sacred name which He actually bears in the mysteries. "I

shall be, that I am become. Tell the people of Israel,"
Moses has Him say, "*I shall be,* who hath sent me unto
you."

In the mysteries, the divinity actually bears this name.
But this name must have been utterly incomprehensible
to the ignorant people of Hebrews. They were hardly
capable of conceiving what was meant, and Moses could
have had far more fortune with a different name; but he
wanted rather to subject himself to this inconvenience,
than to relinquish the idea most important to him, and
this was: to introduce to the Hebrews the true God taught
in the mysteries of Isis. Since it is fairly certain, that the
Egyptian mysteries flourished for a long time before
Jehovah appeared to Moses in the burning bush, it is
surely worth noting, that this apparition bears the very
same name, which it bore previously in the mysteries of
Isis.

But it was not yet sufficient, that Jehovah proclaim
Himself to the Hebrews as a God well-known to them,
as the God of their fathers; He also needed to legitimize
Himself as a powerful God, should they take Him into
their hearts; and this was all the more necessary, as their
fate in Egypt could not have given them a very grand
opinion of their protector. And since, furthermore, He
proclaimed Himself among them only through a third
person, He would have to invest this person with His
power, and make him capable of demonstrating his mission, as well as the power and greatness, by extraordinary
deeds, of Him who sent him.

Thus, were Moses to justify his mission, he must
support his mission by miraculous deeds. That he indeed
performed these miracles, there can be no doubt. How
he performed them, and how they are to be understood—
we leave to each to reflect upon for himself.

The story in which Moses cloaks his mission contains
everything necessary to imbue the Hebrews with faith in
it, and this was all that it was intended to do—among us,
the story need no longer have this effect. We now know,

for example, that it would be irrelevant to the Creator of the world, should He ever decide to appear before a human being in fire or wind, whether such a person appeared before Him barefoot, or not barefoot.—But Moses has his Jehovah command, that he should take his shoes from his feet, for he knew very well, that he had to assist his Hebrews to the conception of divine sanctity by means of some sensuous signs—and just such a sign he had retained from the initiation ceremonies.

He reflected also, no doubt, that his heavy tongue, for example, might be a hindrance—so he anticipated this inconvenience, and wove the objections he might have to fear into his tale, and Jehovah himself would have to overcome them. Moreover, he subordinates himself to his mission only after resisting a long time—the more weight need be laid into God's command, the which then compelled him upon his mission. The most detailed and particular is the portrait in his tale of that which the Israelites, and we, would have the most difficulty to believe, and there is no doubt, he had his good reasons for it.

If we briefly summarize the foregoing, what was the real plan which Moses conceived in the Arabian desert?

He wanted to lead the people of Israel out of Egypt, and help them to possession of their independence and a national constitution in a land of their own. But since he knew the difficulties which stood in his way on this venture quite well; since he knew there could be no reliance upon the latent forces of this people, until they had been given self-confidence, courage, hope, and enthusiasm; for he foresaw, that his eloquence would not take effect upon the soil of the oppressed, slavish minds of the Hebrews: And so he understood, that he must proclaim to them a higher, a supraterrestrial protector, that he must likewise assemble his people under the flag of a divine general.

He thus gives them a God, in order first to lead them out of Egypt. But since that is not the end of it, since he must give them another land in place of the one he takes from them, and since they must first conquer this other land under arms, and sustain themselves in it, it is necessary, that he hold their united forces together in a national body, and he must thus give them laws and a constitution.

As a priest and a statesman, however, he knows, that the strongest and most indispensable pillar of all constitutions is religion; he must thus make use of the God, which he first gives his people only to liberate them from Egypt, as a mere commander of an army, also in the forthcoming legislation; he must thus at once proclaim Him, as he will later make use of Him. For legislation, and for the foundations of the state, he requires the true God, for he is a great and noble man, who cannot found a work which should last, upon a lie. By means of the constitution which he has designed for them, he wants to make his Hebrews a happy, and lastingly happy people, and this can only come to pass, if he founds his legislation upon truth. For this truth, however, their powers of understanding are yet too dull; thus, he cannot bring this truth into their souls upon the pure path of Reason. Since he cannot convince them, he must persuade them, entice, seduce them. He must thus bestow upon the true God he gives them, characteristics which make Him comprehensible and worthy of being received by weak minds; he must cloak his God in heathen robes, and must be satisfied, if they treasure just these heathen features of his true God, and perceive truth only in a heathen way. By this, too, he gains endlessly, he gains, in that the foundation of his legislation is true, so that a future reformer need not collapse the basic edifice of the constitution if he undertakes improvements of conceptions, which are the inevitable consequence in all false religions, as soon as the torch of Reason sheds its light upon them.

All other states of that time, and of times following, are founded upon fraud and error, polytheism, although, as we have seen, there was a small circle which fostered correct conceptions of the Supreme Being. Moses, himself of this circle, and with only this circle to thank for his own better idea of the Supreme Being, is the first who dares not only to proclaim aloud the results of the most secret mysteries, but even to make it the foundation of a state. He thus becomes, for the best for the world and posterity, a betrayer of the mysteries, and lets an entire nation partake of a truth, which until then had been the possession of only a few wise men. Clearly, with this new religion, he could not give his Hebrews the powers of mind necessary to comprehend it, and in that respect the Egyptian *epopts* had a great advantage over them. The *epopts* recognized the truth through their Reason, the Hebrews were at most capable of blindly believing in it.

*Author's note:* I must refer the reader to a work of similar content, *Über die älteste Hebräische Mysterien von Br. Decius*, whose author is famous and of considerable merit, and from which I have taken diverse ideas and facts as the basis for my treatment.

*The*

# JESUIT GOVERNMENT IN PARAGUAY

TRANSLATED BY BRUCE DIRECTOR

In a campaign which preceded the battle of Paraguay, fought on the 12th of September 1759, between the Jesuits and the united Spanish-Portuguese army, two Europeans, who had fought with desperate bravery, were brought in among the different Indian prisoners. Both were dressed entirely differently than the rest of the prisoners. They wore a red Hussar's habit, on which two small sleeves hung down from the shoulder. Their helmet was trimmed with red feathers and both wore a large chain of diamonds around their necks. Just as richly adorned were their horses. Their weapons were a large saber and a flint rifle; when they were undressed, one found a very good breastplate on their bodies, and a small pistol and two daggers as well.

The Indians who were captured with them, fell when they set eyes upon them, reverently went down on their knees before them, and struck themselves on their breast, whereby they repeatedly pronounced the word "Kau." One of the Europeans appeared to accept this homage with annoyance; the Indians around him, however, did not let that disturb them.

---

This sketch first appeared in the October 1788 volume of Wieland's *German Mercury*. Schiller's principal source for this devastating exposé was Christoph Harenberg's *Pragmatic History of the Jesuit Order* (Halle/Helmstedt 1760).

Not a single word could be brought out of him. They hit him, they brought him to be tortured; a few involuntary sounds in the Portuguese language, which pain squeezed out of him, were all that they received from him. The other showed himself more open and free, and soon confessed, that he was a Jesuit. He had, said he, accompanied his Indians around as their chaplain and spiritual assistant in the battle, as he pretended, to keep their excessive fury within bounds, and to implant in them a gentle way of thinking toward the enemy. Finally, he revealed his name was Pater Rennez, and the other, whom the example of his comrade made likewise more talkative, at this point also confessed, that he was a Jesuit and a chaplain of the Indians, and his name was Pater Lenaumez.

When their pockets were searched, a small book was found, at whose discovery they became extremely restless. It was written in an unknown code; on the edge, however, a key in the Latin language was attached thereto. This document contained a law of war of the Indians, or rather the chief tenets of the religion, which the Order had sought to implant in their Indian subjects. I relate them here, because they may interest the curious and, perhaps, give some information about the Jesuit government in Paraguay.

Hear, O man! the commands of God and of the holy Michael:

1. God is the ultimate purpose of all action.
2. God is the source of all bravery and strength.
3. Bravery is a virtue as well of the body as of the soul.
4. God does nothing in vain.
5. Bravery is given to Man, so that he may defend himself.
6. Man must defend himself against his enemies.
7. The enemies are the white men, who come from a far distant region, to conduct war, and are cursed by God.
8. The Europeans, i.e. the Spanish and Portuguese, are such people who are cursed by God.

9. God's enemies cannot be our friends.

10. God commands, that we exterminate his enemies and go forth to their country, to exterminate them.

11. In order that one cursed by God, for example a Spaniard, be destroyed, one must also lose one's temporal life, in order to serve the eternal.

12. Whoever speaks with a European or understands their language, shall be condemned to the infernal fire.

13. Whoever kills a European, will become blessed.

14. Whoever closes a day without having performed a deed of hatred and cursing against a European shall be condemned to the eternal fire.

15. God permits him, who despises temporal goods and is always ready to fight against the friends of the devil, to do everything with a woman.

16. Whoever perishes in an encounter with the Europeans, shall be blessed.

17. Whoever discharges a cannon against the enemies of God, shall be blessed, and all sins of his life be forgiven him.

18. Whoever, at great danger of death, be the cause, of reconquest of a castle and a fortress, which is thus possessed illegitimately, he shall have, from among all the women of the heavens, a very beautiful wife in Paradise.

19. Whoever be the cause, that our empire extend beyond its borders, he shall have four very beautiful wives among all God's daughters.

20. Whoever be the cause, that our weapons extend to Europe, he shall have many beautiful maidens in Paradise.

21. Whoever is devoted to the fruit of the earth, he shall enjoy no fruit of the heavens.

22. Whoever fathers more children, he will have more glory in heaven.

23. Whoever drinks wine, he will not come into heaven's kingdom.

24. Whoever does not obey his Kau and is not humble, shall come into Hell.

25. The Kau are the sons of God, who come out of the heavens over Europe, that they help the people against the enemies of God.

26. The Kau are the angels of God, who descend to the people, to teach them how one comes into heaven, and the art to destroy the enemy of God.

27. One must give to the Kaus all fruits of the land and all labor of mankind, so that they make use of the same, to destroy the people who are the friends of the devil.

28. Whoever dies in disgrace of his Kau, shall not be blessed.

29. Whoever touches the highest Kau, will be blessed.

30. Every man be subservient to his Kau, and go wherever he tells him to go, and give him what he demands, and do what he commands.

31. Men are in the world to fight with the devil and his friends, so that they come into heaven's kingdom, where joy and pleasure are eternal, which no man's heart can grasp.

# AESTHETICS

# ON GRACE AND DIGNITY

TRANSLATED BY GEORGE GREGORY

The Greek myth attributes to the goddess of beauty a belt, possessed of the power to endow the one who wears it with grace, and to obtain love. This goddess is accompanied by the goddesses of grace, or the Graces.

The Greeks therefore *distinguished* grace and the Graces from beauty, for they expressed them by such attributes as were distinct from the goddess of beauty. All grace is beautiful, for the belt of grace is a property of the goddess of Gnidus; but not all that is beautiful is grace, for even without this belt, Venus remains what she is.

According to this very allegory, it is the goddess of beauty alone, Juno, who wears and bestows the belt of grace; Juno, heaven's glorious goddess, must first *borrow* that belt of Venus, when she wants to charm Jupiter on Mt. Ida. Thus majesty, even if a certain degree of beauty adorns it (which one by no means gainsays the wife of Jupiter), is, without grace, not certain to please, since it is not on account of her own charms, but the belt of Venus, that the high queen of the gods expects triumph over Jupiter's heart.

---

Schiller began to write *On Grace and Dignity* in May 1793, after he had completed his correspondence with Körner on the subject of the beautiful. It is the first major published work of Schiller to decisively criticize the perspective of Kant on aesthetics, a fact noted by Humboldt in his intellectual biography of Schiller. *On Grace and Dignity* first appeared in print in July 1793, in the second issue of *New Thalia*.

The goddess of beauty may, after all, part with her belt and cede its power to one less beautiful. Grace is therefore not an *exclusive* prerogative of the beautiful; rather it can also pass, although only from the hand of the beautiful, over to the less beautiful, even to the not beautiful.

These Greeks bid him, to whom grace, or that which pleases, was lacking, whatever other merits of mind he possess, to make sacrifices to the Graces. They thus imagined these goddesses, indeed, as attendants of the fair sex, but yet as such with whom a man, too, might be indulged, and who are indispensible to him if he wishes to please.

But what now is grace, if she indeed loves to unite with beauty, but yet not exclusively? if she is indeed born of beauty, but reveals her effects also in one not beautiful? if beauty can indeed exist *without* her, but *through* her alone can beauty enkindle attraction?

The tender emotion of the Greeks differentiated quite early what reason was not yet able to elucidate, and, searching for an expression, borrowed it from the imagination, since the understanding could as yet offer it no concepts. This myth, therefore, deserves the philosopher's respect, who in any case must content himself with seeking the intuitions in which pure natural sense has laid down its discoveries, or, in other words, with explaining the hieroglyphics of emotions.

If one divests the idea of the Greeks of its allegorical shell, it seems to contain none other than the following meaning.

Grace is a changeable beauty: a beauty of its subject which can come to be and just as well cease to be. She thus distinguishes herself from fixed beauty, which is necessarily existent with the subject itself. Venus can take off her belt and momentarily relinquish it to Juno; her beauty she could surrender only with her person. Without her belt she is no longer the alluring Venus; without beauty she is no longer Venus at all.

This belt, the symbol of changeable beauty, has the extraordinary property, that it confers upon the person it embellishes the objective quality of grace; it thus distinguishes itself from every other ornament which does not change the person himself, but merely the impression which the person makes, subjectively, in another's imagination. It is the expressed meaning of the Greek myth, that grace is transformed into a characteristic of the person, and that the bearer of the belt *becomes* actually charming, and not merely *seems* so.

A belt which is nothing more than a fortuitous outward ornament certainly seems no very fitting image to denote the *personal* character of grace; but a personal characteristic, which is at once thought as separable from the subject, could not be illustrated otherwise than by means of a fortuitous ornament, with which the person may part without detriment to himself.

The belt of grace, thus, does not work its effect *naturally*, since, in that case, it would be incapable of changing the person; rather, its effect is *magical,* that is, its power is enhanced beyond all natural conditions. It is by means of this expediency (which obviously is no more than a contrivance), that the contradiction should be resolved, in which the powers of description inevitably become entangled every time an expression is sought within nature for that which lies outside nature, in the domain of freedom.

If now the belt of grace expresses an objective characteristic, which can be distinguished from its subject without changing anything of its nature, then it can characterize nothing but beauty of movement, since movement is the only change which can occur with an object without dissolving its identity.

Beauty of movement is a concept which satisfies both requirements contained in the cited myth. It is, first of all, objective and belongs to the object itself, not merely to how we perceive it. It is, *secondly*, something fortuitous about the object, and the object remains, even if we think this characteristic away from it.

The belt of grace is not bereft of its magical power even upon those less beautiful, nor yet upon those who are not beautiful at all, and even one who is not beautiful can *move* beautifully.

Grace, says the myth, is something *fortuitous* about its subject; therefore only fortuitous movements can have this characteristic. As far as the ideal of beauty is concerned, all *necessary* movements *must be* beautiful, because, as necessary, they belong to its nature; the beauty of *this* movement is therefore already *given* with the concept of Venus, whereas the beauty of the fortuitous movement is an *enhancement* of this concept. There is a grace of the voice, but no grace of breathing.

But is every beauty of fortuitous movement grace?

That the Greek myth restricts grace and the Graces exclusively to mankind, hardly need be recalled; it goes further, and confines beauty of form to the human species, in which the Greek, as we well know, also included his gods. But if grace is a prerogative of the human form alone, then none of those movements can lay claim to it which mankind has in common with that which is mere nature. Could the locks of hair on a beautiful head move with grace, there were no longer any reason why the branches of a tree, the waves on a river, the seeds in a cornfield, the legs of an animal, should not move with dignity. But the goddess of Gnidus represents the human species exclusively, and where the human being is nothing more than a thing of nature and a creature of sense, she ceases to have any meaning for him.

Grace, therefore, can only characterize willful movements, but also, among these, only those which express *moral* sentiments. Movements which have no other source than sensuousness, be they ever so willful, belong merely to nature, which never elevates herself to grace by herself alone. Could lust express itself with charm, instinct with grace, then were charm and grace no longer capable, nor worthy, of serving as an expression of humanity.

And yet, it is in humanity alone, that the Greek invests all beauty and perfection. Never may sensuousness show itself to him without soul, and to his *human* sentiments it is at once impossible to *sever* raw animality and intelligence. Just as he pictures every idea at the same time with a body, and also strives to embody even things most spiritual, he thus demands of every act of instinct of a person at the same time an expression of his moral destiny. To the Greek, nature is never *mere* nature, for which reason he need never blush to know her; to him, reason is never *mere* reason, for which reason he need never shudder to tread under its rule. Nature and morality, matter and mind, Earth and Heaven, flow together with wondrous beauty in his poems. He introduced freedom, which is at home not merely in Olympus, also into the business of morality, and one will therefore want to indulge him, if he misplaces sensuousness, too, into Olympus.

Now, the tender sense of the Greeks, which only tolerates matter in the constant escort of the mind, knows of no willful movement of man which belongs to sensuousness alone, without that it be at the same time an expression of the morally sentient mind. For him, therefore, grace is but one such beautiful expression of the soul in willful movement. Where grace thus appears, the soul is the moving principle, and *in her* is contained the cause of the beauty of movement. And so every mystical conception of grace resolves itself into the following thought: "Grace is a beauty, the which is not granted by nature, rather brought forth by the subject himself."

Thus far I have restricted myself to develop the concept of grace out of the Greek myth, and, as I hope, without doing it violence. Now I beg leave, that I attempt what can be determined by way of philosophical investigation of the matter, and whether it is true here, too, as in so many other cases, that philosophizing reason can boast of fewer discoveries by far, the which intuition had not already *suspected*, and poetry not already *revealed*.

Venus, without her belt and without the Graces, represents to us the ideal of beauty, such as can come from the hands of *mere nature*, produced by formative forces, and *without the intervention of a sentient mind*. The myth correctly establishes for this beauty its own divine form as representative, since natural sentiment distinguishes her most strictly from the other, whose origin is indebted to the influence of a sentient mind.

Permit me to call this beauty of mere nature, that formed according to the law of necessity, the beauty of frame *(architechtonic beauty)*, in distinction to that which is dependent upon the condition of freedom. By this name, therefore, I want to have that part of human beauty characterized, which is not merely *brought about* by natural forces (which holds good of every phenomenon), but which is *solely determined by natural forces*.

A fortunate proportionality of limbs, flowing contours, a pleasing complexion, tender skin, a fine and free growth, a well-sounding voice, etc., are advantages for which one is indebted to mere nature and fortune: to *nature*, which provided the appropriate predisposition, and itself developed them; to *fortune*, which shielded the forming work of nature from the influence of hostile forces.

This Venus rises already *fully perfect* from the foam of the sea, for she is a completed, strictly balanced work of necessity, and as such, capable of no variety, no enhancement. Since, to wit, she is nothing but a more beautiful enunciation of the purposes which nature intends for man, and therefore each of her characteristics is completely decided by the concept upon which she is founded, so may she—according to her predisposition—be judged as fully present, although this presence must still develop with time.

Architectonic beauty of the human frame must be distinguished from the frame's technical perfection. By the latter is to be understood the *system of purposes* itself, as they are united among themselves toward a highest final purpose; by the former, on the other hand, merely *a characteristic* of the manifestation of these purposes, such as they reveal themselves in their appearance to the observing faculty. If, therefore, we speak of beauty, neither the material value of these purposes, nor the formal artfulness of their composition, is taken into account. The observing faculty is exclusively concerned with the manner of appearance, without taking the slightest account of the logical constitution of its object. Although the architectonic beauty of the human frame depends on the concept upon which it is founded, and on the purposes which nature intends by it, yet aesthetic judgment still *isolates* it completely from these purposes, and nothing but that which properly and immediately belongs to the appearance will be included in the notion formed by aesthetic judgment.

Hence, we cannot say, that the dignity of man increases the beauty of the human frame. In our judgment on the latter, the notion of the former may be included, but then it immediately ceases to be a pure aesthetic judgment. The technology of the human frame is, of course, an expression of the purposes of man's destiny, and as such it may and should fill us with respect. But this technology is not presented to sense, rather to the understanding; it can only be *thought*, but it can never *manifest* itself. Architectonic beauty, on the contrary, can never be an expression of man's destiny, for it is directed at a quite different faculty than that which has to decide upon that destiny.

If, therefore, it is to man, preeminently over all other technical constructions of nature, that beauty is attributed, this is true only insofar as he claims this preeminence in his *mere manifestation*, without that one need be reminded thereby of his humanity. Were it otherwise, since this latter could not but occur as a conception, then it would not be sense, but understanding, which judged of beauty, which entails a contradiction. The human being, therefore, cannot account the dignity of his moral purpose, cannot urge his preeminence as a moral creature, if he wants to claim the prize of beauty; here he is nothing but a thing in space, nothing but one phenomenon among phenomena. His rank in the world of ideas is of no account in the world of sense, and if he wants to claim first place in this world, he can claim it thanks only to that in him which is *nature*.

But just this, his nature, is, as we know, attuned to the idea of his humanity, and so, indirectly, is his architectonic beauty as well. If he so distinguishes himself as preeminent to all creatures of sense around him by greater beauty, then for that he is indebted incontestably to his human destiny, which contains the cause whereof he distinguishes himself at all from other creatures of sense. But it is not on account of its being an expression of this atonement, that the human frame is beautiful, for were it this, then this same frame would cease to be beautiful as soon as it expressed a lesser purpose; then were the contrary of this frame also beautiful as soon as one might assume, that it could express that atonement. But presuming, that one might be able to completely forget in a beautiful human frame what it expresses, and that one could, without changing its appearance, insinuate into it the raw instinct of a tiger, then the judgment of the eyes would be absolutely the same, and sense would proclaim the tiger the most beautiful work of the Creator.

The destiny of man, as intelligent creature, therefore, contributes to the beauty of his frame only insofar as its manifestation, i.e., its expression, *coincides* at once with the conditions under which beauty produces itself in the world of sense. Beauty itself must always remain a free effect of nature, and the idea of reason, which determined the technology of the human frame, can never *bestow* beauty upon it, rather, merely allow it.

One might object, that absolutely everything which manifests itself in appearance is performed by forces of nature, and that this could not, therefore, be an exclusive characteristic of beauty. It is true: all technical forms are brought forth by nature, but it is not because of nature that they are technical; at least we do not judge them to be so. They are only technical because of reason, and this technical perfection, therefore, already has existence in reason, before it steps out into the world of sense and becomes an appearance. Beauty, on the contrary, has that unique characteristic, that she is not merely presented in the world of sense, but also first arises there; that nature not merely expresses her, but also creates her. She is absolutely a characteristic only of the sensuous, and even the artist, who intends to effect her, can achieve that effect only insofar as he preserves the appearance that it is an effect of nature.

In order to judge the technology of the human frame, one needs the assistance of the conception of the purposes to which it is appropriate; one requires no such thing to judge the beauty of this frame. Sense alone is a fully competent judge here, the which it could not be, did not the world of sense (which is its sole object) contain all conditions of beauty, and were it not also thus perfectly sufficient for her production. *Indirectly,* of course, the beauty of man is founded in the conception of his humanity, but sense, we know, only depends upon that which is direct, and so, for sense it is just as much, as if she were a totally independent effect of nature.

From the foregoing, it might seem as if beauty were of absolutely no interest to reason, for she arises merely in the world of sense, and also addresses herself only to the sensuous faculty of knowledge. After having distinguished beauty from the conception of her as alien, from the mixture of which the *idea of perfection* in our judgment on beauty can hardly abstain, then nothing seems to remain to beauty, on account of which beauty could be the object of a reasoning pleasure. Nevertheless, it is as well established, that beauty *pleases reason,* as it is decided, that this is due to no such characteristic of the object, as were solely capable of discovery through reason.

In order to resolve this apparent contradiction, we must recall, that there are two ways by which phenomena become objects for reason, and are capable of expressing ideas. It is not always necessary, that reason *draws* these ideas *from* the phenomena, for reason can *place* ideas *into* them. In both cases the phenomena will be adequate to an idea of reason, but with a difference: in the first case, reason finds the idea objectively within, as if it only receives the idea from the object, because the conception must be posited, in order to explain the constitution, and often even the possibility of an object; whereas, in the second case, it *makes* that which is independent of its conception in the phenomenon, spontaneously into an expression thereof, and thus treats something *merely* sensuous, as if it were more than sensuous. Thus, *in the first case,* the connection of the idea with the object is objectively necessary, whereas in the other, this connection is supremely subjectively necessary. I need not say, that by the former I understand perfection, by the latter beauty.

Since, in the second case, in respect of an object of sense, it is totally fortuitous, whether there is a reason, which connects one of its ideas with the presentation of the object to the senses, it follows, that the objective constitution of the object must be considered totally independent of this idea, and we are absolutely correct, to restrict beauty, *objectively,* to mere natural conditions, and to explain it as a mere effect of the world of sense. But since, on the other hand, reason makes a transcendental use of this effect of the mere world of sense, and impresses its stamp upon it by attributing to it a higher significance, we are also correct to place beauty *subjectively* into the intelligible world. Beauty is, therefore, to be viewed as a citizen of two worlds, belonging to the one by *birth,* to the other by *adoption*; she *receives* her existence in sensuous nature, and *attains* to the right of citizenship in the world of reason. From this it is also explained how it happens, that taste, as a faculty of judgment of beauty, steps into the middle between mind and sense, and connects these two natures, each scornful of the other, in happy concord: as it teaches *matter* respect for reason, it also teaches that which is *rational* its sympathy for sensuousness; as it ennobles perceptions into ideas, it transforms the world of sense in a certain way into a realm of freedom.

But, in respect of the object itself, it is fortuitous, whether reason connects an idea of the object with one of its ideas, yet—for the imagining subject—it is necessary to connect with one such image one such idea. This idea and the sensuous characteristic of its object corresponding to it must stand in such a relationship with each other, that reason is compelled to this operation by its own unalterable laws. The cause must lie in reason itself, why it connects a certain idea exclusively only with a *certain* way of appearance of things, and the cause must lie in the object, why it only calls forth exclusively *this idea* and no other. What kind of idea that might be, which reason implants in a thing of beauty, and by means of which objective characteristic the beautiful object might be capable of serving as symbol to this idea—this is a far too important question to be answered here merely in passing, and so I defer its explication to an analysis of beauty.

The architectonic beauty of man is, therefore, in the manner just mentioned, *the sensuous expression of a concept of reason*; but it is this in no other sense and with no greater right than any other beautiful form of nature in general. *In degree* it indeed surpasses all other things of beauty, but in kind, it is of the same rank, since it too reveals nothing of its subject but what is sensuous, and only receives a supra-sensuous significance in its conception.[1]

That the presentation of purposes turned out more beautifully than in other organic forms, is to be regarded as a *favor,* which reason, the legislator of the human frame, rendered unto nature, the executor of reason's laws. Reason, indeed, in the technology of man, pursues its purposes with strict necessity, but its demands fortunately *coincide* with the necessity of nature, so that the latter carries out the mission of the former, in that she performs merely according to her own inclination.

This, however, can only hold good of the *architectonic* beauty of man, where natural necessity is supported by the necessity of the teleological cause which directs it. Only here was it possible to *set* beauty *in account* against the technology of the construction, which no longer occurs, as soon as necessity is only one-sided and the supra-sensuous cause of phenomena changes fortuitously. Nature *alone* thus provides for the architectonic beauty of man, because here, at once in the first design, the execution of everything which

man *requires* to fulfill his purposes was surrendered to her
once and for all by creating reason, and she therefore need
fear no innovation in this, her *organic* business.

But man is at the same time a *person,* thus a creature
who can be *himself* cause, who can, according to the grounds
he takes from himself, change himself. The manner of his
appearance is dependent upon the manner of his sentience,
and willing, thus, upon circumstances which he decides
himself in freedom, and not nature according to her necessity.

Were man merely a sensuous creature, then had nature
at once dictated the *laws* and determined the *cases* of their
application; now she shares the domain with freedom, and,
although the laws endure, now the mind decides upon the
cases.

The domain of mind extends *as far as nature lives,*
and ends not sooner than where organic life loses itself in
formless mass, and the forces of life cease. It is known, that
all forces in man are interconnected with each other, and
so it is understood how mind—even considered only as
principle of willful movement—can propagate its effects
through his entire system. Not merely the tools of the will,
also those over which the will has no immediate command,
experience at least indirectly its influence. The mind resolves them not merely intentionally when it acts, rather
also unintentionally when it experiences.

Nature by herself, as is clear from the above, can only
provide for the beauty of those phenomena which she alone,
without limitation, determines according to the laws of necessity. But with *willfulness, chance* enters her Creation,
and although the changes which she suffers under the authority of freedom do not succeed according to any other
laws but her own, they do not issue *from* those laws. Since
it depends upon mind, what use it wants to make of its tools,
nature can have no authority any longer over that part of
beauty which depends upon its use, and hence can no longer
be held accountable.

And so, where he elevates himself through use of his freedom to pure intelligence, man would be in danger of being degraded as appearance, and losing in the judgment of taste, what he gained before the seat of reason's judgment. The destiny *fulfilled* by his action would cost him an advantage merely *presaged* in his frame, which destiny had favored; and although this advantage is only sensuous, yet we have found, that reason bestows upon it a higher significance. It is not concord-loving nature who makes herself guilty of such a crude contradiction, and what is harmonious in the domain of reason, will not manifest itself by discord in the world of sense.

While thus the person, or the free principle in man, takes it upon himself to decide the play of phenomena, and by his intervention takes from nature the power to protect the beauty of her works, so he himself steps into the place of nature, and assumes (if I be permitted this expression) together with her rights, a part of her responsiblities. While the mind implicates the sensuousness subordinated to it in its own fate, and lets it depend upon its conditions, it makes itself into a phenomenon to a certain degree, and thus acknowledges itself to be a subject of the law to which all phenomena are subject. And for its own sake, the mind undertakes the obligation to permit nature, dependent upon it, to remain nature, though yet in the service of *mind*, and never to treat her *contrary to* her former duty. I call beauty a *duty* of phenomena, because the requirement corresponding to it in the subject is grounded in reason itself, and is therefore general and necessary. I call it a *former* duty, because sense has already judged, before understanding sets out upon its business.

Freedom thus now governs beauty. Nature provided beauty of form, the soul bequeaths beauty of play. And now we also know what we are to understand by charm and grace. Grace is beauty of frame under the influence of freedom: the beauty of those phenomena upon which the person decides. Architectonic beauty does honor to the

Author of nature, charm and grace honor him who possesses them. The one is *talent*, the latter a *personal* merit.

Grace can belong only to *movement*, since a change in heart can proclaim itself only as movement in the world of sense. But this does not prevent firm and calm lines from manifesting grace. These firm lines were originally nothing but movements, which, by repetition, became habitual, and left their lasting traces.[2]

But not all movements which a person makes are capable of grace. Grace is always solely the beauty of the *form moved by freedom*, and movements *which merely belong to nature* can never deserve this name. It is indeed true, that a lively mind ultimately becomes the master of nearly all movements of its body, but if the chain becomes very long, whereby a beautiful contour joins itself to moral sentiments, it then becomes a characteristic of the frame, and can hardly any longer be accounted to grace. Ultimately the mind *forms* itself a body, and the frame must follow the *play*, so that in the end grace not seldom transforms itself into architectonic beauty.

Just as a hostile mind, at odds with itself, destroys even the most exalted beauty of form, so that under the hand unworthy of freedom we can finally no longer recognize the magnificent masterpiece of nature, so we also occasionally see the merry and harmonious heart come to the aid of a technology fettered by obstacles, to set nature free and scatter even the developed, impressed form with divine glory. The formative nature of man has infinitely many resources within it to harvest nature's shortcomings, and improve her mistakes, if but the moral spirit supports her in her forming work, or sometimes, too, wants not to disrupt it.

Since *congealed movements* (gestures transformed into contours) are not excluded from grace, it might, on the whole, seem as if the beauty of *apparent* or *imitated* movements (veined or serpentine lines) must also be accounted to grace, as Mendelssohn actually claims.[3] But that would extend the concept of grace to the concept of beauty as such;

for *all* beauty is ultimately only a characteristic of a true or apparent (objective or subjective) movement, as I hope to have proven in the explication of beauty. Only such movements can manifest grace, which at once correspond to an emotion.

The person—it is clear what I mean by this—prescribes movements to the body either by his will, if he wants to realize an intended effect in the sensuous world, and in this case the movements are called *willful* or deliberate; or, movements occur without the will of the person, according to a law of necessity, but on the inducement of an emotion. These I call *sympathetic* movements. Although the latter are involuntary and grounded in an emotion, we must not confuse them with those which the moral faculty of sentiment and instinct directs; for instinct is no free principle, and what it accomplishes is no deed of a person. By sympathetic movements, which is what we speak of here, I therefore only want to have those understood, which serve to accompany moral sentiment or moral disposition.

The question now arises, which of these two kinds of movement founded in the person is capable of grace?

That which one must distinguish in philsophizing, is not therefore always distinguished in reality. We thus find deliberate movements seldom unattended by sympathetic ones, because the will, the cause of *the former*, attunes itself according to moral sentiment, from which *the latter* issue. While a person is speaking, we see at once his glances, facial contours, his hands, indeed often the entire body *speaking along,* and the *mimical* part of the conversation is not seldom deemed the most convincing. But even a deliberate movement can at the same time be considered sympathetic, and this happens, when something involuntary interferes with what is willful in the movement.

The way and manner in which a willful movement is performed is not so precisely attuned by its purpose, that there may not be numerous ways in which it can be accomplished. Now, what is left unsettled by the will or the purpose can be sympathetically attuned by the *sentient condition* of the person, and thus serves to express that condition. While I extend my arm to receive an object, I thus fulfill a purpose, and the movement I make is directed by the intention which I thereby want to achieve. But *how* I take my arm to the object and how far I wish to let my body follow, how quickly or slowly, and with how great or how little expenditure of force I want to accomplish the movement—I do not entertain this precise accounting at *that* moment, and something is left to nature in me. But in one way, and one manner or other, that which is not attuned by the mere purpose must be decided, and it is thus here, that my manner of sentiment can settle the issue, and by the *tone* which it sets, attune the kind and mode of movement. Now, the part which the sentient condition of the person takes in a willful movement, is its involuntary part, and is also that wherein one has to seek the Graces.

A *willful* movement, if it does not at the same time combine with a sympathetic one, or, which is to say as much, does not mingle with something *involuntary* which has its ground in the moral sentient condition of the person, can *never* manifest *grace*, for which a sentient condition is always required as the cause. The willful movement *succeeds* upon an act of sentiment, which is also past when the movement ensues.

The sympathetic movement, on the other hand, *accompanies* the act of sentiment and its sentient condition, on account of which it is enabled to this act, and must, therefore, be considered as *running parallel* to both.

From this it is evident, that the willful movement which does not immediately flow from the disposition of the person, also cannot be a manifestation of that disposition. For, between the disposition and the movement steps the *resolution,* which, taken for itself, is a matter of indifference; the movement is the effect of a *decision* and of the purpose, but not of the *person* and his disposition.

Willful movement is fortuitously connected with the preceding disposition, whereas the accompanying (sympathetic movement) is necessarily connected to it. The former stands to sentiment as the conventional signs of speech stand to the thought which they express; sympathetic or accompanying movement are to sentiment, what the passionate tone is to passion. The former, therefore, is not a manifestation of mind by *nature*, but merely of the use to which it is put. Hence, we cannot say, that *mind* reveals itself in a willful movement, for this movement only expresses the *material of will* (the purpose) but not the *form of will* (the disposition). About the latter only the accompanying movement can teach us.[4]

We will be able to conclude, therefore, from the speeches of a person, what *he wants to be held for*, but what *he really is*, we must try to glean from the mimical presentation of his words and from his gestures, thus from movements *which he does not will*. But when one learns, that a person can also *will* his facial expressions, one will not long trust his face from the moment of this discovery, and will no longer take his face for an expression of his disposition.

Now a person may, through art and study, at last succeed, to the extent, that he also subjects the accompanying movements to his will, and, like a skillful magician, can let what form he will fall upon the mimical mirror of his soul. But about such a person everything is a lie, and nature is devoured entirely by art. Grace, on the other hand, must always be nature, i.e., involuntary (or at least seem so), and the subject itself must never look as though *it knew about its grace*.

From this one sees, in passing, what one is to think of *imitated* or *learned* grace (which I would like to call theatric, or dance-master grace). It is a worthy counterpart to that *beauty* which issues from the dressing table from rouge and bleach, wigs, false breasts, and girdles, and is related in approximately the same way to true grace as *toilette beauty* is to *architectonic* beauty.[5]

But although grace must be, or appear to be, something unwilled, yet we seek it only among movements which, more or less, depend upon the will. In fact, one attributes grace to a certain gesture language, and speaks of a graceful smile and a charming flush of color, both of which are but sympathetic movements, whereupon not will, but sentiment decides. Leaving aside that each is in our power, and that it can still be doubted, whether these also belong to grace, still there are by far more numerous cases from the domain of willful movements where grace manifests itself. One demands grace of speech and song, of the willful play of the eyes and mouth, of the movement of the hands and arms, in each free use of the same, of the gait, of the posture of the body, and of position, insofar as it is in a person's power. Of those movements of men which are due to instinct, or an affect which has seized mastery over the person to execute the movement *on its own*, and which in respect of their origin are sensuous, we require something entirely different than grace, as will be discovered hereafter. Such movements belong to *nature* and not to the *person*, from whom alone all grace must spring.

If, therefore, grace is a characteristic which we require of willful movements, and if, on the other hand, everything willful must be banned from grace, then we shall have to seek it out in that which is unintentional in intentional movements, the which also corresponds to a moral cause in sentiment.

This merely characterizes the species of movements among which one must seek grace; but a movement can have all of these characteristics without being graceful. Movement is thereby merely *speaking* (mimical).

I call every manifestation of a body, speaking (in the broadest sense), which accompanies a sentient condition, and expresses it. In this sense, therefore, all sympathetic movements are speaking, even those which accompany mere affects of sensuousness.

Animal forms, too, speak, in that internal processes are outwardly manifest. But here it is mere *nature* that speaks, never *freedom*. In the permanent form and firm architectonic contours of the animal, nature proclaims her *purpose*, in the mimical lines the aroused or satisfied *need.* The ring of necessity passes through the animal as through the plant, without being interrupted by a *person.* The individuality of its existence is only a specific manifestation of a general concept of nature; the particularity of its present condition merely an example of the execution of one of nature's purposes under certain natural conditions. Only the human form is speaking in the *narrower* sense, and it is this, also, only in those of its manifestations which accompany moral sentient condition of the person, and serve as its expression.

Only in *these* manifestations: for in all others, man stands in the same rank with other creatures of sense. In his permanent form and in his architectonic contours, nature displays, as she does with animals and all organic creatures, her intention. The intention nature has with him can indeed reach further than with them, and the combination of means to fulfill that intention be more artful and intricate; all of this is only accounted to *nature,* and can redound to no credit of a person.

Among animals and plants, nature not only sets the tone, *she alone also implements it.* For man she sets the tone, and also leaves its composition to him. This alone makes him into man.

Man alone, as person, has the prerogative over all known creatures to intercede by means of his will into the ring of necessity, which for a mere creature of nature is unbreakable, and to begin an entirely fresh series of manifestations in himself. The act through which he effects this is called preeminently an *intervention* and those of his accomplishments, which flow from such *intervention,* exclusively, his *deeds.* He can prove, therefore, that he is a person only through his deeds.

The animal form expresses not merely the conception of its purpose, but also the relation of its present condition to this purpose. Now since, among animals, nature sets the purpose, and at the same time fulfills it, the form of the animal can, therefore, never express anything but the work of nature.

Since nature provides for the purpose of man, but *places* its fulfillment into *his will*, the present relationship of his condition to his destiny can, therefore, not be the work of nature, but must be his own work. Thus, the expression of this relationship in his form belongs not to nature, but directly to himself; that is, it is a personal expression. If, therefore, we learn from the architectonic part of his form what nature has intended with him, we then learn from the mimical part of his form what he *himself* has done to fulfill this intention.

In respect of the form of man, therefore, we are not satisfied, that it present us merely the general conception of mankind, or what *nature* effected in the fulfillment of that conception with this individual, for that much he would have in common with every technical form. We expect from his form, that it reveal to us at the same time how far he is come, in his freedom, to fulfill nature's purpose: that is, that it bespeak his character. We see in him, in the first case, that nature *aimed* at man, but only from the second is it evident, whether he is really *become* one.

Thus, man's form is only *his*, insofar as it is mimical; but also, *the more mimical it is*, the more it is his. Since, even were the greater part of these mimical lines, yea although all of them, merely the expression of sensuousness, and might hence belong to him as a mere beast, he was yet so attuned as to be capable of limiting sensuousness by his freedom. The presence of such lines proves, therefore, the non-use of that faculty, and the non-fulfillment of his destiny; it is, therefore, speaking morally, to the same extent as the omission of an act dictated by duty is itself an act.

From the speaking lines, which are always an expression of the soul, we must distinguish the mute ones which mere forming nature draws in the human form, insofar as it works its effect independently of any influence of the soul. I call these lines *mute*, because, as incomprehensible ciphers of nature, they say nothing about character. They merely display the idiosyncrasy of nature in the presentation of the species, and by themselves are often sufficient to distinguish the *individual*, but about the *person* they can never reveal anything. For physiognomists these mute lines are by no means void of meaning, because the physiognomist wants to know not only what the man has made of himself, but also, what nature has done for and against him.

Hence, it is not an easy matter, to determine the limits at which the mute lines cease and the speaking ones begin. The uniformly working formative force and the lawless affect incessantly battle over the terrain; and what *nature* constructed in tireless, quiet activity, is often torn asunder by *freedom*, which, like a swelling river, washes over her banks. A lively mind obtains influence over *all* bodily movements, and ultimately succeeds, indirectly, in changing even the fixed forms of nature, which are unreachable by the will, through the power of sympathetic play. With such a person, everything becomes a feature of his character, as we find with many heads, who have fully *worked through* a long life, extraordinary fortunes, and an active mind. In such forms, only the *generic* belongs to formative nature, but the *individuality* of the elaboration belongs to the person; for that reason, one says quite rightly of such a form, that everything is soul.

By contrast, those fashioned students of the *rule* (who indeed bring sensuousness to rest, but are incapable of awakening humanity) demonstrate to us, in their flat and expressionless form, everywhere nothing but the finger of nature. The idle soul is a modest guest in its body and a peaceful, quiet neighbor of the forming powers left to themselves. No strenuous thought, no passion reaches its grip into the calm rhythm of physical life; never is the *edifice* endangered by *play*, never the vegetation upset by freedom. Since the profound quietude of the mind causes no very considerable consumption of energy, so shall the expenditure never surpass the income; animal economy shall instead always show a surplus. For the meager wage of happiness which she casts to him, such a mind is the punctual housekeeper of nature, and its entire glory is to keep her *ledger* in order. That shall be accomplished, therefore, which organization can always acomplish, and the business of nutrition and procreation will flourish. Such fortunate concord between natural necessity and freedom can not but be conducive to architectonic beauty, and it is here that she can be observed in her full purity. But the forces of nature, as we know, wage perpetual war with what is particular, or organic, and artful technology is ultimately defeated by *cohesion* and *gravity*. For that reason, too, beauty of form, as a *mere product of nature*, has its particular golden age of maturity and decay, which indeed accelerates the play, but can never arrest it; and its customary end is, that *mass* gradually becomes master over *form*, and the vital impulse toward form in preserved matter digs its own grave.[6]

While no *single* mute line is an expression of mind, such a silent form, *as a whole*, is characteristic; and indeed for the same reason, that a sensuous line is a speaking one. The mind, to wit, should be active and should be morally sentient; it thus testifies to its failing, if its form leaves no trace of its work. Hence, if the pure and beautiful expression of his destiny in the architecture of his form fills us with pleasure, and even awe, of the most supreme reason as its cause, then shall both sentiments remain unmingled only so long as it is a mere product of nature for us. But, if we think of him as a moral person, then we are justified in expecting that this be expressed in his form, and if this expectation is disappointed, scorn will inevitably follow. Merely organic things are worthy of our respect as *creatures*, the person can only be so as *creator* (i.e., as self-cause of his condition). He should not, as other creatures of sense, reflect the beams of foreign reason, even were it the Divine; rather, like a star, he should glow of his own light.

Thus, we demand a speaking form of man once we become conscious of his moral purpose; but, at the same time, it must be a form which bespeaks his advantage, i.e., a sentient faculty commensurate with his purpose, which expresses a moral faculty. This demand reason makes upon the human form.

But, at the same time, man, as a phenomenon, is an object of sense. Where *moral* sentiment finds satisfaction, the *aesthetical* does not want to be cut short, and concord with an idea must not cost a sacrifice in the appearance. However sternly reason may demand an expression of morality, just as persistently will the eye require beauty. Since both these demands befall the same object, albeit from diverse standpoints of judgment, then satisfaction for both must be provided by one and the same cause. That sentient condition of the person, by which he is most capable of fulfilling his destiny as a moral person, must allow of such an expression, which is also most advantageous to him. In other words, grace must bespeak his moral faculties.

It is here that the chief difficulty arises. It follows from the very notion of morally speaking movements, that they must have a moral cause which lies outside the world of sense; it follows, as well, from the notion of beauty, that she has nothing but a sensuous cause, and must be, or yet seem to be, a completely free effect of nature. But if the final cause of morally speaking movements necessarily lies *without*, while the final cause of beauty necessarily lies *within* the world of sense, then the *Graces*, which are supposed to connect them both, seem to contain an evident contradiction.

In order to resolve it, we will need to assume, that the moral cause in sentiment, which is the cause of grace, must necessarily bring forth just that condition, which contains within it the *natural conditions* of beauty in sensuousness, which depends upon it. Beauty, that is to say, presupposes certain conditions, which is evident of all sensuous things, and, insofar as it is beauty, only sensuous conditions. Now, that the mind prescribes this condition to accompanying nature (according to a law, which we cannot fathom), by the condition in which it finds itself, and that the condition of moral preparedness in the mind is just that through which the sensuous conditions of beauty are brought to fulfillment, makes beauty therewith *possible*, and that alone is the intervention of the mind. But, that beauty is actually begotten of this operation, is the consequence of those sensuous conditions, and thus a *free effect of nature*. But, since nature in *willful* movements, where she is treated as a means to accomplish a purpose, cannot actually be called free, and because *unwillful* movements which express morality also cannot be called free, then the freedom by which she expresses herself, nevertheless in dependency on the will, is a *concession* on the part of the mind. We can therefore say, that grace is a *favor* which morality grants to sensuousness, just as architectonic beauty may be considered the *gift* of nature to her technical form.

Permit me to illustrate this by means of an analogy. If a monarchic state be so administered, that, although everything happens according to one single will, yet the individual citizen can convince himself, that he lives according to his own inclination, then we call this a liberal government. But, one would have considerable reservations, *either* if the regent asserted his will against the inclination of the citizen, *or* if the citizen asserted his inclination against the will of the regent; for in the first case, the government were not *liberal*, in the second, it were no *goverment* at all.

It is not difficult to apply this to the human form under the regime of the mind. If the mind expresses itself in sensuous nature, which depends upon it, in such a way, that nature accomplishes the mind's will most faithfully, and expresses its sentiments most speakingly, yet without violating the demands which sense makes of her, the which it makes of all phenomena, then that which we call grace will ensue. But, we would be far from calling it grace, if either the mind manifest itself in sensuousness by force, or if the free effect of sensuousness fail to express the mind. For in the first case, there were no beauty, and in the second, it were no beauty of play.

It is, therefore, always only the supra-sensuous cause in sentiment which makes grace speak, and always only a merely sensuous cause in nature which makes grace beautiful. We can just as little say, that the mind *produces* beauty, as we can say of the ruler in the cited analogy, that he *creates* freedom, for freedom one may *allow*, but not *grant*.

But yet, just as the reason why a people may feel free under the force of an alien will, lies for the most part in the disposition of the ruler, and a contrary way of thinking would not be very conducive to freedom, for the same reason, we must seek out the beauty of free movements in the moral constitution of the mind which directs them. And now the question arises, what kind of *personal constitution* this might be, which concedes the greater freedom to the sensuous tools of the will, and what kind of moral sentiments best accord with beauty of expression?

This much is evident, that neither the will in respect of deliberate movements, nor emotion in respect of sympathetic movements, may conduct itself as a force against nature, which depends upon it, if she is to accord with beauty. Already the general opinion of mankind makes *ease* the chief characteristic of grace, and whatever requires effort can never manifest ease. It is equally evident, on the other hand, that nature must not conduct itself as a force against the mind, if a beautiful moral expression is to occur, for where mere nature *rules*, humanity must vanish.

In all, three relations are conceivable, in which the person may stand to himself, that is, his sensuous to his rational nature. We must seek that among these relations, which best cloaks him in his appearance, and whose manifestation is beauty.

Either the person represses the demands of his sensuous nature to conduct himself in concord with the higher demands of his reasonable nature; or he reverses this relationship, and subordinates the reasonable part of his being to the sensuous part, and thus merely follows the thrust with which the necessity of nature drives him on, just like other phenomena; or the impulses of natural necessity place themselves in harmony with the laws of reason, and the person is at one with himself.

If a person becomes conscious of his pure autonomy, he thrusts everything sensuous from him, and only by this distinction from matter will he attain to the feeling of his rational freedom. But, because sensuousness stubbornly and powerfully resists, a marked force and effort is required of him, without which it were impossible for him to hold off the appetites and silence insistently urging instinct. A mind so attuned lets nature, which depends upon him, learn, that he is her master in those cases where she acts in service of his will, as well as where she wants to encroach upon his will. Sensuousness, therefore, under his strict discipline, will appear to be supressed, and inner resistance will outwardly betray itself as coercion. Hence, such a constitution of sentiment, in which moral freedom shows itself struggling with matter, cannot be conducive to beauty, which nature brings forth by no other means than her freedom, and this constitution, therefore, also cannot become grace.

If, on the other hand, the person, subjugated by needs, allows natural instinct unfettered rule over himself, then, along with his inner autonomy, every trace of freedom in his form vanishes as well. Only bestiality speaks forth from the rolling, glassy eye, the lusting, open mouth, the strangled, trembling voice, the quickly gasping breath, the trembling limbs, from the entire flaccid form. All resistance of moral power has given way, and nature in him is set in total freedom. But, just this total cessation of self-activity, which usually ensues in the moment of sensuous longing, and even more in the enjoyment of it, also sets raw matter, previously constrained by the balance of active and passive forces, momentarily free. The dead forces of nature begin to take the upper hand over the living ones of organization; form begins to be repressed by mass, humanity by common nature. The soul-beaming eye becomes lustreless, or stares glassily and *vacant* out of its socket; the fine, rosy color of the cheeks thickens into a coarse and uniform bleachy flush; the mouth becomes a mere hole, since its form is no longer the effect of active, but of waning forces; the voice and sighing breath, nothing but noises, by means of which the heavy chest seeks relief, and betrays now merely a mechanical need, but no soul. In a word: with the freedom which sensuousness usurps unto itself, beauty is inconceivable. The freedom of forms, which the moral will had merely *confined*, *overwhelms* the coarse material, which always wins as much of the the field as is torn away from the will.

A person in this condition outrages not merely *moral* sensibility, which unyieldingly demands the expression of humanity; the *aesthetical* sensibility, too, which satisfies itself not with mere matter, rather seeks free pleasure in the form, will turn away in disgust from such a sight, in which only *lusts* can find their account.

The first of these relationships between the two natures in a person reminds us of a *monarchy*, where the strict supervision of the ruler holds every impulse in check; the second, of a wild *ochlocracy*, where the citizens become as little free by suspension of their obedience, as the human form becomes beautiful by the suppression of moral autonomy, rather fall under the sway of the more brutal despotism of the lowest classes, just as the form is subjugated to mass. Just as freedom lies in the middle between *lawful* suasion and anarchy, so we shall now find beauty, too, in the middle between *dignity*, as the expression of the ruling mind, and *wantonness*, as the expression of the ruling insticts.

If, that is, neither *reason, ruling over sensuousness, nor sensuousness, ruling over reason,* accords with beauty of expression, then shall that sentient condition (for there is no fourth case), *where reason and sensuousness,* duty and inclination, *accord with each other,* be the condition under which beauty of play ensues.

In order to become an object of desire, obedience to reason must give us cause to take pleasure in it, for instinct is only set in motion by pleasure and pain. In usual experience, it is indeed the reverse, and pleasure is considered the cause wherefore one acts reasonably. For the fact that morality itself has finally ceased to speak this language, we have to thank the immortal author of the *Critique,* to whom the honor is due to have reestablished healthy reason out of philosophizing reason.

But, in the way the principles of this philosopher are usually presented by him, and also by others, inclination is a very ribald companion of moral sentiment, and pleasure, a regrettable supplement to moral principles. Although the impulse to happiness claims no blind rule over men, it still wants to *have something to say* in the moral business of choice, and thus taints the purity of will, which ought always to follow only the *law* and never an *impulse*. In order, therefore, to be absolutely certain, that inclination not take part, one would rather see it at war with, rather than in accord with the laws of reason, because it might all too easily happen, that the approving intercession of inclination might procure it powers over the will. Since the lawfulness of deeds is not at issue in moral acts, rather only the dutifulness of disposition, one rightly places no value on the consideration, that it might be more to the credit of moral acts, if inclination found itself on the same side as duty. This much, therefore, appears to be certain: that the applause of sensuousness, while it casts no suspicion on the dutifulness of the will, is at least *no guarantee* of a dutiful disposition. The sensuous expression of this approval in grace, will never provide sufficient and valid testimony of the morality of the act with which it is met, and from the beautiful presentation of a disposition or act, one will never learn of its moral value.

As certainly as I am convinced, and just because I am, that the share which inclination has in a free act proves nothing about the dutifulness of this act, I believe, that I may conclude *from this*, that the moral perfection of a person can be manifest only in the share which his inclination takes in his moral action. That is to say, it is not man's purpose, to accomplish individual moral acts, but to be a moral creature. Not *virtues*, but *virtue* is his precept, and Virtue is nothing else than "an inclination to duty." As much as deeds performed from inclination and deeds performed from duty stand opposed to each other, this is not so in the subjective sense, and the person not only *may*, in fact he *must* bring desire and duty into connection: he should obey his reason with joy. Not to cast it away, as a burden, nor to strip it off like a coarse casing, no, to bring it into innermost agreement with his higher self, to this end is a sensuous nature placed beside his pure intellectual nature. In that she made him a reasonable sensuous creature, that is, man, nature announces to him the obligation not to divide asunder what she brought together, not even in the purest expression of his divine part to leave the sensuous part behind, and not to found the triumph of the one on the repression of the other. Only when it flows forth *from his entire humanity* as the united effect of both principles, *when it has become nature for him,* is his moral way of thinking secure from danger. For, so long as the moral mind still applies *force,* natural impulse must still have power to set against it. The enemy merely cast down can arise again, the reconciled is truly vanquished.

In Kantian moral philosophy, the idea of *duty* is presented with a severity which frightens all the Graces away, and a weak reason might easily attempt to seek moral perfection on the path of a gloomy and monkish asceticism.* As much as the great philosopher sought to guard against this misinterpretation, which of all things must be an outrage to his cheerful and free mind, yet it seems to me, that he himself, by the strict and harsh opposition of the two principles working upon the will of a person, gave a strong (although, given his intention, hardly avoidable) inducement to it. On the matter itself, after the proofs he has provided, there can be no argument among thinking minds *who want to be convinced,* and I hardly know how one would not rather surrender his entire humanity, than to want to obtain a different result from reason in this affair. But, as pure as his approach to the *investigation* of the truth was, and as much as everything here explains itself on the basis of merely objective reasons, he yet seems, in the representation of the truth he found, to have been guided by a more subjective maxim, which, as I believe, is not difficult to explain from the circumstances of the time.

Such was the condition of the morality of his time, as he found it in its system and practice, a crude materialism in moral principles on the one hand, which an unworthy complacency of the philosophers had placed like a pillow under the head of the flaccid character of the time, must have aroused his indignation. On the other hand, a no less questionable *principle of perfection*, which, in order to realize an abstract idea of general world perfection, was not very particular about the choice of means, necessarily aroused his attention. He thus aimed the strongest of his arguments where the danger appeared greatest, and re-form, most urgent, made it unto a law, to ruthlessly prosecute sensuousness, both where with brazen impudence it flouts moral sentiment, as well as in the imposing shell of morally laudable purposes, wherein especially a certain enthusiastic monastic mind knows how to conceal it. He had not to instruct *ignorance*, rather to rebuke *perversity*. Violent emotions require the *cure*, not ingratiation and persuasion; and the more severe the contrast which the principle of truth made with prevailing maxims, the more could he hope to stimulate reflection about it. He became a Draco of his time, because to him it seemed not yet worthy and receptive of a Solon. From the sanctuary of *pure reason* he brought forth the alien and yet well-known moral law, and put it on exhibition in its full sanctity before the disgraced century, and inquired little, whether there be eyes, which do not endure its brightness.

But, whereof were the *children of the house* to blame, that he only cared for the *servants*. Because often very impure inclinations usurp the name of virtue, must, on that account, the magnanimous sentiment in the most noble breast be made suspect? Because the moral weakling would like to give the moral law of reason a *laxity* which makes it the toy of his *convenience*, must it therefore be infused with a *rigidity* which transforms the most powerful expression of moral freedom into a merely more glorious kind of slavery? For, has the truly moral person a freer choice between self-esteem and self-condemnation, than the slave of sensuousness between pleasure and pain? Is there then less compulsion for the pure will, than for the corrupted? Must humanity be indicted and degraded by the *imperative* form of moral law, and the most noble document of its greatness be at once the testament to its infirmity? Was it to be avoided in this imperative form, that a precept, which man, as a creature of reason, gives unto himself, which on that account alone binds him, and on that account alone accords with his feeling of freedom, took on the semblance of an alien and positive law—a semblance, which, by its *radical* bias, could hardly diminish the impulse (in that it makes him guilty) to act against that very precept?[7]†

It is certainly no advantage for moral truths to have emotions, to which a person may admit without blushing, *against* them. But, how shall sentiments of beauty and freedom be compatible with the austere spirit of a law, which guides a person more through *fear* than *confidence*, which, although nature *had made him one*, yet always seeks to dismember him, and assures itself dominance over part of his essence only for that reason, that it awakens in him distrust of another? Human nature is a more interconnected whole in reality, than the philosopher, who can achieve something only by dissection, is allowed to let it manifest itself. Never more may reason castigate such emotions as unworthy of itself, which the heart gleefully confesses, and never more may a man, where he were morally degraded, still not rise in his own esteem. Were sensuous nature in morality always only the repressed and never a *collaborating party*, how could she surrender the entire fire of her emotions to a triumph which she celebrates over herself? How could she be a so lively participant in the self-consciousness of a pure mind, were she not capable of so fervently joining with it, that the analytical understanding itself were no longer capable of separating them without violence?

The will, all the same, has a more direct connection with the faculty of sentiment than with knowledge, and it were in many cases bad if it first had to orient itself by *pure reason*. It awakens in me no good judgment of a person if he can trust the voice of impulse so little, that he is compelled to interrogate it first before the court of morality; instead, one will esteem him more, if he trusts his impulses with a certain confidence, without danger of being misguided by them. For that proves, that both principles in him find themselves already in that concord which is the seal of perfected humanity, and is that which we understand by a *beautiful soul*.

We call it a beautiful soul, when moral sentiment has assured itself of all emotions of a person ultimately to that degree, that it may abandon the guidance of the will to emotions, and never run danger of being in contradiction with its own decisions. Hence, in a beautiful soul individual deeds are not properly moral, rather, the entire character is. Nor can one add any individual deed to its account of merit, because the satisfaction of an impulse can never be called meritorious. The beautiful soul has no other merit, than that it is. With such ease, as if mere instinct were acting out of it, it carries out the most painful duties of humanity, and the most heroic sacrifice which it exacts from natural impulse comes to view like a voluntary effect of just this impulse. Hence, the beautiful soul knows nothing of the beauty of its deeds, and it no longer occurs to it, that one could act or feel differently; a trained student of moral rules, on the other hand, just as the word of the master requires of him, will be prepared at every moment to give the strictest account of the relationship of his action to the law. His life will be like a drawing, where one sees the rules marked by harsh strokes, such as, at best, an apprentice of the principles of art might learn. But, in a beautiful life, as in a painting by Titian, all of those cutting border lines have vanished, and yet the whole form issues forth the more true, vital, and harmonious.

It is thus in a beautiful soul, that sensuousness and reason, duty and inclination harmonize, and grace is its epiphany. Only in the service of a beautiful soul can nature at the same time possess freedom and preserve her form, since the former she forfeits under the rule of a strict sentience, the latter, under the anarchy of sensuousness. A

beautiful soul also infuses a form which is wanting of architectonic beauty, and one often sees it triumph even over
frailties of nature. All movements which issue from her
*grace* become light, soft, and yet vigorous. Merry and free
shall the eye gleam, and therein emotions glow. From the
gentleness of the heart shall the heart receive a grace such
as no pretense can feign. There shall be no tension seen in
gestures, no coercion in willful movements, for the soul
knows of none. The voice shall become music, and move the
heart with the pure flow of its modulations. Architectonic
beauty may arouse pleasure, admiration, and amazement,
but only grace can delight. Beauty has worshippers, only
grace has lovers; for we worship the Creator, and love the
person.

On the whole, one will find grace more in the female
sex (beauty possibly more in the male), the cause of which
is not far to seek. Bodily frame, as well as character, must
contribute to grace; the former by its suppleness, to receive
impressions and set them in play, and the latter by the
moral harmony of feelings. In both, nature more favored
woman than man.

The more tender female receives every impression
more quickly, and lets it more quickly vanish once more.
Firm constitutions come in motion only by a storm, and
when strong muscles are tensed, they cannot manifest the
ease which grace requires. That which is still beautiful sensitivity in a woman's face would already express suffering in
that of a man. The most tender fiber of a woman bends like
a thin reed under the softest breath of emotion. In light and
lovely waves the soul glides over the speaking countenance,
soon then smoothing into a calm mirror once again.

Also what the soul must contribute to grace, can be
more easily fulfilled by woman than by man. Seldom will
the female character elevate itself to the highest idea of
moral purity, and seldom, furthermore, will it achieve more
than an affected deed. The female character will often resist
sensuousness with heroic strength, but *through* sensuousness. Since the morality of woman is usually on the side of

inclination, it will appear as if inclination were on the side of morality. Grace will therefore be the expression of female virtue, of which the male may often be wanting.

## DIGNITY

Just as grace is the expression of a beautiful soul, *dignity* is the expression of a noble disposition of mind.

It is, indeed, the person's task to establish an intimate accord between his two natures, always to be a harmonizing whole, and act with his full-voiced entire humanity. But, this beauty of character, the ripest fruit of his humanity, is merely an idea, to be in accord with which, he must strive with persistent vigilance, but which, for all of his effort, he can never entirely achieve.

The reason why he can never achieve it lies in the inalterable constitution of his nature; it is the physical conditions of his very existence which prevent him.

In order, that is, to secure his existence in the world of sense, which depends on natural conditions, the person must (since, as a creature which can willfully change himself, he must provide for his subsistence himself) be enabled to deeds, whereby those physical conditions of his existence may be fulfilled, and if they fall to decay, reestablished. But, although nature had to surrender the task of providing for man, which in her vegetable productions she takes upon herself alone, yet the satisfaction of a so urgent need, where his and his entire species' existence is at stake, could not be entrusted to his uncertain insight. She therefore drew this matter, which in respect of *content* belongs in her domain, also in respect of *form* into the same, in that she laid necessity into the direction of willfulness. This was the genesis of instinct, which is nothing else, than a natural necessity through the medium of sentiment.

Instinct assails the sentient faculty through the double power of pain and pleasure: through pain, where it demands satisfaction, through pleasure where it finds it.

Since the necessity of nature brooks no concessions, man too, regardless of his freedom, must feel what nature wants him to feel, and accordingly, whether the feeling is of pain or of pleasure, there must unalterably ensue in him either abhorrence or desire. In this he is equivalent to an animal, and the most stubborn stoic will feel hunger and abhor it as fervently as the worm at his feet.

But, now the great difference begins. From desire and abhorrence among animals, action follows just as necessarily as desire ensued upon sensation, and sensation upon the outside impression. Here there is a chain, running ever onward, where every ring necessarily links into the other. Among mankind there is yet one more court, the will, which, as a supra-sensuous faculty, is subjugated neither to the law of nature, nor to that of reason, so that a totally free will remains, to direct itself according to the one or the other. The animal *must* strive to be rid of pain, a *person* can decide to keep it.

The will of man is a noble concept, also, when one pays no attention to its moral use. *Mere* will elevates man above beastliness; *moral* will elevates him to divinity. But, he must have left beastliness behind him, before he can approach divinity; hence, it is no small step toward the moral freedom of will, to break the necessity of nature in himself even in matters of no account, to exercise *mere* will.

The legislation of nature binds until it meets with the will, where it ceases and reason begins. Will here stands between both courts of law, and it alone decides from which it wants to receive the law; but will does not stand in the same relationship to both. As natural force, it is as free in respect of the one as the other; that means, it *need* not side with the one, nor with the other. But, it is not free as a moral force, which means, it *should* side with reason. It is not *bound* to either, but to the law of reason it is obliged. In fact, it therefore needs its freedom, even if it acts in contradiction to reason, but then it uses freedom basely, because, irrespective of its freedom, it still remains bound *within nature*, and makes no addition of reality to the operation of mere instinct; for, to *will* out of appetite, means only to desire with more effort.[8]

The legislation of nature through instinct can come into principled conflict with the legislation of reason, if instinct requires for its satisfaction an act which contradicts the moral principle. In this case, it is the immutable duty of the will, to pursue the demand of nature with the verdict of reason, since laws of nature oblige only conditionally, the laws of reason, however, absolutely and unconditionally.

But, nature vigorously claims her rights, and since she never makes demands fortuitously, she thus, unsatisfied, neither withdraws a demand. Since from the first cause, by means of which she is set in motion, until she meets with the will, where her legislation ceases, everything in her is strict necessity, she can therefore not *retreat* in surrender, but must always press *forward* against the will, which stands in the way of the fulfillment of her demand. It, in fact, sometimes seems as if she had shortened her course, and, without bringing her request before the will, it seems as if there were a direct causality for her action, through which she is redressed of her demands. In such a case, where the person not only let instinct take a free rein, rather, where instinct *seizes* the reins, the person were *only* animal; but it is very doubtful, whether this can ever be the case, and were he ever actually so, it is a question whether this blind power of his instinct is not, in fact, a crime of his will.

The faculty of desire insists on satisfaction, and the will is called upon to provide it. But, the will should receive its directing principle from reason, and only make a decision according to what reason allows or prescribes. If, now, the will, in fact, turns to reason before it approves the demands of instinct, then it acts morally; but if it decides directly, then it acts sensuously.[9]

Hence, as long as nature makes her demands, and wants to take the will by surprise by the blind force of emotion, it behooves the will to command nature to hold still until reason has spoken. Whether reason's verdict will turn out *for* or *against* the interests of sensuousness, that is just what the will cannot yet know; but just for that reason, the will must follow this procedure in every emotion without exception, and deny to nature, in every case where she is the instigating element, direct causality. Only by breaking the force of desire, which with overhaste rushes toward its satisfaction, and would most like to scurry past the court of the will entirely, does man demonstrate his autonomy (independence), and prove himself a moral creature, which never merely desires nor merely abhors, but *must always want* his abhorrence and desire.

But, the mere inquiry of reason is already an encroachment on nature, who is a competent judge in her own affairs and will not see her verdicts subordinated to a new and alien jurisdiction. Each act of the will, which brings the affairs of the faculty of desire before the court of morality, is therefore, in reality, *contrary to nature*, because it makes something fortuitous out of what is necessary, and submits the decision to laws of reason in a matter where only laws of nature may speak, and have also actually spoken. For, as little as *pure reason* in its moral legislation considers how sense would like to receive its decisions, just as little does nature in her legislation take account of how she might justify herself to *pure reason*. In each of the two a different necessity holds sway, which, however, would be none at all, were one of them permitted to make fortuitous changes in the other.

For that reason, even the most courageous spirit, for all the resistance which he exercises against sensuousness, cannot repress emotion itself, desire itself, rather he can *merely* deny them influence upon the direction of his will; he can *disarm* instinct by moral means, but only *soothe* it by natural means. He can, by means of his independent power, prevent natural laws from becoming a compulsion for his will, but of these laws he himself can change absolutely nothing.

In emotions, therefore, where *first of all* nature (instinct) acts, and seeks either to *circumvent* the will entirely or to draw it violently to her side, morality of character cannot express itself otherwise than through *resistance*, and, so that instinct not restrict freedom of will, only prevent it by restricting instinct. Accord with the laws of reason in emotions, therefore, is not otherwise possible than by contradiction of the demands of nature. And since nature never withdraws her demands for reasons of morality, everything consequently remains the same on her side, however the will, in view of that, may comport itself; there is, therefore, no congruity possible between inclination and duty, between reason and sensuousness, so that man here cannot act with the totality of his harmonizing nature, rather, exclusively and solely with his reasonable nature. In such cases, therefore, he also does not act *morally beautiful*, because inclination, too, must take part in the beauty of a deed, whereas here inclination is in conflict. But, he acts *morally great*, because all that, and only that is great, which testifies to the superiority of the higher faculty over the sensuous faculty.

The *beautiful* soul must, therefore, transform itself in emotion into a *noble* soul, and that is the unerring hallmark, whereby one can distinguish it from the *good heart* or *virtue of temperament*. If inclination in a person is only, therefore, on the side of justice, because justice fortunately finds itself on the side of inclination, then will the natural impulse in emotion exert a totally dominating force of compulsion over the will, and, where a sacrifice is necessary, morality and not sensuousness will bring it. If, on the other hand, it were reason itself which, as is the case in a beautiful character, binds inclination to the directions of *duty*, and *only entrusts* the rudder to sensuousness, then reason will take it back in the very moment when instinct wants to misuse its power. Virtue of temperament in emotion is, therefore, reduced to a mere product of nature; the beautiful soul passes over into the heroic, and elevates itself to pure intelligence.

Mastery of instinct by moral force is *freedom of mind*, and *dignity* is the name of its epiphany.

Strictly speaking, the moral force in man is capable of no representation, since that which is supra-sensuous cannot be made sensuous. But, it can be indirectly represented to the understanding by sensuous signs, which is in fact the case with the dignity of the human form.

Aroused natural impulse, just as the heart in its moral emotions, is accompanied by movements in the body which partly rush ahead of the will, partly, as merely sympathetic movements, are not subject to its governance whatsoever. Since neither sentiment, nor desire and abhorrence, lie within the will of a person, he thus cannot exert command over those movements which are immediately connected to them. But, impulse does not remain standing at mere desire; precipitously and urgently it seeks to realize its object, and, if it is not insistently withstood by the independent mind, will itself *anticipate* such deeds, about which the will alone ought to speak. For the impulse to self-preservation wrestles incessantly for legislative authority in the realm of the will, and its endeavor is to rule as unfettered over man as it rules over animals.

Hence, one finds movements of two kinds and origins in each emotion, which enkindle the impulse to self-preservation in man; firstly such, which directly proceed from sentiment, and are unwillful; secondly such, which, according to their kind, ought to be and can be willful, but which the blind impulse of nature exacts from freedom. The first relate to the emotion itself, and are therefore necessarily connected to it; the second correspond more to the cause and object of emotion, and are therefore fortuitous and changeable, and cannot be taken to be infallible signs of the same. But, since both, as soon as the object is fixed, are necessarily equivalent to the impulse of nature, they each contribute, to make the expression of emotion a complete and harmonic whole.[10]

Now, if the will possesses sufficient independence to lay restraints on encroaching natural impulse, and to maintain against its furious power its own just power, so shall all those appearances remain in force which aroused natural impulse effected in its own domain, but all those shall now be lacking which, in the domain under the jurisdiction of another, it had despotically wanted to usurp. The appearances are no longer in accord, but in their contradiction lies the expression of moral force.

Assume that we notice in a person signs of the most painful emotions from the class of those first entirely unwillful movements. But, while his veins swell, his muscles are cramped in tension, his voice is strangled, his chest swollen, his belly pressed inward, gentle are his willful movements, the lines of his face free, and his eyes and brow are joyful. Were the person merely a creature of sense, then all of his features would be in accord with one another, since they have a common source, and therefore they must all, in the present instance without exception, express suffering. But, since features of calm are mingled with features of pain, and since a single cause cannot have opposite effects, then this contradiction of features proves the existence and influence of a force which is independent of suffering, and superior to the impressions to which we see that which is sensuous succumb. And in this way, *calm in suffering*, wherein dignity actually consists, although only by a decision of reason, becomes the demonstration of intelligence in man and the expression of his moral freedom.[11]

But, it is not merely in suffering in the narrow sense, where the word signifies only painful emotions, but at every moment the desiring faculty shows a strong interest, that the mind must prove its freedom, and thus dignity be its expression. The pleasant emotion requires it no less than the painful, since nature in both instances would gladly play the master, and ought to be reined in by the will. Dignity relates to the *form* and not to the *content* of emotion, for which reason it can happen, that often, in respect of the content, laudable emotions, if the person surrenders himself to them blindly, for lack of dignity, are reduced to the common and low; but not seldom, reprehensible emotions approximate to nobilty, as soon as they bespeak mastery of the mind over its sentiments in respect of form.

In respect of dignity, therefore, the mind conducts itself in the body as *master*, for it is here that it must maintain its independence against imperious impulse, which without it strikes to action, and would gladly cast off its yoke. In respect of grace, on the other hand, the mind governs *liberally*, for here it is the mind which sets nature into action, and finds no resistance to vanquish. But, only obedience deserves forbearance, and only *insubordination* can justly deserve sternness.

Hence, grace lies in the *freedom of willful movements*; *dignity* in *mastery over unwillful movements*. Grace inclines toward nature, where she carries out the commands of the mind, a semblance of the willful; where nature wants to rule, dignity subjugates her to the mind. Everywhere instinct begins to act, and makes so bold as to intercede into the office of the will, there may the will show no *indulgence*, rather must prove its independence (autonomy) by insistent resistance. Where, on the other hand, the will *begins*, and sensuousness *follows*, there may the mind show no sternness, and instead must show indulgence. This, in few words, is the law for the relationship of the two natures in man, just as it manifests itself in appearance.

Dignity is more required and manifest in *suffering* (pathos), grace more in ethos; for only in suffering can freedom of sentiment reveal itself, and the freedom of the body only in action.

Since dignity is an expression of resistance, which the independent mind exerts against natural impulse, this latter, therefore, necessarily viewed as a force which makes resistance necessary, so where there is no such force to be subdued, it is ridiculous, and where there ought no longer be such a force, contemptible. One laughs about the comedian (of whatever rank and station he might be), who affects a certain air of dignity even on occasions of no consequence. One has contempt for the small soul, who assumes the honor of dignity for the exercise of a common duty which is often only the omission of a base act.

On the whole, it is not in fact dignity, rather grace, that one demands of virtue. In the case of virtue, dignity comes of its own, which, in respect of its content, presupposes the

mastery of the person over his impulses. In the exercise of
moral duties, moreover, sensuousness will find itself in a
condition of coercion and repression, especially where a
painful sacrifice must be made. But, since ideally perfect
humanity requires, that there be no discord, but concord
between the moral and the sensuous, so it is not commensurate with dignity, which, as an expression of the discord
between the two, makes visible either the particular restraints of the subject, or the general ones of mankind.

If it is the former, and it is due merely to the incapacity
of the subject, that inclination and duty in an act do not
accord, so will this act always lose just so much in moral
esteem as struggle mingles in its exercise, thus dignity in
its execution. For our moral judgment applies the standard
of the species to every individual, and there are no other
restraints laid upon a person than those of humanity.

If it is the latter, and if a deed of duty cannot be brought
into harmony with the demands of nature without annulling
the conception of human nature, then resistance against
inclination is necessary, and it is the sight of struggle which
can convince us of the possiblity of triumph. Here we therefore expect an expression of discord in the appearance, and
will never permit ourselves to be convinced to believe in a
virtue where we do not catch sight of humanity. Where,
therefore, moral duty demands an act which necessarily
makes sensuousness suffer, there everything is serious, and
not play, there the ease of execution would outrage us more
than please us; therefore, the expression cannot be grace,
rather dignity. On the whole, the law holds here, that
the person must do with grace everything which he can
accomplish within his humanity, and with dignity everything, in order to accomplish the which, he must transcend
his humanity.

Just as we require grace of virtue, so we also require
dignity of inclination. Grace is as natural to inclination, as
dignity is to virtue, for by its very content it is sensuous,
favorably disposed to natural freedom, and adversary to all
exertion. Even the coarse person does not lack a certain

degree of grace, if love or a similar emotion besouls him, and where do we find more grace than among children, who yet are entirely under the guidance of the senses? There is far more danger, that inclination makes the condition of suffering a prevailing one, which suffocates self-activity of the mind, and results in a general disability. In order, therefore, to attain to esteem in a noble feeling, which only a *moral* cause can provide to it, inclination must always ally itself to dignity. For that reason, the loving one expects dignity from the object of his passion. Dignity alone is his guarantee, that it was not desire which compelled the object of his passion toward him, rather, that it was freedom which chose him—that he is not *desired as a thing*, rather *esteemed highly as a person.*

One expects grace of him who demands a commitment, and dignity of him who makes one. The former, in order to avoid an insulting judgment of the other, ought to reduce the act of his disinterested decision by the share which he lets inclination take in it, to an *affected* act, and give himself the semblance of the victorious part. The other, in order not to dishonor humanity in his person (whose sacred palladium is freedom) by the dependency he enters, ought to elevate the mere *approach* of inclination into an act of his will, and in this way, by receiving a favor, grant one.

One must chastise a mistake with grace, and confess one with dignity. If one reverses it, it will seem as if the one too much appreciates his merit, and other, too little his failing.

If the strong will be loved, he shall soften his superiority by grace. If the weak will be esteemed, so may he succour his weakness with dignity. One is otherwise of the opinion, that dignity belongs upon the throne, and, as we know, those who sit on it, in their councils, confessionals, and parliaments, love—grace. But, what is perhaps good and laudable in a political kingdom, is not always so in the kingdom of taste. Into this kingdom the king, too, steps, as soon as he steps down from his throne (for thrones do have their privileges), and the cowering page at court dons his sacred freedom, too, as soon as he stands up straight as a person. Then might the former be advised to replenish what he lacks from the surfeit of the other, and render the latter so much of dignity as he himself has need of grace.

Since dignity and grace have their diverse domains wherein they express themselves, they yet do not exclude one another in the same person, nor in fact, in the same condition; it is rather only from grace, that dignity receives its certification, and it is only from dignity, that grace receives its worth.

Dignity, indeed, everywhere proves, when we meet with it, a certain restraint of desires and inclinations. But, whether it might not rather be dullness of the sentient faculty (severity), which we take for self-restraint, and whether it be really moral self-activity and not the preponderance of another emotion, thus deliberate exertion, our doubts on this account can only be lifted by accompanying grace. Grace, that is, bespeaks a calm disposition, harmonious with itself, and a sensitive heart.

In the same way, grace of its own bespeaks a receptivity of the sentient faculty, and a concord of sentiments. But, that it be not indolence of the mind which leaves the senses so much freedom, and that it be morality which brought these sentiments into concord, this, in turn, only allied dignity can guarantee us. It is, that is, in dignity, that the subject proves his legitimacy as an independent force; and in that the will *restrains the license* of unwillful movements, it proclaims, that it merely *permits the freedom* of willful ones.

If grace and dignity are supported, the former by architectonic beauty, the latter by force, *united* in the same person, then the expression of humanity in the person is complete, and he stands there, justified in the world of mind, and exonerated in that of appearance. Both legislators here touch one another so closely, that their borders flow together. With softened lustre there rises in the smile of the mouth, in the tender animated look, in the cheerful brow, *freedom of reason*, and with sublime dispatch, *necessity of nature* is lost in the noble majesty of the countenance.

It was according to this ideal of human beauty that the art of antiquity was framed, and one recognizes it in the divine form of a Niobe, in Belvederean Apollo, in the Winged Genius of Borghesi, and in the Muse of the Barberini Palace.[12]

Where grace and dignity unite, we are alternately attracted and repulsed; attracted as intellects, repulsed as sensuous natures.

In dignity, that is, an example of the subjection of the senses to morality is held up to us, the imitation of which is for us at the same time law, but surmounting our physical capacities. The discord between the needs of nature and the requirement of the law, whose validity we yet acknowledge, strains sensuousness, and awakens the feeling called *respect*, which is inseparable from dignity.

In grace on the other hand, as in beauty generally, reason sees its demands fulfilled in sensuousness, and suddenly strides to meet it as the sensuous appearance of one of its own ideas. This unexpected concord of the fortuitousness of nature with the necessity of reason, awakens an emotion of joyous approbation, *good will*, which is relaxing for the senses, but animating and engaging for the mind, and an attraction of the sensuous object must follow. This attraction we call benevolence—*love*; an emotion which is inseparable from grace and beauty.

With *allurement* (allurement of love, or voluptuousness, stimulus), a sensuous thing is held up to the senses, which promises the satisfaction of a desire, that is, lust. Sense, therefore, strives to unite itself with sensuousness, and sensuous desire arises; an emotion, which is an excitement for the senses, but dulling for the mind.

One may say of respect, that it *bows down before* its object; of love, that it *inclines toward* its own. For respect, the object is reason and the subject is sensuous nature.[13] In love, the object is sensuous, and the subject is moral nature. In sensuous desire, object and subject are sensuous.

Love alone, therefore, is a free emotion, for her pure source flows from the seat of freedom, from our divine nature. Here it is not the petty and low which mingle with the great and high, not sense, which gazes dizzily aloft at the law of reason; it is the *absolutely grand* itself, which finds itself imitated in grace and dignity, and satisfied in sensuousness, it is the Legislator himself, the *God* in us, who plays with his own image in the world of sense. Sentiment is therefore relaxed in love, for it is strained in respect; here there is nothing which sets restraints, for absolute greatness has nothing above it, and sensuousness, from which alone restraints could come, accords in grace and beauty with the ideas of the mind. Love is a descent, for respect is a climbing upward. The bad person therefore can love nothing, although he must respect much; the good person therefore can respect little which he cannot embrace at the same time in love. The pure mind can only love, not respect; sense can only respect, but not love.

If the conscience-striken person is suspended in eternal fear of meeting the Legislator in himself in the world of sense, and catches sight of his enemy in everything great and beautiful and excellent, so the beautiful soul knows no sweeter happiness than to see that which is sacred in himself imitated or realized outside of himself, and to embrace in the world of sense his immortal friend. Love is that which is at once the most magnanimous and the most selfish in nature: the former, for she receives from her object nothing, rather gives him everything, for the pure mind can only give, and not receive; the latter, because it is always only her own self, which she seeks and esteems in her object.

But, just for the reason that the lover receives from the beloved only what he himself gave, so it often befalls him, that he gives what he does not receive. External sense believes it sees what only the internal sense may perceive, the fiery wish becomes belief, and the lover's own surfeit conceals the poverty of the beloved. That is why love is so often deceived, which seldom happens to respect and desire. As long as internal sense exalts the outer, just so long does the blissful enchantment of platonic love last, to which only the permanence is lacking for it to become the ecstasy of the immortals. But, as soon as inner sense no longer insinuates *its own* view into that without, the external steps into its rights again, and demands its due, *matter*. The fire which enkindled heavenly Venus is employed by the earthly one, and natural impulse takes vengeance of long neglect, not seldom by an all the more unrestrained domination. Since sense is never deceived, it presses its advantage with coarse arrogance against its more noble rival, and makes bold to claim, that it has held what enthusiasm still owed.

Dignity prevents love from becoming desire. Grace takes care, that respect does not become fear.

True beauty, true grace should never arouse desire. Where the latter mingles, its object must either lack dignity, or the observer, morality of sentiment.

True greatness should never arouse fear. Where this occurs, one can be certain, that either its object lacks taste and grace, or the observer, a favorable testimony of his conscience.

Allurement, charm, and grace are in fact usually taken to be equivalent; but they are not, or should not be, for the concepts they express are of diverse species, which deserve a different characterization.

There is an animating and a calming grace. The first borders on excitement of the senses, and pleasure in the same can, if it is not restrained by dignity, easily degenerate into yearning. This can be called allurement. A langorous person cannot set himself in motion by inner force, rather, he must receive the material from the outside, and, by easy exercises of the fantasy, and rapid transitions from sentience to action, attempt to restore his vitality. This he accomplishes in the company of an *alluring* (enticing) person, who brings the stagnating sea of his powers of imagination into swing by discussion and glances.

Calming grace borders more closely on dignity, since it expresses itself by moderating agitated movements. To it the tensed person turns, and the wild storm of emotions dissipates itself upon its peacefully breathing chest. This can be called *grace*. With enticement, laughing wit and thorns of mockery gladly go hand in hand; with grace, compassion and love. Unnerved Soliman pines away in the chains of Roxanne, while the tumultuous mind of an Othello lays itself to rest on the soft breast of a Desdemona.

Dignity, too, has its several shadings, and where it approaches grace and beauty, becomes *noble*, and where it borders on the timorous, *majesty*.

The highest degree of grace is *enchanting*; the highest degree of dignity, *majesty*. We lose ourselves at once in the enchanting, and flow over into the object. The highest enjoyment of freedom borders on its complete loss, and the intoxication of the mind, on the tumult of sensuous desire. Majesty, on the other hand, holds up to us a law, which obliges us to look into ourselves. We cast our eyes to the ground in the presence of God, forget everything outside ourselves, and feel nothing but the heavy burden of our own existence.

Only what is sacred has majesty. If a person can represent this to us, he has majesty; and although our knees do not follow, our mind will yet fall down before him. But, the mind will quickly rise again as soon as only the slightest trace of *human guilt* becomes visible in the object of our worship; for nothing, which is only *comparably* great, may cast down our courage.

Mere power, be it however terrible and limitless, can never lend majesty. Power impresses only the creature of sense, majesty must seize the freedom of the mind. A man who may write my death sentence, has no majesty as far as I am concerned on that account, as soon as I am but what I should be. His advantage over me is gone as soon as I will it. But, whoever presents me the pure will in his person, to him shall I bow down, even in the world to come.

Grace and dignity stand in too high value, not to entice vanity and folly to imitation. But, there is only *one* way to do that, that is by imitation of the disposition whereof they are the expression. Everything else is *mimicry*, and will make itself known soon enough through exaggeration.

Just as *pomposity* comes from mimicry of the sublime, the *precious* issues from imitation of the noble, affected grace becomes *airs*, and affected dignity, stiff *ceremony* and *gravity*.

Genuine grace *merely yields* and is willing to oblige; the false, on the other hand, *melts away*. True grace merely *indulges* the tools of willful movement, and wants not unnecessarily to encroach upon the freedom of nature; false grace has no heart at all to properly use the toils of the will, and, in order not to become severe or ponderous, rather sacrifices something of the purpose of the movement, or seeks to achieve it by *digression*. If the clumsy dancer in a minuet expends so much force, that it seems as though he were treading a mill-wheel, and cuts such sharp corners with his hands and feet, as if it all had to do with matters of geometrical precision, then the *affected* dancer will perform so weakly, that it seemed he feared the floor, and described nothing but serpentine lines with his hands and feet, though he were never to move from the spot. The fair sex, which is preeminently in possession of true grace, is also most often guilty of false grace; but nowhere does false grace greater insult, than where it serves as a fish-hook for desire. The smile of true grace then becomes the most repugnant grimace, the beautiful play of the eyes, so enchanting when it bespeaks true emotion, becomes a perversity, a melting modulating voice, so irresistable in a true mouth, becomes a studied tremulo noise, and the full voice of female charms a fraudulent artifice of the toilette.

While one has the opportunity to observe affected grace at the theater and in ballrooms, one can just as frequently study false dignity in the cabinets of ministers and the study rooms of scholars (especially from universities). While true dignity is satisfied to prevent emotion from becoming governor, and only sets restraint upon natural impulse where the latter wants to play the master in unwillful movements, false dignity governs even willful movements with an iron scepter, suppresses moral movements which are sacred to true dignity, as well as sensuous ones, and extinguishes the entire mimical play of the soul in the lines of the face. False dignity is not merely stern against reluctant nature, but also severe against submissive nature, and seeks its ridiculous grandeur in the subjugation of, and, where that will not succeed, in the submersion of nature. It is not much different than if this false dignity had praised everything which is nature with irreconcilable hate, sticks the body in long folded robes, which conceal the limbs and form of the person entirely, constrains the use of the limbs with a burdensome apparatus of ornamentation, and shaves off the hair, to replace a gift of nature with an artificial contraption. While true dignity is never ashamed of nature, only coarse nature, also where it keeps to itself, yet remains free and open when emotion shines in the eyes, and a merry, calm spirit rests upon its speaking brow, *gravity* lays the brow of false dignity in folds, becomes closed and mysterious, and scrupulously supervises the features like a comedian. All facial muscles are tensed, all true natural expression vanishes, and the entire person is like a sealed letter. But, false dignity is not always wrong to keep sharp discipline over the mimical play of its features, because they might well reveal more than wants to be heard aloud—a precaution of which true dignity obviously has no need. The latter will only govern nature, not conceal her; with false dignity, nature rules all the more violently from within, because she is coerced from without.[14]

## AUTHOR'S NOTES

1. Because—to repeat it once more—everything about beauty, which is *objective*, is given in *mere perception*. Since that which gives man precedence over all other creatures of sense does not *present itself* to mere perception, then a characteristic, which reveals itself to mere perception, cannot make this preeminence visible. His higher destiny, which alone is the cause of this preeminence, is thus not expressed by his beauty, and a sensuous concep-

tion of his beauty can, therefore, never furnish an ingredient of the former destiny, cannot be admitted in aesthetic judgment. It is not the thought itself, of which the human frame is the expression, but merely the effects thereof in its appearance, which reveal themselves to sense. Mere sense elevates itself to the supra-sensuous cause of these effects as little, as (if one will permit me this example) the merely sensuous man rises aloft to the idea of the supreme cause of the world, when satisfying his carnal impulses.

2. Therefore, Home takes the concept of grace too narrowly, when he says (*Grundsätze d. Kritik II*, 39): "that, if the most charming person is at *rest*, and neither moves nor speaks, we lose sight of the quality of charm, like colors in the dark." No, we do not lose sight of it, as long as we perceive those lines upon the sleeping person, which a benevolent and mild mind formed; and precisely the most treasured part of grace remains, that very part, which congealed *demeanor into lines,* and thus reveals the *preparedness* of mind in beautiful emotions. If, however, Mr. *Rectifier of the Works of Home* believes he sets his author aright with the remark, (pg. 459 of the same work) "that charm is not limited to willful movements, that a sleeping person does not cease to be charming"—and why?, "because, while he is in this condition, the involuntary, soft, and, for that very reason, the more graceful movements first become evident," he thus abolishes, annuls the concept of grace altogether, which Home merely conceived too narrowly. Involuntary movements in sleep, if they are not mechanical repetitions of willful ones, can never be graceful, far from their being preeminently such, and if a sleeping person is charming, this is by no means on account of the movements which he makes, but because of the *lines*, which attest to previous movements.

3. Philosophical writings, I. 90.

4. When something happens in front of a numerous company, it can befall, that each of those present has his own opinion about the disposition of the acting person, so fortuitously are willful movements connected with their moral cause. If, on the other hand, one out of this company unexpectedly catches sight of a very beloved friend or a very hated enemy, the unequivocal expression on his face would certainly and quickly betray the sentiments of his heart, and the judgment of the entire company on the present sentient condition of this person would probably

be completely unanimous: for here the expression is connected with its cause in the sentiment by natural necessity.

5. Upon a practiced sensibility, both can have the same effect as the original which they imitate, and if the art is great, they can even deceive the expert for a time. But, from some motion or other will the compulsion and intention ultimately shine forth, and then indifference, if not even contempt and disgust, are the inevitable result. As soon as we notice, that the architectonic beauty is affected, we see just that much of humanity (as appearance) disappear, as has been added from a foreign source—and how shall we, who do not forgive the surrender of yet a single fortuitous excellence, take pleasure in, yea even look upon an exchange indifferently, whereby a part of humanity is surrendered for base nature? How shall we, although we might pardon the effect, not despise the deceit?—as soon as we notice, that the grace is artificed, our heart closes suddenly, and the soul rising up to meet it flees in retreat. We see matter having suddenly been created out of mind, and an image of clouds out of a divine Juno.

Far be it from me, in this compilation, to deny the dance-master his merits on behalf of true grace, or the actor his claim thereto. The dance-master incontestably comes to the aid of true grace, in that he empowers the will with mastery of its tools, and sweeps aside the hindrances, which *mass* and *gravity* pose against the play of vital forces. He cannot accomplish this other than according to *rules*, which maintain the body in healthy discipline, and for as long as inertia resists, stiffly, these must be *compelling* and so may also appear to be such. But, when he discharges the apprentice from his school, the rules must already have performed their service upon him, so that they *need not accompany* him into the world: in brief, the work of rules must pass over into nature.

The low estimation, with which I speak of theatric graces, holds only for those that are *imitated*, and these I do not hesitate to castigate, on the stage just as in life. I confess, that the actor does not please me, who, however successfully he accomplishes his imitation, has studied his *Graces* at the toilette. The demands we make upon the actor, are: 1. *truth* of performance, and 2. beauty of performance. Now, I claim, that the actor, as far as *truth of performance* is concerned, must bring forth everything through art and nothing through nature, for otherwise he is no artist; and I shall admire him, if I hear or see, that he, who masterfully played an enraged Guelfo, is a person of tender character; on the other hand, I claim, that, as far as *grace of performance* is concerned, he must needs owe his art nothing, and that here everything about him must be a freely-willed work of nature. If it occurs to me, in respect of the truth of his playing, that this character is not natural to him, then I shall esteem him all the more; if I notice, in respect of the beauty of his playing, that these graceful movements are not natural to him, I shall not be able to restrain myself from being angry at him who had to avail himself of the resources of the *artist*. This is because grace vanishes where there is no naturalness, and because grace is still a demand which we believe ourselves justified in making of mere human beings. What shall I now answer to the mimic artist, who would like to know, since he cannot *learn* it, how he may come into possession of grace? He should—this is my view—first of all ensure, that the humanity in him comes to maturity, and then he should go hence and (if it is his profession) represent it upon the stage.

6. Hence we often find, that such beauty of form is considerably enlarged already in middle age by obesity, that, instead of those barely suggested tender lines of skin, *cavities* sink in and sausage-like folds protrude, that *weight*, unnoticeably, exerts its influence on the form, and that the alluring manifold play of beautiful lines upon the surface loses itself in a uniform swelling cushion of fat. Nature takes, what she once had given.

I mention in passing, that something similar happens to *genius*, which in its origin in general, as in its effects, has much in common with architectonic beauty. Like the latter, the former is a mere *product of nature*, and according to the perverse way of thinking of people, who esteem that most, which cannot be imitated according to any rule, and cannot be obtained through any merit, beauty is more admired than charm, genius more than the acquired power of mind. Both *favorites of nature*, for all of their bad manners (on account of which they are not seldom the object of deserved contempt), are considered as a kind of nobility by birth, as a higher caste, because their advantages depend upon nature, and therefore lie beyond all choice.

But, just as it befalls beauty, when she does not take timely care, to draw forth *grace* for support, so it also befalls *genius*, if it neglects to strengthen itelf by principles, taste, and science. Fitted out with lively and flourishing powers of imagination (and nature can grant nothing but sensuous advantages), so betimes may it consider, to secure itself this ambiguous gift by the sole use, whereby natural talents can become possessions of mind; I mean, by giving form to matter; for the mind can call nothing but form its own. Governed by no proportionate force of reason, the uncultivated, sumptuous *power of nature* will outgrow the freedom of understanding, and suffocate it, just as in the case of architectonic beauty, mass ultimately suppresses form.

Of this, experience, I think, provides ample proof, especially in respect of those poetic geniuses, who become famous, sooner than they are mature, and where, as is often the case with beauty, the entirety of talent is often only *youth*. But, when the short spring is past, and one asks after the fruits of which it offered hope, then these are spongy and often crippled offspring, which a misguided, blind forming impulse produced. Precisely there, where one can expect, that matter ennobles itself into form and the forming mind lays its ideas into the appearance, they are, like any other product of nature, fallen back into the matter, and the meteors so promising appear very common lights—if not quite less. For the poeticizing power of imagination [*Einbildungskraft*] often sinks utterly back into the matter, from which it had disentangled itself, and does not disdain, to serve nature with another *more solid* edifice, if poetical production will no longer quite succeed.

7. See the confession on the subject of human nature by the author of the *Critique* in his latest book, *Revelation Within the Limits of Reason*, Part 1.

8. On this matter, see the theory of will, most worthy of attention, in the second part of Rheinhold's *Letters*.

9. One must not, however, confuse this interrogation of will at the gate of reason with that, where it should learn of the *means* through which it is to satisfy a desire. The issue here is not, how satisfaction is to be *accomplished*, rather, whether it is *permitted*. Only this belongs in the moral realm, the former is an issue of cleverness.

10. If one finds only movements of the second kind, without those of the first, this indicates, that the person wants the emotion, but nature gainsays it. If one find movements of the first kind, without those of the second, this proves, that nature manifests itself in the emotion, but the person prohibits it. The first case one sees every day in affected persons and bad comedians; the second more rarely and only in strong dispositions.

11. This is dealt with more comprehensively in the third edition of *Thalia*, in an investigation of representations of pathos.

12. With that fine and grand insight which is his, Winkelmann (*History of Art*, Part I. pp. 280 ff.) described this high beauty, which issues from the combination of grace and dignity. But, that which he found united, he took and presented to be, in fact, one, and remained fixed upon what his senses alone had taught him, without investigating whether it should be separated. He confuses the concept of grace, because he comprehends the characteristics which obviously belong to dignity alone in this conception. But, grace and dignity are fundamentally different, and it is unjust to make that which is a *limitation* of grace into its characteristic. What Winkelmann calls the high, heavenly grace is nothing but beauty combined with grace, with predominant dignity. "Heavenly grace," he says, "appears self-sufficient, and does not offer itself, but wants to be sought after. She encloses in herself the movements of the soul, and feeds upon the sacred stillness of divine nature.—Through her," he says in another place, "did the artist of Niobe dare the kingdom of incorporeal ideas, and reached the secret of combining the fear of death with the highest beauty." (It would be difficult to make any sense of this, were it not obvious, that only dignity is meant here.) "He became a creator of pure spirits, which awaken no desire of the senses, for they seem not to be made for passion, but only to have assumed the shape of passion."—In yet another place, he says, "the soul expressed itself only beneath the calm surface of the water, and never erupted in passion. The greatest pain remains enfolded in the idea of suffering, and joy wafts like a gentle breeze, which hardly stirs the leaves, upon the face of a Leukothea." All of these characteristics belong to dignity, and not to grace, for grace does not enfold herself, but steps forth, and grace is not sublime, but beautiful. But, dignity is that, which holds nature back in her expressions, and commands calm to the features, even in the fear of death and in the bitterest suffering of a Laocoon. Home succumbs to the same mistake, which is less astonishing for this writer. He, too, takes characteristics of dignity to be those of grace, although he strictly distinguishes grace and dignity. His observations are usually correct, and the rules he constructs from them, true: but one cannot follow him further (*Grundsätze d. Kritik II*, Anmut und Würde).

13. One must not confuse *respect* with *esteem*. Respect (according to its pure concept) only applies to the relationship of sensuous nature to the demands of pure practical reason in general, without regard to an actual fulfillment. "The feeling of inappropriateness to the accomplishment of an idea, which is a law for us, is called respect" (Kant's *Critique of Judgment*). Respect is therefore not a pleasant, but an oppressive sentiment. It is the feeling of the distance of the empirical will from the pure one.— It therefore ought not to be surprising, that I make sensuous nature the subject of respect, although this only applies to *pure reason*; for the inappropriateness to the realization of the law can only lie in sensuousness. Esteem, on the other hand, applies to the real fulfillment of the law, and is felt, not on account of the law, rather on account of the person, who acts in accordance with the law. Esteem is, therefore, something delightful, because the fulfillment of the law must delight creatures of reason. Respect is compulsion, esteem is already a free sentiment. But, the source of that is love, which constitutes an ingredient of esteem. Even the good-for-nothing must respect the good, but to esteem him, who has done the Good, he would have to cease to be a good-for-nothing.

14. Nonetheless, there is *ceremony* in a good sense, whereof art can make use. This arises not from the arrogance, to make oneself important, rather, it aims at *preparing* emotion for something important. Where a great and deep impression is to be made, and the poet's chief concern is, that nothing of it be lost, he tunes emotion to be receptive of the impression beforehand, removes all distractions, and sets the powers of the imagination in an expectant tension.

Now, to this effect, *ceremony* is quite appropriate, where there is an accumulation of preparations, which do not betray their purpose, and an intentional delay of the progress of events, where impatience demands dispatch. In music, the ceremonious is brought forth by a *slow*, uniform sequence of strong tones; the intensity awakens and tenses emotion, the slow beat delays satisfaction, and the uniformity of the beat lets impatience see no end.

*Ceremony* supports the impression of greatness and sublimity not a little, and is used with success in religious rituals and mysteries. The effects of bells, choral music, and the organ are known; but there is also something *ceremonious* for the eye, that is, *pomp*, combined with the awesome, as in funereal ceremonies, and on all public occasions, which observe a grand style and a slow beat.

## TRANSLATOR'S NOTES

\* The second edition of Immanuel Kant's *Religion innerhalb der Grenzen der Blossen Vernunft*, was published in 1794, one year after the completion of *Über Anmut und Würde*, published in *Thalia*, 1793. (The translation is not mine, but by Theodore M. Greene, who studied under Norman Kemp Smith in the early 1920s in Edinburgh.)

Kant inserted the following footnote in the first part of *Religion . . .*, "On Radical Evil In Human Nature: 'Professor Schiller, in his masterly treatise (*Thalia*, 1793, Part III) on grace and dignity in morality, objects to this way of representing obligation, as carrying with it a monastic cast of mind. Since, however, we are at one upon the most important principles, I cannot admit that there is disagreement here, if only we can make ourselves clear to one another. I freely grant that, by very reason of the dignity of the *idea of duty*, I am unable to associate *grace* with it. For the idea of duty involves absolute necessity, to which grace stands in direct contradiction. The majesty of the moral law (as of the law on Sinai) instills awe (not dread, which repels, nor yet charm, which invites familiarity); and in this instance, since the ruler resides within us, this *respect*, as of a subject toward his ruler, awakens a *sense of the sublimity* of our own destiny, which enraptures us more than any beauty. *Virtue*, also, i.e., the firmly grounded disposition strictly to fulfull our duty, is also *beneficent* in its results, beyond all that nature and art can accomplish in the world; and the august picture of humanity, as portrayed in this character does indeed allow the attendance of the *Graces*. But, when duty alone is the theme, they keep a respectful distance. If we consider, further, the happy results which virtue, should she gain admittance everywhere, would spread throughout the world, we see morally directed reason (by means of the imagination) calling the sentiments into play. Only after vanquishing monsters did Hercules become Musagetes, leader of the Muses—labors from which those worthy sisters, trembling, draw back. The attendants of Venus Urania become wantons in the train of Venus

Dione, as soon as they meddle in the business of determining duty and try to provide springs of action thereof.

"Now if one asks, what is the *aesthetic character*, the *temperament*, so to speak, of *virtue*, whether courageous and hence *joyous*, or fear-ridden and dejected, an answer is hardly necessary. This latter, slavish frame of mind can never occur without a hidden *hatred* of the law. And a heart which is happy in the *performance* of its duty (not merely complacent in the *recognition* thereof) is a mark of genuineness in the virtuous disposition—of genuineness even in *piety*, which does not consist in the self-inflicted torment of a repentant sinner (a very ambiguous state of mind, which ordinarily is nothing but an inward regret at having infringed upon the rules of prudence), but rather in the firm resolve to do better in the future. This resolve, then, encouraged by good progress, must needs beget a joyous frame of mind, without which man is never certain of having really *attained a love* for the good, i.e., of having incorporated it into his maxim."

†*Religion* . . . Part I, Section III, "Man is Evil by Nature," begins with the quote "*Vitiis nemo sine nascitur*," Horace ("No one is born free of vices"), and continues: ". . . He is evil *by nature*, means but this, that evil can be predicated of man as a species; not that such a quality can be inferred from the concept of his species (that is, of man in general)—for then it would be necessary; but rather, that from what we know of man through experience we cannot judge otherwise of him, or, that we may presuppose evil to be subjectively necessary to every man, even to the best. . . . Hence, we can call this a natural propensity to evil, and as we must, after all, ever hold man responsible for it, we can further call it a *radical*, innate *evil* in human nature (yet nonetheless brought upon us by ourselves). . . ." And further on, ". . . Now if a propensity to this (inversion of the ethical order) does lie in human nature, there is in man a natural propensity to evil; and since this very propensity must in the end be sought in a will which is free, and can therefore be imputed, it is morally evil. This evil is *radical*, because it corrupts the ground of all maxims; it is, moreover, as a natural propensity, *inextirpable* by human powers, since extirpation could occur only through good maxims, and cannot take place when the ultimate subjective ground of all maxims is postulated as corrupt; yet, at the same time, it must be possible to *overcome* it, since it is found in man, a being whose actions are free. We are not then to call the

depravity of human nature *wickedness*, taking the word in its strict sense as a disposition (the subjective *principle* of the maxims) to adopt evil, *as evil*, into our maxim, as our incentives (for that is diabolical); we should rather term it the *perversity* of the heart, which, then, because of what follows from it, is also called an *evil heart*. Such a heart may coexist with a will which in general is good: it arises from the frailty of human nature, the lack of sufficient strength to follow out the principles it has chosen for itself, joined with its impurity, the failure to distinguish the incentives. . . ."

# ON MATTHISSON'S POEMS

TRANSLATED BY JOHN SIGERSON

Landscape painting, as is well known, was not exactly in high regard among the Greeks, and even our present-day artistic rigorists have yet to decide whether the landscape painter should even be accepted as a genuine artist. But the ancients' works tell us nary a thing about a genre which has not as yet achieved much recognition: Landscape *poetry*— whose relation to epic, lyrical, and dramatic poetry parallels landscape painting's relation to the portrayal of animals and human beings.

There is a world of difference between merely incorporating inanimate nature into a scene—thereby providing a backdrop for a particular action, and, where necessary, lending its colors to the representation of things animate, as is often done by historical painters and epic poets—and the diametrically opposite procedure employed by such artists as the landscape painter, who makes inanimate nature itself into the scene's central figure, relegating man to a mere auxiliary role. We find countless examples of the

---

Friedrich Matthisson (1761–1831) is probably best known for his poem *Adelaide,* which was set to music by Ludwig van Beethoven in 1796. Schiller met Matthisson on February 2, 1794 in Ludwigsburg, and probably wrote this review shortly thereafter. From Schiller's letters to Körner, it is clear that he considered Matthisson an inferior poet, but one whose defects were a useful foil to elaborate on his theory of aesthetic composition.

first approach in Homer; and who can match the truth, individuality, and vitality with which that great portrayer of nature regales our senses in the backdrops of his dramatic tableaux? But it was reserved for the more modern poets (extending back to some of Pliny's contemporaries) to produce landscape paintings and landscape poetry in which this aspect of nature, for itself, is made into the object of its own representation, thereby enriching art's domain—which the ancients seem to have restricted to man and his semblances—through the addition of this new province.

What, then, might be the origin of this indifference evinced by the Greek artists toward a genre which we moderns hold in such universal esteem? Should we perhaps assume that the Greek—this connoisseur and passionate partisan of everything beautiful—was somehow insensible to the allures of inanimate nature? Or, must we not rather suspect, that he deliberately rejected this material, because he found it incompatible with his own conception of fine art?

We ought not be disconcerted to hear this question brought up in the instance of a poet whose great strength—perhaps greater than that of any other representative of this genre—lies in his rendering of natural landscapes, and who can indeed serve as a general example of what this department of poetry can do. Thus, before we deal with the poet himself, we must first focus our critical eye on the genre to which he has applied his powers.

Certainly anyone who still has the magical impression of Claude Lorrain's paintbrush freshly in mind, will not be easily brought around to the view, that it was not a work of fine art, but merely of agreeable art, which sent him into such transports; and anyone who has just laid aside one of Matthisson's tableaux, will indeed find it quite disconcerting to ask himself whether he had really been reading the work of a poet.

We leave it to others to vie for the landscape *painter's* standing amongst the community of artists, and from this material we shall extract only that which immediately concerns the landscape *poet*. In the process, our inquiry shall reveal the principles according to which we are to determine the worth of his poems.

It is, as we know, never his theme, but rather the manner in which he treats it, which distinguishes the artist and poet; a household object or a moral lesson, if executed with taste, can be elevated into a free work of art with equal facility, while an unskilled hand can easily degrade the portrait of a human being into a crude parody. Thus, if we hesitate here to recognize paintings or poems whose only object is soulless natural things, as genuine works of art (i.e., works in which an ideal is possible), then it is because we doubt that these objects are susceptible of being treated as befits the character of fine art. What, then, is this character, with which we supposedly can not entirely reconcile landscape nature? It must be the same which distinguishes fine art from that which is merely agreeable. Now, it so happens that the character of *freedom* is common to both; and from this it follows, that if a merely agreeable work of art is also to be at the same time beautiful, it must also be clothed with the character of *necessity*.

If we understand poetry in general as the art "of putting us into specific emotional states by means of the free action of our productive powers of imagination" (a definition which certainly holds its own against the many others in circulation on this topic), we come up with two requirements which no poet may shirk, if he wishes to deserve the name. Firstly, he must permit the free play and self-activity of our own imaginative powers; and secondly, he must be no less certain of achieving his intended effect upon us, arousing within us a determinate emotion. These two requirements may initially seem mutually contradictory, since according to the first, our own imaginative powers must rule, and must obey none other than their own law; whereas according to the second, those powers must serve and obey the poet's law. How, then, does the poet resolve this contradiction? By prescribing to our imagination, no other course but that which it would have had to take in full freedom and according to its own laws, such that the poem's purpose is achieved *through nature*, thereby transforming external into internal necessity. And thus we discover, that both requirements not only mutually resolve one another, but that each in fact contains the other within itself, and that the highest degree of freedom is possible only through the highest degree of determinacy.

And here the poet is confronted with two great obstacles blocking his progress: As we know, the imagination, if left to roam freely, will simply follow the law of idea-association, which in turn is ultimately based on some purely accidental concatenation of perceptions—that is, on something entirely empirical. The poet must nevertheless know how to act to enrich that empirical associative activity, because he remains a poet only insofar as his purpose is achieved through the free self-activity of our own imaginative powers. In order to calculate his effect, within that activity he must discover some lawfulness, and he must be able to trace back from the empirical context of the mental image, to that which makes it necessary. Our mental images, however, are necessarily connected only insofar as they are based upon an objective connectedness among phenomena—and not upon some purely subjective, random interplay of thoughts. The poet must therefore strictly adhere to that objective connectedness among phenomena, and only after he has carefully cleansed his material of everything of purely accidental and subjective origin—only once he is certain he has attached himself to the pure object, and has subordinated himself to the law that governs the imaginations of all subjective individuals—only then can he be assured that everyone else's imagination will in freedom follow the course he has prescribed for them.

But the poet's only purpose in evoking a determinate imaginative interplay, is in order to have a determinate effect on the human heart. As difficult as it may be to determine the imagination's interplay without thereby impinging upon its freedom, that first task is no less taxing than this second one, namely, to wield this imaginative play so as to determine the subjective individual's emotional state. We know that the same set of circumstances can move different people in entirely different ways, and even the same individual's response will be different at different times. But irrespective of our emotions' dependency upon accidental influences beyond the poet's power to control, the poet must nevertheless determine what our emotional state is to be; he must therefore create the conditions out of which a determinate stirring of the soul will necessarily result. Now, there is nothing necessary about any particular person's subjective character, save his species-character; therefore, the poet can only determine our emotions insofar as he elicits them from the species within us, and not from our specifically delineated selves. But in order to be certain, that he is indeed addressing the pure species within the individual, he himself must have already extinguished the individual within himself, and must have elevated himself to species-being. Only when he no longer experiences emotion as belonging to this or that specific person (in whom the notion of species would always remain limited), but rather as belonging to man as a universal, can he then be certain that the emotions of the entire human species will follow his own; indeed, he is just as entitled to strive for this effect, as he is to demand pure humanity from each human individual.

Two qualities are therefore indispensable in every work of art: a necessary relationship to its object (i.e., objective truth), and second, a necessary relationship between that object or its description, and the emotional faculties (i.e., subjective universality). Everything in a poem must be true nature, since the imaginative powers obey no other law, and tolerate no other compulsion, than that which the natural order prescribes; but also, nothing in a poem must be actual (historical) nature, since all actuality imposes some sort of restriction upon that universal natural truth. Every individual human being is less human, to the extent that he is a mere individual; every type of emotion ceases to be necessary and purely human, insofar as it remains peculiar

to a particular person. Only by discarding what is accidental
and by expressing unalloyed necessity, do we develop true
greatness of style.

We can gather from these remarks, that the realm of
truly fine art can extend only as far as we can discover
necessity in the connectedness of phenomena. The area
falling outside this region is governed by caprice and accident, and there is neither freedom nor determinacy; for,
whenever the poet becomes unable to guide our own imaginative play by means of an internal necessity, either he
must guide it externally, in which case it is no longer *our*
action; or, he does not guide it at all, in which case it ceases
to be *his* action; and yet, both must coexist side by side in
a work of art, if we are to call it poetry.

This may account for why the wise ancients restricted
both poetry and the plastic arts to the human domain,
because only those phenomena appertaining to (internal
and external) man seemed to contain this lawfulness. An
intellect better informed than ours, might perhaps demonstrate a similar lawfulness with respect to other natural
things; but in our own experience they do not demonstrate
this, but instead merely open up infinite vistas for sheer
arbitrariness. The realm of determinate forms does not extend beyond our animal body and our human heart; hence
it is only within these, that an ideal can be set forth. For art
(as distinct from science), there exists no higher object in
the world of phenomena than man himself; art's province
extends no further. For fine art (as distinct from agreeable
art), there exists no object inferior to man himself, because
below him, we are forever barred from the realm of necessity.

If the principles we have set forth here are indeed the
correct ones (a judgment which we leave to connoisseurs of
art), then our initial suspicions seem confirmed, namely,
that very little good is to be had from landscape representations, and it becomes rather questionable whether the an-
nexation of this vast province can be regarded as a true
extension of the boundaries of fine art. Within those natural

environs wherein the landscape painter and landscape poet have taken up residence, we already see quite a marked slackening in the determinacy of forms and mixtures thereof; not only are the images more random here, let alone their aura of arbitrariness; in their interconnection as well, the role played by accidental features becomes quite troublesome for the poet. Thus, whenever he presents us with determinate images in a determinate order, it is he, and not we, who does the determining, since in this case no objective standard is available by which the viewer's free fantasy can coincide with the artist's own idea. And so, we end up receiving from the poet's hands the law which we should have been giving ourselves, and the effect is not a purely poetic one, to say the least, because it is not the perfectly free self-activity of our imaginative powers. But if, on the other hand, the artist wishes to preserve that freedom, he can do so only by dispensing with determinacy altogether, in which case he renounces all true beauty.

Nevertheless, this region of nature is by no means forever lost to fine art, and indeed, the principles we have just set forth reserve a very honorable rank for the poet who goes there for his thematic material. First of all, we cannot deny that, for all its seeming arbitrariness of forms, this realm of phenomena is nevertheless governed by a great unity and lawfulness, which the wise artist, in his imitations of nature, can guide along the proper pathways. Moreover, it must be noted that, although a great deal of determinacy must be abandoned in this field of art (because the parts tend to become engulfed by the whole, and the effect is only achieved through composites), it is still possible for the composition as a whole to be ruled by a great overriding necessity—as we see, for example, in painting, in the softening of harsh outlines and the blending of one color into the next.

But landscape nature does not exhibit this strict necessity in all its constituent parts, and even after the most profound study, the artist and poet will always be left with a very large residue of arbitrariness, shackling him to a lower level of perfection. The high degree of necessity which alone can satisfy the genuine artist and poet, but which he does not find here, lies within *human* nature, and therefore he will not rest, until he has succeeded in coaxing his object into the realm of supreme beauty. To be sure, he will, as much as possible, elevate landscape-nature for its own sake, and as befits the situation, he will seek within it the characteristic of necessity and attempt to represent this; but all his efforts notwithstanding, by this route he will never be able to place it on an equal footing with human necessity, and therefore he will ultimately resort to a symbolic operation which transforms that characteristic into human necessity, in order that he may partake of all the latter's inherent artistic advantages.

But how can he bring this about, without thereby forcing a break with nature's truth and its distinguishing characteristics? All true artists and poets working in this genre, perform this operation successfully, though in most cases they are unable to clearly account for what they are doing. There exist two routes by which inanimate nature can come to symbolize human nature: either as a representation of emotions, or as a representationa of ideas.

Emotions, of course, are by their very nature impossible to represent directly; but they *can* be represented with respect to their form, and indeed there already exists a much beloved and effective type of art, which derives its thematic material from just such forms of emotion. This art is called music, and insofar as landscape poetry acts musically upon us, it is a representation of our emotional faculties, and thus an imitation of human nature. Indeed, we may regard every pictorial or poetic composition as a species of music, which to some extent can be subjected to the same laws. We demand that the painter's colors have tone and harmony, and even something resembling modulation. In every poem, we recognize a distinction between its unity of thought and its unity of emotion, between its musical attitude and its logical construction—in short, we demand that in addition to what it expresses through its content, the poem's form must be an imitation and expression of emotions, and must affect as a piece of music does. From the landscape painter and the landscape poet, we demand this to an even greater degree, and more consciously so, since in their case we must somewhat lower the standards we customarily apply to works of fine art.

The overall effect of music (by which we mean music as fine, and not merely agreeable, art), consists in its ability to accompany the internal movements of the soul, and to make them sensuous by means of analogous external movements. Now, since these internal movements (i.e., human nature) proceed according to strict laws of necessity, this necessity and determinacy also becomes transferred to the external movements through which they are expressed, and in this way it becomes clear to us how, through the mediation of this symbolic act, the common natural phenomena of sound and light can participate in the aesthetic dignity of human nature. Thus, once the composer and the landscape painter has fathomed the secret of the laws governing the internal movements of the human heart, and has studied the analogies which emerge between these movements and specific external phenomena, he becomes transformed from a mere portrayer of common nature, into a true painter of human souls. Quitting the realm of arbitrariness and entering the realm of necessity, he may then confidently take his rightful place, not alongside the plastic artist whose object is external man, but alongside the poet, whose object is that which lies within.

But there is also a second route by which landscape-nature can be brought within humanity's purview, namely, by having it become an expression of ideas. By ideas, however, we definitely do not mean whatever is aroused as the result of accidental associations; such a practice is arbitrary and altogether unworthy of art. Rather, we mean those ideas which necessarily proceed from the lawful operations of our imaginative powers. Within active souls, awakened to the feeling of their own moral dignity, reason is by no means a passive observer in the interplay of the imagination; rather, it unceasingly strives to reconcile this accidental interplay with its own operations. If among these images, reason locates one which can be treated according to its own (practical) maxims, then that image will become a sensuous representation of reason's own actions; nature's mute text will become a living language of the mind, and the same book of phenomena will be read in entirely different ways by the inward and by the outward eye. And now, that lovely harmony of shapes, of tones, and of light, which delights man's aesthetic sense, will in that same moment also satisfy his sense of morality. The unbroken continuity with which lines in space, or tones in time merge into one another, is a natural symbol of the soul's inner harmony with itself, and of the ethical connectedness of feelings and actions; and within the beautiful attitude evinced by a pictorial or musical work of art, we see the reflection of an even more beautiful, morally attuned soul.

The composer and the landscape poet achieve this effect solely by means of the form of their representation, and they merely attune the mind to certain types of emotions and ideas; it is left to the listener or observer's own imaginative powers, to discern a content therein. The poet, for his part, enjoys one additional advantage: He can underlay those emotions with a specific text, i.e., he can utilize content to selectively reinforce and guide those symbolic forms within the imagination. But let him not forget, in the meantime, that there are well-defined limits to his intervention here. He may hint at those ideas, and he may allude to those emotions, but he must never lay them out explicitly, lest he encroach upon the reader's own imaginative powers. Any further specification here would inevitably be perceived by the reader as an irksome restriction, since what makes such aesthetic ideas so appealing is precisely the fact, that we look at their content as into a bottomless depth. Whatever actual and explicit content the poet does incorporate, will always remain finite; the potential content which he leaves us to fill in, is infinitely great.

Our purpose in ranging this far afield, was not to distance ourselves from our poet, but on the contrary, it was so that we may approach him more closely. In most of his tableaux, Mr. M. unites all three of the above-named requirements for the representation of landscape. His works have a pleasing vividness and truth about them; we are tantalized by their musical beauty, and we become fully engaged by the spirit which breathes through them.

Provided we confine ourselves to examining how he faithfully imitates nature in his landscape tableaux, we can only marvel at the artistry with which he is able to challenge our imaginative powers to summon up these scenes, and how he can rule over our imagination without thereby depriving it of its freedom. We find all individual parts of these works ordered according to a single law of necessity; nothing has been extraneously introduced, and in one most happy glance, he has captured the universal character of these natural shapes. This is the reason why our imagination finds it so uncommonly easy to follow him; we believe we are beholding nature itself, and it seems as if we are merely abandoning ourselves to recollections of scenes we have witnessed in the past. He is also perfectly acquainted with the devices for giving his scenes life and sensuousness, and has an excellent knowledge of both the advantages and natural limitations of his art. Namely, he knows that, in this type of composition, the poet is put at a certain disadvantage with respect to the painter, because whereas his own ability to produce a desired effect relies in large part upon the immediate and simultaneous impression of the whole, he can only construct that whole sequentially over time within the reader's imagination. His business is to represent not what exists, but what occurs, and provided he knows how to put this advantage to good use, he will always limit himself to that portion of his thematic material which can be represented genetically. Landscape-nature is by definition an entirety of phenomena beheld simultaneously, and in this respect it is a more propitious medium for the painter;

but it is also an entirety when taken in succession, because
it is in continuous flux, and to that extent it gives the poet
the advantage. Mr. M. has displayed much good judgment
by attuning himself to this distinction. He always selects as
his object a complex of phenomena existing in time rather
than in space, and he favors nature in motion over nature
which is fixed and at rest. Before our eyes he unfolds her
eternally changing drama, and her various phenomena are
made to flow into each other with the most appealing continuous harmony. What tremendous life and movement greet
us, for example, in his lovely *Moonshine Scene*, page 85:


Der Vollmond schwebt im Osten,
    Am alten Geisterturm
Flimmt bläulich im bemoosten
    Gestein der Feuerwurm.
Der Linde schöner Sylphe
    Streift scheu in Lunens Glanz;
Im dunkeln Uferschilfe
    Webt leichter Irrwischtanz.

Die Kirchenfenster schimmern;
    In Silber wallt das Korn;
Bewegte Sternchen flimmern
    Auf Teich und Wiesenborn;
Im Lichte wehn die Ranken
    Der öden Felsenkluft;
Den Berg, wo Tannen wanken,
    Umschleiert weißer Duft.

Wie schön der Mond die Wellen
    Des Erlenbachs besäumt,
Der hier durch Binsenstellen,
    Dort unter Blumen schäumt,
Als lodernde Kaskade
    Des Dorfes Mühle treibt,
Und wild vom lauten Rade
    In Silberfunken stäubt. Etc.

The full moon is hovering in the East,
    On the old ghost-tower
Is the bluish flicker
    Of fireflies among the moss-grown walls.
The linden-tree, beauteous sylph,
    Shyly flits in Luna's light.
Among the rushes by the shadowy bank
    Weaves the dancing will-'o-the-wisp.

The church-windows are a-gleaming;
    The corn sways in the silvery light;
The stars flicker, as if alive,
    On pools and meadow-springs;
Moonlight-lit vines rustle
    In the desolate ravine;
The mountain-top, where pine-trees sway,
    Is veiled in white mist.

How beautifully the Moon fringes
    The waves on the alder-brook;
It foams, here through sedgy places,
    There among the flowers,
And, as a blazing cascade,
    Drives the village mill,
And wildly leaves the noisy wheel
    In sprays of silver sparks. Etc.

But also in those instances where he sets out to place
the entire scene before us in a single moment, he knows
how to use continuous connectedness in order to bring it
easily and naturally within our grasp, as in the following
tableau:

Die Sonne sinkt; ein purpurfarbner Duft
    Schwimmt um Savoyens dunkle Tannenhügel,
Der Alpen Schnee entglüht in hoher Luft,
    Geneva malt sich in der Fluten Spiegel.

The sun is setting; a purple-hued mist
    Floats around Savoy's dark, pine-wreathed hills,
The alpine snow flares up in the mountain air,
    Geneva is painted below in the watery mirror.

Even though we take these images into our imagination successively, we find that they easily fuse into a single totality, because each image reinforces, and, as it were, makes necessary the image which follows. In the next strophe, we find it somewhat more difficult to make this synthesis, since continuity is less strictly observed:

> In Gold verfließt der Berggehölze Saum;
> Die Wiesenflur, beschneit von Blütenflocken,
> Haucht Wohlgerüche; Zephyr atmet kaum;
> Vom Jura schallt der Klang der Herdenglocken.

> The tips of the mountain-forest melt into gold;
> The meadow, snowy with flower-flakes,
> Exhales sweet odors; Zephyr barely breathes;
> From the Jura one hears the herd-bells ringing.

Here a leap is required on our part, in order to bring ourselves from the gilded mountain-tops to the fragrant, flower-strewn meadow; and we become all the more sensible of this leap, in that we must bring another of our five senses into play. But now again, how we admire his success in the following strophe:

> Der Fischer singt im Kahne, der gemach
> Im roten Widerschein zum Ufer gleitet,
> Wo der bemoosten Eiche Schattendach
> Die netzumhangne Wohnung überbreitet.

> The fisherman sings in his bark, which gently,
> In the red after-glow, glides to shore,
> Where the mossy oaks' shady roof
> Spreads above the net-draped cottage.

If nature herself offers him no motion, then the poet will borrow motion from his own imaginative powers, and will populate that tranquil world with spirits, flitting about in the nebulous mist, or dancing in the shimmering moonlight. Or, it is the figures of classical antiquity who awaken within his memory to infuse a desolate landscape with artificial life. Associations such as these do not come to him willy-nilly; they arise as if out of necessity, either from the landscape's locale, or from the nature of the emotions which that landscape arouses within him. Such associations, of course, are merely a subjective parallel to the landscape itself, but that parallel is so broadly universal, that the poet may confidently venture to give them an objective significance.

Mr. M. is no less conversant with the musical effects that can be produced through the appropriate choice of harmonizing images, and through the artful employment of eurythmy in their ordering. Who, for example, can help but experience something analogous to the impression left by a beautiful sonata, when he hears the following little song found on page 91:

### Abendlandschaft

Goldner Schein
Deckt den Hain
Mild beleuchtet Zauberschimmer
Der umbüschten Waldburg Trümmer.

Still und hehr
Strahlt das Meer;
Heimwärts gleiten, sanft wie Schwäne,
Fern am Eiland Fischerkähne.

Silbersand
Blinkt am Strand;
Röter schweben hier, dort blässer,
Wolkenbilder im Gewässer.

Rauschend kränzt
Goldbeglänzt
Wankend Ried des Vorlands Hügel,
Wild umschwärmt vom Seegeflügel.

Malerisch
Im Gebüsch
Winkt mit Gärtchen, Laub und Quelle
Die bemooste Klausnerzelle.

Auf der Flut
Stirbt die Glut,
Schon erblaßt der Abendschimmer
An der hohen Waldburg Trümmer.

Vollmondschein
Deckt den Hain,
Geisterlispel wehn im Tale
Um versunkne Heldenmale.

## Evening Landscape

Golden light
Bedecks the grove.
An enchanting twilight gently illuminates
The castle's o'ergrown ruins.

Still and sublime,
The ocean gleams
Homeward there glide, gentle as swans,
Fisher-boats near the far-off isle.

Silvery sand
Glitters on shore
Redder here, paler there,
Cloud-images float upon the waves.

Fluttering, rustling,
Crown'd with gold,
The reeds encircle the foreland-hillock,
Wildly swarming with sea-fowl.

Picturesquely,
From the thicket,
There beckons, with garden, foliage, spring,
The hermit's moss-grown shanty.

On the water
The glow dies out,
Already the evening glimmer grows pale
Across the lofty castle's ruins.

Light of the full moon
Bedecks the grove,
In the valley float lisping spirit-voices
'Round fallen heroes' crumbled monuments.

We do not mean to imply that this poem's felicitous construction is the sole reason why it has such a musical effect on us. Its metrical euphony certainly does act to support and elevate that effect; but that is not its cause. Rather, it is the poem's felicitous juxtaposition of images, and the lovely continuity as each is succeeded by the next; it is the poem's modulation, and its beautiful manner, which permits it to become the expression of a determinate mode of emotion, and thus to become a portrait of the human soul.

A similar effect, though with an entirely different content, is also evoked by *The Mountain-Wanderer* on page 61, and *The Alpine Journey* on page 66—two compositions in which the most successful representation of nature is united with the most elaborated expression of emotion. We imagine we are listening to the musical composer as he tests the limits of his power over our emotions; and what better vehicle for this, than a ramble through the Alps, where the great and the beautiful, the terrifying and the ridiculous, succeed each other with such surprising abruptness.

Lastly, we find among these landscape tableaux, many which move us because of a certain pervading spirit or mode of expressing ideas, as in the very first poem in the collection, *Lake Geneva*. In this poem's magnificent prelude, the victory of the living over the lifeless, of form over amorphous mass, is quite successfully placed before our senses. The poet opens the beautiful scene with a rearward glance into an earlier time, when the expanse now before him was still a wasteland:

Da wälzte, wo im Abendlichte dort
Geneva, deine Zinnen sich erheben,
Der Rhodan seine Wogen traurend fort
Von schauervoller Haine Nacht umgeben.

Da hörte deine Paradiesesflur
Du stilles Tal voll blühender Gehege,
Die großen Harmonien der Wildnis nur
Orkan und Tiergeheul und Donnerschläge

Als senkte sich sein zweifelhafter Schein
Auf eines Weltballs ausgebrannte Trümmer,
So goß der Mond auf diese Wüstenein
Voll trüber Nebeldämmrung seine Schimmer.

Where, now, in the twilight,
Geneva, your rooftops rise skyward,
The Rhodan's waves rolled mournfully on,
Wrapt in eerie forest-night.

You paradisiacal region,
You hushed valley filled with verdant gardens,
Heard only the great harmonies of the wild:
Gale and howl of beast and thunderclaps,

As if its dubious light were falling
Upon a planet's charred ruins—
So did the moon pour its glimmering
Onto these desolate reaches, filled with turbid
      twilight-mist.

And now the magnificent landscape is revealed to him,
and in it he recognizes the site of those poetic scenes which
remind him of the creator of Heloise:

O Clarens! friedlich am Gestad erhöht,
Dein Name wird im Buch der Zeiten leben.
O Meillerie! voll rauher Majestät!
Dein Ruhm wird zu den Sternen sich erheben.

Zu deinen Gipfeln, wo der Adler schwebt,
Und aus Gewölk erzürnte Ströme fallen,
Wird oft, von süßen Schauern tief durchbebt,
An der Geliebten Arm der Fremdling wallen.

O Clarence! Thy name, peacefully erected on the
 river-shore
Will live on in the Book of Ages.
O Meillerie! Full of rough-hewn majesty!
Your fame will rise up to the stars.

To thy summits, where the eagle hovers
And angry storms fall from the clouds,
Will the stranger, quaking with a sweet shudder,
Often make his pilgrimage, his loved one leaning on his
 arm.

How spirited, how heartfelt and picturesque he is up to
this point! But now, the poet attempts to outdo himself, and
this becomes his undoing. The strophes which follow, quite
beautiful in themselves, come from the coldly calculating
poet—not from his overflowing emotions, utterly enthralled
with the here-and-now. If the poet's heart had been entirely
with his object, he would have found it impossible to tear
himself away and transport himself elsewhere—now to Mt.
Aetna, now to the Tibur, now to the Gulf of Naples, etc.—
and this, not with mere passing references, but with a
lingering attendance. We certainly admire his magnificent
brushstrokes, but they blind us, rather than refresh us; a
straightforward representation would have had much
greater effect. All these changes in scenery end up distracting the mind to such an extent, that when the poet finally
does return us to his main theme, we have lost all interest
in it. And instead of reviving that interest, he weakens it
still further, with the rather abrupt falling-off at the poem's
conclusion, which is so obviously at odds with the impetus
with which he initially vaulted aloft and managed to sustain
himself over such a long span. This is the third time Mr.
M. has revised this poem, and we fear that in doing so, he
has made it all the more necessary to undertake a fourth.
The many different emotional dispositions which he allowed
to influence him in these alterations, have done violence to
the spirit which initially dictated it, and in becoming too

richly endowed, the poem has lost much of its true content, which lies in its very simplicity.

But though we characterize Mr. M. as an excellent poetic composer of landscape scenes, far be it from us, to limit him to that sphere of endeavor. Even in this small collection, his poetic genius shines forth with equal success in quite diverse fields. His has quite successfully ventured into into the genre which involves free inventions of the imagination, and he has perfectly captured the spirit which must in fact govern this sort of poetry. Here, his imaginative powers appear in their unshackled splendor; but they are also evident in how they they harmonize most beautifully with the idea to be expressed. In the song entitled *The Fairyland,* the poet derides his own wayward fantasies with a great deal of good humor; everything here is just as color-ful, just as lush, just as overladen, just as grotesque as is required by the character of this unruly genre of poetry; and in the *Song of the Elves,* everything is just as light, just as nebulous, just as ethereal as it ought to be in this little moonshine-world. Carefree, blissful sensuousness breathes throughout the pleasing little *Song of the Fauns,* and the gnomes show much candor as they blurt out the secret of their (and their consorts') profession (see page 141):

Des Tagscheins Blendung drückt,
Nur Finsternis beglückt!
Drum hausen wir so gern
Tief in des Erdballs Kern.
Dort oben wo der Äther flammt,
Ward alles, was von Adam stammt,
Zu Licht und Glut mit Recht verdammt.

We are oppressed by the day's blinding light,
Only darkness makes us happy!
That's why we like so much to live
Deep in the globe's core.
Up above, where the ether burns,
Everything which issued from Adam
Was justly condemned to light and heat.

Mr. M. is a very successful painter of emotions—not merely indirectly, through how he treats landscape scenes, but also in an immediate sense; and we can already anticipate in advance, that the poet who knows how to interest us so deeply in the inanimate world, will not emerge empty-handed from the the world of the animate, where the material is so much richer. We can likewise determine in advance, the approximate range of emotions upon which a muse so devoted to nature's beauty, will doubtless dwell. Our poet will seek humanity, not within the bustling world at large, not in contrived society, but rather in solitude, within his own heart, in the simple situations of man's original state. Friendship, love, religious emotions, childhood recollections, the joys of rural life, and the like will be the content of his songs—simple themes, those most closely allied with landscape nature, and with a clearly defined relationship to it. His muse is characterized by a touch of melancholy and a certain contemplative *Schwärmerei*, to which all sensitive individuals are inclined in the presence of nature's beauty and solitude. In the tumult of society, each new mental image is ever crowding in upon the previous one, and our diversified nature does not always work to our own advantage; all the more reason to let simple nature around us stand in confirmation of our emotions, which we make into nature's intimate friends; and through those emotions' eternal unity, we rediscover our own unity as well. Herein lies the reason for the narrow scope within which our poet revolves—his long, drawn-out echoing of every sense-impression, his frequent recourse to the same feeling-states. The emotions which flow from nature's wellspring lack variation, and are rather sparse; whereas the elements which coalesce into more subtle nuances and synthesized mixtures in the course of the world's tangled interplay, constitute an inexhaustible source of material for the painter of human souls. The simple emotions can easily become tiresome, because there is too little to work through; but we like to return to them ever and again, and we rejoice whenever we see those synthetic manners—

which frequently are mere degenerations—restored to their original state of humanity. If the cultured individual is to benefit from this reversion to the Saturnine age and to nature's simplicity, then that simplicity must appear as a work of freedom—not of necessity; it must be that nature, which culminates in the moral human being—not that which begins with his physical being. Therefore, if the poet wishes to draw us away from the crowd and into his own solitary world, his revulsion toward all artifice, and his love for nature, must arise from a need, not for relaxation, but for a heightening of tension, and from a yearning, not for peace, but for harmony. It is not because the moral world conflicts with the poet's theoretical world, but rather, because the moral world conflicts with his own practical potential, that he must look around for a Tiber, and must seek refuge in the world of inanimate things.

This certainly requires, that the poet apply something more than the paltry skill of contrasting nature with artifice—a talent which frequently comprises the idyllic poet's entire instrumentarium. The poet's heart must be on intimate terms with the highest beauty, if, amid all the influences of the most refined culture, it is to keep that simplicity of emotions, which alone lends them dignity. Such a heart betrays its presence through the richness which it manages to conceal within even the most modest form; through the nobility which it imparts even to flights of fancy and mood; through the discipline with which it reins itself in, even in its most glorious triumphs; through the unspoiled innocence of its emotions. It betrays its presence through its irresistible and truly magical power, which draws us toward it, holds us fast, and, as we do homage to its dignity, in effect, obliges us to remember our own.

Mr. M. has laid claim to this title in a manner which should satisfy even the severest judge. Anyone who can compose a fantasia such as his *Elysium* (page 34), who is an initiate into the innermost secrets of the art of poetry, and a disciple of true beauty—is fully entitled to this distinction. Through his intimate intercourse with nature and with clas-

sical models, his spirit has been nourished, his taste purified, and his moral grace preserved; his poems are alive
with a cheerful, genuine humanity, and the beautiful images
of nature are flawlessly reflected in the becalmed clarity of
his mind, as in a mirror-smooth pool of water. In every one
of his works, we observe a discrimination, a sense of what
is fitting, an internal rigor, an untiring quest for the maximum of beauty. He has already accomplished much, and
we might hope, that he has yet to reach his limits. But now
that he has tested his wings in more humble surroundings,
it is up to him to soar higher; to place a profound meaning
within the raiments of his imagination's graceful forms and
the music of his language; to people his landscapes with
human figures, and to paint active humanity upon this attractive ground. A humble distrust in one's own powers is
always the mark of a true talent; but courage is also in order,
and as *beautiful* as it is, when the conqueror of Python
exchanges his fearsome bow for a lyre, so it is *great* to behold
Achilles when, from amongst a group of Thessalonian maidens, the hero all at once straightens himself and stands
upright.

# ON BÜRGER'S POEMS

TRANSLATED BY JOHN SIGERSON

The indifference with which our philosophizing age has now begun to treat the muses' playful games, has, it appears, dealt a blow more painful to lyrical poetry, than to any other poetic species. The art of dramatic poetry has, at least to some degree, been shielded by social usages, and as for the ballad, its freer form permits it to adapt to the spirit of the times, incorporating that spirit as its own. But all our ladies' almanacs, social singing, and enthusiasm for music are but a fragile bulwark against the collapse of our lyrical poetry. And yet, it would be a depressing thought indeed, if these youthful blossoms of the human spirit were to shrivel and die on the vine, and if a more matured culture had to be purchased with the sacrifice of even a single enjoyment of beauty. And just as with poetry in general, even in these so

---

Gottfried August Bürger (1747–1794) was an enthusiastic German republican patriot and a great admirer of Schiller. The two poets met in Jena in April 1789, but Bürger was apparently more impressed by Schiller than the other way around. Only a few months later, Bürger sent Schiller the second edition of his collected poems, with a new dedication to "Schiller, the man who gives my soul new wings." Schiller's brutally frank review, translated here, appeared in 1791, and stung the "popular" poet to the quick, moving him to write an "anti-critique" in which he claimed that Schiller's criterion of idealization of the poetic object is invalid and unnecessary. Despite this, Bürger maintained the highest respect for Schiller's own poetic works.

unpoetical times, we can discover a very worthy mission for
lyrical poetry, and perhaps we can demonstrate, that if, on
the one hand, she must stand aside for higher intellectual
pursuits, she is, for that reason, more necessary now than
ever before. In a time when our mental powers have been
compartmentalized and their effectiveness scattered, as a
necessary consequence of the expanded scope of our knowledge and the specialization of professions, poetry is virtually
unique in its power to reunify the soul's sundered forces,
to occupy heart and mind, activity and wit, reason and the
power of imagination in harmonious alliance, and, as it
were, to restore the entire human being within us. She
alone can avert the most wretched fate which can ever
overtake the philosophizing intellect: to lose the reward of
one's diligence in the very effort to attain it, and, in the
reclusive world of reason, to become insensible to the joys
of the actual world. With poetry's aid, the mind might once
again find its way out of such aberrant pathways, and, in
her rejuvenating light, might escape an early senility. She
would be the beaming, youthful Hebe, waiting upon the
immortal gods in Jupiter's hall.

For her to do this, however, she herself would have to
stride forward along with the era for which she would perform that important service, and she would make all that
era's advantages and acquisitions into her own. Whatever
riches experience and reason had amassed for humanity,
would have to become living and fecund, and, in poetry's
creative hand, would become clothed in grace. Into her
mirror, she would have to assemble all the wisdom, culture,
and character of her era, and, out of the century itself,
using her idealizing art, she would create a model for that
century—all this, however, under the assumption that she
herself would fall into none but mature and educated hands.
For, as long as that is not so—as long as there exists between
the poet and the morally developed, unprejudiced mind
some other difference than the former's possession of poetic
talent over and above all the latter's fine qualities—the art
of poetry will fail to have an ennobling influence on the

century, and each advance made by scientific culture will merely reduce the ranks of that culture's admirers. It is inconceivable that a man whose knowledge has matured will seek refreshment for heart and mind from an immature youth; nor will he desire to encounter in a poem the very same prejudices, brutish customs, and vacuousness which plague him in his daily life. Such an individual is fully justified in demanding that the poet be as Horace was for the Romans, a trusted guide through life, and that the latter be on his own moral and intellectual level—since he desires never to sink below himself, not even in the hours he sets aside for recreation. It is therefore not enough to merely depict sentiments with elevated colors; our sentiments must themselves be elevated. Enthusiasm alone is not enough; we demand the enthusiasm of a matured mind. All that the poet can give us, is his own personality; it must therefore be worthy of being presented to the scrutiny of society and posterity. The task of ennobling that personality to the highest degree, of refining it into the purest, most splendid humanity, is the first and most important business he must address, before he may venture to stir members of the elite. There can be no greater value to his poetry, than that it is the perfected imprint of a truly interesting disposition of a truly interesting, perfected mind. Only a mind such as this, should peer out at us from particular works of art; we notice it in the subtlest innuendo, and he who is not such a mind seeks in vain to conceal this critical lack through mere artifice. In the realm of aesthetics, it is the same as with morality: Just as it is the human being's morally upstanding character, which alone can place the stamp of moral goodness upon each of his particular actions, so it is only the mature, perfected mind which pours forth maturity and perfection. No mere talent, no matter how great, can imbue a work of art with what its creator never possessed, and no file can remove imperfections arising from this source.

We would be hard put indeed, if, with this measuring rod in hand, we were now asked to explore the entire landscape of our contemporary muses. But that exercise would, we believe, surely demonstrate how deeply the majority of our not-unsung lyric poets have touched the more discerning among the public; it even sometimes happens, that one or another of them, whose poems themselves have not particularly struck us, surprises us with his confessions, or provides us evidence of his moral goodness. At present, we shall confine ourselves to applying what has just been said, to Mr. Bürger.

But is it permissible to apply this rule to a poet who explicitly proclaims himself a "popular singer," and who has made popularity into his supreme law (see his Preface to Part I, pp. 15f.)? Far be it from us to quibble with Mr. Bürger over the hazy word "popular"; indeed, perhaps only a few words will suffice for us to agree on this, namely: In our day and age, it would be an exercise in futility to seek a popular poet in the same sense Homer was for his age, or the troubadours were for theirs. Ours is no longer an Homeric society, all of whose members were on approximately the same emotional and critical level, who could therefore easily recognize themselves in one and the same depiction, and could see themselves experiencing the same emotions. There now exists a very great disparity between a nation's select few and the mass of people, a disparity ascribable to the fact, that conceptual enlightenment and moral ennoblement now constitute a coherent whole, whose mere fragments yield us nothing. Besides this difference in culture, also social conventions establish distinct types and modes of expressing sentiment, thereby giving rise to the acute discrepancies between the nation's various parts. Hence it would be futile to arbitrarily amalgamate into a *single* notion, what has long since ceased to be a unity. A popular poet today would thus have to choose between the easiest of all, and that which is most difficult: either adapt himself exclusively to the limited faculties of the common herd, and forego any applause from the educated class—or, through the greatness of his own artistry, bridge that great chasm separating the two, and pursue both goals simultaneously. We certainly have no dearth of poets who have enjoyed success in the first kind of poetry, and who have elicited warm applause from their intended public; but a poet of Mr. Bürger's genius could never have denigrated his artistry and talent in the mere pursuit of such a lowly objective. On the contrary, far from being a means of simplifying the poet's work or concealing a mediocre talent, popularity for Bürger is an additional hurdle, and indeed such an imposing one, that surmounting it may be called the highest triumph of genius. What a grand undertaking: to satisfy the jaded tastes of the connoisseur, without thereby becoming unpalatable to the great masses, and to nestle up to the common people's childish comprehension without thereby depriving art of its dignity! This difficulty, and the whole secret to its solution, is great, but not insurmountable; it involves a careful choice of material, and utmost simplicity in its treatment. The poet would have to choose exclusively from among those situations and sentiments which belong to man as man. He would have to systematically renounce everything associated with particular experiences, items of information, or fluencies acquired only by special arrangement, and in this way, extracting what makes man simply man, he may, so to speak, recall our lost original natural state. In tacit alliance with the elite of his era, he would then touch the people's hearts in their most tender and impressionable spot; he would bolster their moral impulses by exercising their feeling for beauty, and would bend their appetite for passion—which the run-of-the-mill poet satisfies so meagerly, and often so harmfully—toward the refinement of that passion. Acting as the enlightened, polished spokesman for popular feelings, he would underlay the gushing, wordless, yet word-seeking affects of love, joy, devotion, melancholy, hope, etc., with a more refined and inspiring text, and, in the course of expressing those affects, he would have mastered them, so that the people's raw, amorphous, often bestial eruptions would become ennobled even as they left their lips. Such a poet would resolve even the most sublime philosophy of life, into simple natural emotions; he would deliver the results of the most painstaking investigation over to the power of imagination, and would render the philosopher's secrets in a language of images, as easy puzzles to be solved by childish minds. This presager of distinct knowledge would have already instilled the people with reason's most daring truths, attractively and innocently garbed, long before the philosopher and the legislator will have dared to bring them forth in their full splendor. And long before those truths had become the property of conscious conviction, through him they will have already effected their silent power on the heart; and, on its own accord, an impatient, universal yearning will finally demand reason's satisfaction.

Taken in this sense, it would seem that the popular poet—whether he be measured according to his initial abilities, or by the scope of his influence—deserves a very high rank. Only the truly great talent is gifted with this ability to play creatively with the results of profound thinking, to separate the thought from the form to which it adheres, and from which it perhaps arose; and then to graft it onto an unfamiliar chain of ideas, concealing so much art with so little expenditure, such great wealth within such a simple raiment. Thus, Mr. B. is by no means saying too much, when he declares that "a poem's popularity is the proof of its perfection." But in asserting this, he lets pass a tacit assumption, which may completely escape many who read him, namely, that the first indispensable prerequisite for a perfect poem, is that it possess an inner worth, entirely independent of the extent of the individual reader's comprehension. "If a poem," he seems to want to say, "passes the test of genuine taste, and unites with this advantage a clarity and comprehensibility which enables it to live on the people's lips, then that poem bears the seal of perfection." This statement is identical with the following: What pleases the cultured elite is good; and what equally pleases all, is all the better.

Therefore, with poems aimed at appealing to the populace at large, by no means do we relax the demands of art somewhat; rather, if we are to ascertain the poem's true value (which can only consist in a successful fusion of such diverse characteristics into a whole), it is both essential and necessary to begin by asking: Has nothing of higher beauty been sacrificed for popularity's sake? Has it not lost for the connoisseur, the interest which it gained from the popular masses?

And here we must admit that for us, Bürger's poetry has left us with much to be desired, and that, by and large, we miss that gentle, ever self-same, ever transparent, manly intellect who, initiated into the mysteries of the beautiful, noble, and true, strides down to the people with his creative powers, but who never, even in his most intimate dealings with them, denies his own heavenly origins. Mr. B. not infrequently merges himself with the people to whom he ought merely to descend, and rather than drawing them upward toward him, through jokes and games, is often content to make himself their equal. Moreover, the "people" for whom he composes is unfortunately not always what he would like to be considered under that rubric. It will never be the same audience for whom he wrote his *Venus' Nocturnal Fest*, his *Leonore*, his *Song to Hope*, *The Elements*, *The Joyful Festival at Göttingen*, *Manly Virtue*, *Premonition of Health*, and others, not to mention a *Mrs. Schnips*, *Fortuna's Rack*, *Menagerie of the Gods*, *To People's Faces*, and the like. If ever we have reason to hold a popular poet in high regard, then his merit must consist not in his ability to furnish songs to please members of particular social classes, but rather in his ability to satisfy all social classes with every one of his poems.

We do not wish to dwell upon faults which owe their origin to an hour of weakness, and which could be obviated by making a more rigorous selection from among his poems. However, the fact that we often find this same aesthetic inconsistency within a single poem, is as unpardonable as it is difficult to remedy. The reviewer must concede, that of all Bürger's poems (we are referring to those which he has most profusely bestowed upon us), the reviewer can not name a single one which yielded a completely pure

enjoyment, uncorrupted by offensive aspects. Whether it
was a lack of agreement between the image and the thought,
or an affront to the dignity of the subject matter, or an
uninspired turn of phrase; whether it was one single, igno-
ble image distorting the beauty of the idea, an expression
which fell flat, a superfluous flourish, a false rhyme or rough
verse (though these we encounter quite seldom) disrupting
the harmonious effect of the whole—such a disruption was
all the more irksome to our full enjoyment, in that it forced
us to judge that the mind presenting itself in these poems
is still immature, unperfected—that the final strokes are
missing from his works, because he lacks those final strokes
within himself. One of the poet's indispensable functions is
to idealize his object; failing this, he deserves not the name.
It is his office, to free all that is excellent about his object
(whether this be a physical shape, a sentiment, or an action,
either internal or external) from coarser, and even from
merely extraneous substances; to gather the beams of perfection scattered among many objects, into a single beam;
to subordinate asymmetrical features to the harmony of the
whole; to elevate what is individual and local, into what is
universal. All particular ideals which he develops in this
fashion, are, as it were, outpourings of an inner ideal of
perfection abiding within the poet's soul. And the more he
has brought this inner, universal ideal to fullness and purity,
the more, too, will all those particulars approach the highest
degree of perfection. But all too often, we miss this art of
idealization in Mr. Bürger's works. In addition to the fact,
that his muse generally seems to have an all too sensuous,
often vulgarly sensuous character; and that for him, love is
seldom anything but pleasure or a feasting of the eyes,
beauty is often only youth, felicity and good health merely
physical well-being—we would have to characterize the
pictures he presents more as a jumble of images, a compilation of specific features, a kind of mosaic, rather than as
ideals. When, for example, he wants to paint us an image
of feminine beauty, he looks around in Nature for images,
each of which correspond to each of his beloved's particular

allures, and out of this conglomeration he creates his goddess. See Part I, page 124 for *The Maid I Fancy, The Song
of Songs,* and many others. And when he wants to present
her as a universal example of perfection, he merely borrows
and assembles her qualities from an entire legion of goddesses. For example, page 86, *The Two Lovers*:

> Im Denken ist sie Pallas ganz,
> Und Juno ganz am edelm Gange,
> Terpsichore beim Freudentanz,
> Euterpe neidet sie im Sange,
> Ihr weicht Aglaja, wenn sie lacht,
> Melpomene bei sanfter Klage,
> Die Wollust ist sie in der Nacht,
> Die holde Sittsamkeit bei Tage.

> In her thinking she is entirely Pallas,
> And all Juno in her noble step,
> Terpsichore in her joyful dancing,
> Her singing is Euterpe's envy,
> Aglaya yields whene'er she laughs,
> And Melpomene to her gentle plaint,
> Unbridled lust is she by night,
> By day most gracious chastity.

We cite this particular strophe, not because we believe,
that it disfigures the poem in which it appears, but because
it seems the most appropriate example of the general manner in which Mr. B. idealizes his objects. This extravagant
rush of color cannot fail to dazzle and transfix the viewer at
first sight—especially in readers who are receptive only
to sensual imagery, and who, like children, are drawn to
brightly colored objects. But paintings of this sort have little
to say to the refined artistic sensibility, whose satisfaction
lies never in mere riches, but in wise economy; never in
the material, but in the beauty of its form; never in the
ingredients, but in the quality of the mixture. We do not
intend to investigate how much, or how little art goes into
this sort of inventiveness; but we do take this occasion to
discover, within ourselves, how such youthful *tours de force*

scarcely meet the demands of an adult sense of taste. And for this reason, it might come as a not very pleasant surprise, that in this collection (assembled in his more mature years) we encounter entire poems, as well as certain passages and isolated expressions (not to mention *The Klinglingling, Hop, Hop, Hop, Hoho, Huzzah, Trallarum-Larum,* and the like) whose only excuse is their author's poetic immaturity; and it is this immaturity which constitutes the basis for the acclaim they have drawn from the popular masses. Now, if a poet such as Mr. B. puts the magical power of his paint-brush, the weight of his own example, in the service of such frivolities, how, then, are we to counteract the unmanly, childish tone which an army of incompetents has succeeded in insinuating into our lyrical poetry? For the same reason, the reviewer can give only qualified praise to the otherwise so wonderfully sung poem, *Wondrous Blossom.* As much as this device may have personally pleased Mr. B., a magical blossom at the beloved's bosom is an entirely unworthy, and not very spiritually uplifting symbol for modesty; it is, to be blunt, flirtation. And when it is said of this blossom that

> Du teilst der Flöte weichen Klang
> Des Schreiers Kehle mit,
> Und wandelst in Zephyrengang
> Des Stürmers Poltertritt.

> Thou impartest, as the flute's soft sound,
> The cryer's throaty tones,
> And transformest into Zephyr-like movements
> The stormer's crashing footsteps.

This is giving modesty altogether too much credit. The ill-suited expression, "her nose is gasping for ether," and a false rhyme—*blähn* with *schön*—disfigure the easy and beautiful gait of this song.

Mr. B. is most wanting in the art of idealization when he is describing sentiments, and this reproach is especially pertinent to his more recent poems—most of them addressed to Molly—with which he has filled out this edition. Incomparably beautiful though most of these may be in their diction and versification, and as poetically though they may be sung, the way they are *felt* seems unpoetic to us. What Lessing set down somewhere as a law for the tragedian, namely, that he must avoid presenting idiosyncrasies or rigidly delineated character traits, is all the more applicable to the lyrical poet. The latter is all the more enjoined from abandoning a certain universality in the emotions he describes, the less leeway is given him to expand upon the unique set of circumstances which gave rise to those emotions. For the most part, Bürger's poems are the product of one such entirely peculiar situation—one which is admittedly not as rigidly individual nor as exceptional as a Heautontimorumenos of Terentius, but which is just individual enough, so that the reader grasps it neither completely, nor clearly enough to remain undisturbed by its inherent non-ideal features. Now, taken by itself, such a defect would merely mar the perfection of a poem wherein it is encountered; but on top of this, comes yet another defect, which harms its very substance. Namely, these poems are not simply depictions of his own peculiar (and quite unpoetical) disposition, they are also clearly the offspring of that disposition. The poet's sensitivity, his indignation, his melancholy are not merely the subject of his song; unfortunately, they are frequently also the Apollo of his inspiration. But the goddesses of beauty and allure are very obstinate deities. They reward only those passions which they themselves would inspire; upon their altar they will not suffer any other fire than the fire of a pure and disinterested enthusiasm. An angry actor can scarcely be expected to be a noble personification of indignation; let the poet beware of singing of sorrow while he is wallowing in his own. Otherwise, just as the poet himself becomes but a passive object, so will his own emotion inevitably descend from its idealizing universality, into imperfect individuality. He may well compose from memories tempered with time, and the more he has experienced that of which he sings, the better; but he must never do so while under the immediate sway of the affect he is supposed to be rendering, sensuously and beautifully, for us. Even in those poems, about which it is customarily said that love, friendship, etc. guided the poet's brush, the poet always had to commence by going outside himself, by stripping away the individuality of the object of his enthusiasm, and by viewing his passion from a moderating distance. Ideal beauty is possible in no other way than through spiritual freedom, through a kind of self-activity which rescinds the rule of the passions.

Mr. B.'s more recent poems convey a certain bitterness, an almost morbid melancholy, and, on this account, the most excellent piece in this collection, *The Song of Songs of the Only One*, loses much of its otherwise incontestible merit. Other judges of art have already discoursed at great length about this beautiful product of Bürger's muse, and we are pleased to concur with a good portion of the praise they have given it. And yet, we can only marvel at how it was possible for them to forgive the poet's sweep, the fire of his emotions, his wealth of imagery, the power of his language, the harmony of his verse, for so many rude offenses against good taste—how it was possible to overlook the fact, that this poet's enthusiasm often verges on insanity, how his fire often turns into fury, and that for this very reason, the frame of mind in which this song comes across, is absolutely not the benign, harmonious mood into which we would expect to see the poet set us. We can well understand how Mr. B., carried away by the affect which dictated this song to him, was lured by the song's close relationship to his own situation, which he then proceeded to enshrine within that song; and how, at its conclusion, he could proclaim to himself that it bears the seal of perfection. But for this very reason—and all its brilliant strokes notwithstanding—we would prefer to describe it as merely a very excellent incidental poem—to wit, a poem whose immediate inspiration and intent gives us grounds to pardon its lack of the ideal purity and perfection which alone can satisfy our good taste.

We note in passing, that it is precisely this poet's great personal empathy with this and other songs in this collection, which explains why we are reminded of him, the author, with such excessive frequency. Among the more modern poets, the reviewer knows of no one who has rehearsed Horace's *sublimi feriam sidera vertice* to such ill purpose. We do not mean to imply, that on such occasions, the wondrous blossom has fallen from his beloved's breast; we realize, that only in jest could anyone lavish so much praise upon himself. But even assuming he were serious in only one-tenth of all such jesting expressions, still that one-tenth, repeated ten times over, adds up to one full share of bitter seriousness. Self-praise can scarcely be pardoned, even in the mouth of Horace, and an engrossed reader will not readily pardon a poet whom he would so dearly like to just sit back—and admire.

These general remarks concerning this poet's spiritual mettle, seem to be all that can be said in the confines of a journal article about a collection of over one hundred poems, many of which merit a more detailed analysis. The unanimous judgment, long since uttered by the public, spares us the task of discussing his ballads, a poetic genre in which other poets will not have an easy time outshining Mr. B. As for his sonnets—exemplars of this genre, which are transformed into song the moment they touch the reciter's lips—we wish along with him, that they may find no imitators save those who, like him and his outstanding friend Schlegel, are skilled enough to play the lyre of the Pythian god. We would have gladly seen all those pieces of mere wit, especially the epigrams, omitted from this collection, and would likewise prefer to see Mr. B. abandon the light, jesting genre, which is not in keeping with his strong, pithy style. To convince the reader of this, let him compare, for instance, his *Drinking Song*, Part I, p. 142, with songs of similar content by Anacreon or Horace. If, after this, one were to ask in good conscience, which of Mr. B.'s poems should be ranked the highest—the serious or the satirical ones, the exclusively lyrical or the lyrical-narrative ones—

our verdict would have to favor the serious, the narrative, and the early poems. It is beyond question, that over time Mr. B. has grown in poetic strength and breadth, in his power over language, and in the beauty of his verse; but his style has not become more elevated, nor has his taste grown more refined.

If we have pointed out only the defects of poems about which infinitely many beautiful things could likewise be said, let it be known that we would only commit this injustice against a poet of Mr. B.'s gifts and stature. Only when dealing with a poet whom so many are poising their pens to imitate, is it worth troubling ourselves to take definite sides in the defense of art, and only a great poetic genius such as he, is capable of reminding beauty's friends about art's highest exigencies, which, when confronted with a mediocre talent, they may either voluntarily put out of mind, or are in danger of forgetting entirely. We freely concede, that the entire legion of poets vying with Mr. B. for the crown of laurels, in our opinion stand just as far beneath him, as he himself remains below the pinnacle of beauty. We also know full well, that much of what we have found to be objectionable in his works, can be laid to external circumstances, which have restricted the power of his genius to effect the greatest beauty—as we can see from the moving testimony contained within his own poems. But only the unbeclouded, serene soul can give birth to perfection. Of all people, the poet can least afford to burden his soul with external woes and problems of personal health—struggles which certainly sap anyone's mental powers. The poet must be able to extricate himself from the here-and-now, so as to soar aloft, boldly and freely, into the world of ideals. No matter how much tumult rages within his breast, his brow must remain bathed in clearest sunlight.

If, in the meantime, any of our poets has ever deserved to perfect himself in order that he may produce perfected works, then Mr. Bürger is that poet. This richness of poetic imagery, this energetic language of the heart, this flood of poetry, now majestically undulating, now gently lilting, pouring forth such excellently varied works; and, lastly, this honest heart which, one might even say, speaks out to us from every line—all this deserves to become wedded with eternally changeless aesthetic grace, with manly dignity, with thought-content, and with lofty, quiet greatness, so that it may attain classicism's supreme crown.

And now, the public has a beautiful opportunity to earn this prize for art here in our fatherland: We hear that Mr. B. is working on a new, expanded edition of his poems, and it will be the amount of support afforded him by the friends of his muse, which will determine whether it shall at the same time be an improved, perfected edition.

Thus was the reviewer's verdict on Bürger's merit as a poet eleven years ago; and today, he can not alter that opinion, although he would probably support it with more conclusive proofs, since, at the time, his feelings were more on the mark than was his reasoning. Partisan passions have become mingled in this dispute, but if the reader will set aside his personal interest, he may do justice to this reviewer's basic intent.

*Of the*

# AESTHETIC ESTIMATION
# OF MAGNITUDE

TRANSLATED BY SUSAN JOHNSON

I can form four mental images, quite different from one
another, of the quantity of an object. The tower which I see
before me, is a magnitude.

It is 200 ells high.

It is high.

It is a high (sublime) object. It is striking, that something
quite different is expressed in each of these four judgments,
all of which, however, refer to the quantitative nature of
the tower. In the first two judgments, the tower is regarded
simply as a quantum (as a magnitude), in the two remaining
ones as a magnum (as something large).

Everything which has parts, is a quantum. Every perception, every idea formed by comprehension, has a magnitude, just as the latter has a domain and the former a
content. Quantity in general, therefore, cannot be meant,
if one speaks about a difference of magnitude among objects.

---

Schiller wrote this essay in 1793. Its significance lies in its opposition to Immanuel Kant, the hegemonic philosopher of the time,
who denied any connection between beauty and science. In this
essay, Schiller demonstrates the coherence of beauty and mathematical science, in particular. In so refuting Kant's conception of
beauty as subjective, Schiller created the conceptual basis for the
advances later made in mathematical physics by German scientists
Bernhard Riemann and Georg Cantor.

Here we speak about such a quantity as characteristically belongs to an object, that is to say, that which is not simply a *quantum*, but is at the same time a *magnum*.

Given any magnitude, one thinks of a unit to which various parts of the same kind are conjoined. Thus, if two magnitudes differ, it can only be because in one of them more parts are conjoined in the unit, in the other, fewer, or, that the one constitutes merely a part of the other. That quantum which contains in itself another quantum as a part, is, with respect to the latter quantum, a *magnum*.

To investigate how many times a certain specific quantum is contained in another, is to *measure* that quantum (if it is continuous), or to count it (if it is not continuous). What we take as a unit of measure each time depends upon whether we are to consider an object as a magnum, that is to say, all magnitude is a relative concept, an idea of proportion.

Held up against its own measure, every magnitude is a magnum, and still more so, held up against the measure of its own measure, compared with which its own measure is itself again a magnum. But, just as the process descends, it also ascends. Every magnum is small in turn, as soon as we think it contained in another, and where is there a limit, since we can once more multiply any number series, however large, with itself?

By means of measurement, thus, we indeed arrive at the *comparative*, but never at the *absolute magnitude*, at that, to wit, which cannot be included in any other quantum, but subsumes all other magnitudes. Nothing, of course, would hinder the same action of the mind which provided us with such a magnitude, from providing us with its *double*, for the mind proceeds successively, and, guided by ideas of number, can continue its synthesis into infinity. So long as it is still possible to determine how *large* an object may be, the object is still not (simply) large, and can, through the same operation of comparison, be diminished into something very small. Accordingly, there could exist in Nature only one single magnitude *per excellentiam*, to

wit, the infinite totality of Nature herself, to which, however, no one perception ever corresponds, and whose synthesis cannot be completed in any span of time. For, since
the realm of numbers can never be exhausted, it would have
to be the mind which brings its synthesis to a conclusion.
The mind itself would have to establish or create some
unit as the highest and maximum measure, and whatever
exceeds that, simply define it to be large.

This also happens in practice, when I say of the tower
which stands before me, *it is high,* without *determining* its
height. I give no measure of comparison here, and yet I
cannot ascribe absolute magnitude to the tower, since nothing at all prevents me from assuming it to be still larger.
Simply by looking at the tower, therefore, a maximum measure must already be given to me, and I must be able to
presume, that by saying *this tower is high,* that I have
prescribed this maximum measure to every other observer
as well. This measure, therefore, already lies in the idea of
a tower, and it is nothing other than the idea of its *species-
magnitude.*

A certain maximum magnitude is prescribed to every
thing, either through its *species* (if it is a work of nature), or
(if it is a work of freedom) through the *constraints* arising
from its underlying cause and purpose. We employ this
measure of magnitude, more or less consciously, in every
observation of objects; but our perceptions are very different, depending upon whether the measure we apply is more
fortuitous or more necessary. If an object exceeds the idea
of its species-magnitude, it will, to a certain degree, put us
into a state of *bewilderment.* We will be surprised, and our
experience expands, but insofar as we take no interest in
the object itself, what remains is simply a feeling, that the
magnitude which we expected has been exceeded. We have
derived this measure merely from a series of empirical
experiences, and there is no necessity whatever at hand that
it must always fit. If, on the other hand, a product of freedom
exceeds the idea which we established for ourselves about
the constraints of its cause, we will no doubt feel a certain

sense of *admiration*. What startles us in such an experience is not merely the exceeded expectation, it is at the same time that the constraints have been cast off. There, in the earlier case, our attention simply remained on the *product*, which was of indifferent concern in itself; here, our attention is drawn toward the *generative force*, which is moral, or is at least associated with a moral being, and as such it must necessarily interest us. This interest will increase just to that degree, that the force constituting the active principle is the more noble or more weighty, and the constraint which we find exceeded is the more difficult to overcome. A horse of uncommon size will pleasantly surprise us, but still more the adept and powerful rider who tames him. If we now see him leap with this horse over a wide, deep gully, we are astonished, and if it is an enemy front which we see him charge, respect shall join with this astonishment, and turn into admiration. In this latter case, we treat his action as a dynamic magnitude, and apply our idea of human valor as a metric, where it is now a question of how we are conscious of our own worth and what we consider the maximum limit of courage.

Things are totally different, if the idea of the magnitude of the purpose is exceeded. Here we employ no empirical and fortuitous metric as the basis, but, on the contrary, a rational and thus necessary one, one which cannot be exceeded without negating the purpose of the object. The magnitude of a house is solely determined by its purpose; the magnitude of a tower can be determined merely by the constraints of architecture. Hence, should I find the house too large for its purpose, it must necessarily displease me. Should I, on the other hand, find that the tower exceeds my idea of a tower's height, it will but delight me all the more. Why? The one is a contradiction, the other only an unexpected accordance with what I seek. I can still reconcile myself where a constraint is relaxed, but not where an intention is not carried out.

If, now, I merely say of an object, *it is large*, without adding *how large* it is, I am not at all thereby proclaiming it to be something absolutely large, to which no metric can measure up; I am simply saying nothing about the measure to which I subject it, on the assumption, that it is already contained in the mere idea of it. I do not determine its magnitude completely in contrast to all other things conceivable, but I do so partially, and with respect to a certain class of things, yet, therefore, always objectively and logically, because I affirm a proportional relationship, and proceed according to an idea.

This idea, however, can be empirical, and therefore contingent, and my judgment in this case will have only subjective validity. I perhaps make into the species-magnitude, that which is only magnitude of a certain kind; perhaps I see an objective limit in what is but my subjective limitation; perhaps I smuggle my private idea of the use and purpose of the thing into my judgment. As regards substance, my estimate of magnitude can thus be quite subjective, although in respect of form, it is objective, i.e., an actual determination of proportions. The European takes the Patagonian to be a giant, and his judgment is entirely valid among that stock of people from whom he derives his concept of human magnitude; in Patagonia, however, he will find disagreement. Nowhere does the influence of subjective principles on men's judgment become more apparent, than in their estimation of size regarding corporeal as well as incorporeal things. Everyone, one may assume, has a certain measure for strength and virtue within himself, which guides his estimation of the magnitude of moral acts. The miser will look upon the donation of a guilder as a very large strain on his generosity, while the generous man believes threefold the sum is too little to give. The man of common stamp celebrates his lack of criminality as a great proof of his honesty; another of fine sensibility may sometimes scruple over whether to take a legitimate profit.

Although in all these cases, the measure is subjective, the act of measuring is itself always objective; for one need only generalize the measure, and a general standard of magnitude will be introduced. This is actually the case with the objective measures which are in general use, even though they all have a subjective origin and are derived from the human body.

All comparative estimation of magnitude, however, be it abstract or physical, be it wholly or only partly determinant, leads only to relative, and never to absolute magnitude; for if an object actually exceeds the measure which we assume to be a maximum, it can still always be asked, by how many times the measure is exceeded. It is certainly a large thing in relation to its species, but yet not the largest possible, and once the constraint is exceeded, it can be exceeded again and again, into infinity. Now, however, we are seeking absolute magnitude, for this alone can contain in itself the basis of a higher order, since all relative magnitudes, as such, are like to one another. Since nothing can compel our mind to halt its business, it must be the mind's power of imagination which sets a limit for that activity. In other words, the estimation of magnitude must cease to be logical, it must be achieved aesthetically.

If I estimate a magnitude in a logical fashion, I always relate it to my cognitive faculty; if I estimate it aesthetically, I relate it to my faculty of sensibility. In the first case, I experience something about the object, in the second case, on the contrary, I only experience something within me, caused by the imagined magnitude of the object. In the first case I behold something outside myself, in the second, something within me. Thus, in reality, I am no longer measuring, I am no longer estimating magnitude, rather I myself become for the moment a magnitude to myself, and indeed an infinite one. That object which causes me to be an infinite magnitude to myself, is called sublime.

The power of imagination, as the spontaneity of emotion, accomplishes a twofold business in conceptualizing magnitude. It first gathers every part of the given quantum into an empirical consciousness, which is *apprehension*; secondly, it assembles the *successively collected* parts into a pure self-consciousness, in which latter business, that of *comprehension*, it acts entirely as pure understanding. The concept of my "I" (empirical consciousness), in other words, combines with each part of the quantum; and through reflection upon these successively performed syntheses, I recognize the identity of my "I" (pure self-consciousness) in this series as a whole; in this way, the quantum first becomes an object for me. I link A to B, and B to C, and so forth, and while I watch my activity, as it were, I say to myself: in A, as well as in B, and in C, I am the acting subject.

Apprehension takes place *successively,* and I grasp each partial conception after the other. Since, after every moment in time, another constantly follows, and so forth into infinity, there is no danger in this procedure, that I would not be able to bring even the quantum with the highest numerical value to completion. Simply give me time, and there is no number, in apprehension, which shall exceed my reach. The synthesis, however, takes place *simultaneously,* and through the concept of the self-identity of my "I" in all preceding syntheses, I transcend anew the temporal conditions under which they had occurred. All those different empirical conceptions held by my "I" lose themselves in the single pure self-consciousness: the subject, which had acted in A, and B, and C, and so forth, is I, the eternally identical self.

For this second act, that is to say, for the reduction of different empirical apperceptions into pure self-consciousness, it is now absolutely not a matter of indifference, how many such empirical apperceptions are to be resolved into pure self-consciousness. Experience at least teaches us, that the power of imagination has a limit here, however difficult it may be to find out its necessary ground. This limit may differ for different persons, and can perhaps be extended by deliberate practice and energetic effort, but it can never be dissolved. If the power of reflection transgresses this limit, and seeks to bring together mental images, which already lie beyond the limit, into one unity of self-consciousness, it will lose as much in clarity as it gains in scope. Between the circumference of the entirety of a mental image and the distinctness of its parts, is an ever insuperable, specific relationship, wherefore in each addition of a large quantum we lose as much backward as we gain forward, and when we have reached the end-point, we see the starting-point vanish.

That number of mental images with which the distinctness of the individual parts can still perfectly subsist, would thus be the maximum of the human power of comprehension. This maxiumum can be exceeded, and indeed very considerably so, but each time at the cost of distinctness; and to the disadvantage of the mind, which must rigorously depend upon that distinctness. Fewer than three this number cannot truly be, for the original act of comparison upon which all determinate, precise thinking is based, makes this three-ness necessary. Whether this number may be greater than three may be doubted, and experience at least provides nothing by means of which it could be proven. And so certainly the number *three* may be called the holy number, for through it our orbit of thought would be determined.

The aesthetic measure is directed according to this logical base-measure, as well, in the estimation of magnitude, which, to be sure, cannot be understood so narrowly. It is agreed, at least, that we are able to take in and distinguish more than three units at a time, although the further we enlarge the summation, the more the clarity decreases. Yet since, in the estimation of magnitude, all parts are taken to be of the same kind, here the requirement for clarity is somewhat less rigorous. We may perhaps perceive twenty persons at one glance, but to recognize more than three among them at one instant will be difficult. Generally, here we must take heed, that we do not take as simultaneous, that which is simply a rapid succession. The rapidity with which the mind makes nine out of three-times-three, no longer allows us to distinguish whether these nine units appear to us all at once, or in a succession of three moments. We often fancy, that we grasp with our senses, when we but comprehend with our mind. We need but only make the experiment, whether that which we take in all at once with a rapid ordering makes the same effect when it is in disorder. Classification and order can only aid the mind, never the power of imagination; thus what we easily take in under the foregoing condition, we have not perceived at one stroke, but counted or measured.

This maxiumum of comprehension, determined by the constraints of our subjectivity, governs us in all estimation of magnitude, also the mathematical, as the ultimate base-measure. Since each magnitude is only determinable by means of comparison, the mind, without such a maximum base-measure, would lack a fixed point of reference on which, by necessity, it must ultimately rest in order to be able to distinguish any magnitude at all. Now, every quantum in Nature will be estimated according to this subjective base-measure, and the sameness of this measure in all human beings is the sole cause of why men's judgment about magnitude can agree. Were this base-measure to be expanded, all objects, at least aesthetically considered, would move into a different relationship to us; calculations which now proceed only discursively according to concepts, would be the work of a glance; and objects which now move us by their sublimity, would shed their entire enchantment and vanish into the common rank.

Let us assume for the moment, that this maximum of sensuous comprehension is *ten*. The power of imagination can thus grasp ten units in one, without missing a single unit. Now, however, let a given magnitude contain a thousand such units, and the entire thousand is to be absorbed by consciousness. To apprehend the quantum, i.e., to take each of these thousand units individually into consciousness, is not difficult at all, for nothing but time is required; but to comprehend the quantum, i.e., to recognize the consciousness strewn into all these thousand mental images of units as self-identical, to grasp a thousand different apperceptions in a single one, that is the difficult task to be solved. Now there is no other way out, but to reduce these thousand units to ten, for ten is the highest unit which the power of imagination can take in all together.

But how can a thousand units be represented by ten?—In no other way than through concepts, which are the unique and invariant representatives of perceptions. The power of imagination thus relinquishes its intuitive business, and the mind begins its discursive (here, actually symbolic) work. Number must assist where perception no longer suffices, and thought must subdue, where the eye's vision can no longer become master.

From those ten units, which are the maximum of sensuous comprehension, the mind forms a new logical unit, the number-concept 10. Now, however, the power of imagination can, as we assume, comprehend ten units at the same time; every number-concept 10, thought of as a unit, can thus, taken ten times, fuse together in one intuition of the power of imagination. Admittedly, these logical units formed by the mind are appropriated in this second act of comprehension not as multiples but as units, and the ten units, which each contains, are no longer seen as individuals. All that is accounted is the concept simply as representative, and what is represented loses itself in darkness or disappears. These ten logical units are now compressed by the mind into a new unit, the number 100, which, repeated 10 times, can once more be conceived at a single stroke by the power of imagination, producing the number 1,000, which fully provides the measure of the given quantum. In this third act of comprehension, those original units must still be extinguished far more, because their immediate representatives, the number-concepts 10, have become represented by others, and themselves have vanished into darkness.

Throughout this operation, the power of imagination has in no way enlarged the scope of its comprehension, and it was always just the same quantum of 10 units which hovered before it at any one point in time. Yet, by virtue of the fact, that the mind, in three successive operations, replaced those sensuous units with logical ones, and constantly brought the latter under the sway of other, higher logical units, the mind subdued for the power of imagination the whole quantum of that 1,000, and in this fashion concealed her aesthetic impoverishment from her in a logical profusion.

Nevertheless, in order to know, that one is not counting ten, but a thousand, and that each of the last ten units contains within it a hundred others, the mind's spirit must quickly recall the preceding synthesis through which it produced these units. At least a dim intuition of the content of the number-concepts must accompany the ongoing synthesis, as anyone who has watched himself making calculations can observe in himself. Only it cannot but come to pass, that the more the number-concepts increase, the more logical the operations of the mind's spirit constantly become, and clarity of perception must fade away; from this it also follows, that the highest number-concepts ultimately tell us far less than the lower ones, for we still associate a content with the latter. In order to be moved by the concept of a million pieces of gold, one must at least dimly recall how large a content already lies in the number thousand, and how many smaller coins a single gold-piece contains.

A regiment of 2,000 men, stationed along a broad front, three men deep—let us quickly form a mental image of its magnitude. To facilitate the act of perception, I shall assume, that they are all arranged in groups of 10. Let a small segment "a" stand for every 10, and a larger one, "aa," for every 100, and our eyes shall survey the entire length of the front. The first segment, up to "a," we shall thus take in, according to our previous assumption, in one simultaneous glance, wherein each individual man can still be distinguished. This segment is now at the same time a unit for the reflecting mind; and when our gaze has passed over 10 such segments, and the power of imagination has accomplished her act of comprehension ten times successively, the mind attempts once more to realize for itself the identity of consciousness in these ten acts of comprehension, i.e., to make from these ten logical units a new unit. The mind succeeds in this, too, but at the cost of the first intuition, which conceals its parts, in the same proportion as it transforms itself into a part of another whole. As the successive acts of comprehension are made simultaneous by means of the reflecting mind, so the simultaneous intuitions of the power of imagination lose their clarity, and now appear before the soul simply as masses. If this synthesis is now brought to a still higher level, and new units are again generated out of the ones already produced, the individual entity disappears altogether, and the entire front simply melts into a continuous length, in which it is impossible to distinguish a segment, much less a particular head. It follows from this, that the clarity of intuition always remains confined only in a specific number; that for all discursive progression on the part of the mind, the power of imagination never expands its real wealth (as far as the simultaneity of perception is concerned); and that, even if the process of calculation goes into the millions, only a specific number contained therein will always be the governing number in which the others, as it were, are submerged. Now, if one wishes to obtain an aesthetic impression of a large quantum, one must try to quickly reconstitute the original units out of the concept representing them, which, e.g., in the preceding case, will occur when one tries to constantly keep the first segment in mind, while looking down at the entire front.

But it is precisely here, in this attempt of the power of imagination to restore the sensuousness of the mental image out of the logical representation provided by number-concepts, and so to grasp length with breadth, simultaneity with succession in one intuitive act, that the limit of this ability comes to light; yet, at the same time, so does the strength of another capacity, through which latter discovery that lack will be more than recompensed.

Reason insists, in accordance with its necessary laws, upon absolute totality of perception, and without letting itself be rebuffed by the necessary limitation of the power of imagination, the mind requires from it a complete summation of all the parts of a given quantum in one simultaneous mental image. The power of imagination is thus compelled to exhaust the entire scope of its comprehensive capacities, but because it nevertheless does not complete this task to the end, and, all exertions notwithstanding, cannot extend its scope, the power of imagination sinks back into itself exhausted, and sensuous man experiences with painful disquiet his limitations.

But is it an external force, which gives him this experience of his limitations? Is it the fault of the measureless ocean, or the infinite star-sown heaven, that I become self-conscious of my impotence while representing their greatness? Whence, in that event, do I know, that their greatness exceeds the reach of my representation, and that I can obtain no totality of their image? Do I, indeed, know of these objects, that they are supposed to constitute a totality of a mental image?—I could only know this by virtue of my mental image of them, and in no other way, and yet it is presupposed, that I cannot imagine them as a totality. They are thus not presented to me as a totality, and I myself am the very one, who first put the concept of totality into them. I thus already have this idea in me, and I myself, the thinking being, am the very one, by which I, the being who makes representations of images of the intellect, am vanquished. In contemplating these great objects, I indeed experience my *powerlessness,* but I experience it through my *strength.* I am not vanquished by Nature, *I am vanquished by mine own self.*

In wanting to comprehend all individual parts of an apprehended quantum, what do I actually want to do? I want to recognize the identity of my self-consciousness in all the partial conceptions, I want to find myself in everything. I want to say to myself: "All these parts have become conceived through me, the eternally self-same subject." One must remember, that reason always requires the comprehension of only those parts which are already apprehended, thus already presented in empirical consciousness; for a magnitude only begins to affect me, if I have scanned it with my power of imagination, thus apprehending its parts, yet cannot entirely comprehend it.

Thus I want to dissolve images of the intellect, which I already have, into a single one, and cannot do it, and I am pained, that I cannot. But in order to experience, that I cannot fulfill a requirement, I must at once have the idea of this requirement and that of my incapacity. But this requirement is present: totality of the parts in the act of comprehension, or unity of my "I" in a certain series of transformations of my "I." Thus I must only imagine, that I cannot generate in consciousness a mental image of the unity of my "I" in all these transformations; but precisely in so doing I do produce this idea. Precisely in so doing, I think the totality of the whole series, and that I *want* to think it, for I can want nothing of which I do not already have an idea. I thus already bear within myself this totality which I seek to represent, just because I seek to represent it. Greatness, therefore, is in me, not outside me. It is my eternally self-same subject, persistent through every change, finding itself once more in every transformation. I can continue the act of apprehending into infinity: this means nothing else, than that, in endless transformations of my consciousness, my consciousness is self-identical, the entire infinity lies in the unity of my "I."

This solution can be expressed in another formulation. In all ideas about objects, including magnitude, the mind's spirit is never simply what is *determined*, rather it is at the same time always what *determines*. It is indeed the object which changes me, but I, the conceiving subject, am what makes the object into an object, and through its generation, changes itself. In all these transformations, however, there must be something which does not change, and this eternally immutable *principium* is precisely the pure and self-identical "I," the ground of the possibility of all objects, insofar as they become represented to the intellect. Whatever of greatness lies in the idea, lies in us, who bring forth these ideas. Whatever law may be given to us for our thoughts and actions, it is given us *by us*; and even if, as sensuously constrained beings, we *must* leave unfulfilled, as we do, the law of totality here in the theoretical realm in the portrayal of magnitude, or when, as free beings endowed with will, we break the law, as we do the moral law in the practical realm, still it is always *we* who have established the law. I may thus lose myself in the dizzying idea of omnipresent space, or never-ending time, or I may feel my own nothingness in the idea of absolute perfection—it is after all only I, myself, who gives space its infinite breadth, and time its eternal length, it is I, myself, who bear within me the idea of the Holy of Holies, for I create them; and the Godhead, which I conceive, is my creation, so surely as my thought is my own.

The sublimity of the magnitude is therefore no objective property of the object to which it is attributed; it is purely the effect of our own subjectivity, occasioned by that object. It arises in one part out of the imagined incapacity of the power of imagination of the mind to achieve the totality demanded by reason in portraying magnitude, partly again from the imagined capability of reason to make such a demand. On the first is based the repulsive, on the second the attractive power of great magnitude and of the sensuous-infinite.

Although the sublime is a phenomenon which is first produced in our subjectivity, yet the object itself must contain the reason why only this object and no other gives us occasion to make this use of it. And since, furthermore, we posit the predicate of the sublime in our judgment *into the object* (by which we indicate, that we do not simply resolve upon this connection arbitrarily, but rather thereby intend to establish a law for everyone), so our subjectivity must contain a necessary reason why we make precisely this use of a certain class of objects, and no other.

There exist accordingly *internal* and *external* necessary conditions of the mathematical-sublime. To the former belongs a certain specific relationship between the mind and the power of imagination, to the latter a specific relationship of the perceived object to our aesthetic measure of magnitude.

The power of imagination as well as reason must express themselves with a certain degree of intensity if something of great magnitude is to affect us. It is required of the power of imagination, that it summon up all its resources of comprehension to set forth the representation of the absolute, toward which Reason unremittingly presses. If the imagination is sluggish and dull, or if the emotive tendency of one's mind is more toward conceptual formulations than intuitive vision, even the most sublime thing remains merely a logical object, and will not be brought before the aesthetic tribunal at all. This is the reason, why those with overbearing intensity of analytical understanding seldom prove to be very receptive to that which is aesthetically great. Either their power of imagination is not lively enough to so much as venture toward the representation of reason's absolute, or their mind too preoccupied to appropriate the object itself, and play it over from the field of intuition onto the mind's discursive terrain.

Without a certain intensity of imagination, great objects do not become aesthetic at all; without a certain strength of reason, on the other hand, that which is aesthetic does not become sublime. The idea of the Absolute certainly requires a more than ordinary development of the higher faculty of reason, a certain richness of ideas, and a more rigorous acquaintance on the part of the individual with his noblest self. He whose reason has undergone no cultivation at all, will never know how to make a supra-sensual use of the grandness of the senses. Reason will not become involved in the business at all, and it will be left to the power of imagination alone, or to the mere understanding alone. The power of imagination, however, for itself, is not about to tolerate a process of synthesis which becomes embarrassing for it. It thus contents itself with the mere apprehension of something, and it never even occurs to it to want to give its representations universality. This is the source of that most stupid insensibility with which the savage can dwell in the lap of most sublime Nature, and amidst the symbols of the Infinite, without thereby being awoken from his bestial slumber, without revering even from afar the great spirit of Nature, which speaks to a feeling soul out of the sensuous-immeasurable.

What the crude savage gapes at with dull insensibility, the unnerved weakling flees as an object of horror, one which shows him not his strength, but only his impotence. His straitened heart feels painfully pulled asunder by great ideas. His imagination is sufficiently excitable to make an attempt at representing the sensuous-infinite, but his reason is not sufficiently independent to complete this undertaking with success. He wants to scale the summit, but goes to his knees halfway, fainting. He does combat with awesome Genius, but only with earthly weapons, not immortal ones. Conscious of this weakness, he prefers to withdraw from a sight which would vanquish him, and seeks succor from the consolatrix of all weak men, the *rule*. If he cannot stand up straight to the greatness of Nature, then Nature must climb down to his small powers of comprehension. She must exchange her bold forms for those of artifice, those alien to her, but which are yet what his spoiled senses require. She must subject her will to his iron yoke, and cringe within the shackles of mathematical regularity. That is how the earlier French taste in gardens arose, which at last has almost entirely given way to the English, without in its course having come appreciably closer to true taste. For Nature's character has just as little to do with sheer variety as with uniformity. Her lawful, tranquil seriousness accords just as little with these sudden, frivolous transitions, which in the new gardening style have her hopping from one decoration to another. As Nature transforms herself, she does not relinquish her harmonious unity, in modest simplicity she conceals her fullness, and even in the most exuberant freedom, we see her uphold the law of continuity.[1]

Among the objective conditions of the mathematical-sublime are, first, that the object deemed by us to be such, constitute a whole, and thus manifest unity; second, that it make the largest sensuous measure, which we habitually use to measure all magnitudes, utterly useless to us. Without the first condition, our power of imagination would not be challenged at all to attempt a representation of its totality; without the second, it would not be possible for this effort to fail.

The horizon surpasses any magnitude which can ever come before the mind's eye, since all magnitudes in space must lie within it. Nevertheless, we often observe, that one particular mountain, rising over the horizon, can give us a far stronger impression of the sublime than our entire field of vision, which encompasses not only this mountain, but also thousands of other magnitudes. This comes about, because the horizon does not appear to us to be a single object, and thus we are not invited to comprehend it and represent it as a totality. But if one removes all objects from the horizon which especially attract our attention, if one conceives of a wide, continuous plain, or an open sea, the horizon itself becomes an object, and indeed the most sublime which can ever appear before our eyes. The circular shape of the horizon especially contributes to this impression, because, in itself, it is so easy to grasp, and all the less can the power of imagination abstain from seeking to complete the shape.

The reason for the aesthetic impression of magnitude, however, is that the power of imagination attempts in vain to give a complete representation of the given object, and this can only come to pass in such a manner, that the maximum measure of magnitude which the power of imagination can grasp clearly at one strike, adding to itself as many times as the mind can clearly think all together, is too small for the object. But from this it seems to follow, that objects of like magnitude would also have to make an impression of like sublimity, and smaller size would elicit a lesser impression, which, however, is contrary to experience. For according to experience, the part often seems more sublime than the whole, the mountain or tower more sublime than the sky it stretches toward, the cliff upon which the waves wash more sublime than the ocean. Here one must recall the condition mentioned above, by force of which the aesthetic impression only ensues when the imagination is receptive for the totality of the object. If it omits to do so with respect to the far larger object, and on the other hand carries it out with respect to the smaller one, it may be aesthetically stirred by the latter, and yet insensitive to the former. If it thinks this larger object as a magnitude, however, the imagination thinks it, at the same time, as a unity, and then it must necessarily make a relatively stronger impression, the more it exceeds the other in size.

All sensuous magnitudes exist either in space (extended magnitudes) or in time (numerical magnitudes). Although every extended magnitude is at the same time a numerical magnitude (for we must also apprehend in time that which is given in space), numerical magnitude is yet itself sublime only insofar as I transform it into a spatial magnitude. The Earth's distance from Sirius is certainly an enormous quantum with respect to time, and if I want to grasp it in its totality, it overwhelms my imagination; but it would never occur to me to behold this temporal magnitude; on the contrary, I avail myself of numbers, and that, only when I call to mind, that the maximum spatial magnitude I can comprehend as a unity, e.g., a mountain-range, is nevertheless a much too small and utterly useless measure for this distance, do I receive the impression of sublimity. Thus, I do take the measure for this distance from extended magnitudes, and it depends upon just this measure, whether or not an object is to seem large to us.

Great magnitude in space appears either in *lengths* or in *heights* (which also include depths, for depth is only a height below us, just as height can be termed a depth above us). Accordingly, Latin poets did not hesitate to use the expression profundus [deep] for heights as well:

ni faciat, maria ac terras caelumque profundum
quippe ferant rapidi secum. . . .[2]

—*Aeneid, I, 58*

Heights indeed seem more sublime than equally great lengths, partly for the reason that the dynamic-sublime combines with the vision of the height. A mere length, however impossible it may be to see its end-point, has nothing at all terrifying about it, but a height surely does, for we could fall down from it. For the same reason, a depth is still more sublime than a height, because the idea of the terrible immediately accompanies it. For a great height to frighten us, we must first think ourselves aloft, and thus transform it into a depth. One can readily experience this if one beholds a blue sky intermixed with clouds in a well, or in dark water, where its infinite depth gives an incomparably more terrifying appearance than its height. The same thing happens to a still greater degree, when one looks upside-down at the sky, which in the same way becomes a depth, and, because it is the only object which strikes our view, it irresistibly compels our power of imagination to represent its totality. Heights and depths affect us more intensely for exactly this reason, because no process of comparison weakens the estimation of their magnitude. A length always has a metric on the horizon, before which it pales, for, however far a line may extend, the heavens also extend so far. The highest mountain range is indeed small against the height of the firmament, but that is merely what the understanding teaches, not the eye, and it is not the heavens whose height makes the mountains low, rather it is the mountains which, by their magnitude, show the elevation of the sky.

It is, accordingly, not merely an *optically* correct, but also a *symbolically* true idea, when it is said, that Atlas holds up the heavens. Just as the heavens themselves literally seem to rest on Atlas, so our idea of the height of the heavens rests upon the height of Atlas. Thus the mountain, in the figurative sense, really holds up the heavens, because it holds the heavens aloft for our sensuous comprehension. Without the mountain, the heavens would fall, that is, it would sink before our eyes and be brought low.

## Author's Notes

1. The art of gardening and the art of drama have had in recent times somewhat the same fate, and indeed in the same nations. The same tyranny of rules in French gardens and French tragedies; the same motley, wild unruliness in the parks of Englishmen and in their Shakespeare; and, as German taste from time immemorial has had the law laid down by foreigners, in this case, too, it was compelled to swing back and forth between those two extremes.

2. Translation, from *Der Sturm auf dem Tyrrhener Meer*: "Thät er das nicht, sie brächen hervor, durchwühlten die Meere, | Schleiften den Erdball, und schleiften den ewigen Himmel | Mit sich dahin. . . ."

*From the*

# AESTHETICAL LECTURES
## (1792–93)

**TRANSLATED BY WILLIAM F. WERTZ, JR.**

Aesthetics is not able, to *bring forth* artists, but rather only, *to judge* art.

Nothing is more difficult, than to philosophize concerning *sentiments* and concerning art, which has to do with sentiments.

One sought until now to bring art works into the aesthetical provinces, without considering, whether genius had not broken its own course. Psychological empirical rules without completeness and an anxiously formed theory according to existing models constituted about the most important achievements, which one accomplished before Kant for the doctrine of taste.

### CONTENT OF AESTHETICS,
### ITS WORTH AND USEFULNESS
### ON TASTE

Aesthetics investigates the nature of the capacity, that is effective in the judgment of the beautiful; it seeks to draw the boundaries of taste exactly and rightly.

---

*The Aesthetical Lectures* is the transcript of a lecture series Schiller gave during the winter of 1792–93 at Jena University. Schiller had first read Immanuel Kant's *Critique of Judgment* in March 1791, and this transcript, prepared by one of his students, Chr. F. Michaelis, reflects Schiller's intellectual preparation for presenting his own theory of aesthetics, as distinct from that of Kant.

Every beauty of art requires, as imitation of nature, *truth*, and stands therein under objective judgment. In the area of *concepts* the *understanding* gives laws, which thus decides in the *logical* part of art.

Indispensible conditions of the beautiful presentation are truth and errorlessness (the correct). These, however, do not yet encompass beauty itself.

The doctrine of taste can hold back the artist before the errors of his genius, and through the reasoning of the self-active understanding occasioned therefrom, contribute to the ennoblement of the pleasures.

Taste does not only promote our felicity, but rather also *civilizes* and *cultivates* us. Man is not permitted to enjoy entirely *alone*, but must also take care, to communicate his enjoyment. Not every enjoyment, however, is capable of being communicated, and meet thereto. Also a virtue, which is not sparing of the weaknesses of society, offends against its own laws; it should also express itself with a certain *grace*. Man must make into law *universal communicability* of his sentiments. *Taste* shows itself in the capacity, to express this property (for example in the observation of the appropriate means in speech between saying too little and too much, in order not to rob the other of the enjoyment of thinking for himself).

To seek felicity, is not the highest aim of man. A frivolity of taste can easily enter, where one sacrifices duty to enjoyment. Everything depends hereby upon the concept of the *dignity of man*, which rests upon the self-activity of his reason, upon his freedom from sensuous impulses.

Shall a sentiment of pleasure be *universally communicable*, so must everything empirical, material, all influence of inclination be separated therefrom. The judgment of taste must be taken without inclination, like the *moral*; for both limit themselves only to the *form* and decide *immediately*. *Taste* has, like the *practical reason*, an *inner principle of judgment*, combines both natures of man and facilitates for him thereby the transition to morals, that he maintains alongside sensuous objects a certain *freedom* and impresses upon its treatment the character of *universality* and *necessity*. As *animal* being, man loves only himself, dependent on the laws of matter, from which only *rationality* tears him away as by the force of nature, in order to subjugate him to the dominion of reason.

Taste is the capacity, to judge the universal *communicability* of sentiments. Nothing material, empirical is universally communicable; for it is accidental. Taste, however, refers something empirical to the rational; accordingly were taste the capacity, to refer a sensuous representation to something supersensible. It leads from the *sensuous world* to the *intelligible* and wins the attention of reason to the sensuous through the reference to the super-sensible. Taste rests upon a sensuous impression-receiving capacity and upon a supersensible self-active capacity, upon phantasy and understanding.

## INFLUENCE AND VALUE OF TASTE

Taste secures man before raw sensuousness and before the savage state. So soon as love of adornment expresses itself in the savage, so does his culture also already begin. Even the still so bad taste betrays already a higher activity, the longing to make a favorable impression on another, which already assumes the opinion of the *worth* of the other. Now man is no longer a *savage*, rather a *barbarian*, since he is not without all taste, if he even possesses a false one. The embellishment of the needy already betrays the beginning civilization. The worth, which one places on the opinion of others, makes one more dependent upon them and necessitates holding back the raw instincts, leading thus to the refinement of the mode of living.

With the ennoblement of taste, religion also ennobled itself. Taste laid the basis for humanity.

Its influence shows itself also in the advancement of the activity of the higher spiritual capacity, whereby it facilitates the dominion of reason over sensuousness. For its presentations soften or make good the violence, which is dealt to sensuousness. Through taste, fantasy enjoys its whole freedom and is led back finally by means of a hidden bond to unity of the understanding. Taste also weakens sensuousness itself, whilst it requires *decency* and *moderation,* whereby much is won not only for *civilization,* but also for *morals,* whilst man not merely according to feelings, rather according to precepts of pure reason is accustomed to act so.

Individual men and entire nations have in reality only an *aesthetical virtue.*

Since morality demands *autonomy,* how can one counter the objection, that taste falsifies morality through the influence of the material? Does not religion also work against the resistance of the sensuous capacity, whilst religion wins it to the benefit of morals?

Taste brings the higher and lower *mental* capacities into union; it calls the philosophizing reason back from reflection to perception; it gives *humanity,* that is, it unites in man the natural being with the intelligence and promotes their reciprocal influence, so that sensuousness is ennobled through morality.

Taste conducts itself as the judgment of the beautiful just as the tasting of a meal, in that one must have first sampled this one, inspected and perceived that one, in order to be able to declare his feeling and judgment of both.

Taste is a capacity of the power of judgment, applied to universally communicable sentiments. The sentiments assumed to be universally communicable stand under inner subjective conditions, which must necessarily be common to all men. A universally communicable sentiment is *conditioned,* if it arises from concepts; the universal communicability of such a sentiment is never entirely certain. Taste is opposed to the sensuous *cognitive capacity,* is applied to *sentiments,* to something subjective-universal and necessary, and is the capacity, to judge the universal communicability of a feeling.

## DIVISION OF THE DOCTRINE OF TASTE

The doctrine of taste is *pure* or *applied*. The former treats of universal subjective conditions, under which judgments of taste are possible, and seeks to discover the kind of effectiveness, in which beautiful works of nature and art place the human mind. The second, practical part, concerns special determinations, under which certain aesthetical ends are achieved, the branches of art itself.

## DIFFERENCE BETWEEN SENTIMENT AND FEELING, PLEASURE AND DISPLEASURE, ETC.

Sentiment, which is *objective*, one can simply call sentiment, the *subjective*, however, one can call feeling. Sentiment is a representation, which refers to the subject, and distinguishes itself thereby from *cognition*. *Pleasure* is a sentiment, in which I wish to persist, *displeasure* one such, which I wish to avoid. A real ground is not indicated therefrom, but these sentiments are nonetheless distinguished from the representation and from desire. The formal ground, the universal condition of pleasure and displeasure is free or hindered efficacy of the power of the soul, which the soul must feel, in order to determine itself, and hereto it stands in need of the instinct or the representation. Pleasure should not be the end, but rather the *means* of efficacy, although many people reverse it. *Pleasure* is the self-consciousness of the acting—*displeasure* the self-consciousness of the hindered power. Displeasure may not be confused with negative pleasure.

Pleasure must be differentiated according to the difference of capacity, which can come to efficacy. The *sensuous* pleasure corresponds always to the perfect condition of a part of the body or the whole body. The well-being of the body can not be entrusted alone to freedom, rather needs the instincts and the sensuous pleasure as means to the activity of man.

*Intellectual* pleasure or pleasure of the cognitive capacity is a) pleasure of the *capacity of the intuition* or of sensuousness as the receptivity for matter, b) pleasure of the understanding, which forms the matter, as capacity of concepts, which separates or binds, observes agreement or contradiction, and c) pleasure of *reason,* of the capacity of ideas, of the striving toward the whole and toward harmony.

The *lower capacity of desire* strives for *pleasure* and determines itself according thereto; the *higher* determines itself according to *concepts.* The *moral* enjoyment is always accompanied with pain through the violence done to sensuousness, and is therefore mixed.

*Mental* pleasure grounds itself upon representations with consciousness; the *sensuous,* either upon none or upon representations without consciousness. Both accompany one another, as both kinds of displeasure, almost in all men, due to the reciprocal action between soul and body, in which even the body participates in the purest enjoyment. The mental pleasure is wont to be weaker, but more enduring than the sensuous.

Mere *sense perceptions,* as well as the entirely pure *rational perceptions,* are capable of no universal communicability and therefore are excluded from the realm of taste. In the same realm belong merely the *mixed,* which ground themselves upon the efficacy of the *cognitive* or of the *will-power*: of the former kind is the *perfect* and *beautiful,* of the latter the *moving* and *sublime.*

The *purposive, perfect* and *good* belong to the indispensible conditions of art work and constitute no characteristic property of the same, as a beautiful artwork.

The pleasure in the *sublime* is directly opposite to sensuousness and grounds itself upon this opposition, which the power of reason excites.

The pleasure in the *beautiful* arises from the *united* interest of reason and sensuousness. The beautiful alone affords a fully unconstrained pure enjoyment. Neither the moving nor the sublime can, as objects of *taste*, do without the beautiful, and both must subordinate themselves to the same. The beautiful alone makes the mere work of art into a product of taste. The beautiful endures in the form, which, however, can only become visible in a material. The material of beauty is an idea brought into presentation. Beauty is only a property of *form* and cannot be presented immediately in the mass.

Art *in general* has the aim of truth or perfection, of the relationship of the manifold to unity, and realizes it with the understanding. *Beautiful* art realizes this end moreover with beauty and taste: the former end one can call the *proclaimed*, the latter the *silent*.

The *earnestly intended, for-itself-perfected, logical purpose* of an art work can subordinate itself to the *aesthetical*, to the aim of beauty, as in the products of *eloquence*. Here beauty serves perfection. If the logical aim be merely *imagined*, then beauty *rules*; then nothing depends on the achievement of the proclaimed end; the artist *plays*, as it were, with his objects. Hence can the entire *art of poetry* be reckoned. If the poet fully achieves the aim of beauty, then he has in addition already attained the *moral*.—Beauty tolerates no dependence from logical aims, rather follows her own laws. Through her *play* with the earnest, logical aim, she achieves it best herself. Since she, however, persists only in the *form*, so she herself loses nothing by the treatment of light-minded objects.

The works of art of the first class (the earnestly intended aim) have to do either with *physical* or with *moral* aims. In the first case beauty indeed ennobles the works (for example, the beautiful tools and clothing of common architecture); but they are, through the shimmer, which beauty casts upon them only in passing, merely related to the works of beautiful art. If the works of art have *moral* aims, they stand in relationship with the aesthetical works, cultivate nevertheless even through their logical aim, thus their beauty works only yet more ardently. If beauty, through compliance with the purpose of sympathy, has suffered nothing at all, then have such art works the greatest perfection (as for example the group of Laocoon). Beauty takes delight in itself only through *contemplation*, not through *movement*. If it unite with the exertion of pathos, then must the latter suffer a certain moderation.

## THE DIFFERENCE BETWEEN THE BEAUTIFUL, PLEASANT, AND GOOD

One distinguishes the beautiful from the pleasant and good. The beautiful is perceived, like pleasantness, before the concept of the consequence of enjoyment; the good, first through the concept of capability of usage. With visible objects the beautiful seems to indicate the freedom of the mind in the intuition, and it seems chiefly to be characteristic of them. There is, however, also an *intellectual* beauty and a *moral*. Where a universal concept in an immediate intuition, an idea is represented through an action, where our disposition during contemplation is in freedom and the results are not obtained as given, but rather develops itself, here we find beauty. The immediate pleasure through the mere impression characterizes the judgment of beauty, in so far as it is free of material grounds of determination, of the determining influence of sentiments and concepts, grounds itself therefore upon a *freedom* of the disposition.

A character is then beautiful, if he instills in us more *love* than respect, as the character of Caesar as against that of Cato, which shows more deterring, humiliating severity, or as that of Tom Jones as against that of Grandison. Hence, one often confuses deeds of *preference* with the *beautiful*, because they seem to require less of nature. Sensuousness must also appear free in moral deeds, even though it is not; freedom also acquires here the predicate of beauty.

The concept *beautiful* is not empty, rather it also has its determined and unchanging meaning with heterogeneous objects.

Those who have dismissed the *objective* concept of beauty, hold beauty to be entirely *subjective*. Those who have accepted it, attempt to explain the concept either objectively or subjectively. Both accept, that the beautiful arouses *satisfaction*. To the former, the beautiful is merely a property of the object; the others only attach themselves to the sentiment, although they do not deny certain grounds of the sentiment of the beautiful in the object. The latter party promises very much through the removal of everything arbitrary: in its lead stands Kant.

The beautiful stands directly in a reciprocal relationship with the *useful*. That both amount to the same thing, indeed contradicts the common experience. Moreover, the beautiful pleases immediately through the impression, whereas the useful presupposes the concept of use.

Others place the beautiful in *proportion*. But the judgment about this, so far as it refers to use, would be a *cognitive* judgment, not a judgment of taste. Or if we have merely a certain universal ratio in mind for all kinds and species of object, so would the claim of such a proportion contradict the manifoldness and inequality, which nature observes in all beauty. Yet for every species of natural object we have in mind a certain measure, a medium size, according to which we judge the beauty of an individual, and which we unconsciously lay as the basis for this judgment. If this ratio is violated, so we name the object *deformed*. Yet the *ugly* should be in opposition to the beautiful. The degree of our dissatisfaction in regard to violated proportion depends upon custom and is much strengthened by it. Even with the best proportion an object can be unpleasant to us. *Correctness* is indeed the first condition of beauty, however, it does not itself constitute it. The most regular of all forms are not precisely the most beautiful (for example, the canon of Polyclitus, the most regular, but not beautiful figure). A small transgression of regularity can subsist very well with the most perfect beauty. Mere regularity in the production and judgment requires often only a mediocre mind.

Where the rule, which must be observed with beauty, *reigns,* there it smothers beauty.

One gave *sensuous perfection* as the ground of beauty. Perfection one called manifoldness, bound to a whole. The judgment of the same, however, is *logical,* not *aesthetical,* since it presupposes a concept. Perfection is purposiveness. *Inner* purposiveness is called actual perfection, which we attribute to the world structure or to a morally good deed, which have their end in themselves. *External* purposiveness is utility, in which judgment we do not merely have need of the object, but rather also the concept of its use. Such a (merely useful) object is for itself never a whole in the judgment. Ennobled is something thereby, if it is elevated from a mere means to a self-end. Everything useful is elevated thereby to perfection, if the external use is made unnecessary, to explain its existence. In order to know, how the manifold comes to agreement with the whole, one must know, to what end it agrees. Since, however, the utility is excluded from the beautiful, so we have to do here merely with the *inner* purposiveness.

*Free beauties* are those, with which we presuppose no characteristic purpose. For example, with a rose we are conscious of no determined purpose of its form and constitution. The *adhering* beauty, however, stands under the constraint of a concept, which exclusively permits only certain kinds of beauty and presupposes a purpose in the object. An unmixed, pure judgment of beauty is passed only in regard to *free* beauty.

Unity only takes place in a concept. Now the question is, whether we place a concept at the basis of the judgment of beauty? Yet even after long reflection this is not to be found here. No trace of a concept or the reference to a purpose reveals itself in the approval, which we afford the beauty of a flower, a landscape, a human face. Yes, with more exact dissection beauty would often only be lost.

*Dark* representations are such, whose consciousness would quickly be forgotten. Only in the condition of dark representations is pleasure or displeasure possible. For the attention to the object weakens the attention to the subject. Also with the *confused* representation, the partial representations must at least have been formerly at hand: yet one can pass a judgment of beauty, without any regard to the agreement of the part. Also in that theory, which places beauty in sensuously represented perfection, the difference between satisfaction in purposiveness and satisfaction in the beautiful would fall away. This theory would suit only some beauties, but not free, least of all poetical. Either the judgment of taste were intellectual and not pure, or it were by no means actually judgment of taste.

All painful, mathematical regularity is for us not beautiful. Since imperfection oppresses beauty, so one held perfection and regularity for the essence of beauty. A beautiful landscape must indeed be correct; correctness, however, still gives it no beauty.—Unity of the manifold, as simplicity in fullness and rest in business, is only relative beauty.—There are confused representations of perfection, which yet awaken directly no feeling of beauty; also, every judgment of beauty is not combined with the judgment of perfection.

## EXPLANATION OF THE BEAUTIFUL ACCORDING TO BURKE

Burke says, beauty arouses inclination, without desire for possession; a true, but only subjective explanation. The predicate of beauty is used more by small than by large things. So also the large awakens more awe than love, perhaps because the large has for us something diminishing, often arouses fear and strains us, while the opposite occurs with the small. Burke says, not unjustly, that the smooth be essential to the beautiful; this smoothness relates to all five senses. But Burke also here includes the *pleasant* in the beautiful. The soft, gradual transition of the wavy line, the avoidance of all angles, gracefulness constitutes beauty. Burke explains this merely from the inflow upon the eye, which can be explained from the understanding. Further,

Burke reckons *delicacy* with beauty, the gentle and nearly feeble. The beautiful must be proportionately small, have smooth surface, mild colors, gradual changes in the direction of lines, be more tender than strong; this is approximately Burke's description of the beautiful. Relaxing effect is the characteristic, which Burke bestows upon beauty. Yet the *pleasant* is here included incorrectly, whereby the *universal communicability* of the beautiful is limited; further, he derives true beauty also merely from *physical* causes, since it must still be supported upon a principle of reason.

## EXPLANATION OF THE BEAUTIFUL ACCORDING TO MORITZ

Moritz places the *useful*, *good* and *beautiful* next to one another. In the first case, the object is related to a use; it has merely external worth. The *good* object has inner and external worth. The *beautiful* is without all external relationships, and possesses its worth in itself. *Noble* is the *morally beautiful*. Quite well can the useless and the beautiful subsist next to one another. The beautiful is recognized in the useful as superfluous. The useful receives its worth through its contribution to perfection of a whole. A whole is, what is completed in itself. Only the whole, which strikes the senses or can be embraced with imaginative power, is *beautiful*.—Up to here one can regard Moritz as right. Yet after that he confuses the effects of our reason with the effects of objects, the whole of nature, which we can never grasp, with the whole of reason, which to be sure always aims at unity.

Presentation of the whole of nature in the appearance, according to Moritz, constitutes a work of art.

## Explanation of the Beautiful
## According to Kant

If we name an object *beautiful*, says Kant, then is the ground of determination of our judgment merely *subjective*. This satisfaction is without all interest and has nothing to do with the capacity of desire; it exists even with sensuous pain or moral dissatisfaction. With the beautiful, the bare *representation* pleases us, with the pleasant, its *existence*. The pleasant and the good include an *interest*, are grounded upon a need; the satisfaction therein is therefore not free. Just because the satisfaction in the beautiful rests on no interest, on no private ground, we impute to this satisfaction *universal validity*. The pleasant does not have this universal validity. The unity of the unchangeable in human nature is the ground of this universality, and it rests upon the laws of thought of the soul.—The concept *beautiful* lacks the *objective* ground of agreement; its ground must therefore be sought in the judging subject. A judgment about the beautiful is no immediate judgment of the senses, but rather a *judgment of reflection*, a judgment *a priori*, since it includes a universal claim on all thinking and has universality *a priori*. This claim grounds itself upon the universal ability to communicate of the condition, about which I reflect. Every cognition rests upon an indispensible condition and can be communicated; so must also this condition, which lays the basis for the judgment of taste, be able to be communicated. The *imaginative power* for the representation of the manifold and the *understanding* for the union of the same—the former has *freedom*, the latter has *lawfulness*—the latter with the highest possible freedom of the former, perceived through reflection, produces pleasure in the object and the judgment of the *satisfaction*. This agreement of both representing capacities can only be observed through the *inner sense*. Taste judges the beautiful *subjectively*, through a *feeling*.

The beautiful pleases without all interest. *Interest* grounds itself upon a connection of the object to us. The beautiful, however, pleases *unconditionally*. A satisfaction, dependent upon no private connection, must be *universal*; the beautiful must please *everyone*. The *good* indeed also pleases everyone, but through a *concept*. While the good only pleases universally through its *objective* constitution, pleasure in the beautiful supports itself upon a *subjective* ground, upon the universality of the laws of thought.

Since beauty consists merely in the *form* of purposiveness, so beauty consists in general only in the *form*. *Pure* then is a judgment of beauty, if neither *charm* nor *sympathy* is thereby in play. Therefore, all ennoblement of art subsists in *simplicity*.—*Charm* is in general an invitation to activity. A painting can *charm* through its colors, but is beautiful only through *composition* and *design*.—*Sympathy* arises from *suffering*, and subsists in men from moral feeling and active spirit not from out of merely *physical* effects. Also, the sympathetic suffering of a moral man cannot long remain *bodily*; reason awakens soon in its sublimity above all sensuous interest.—Also, the moral sympathy, which grounds itself upon a very lively interest of reason, can falsify the judgment of beauty.

All sensuous beauty is either *form of rest* or *form of motion*. The former is the design in general; the colors merely accentuate the outlines more, awaken the attention and produce agreement with nature. The form of *motion* is a) the *play of figures in space,* b) *the play of sentiments in time*. To the former belongs *miming*, to the latter, mainly *musical art*. The single tone pleases merely in the *sense perception*. The beautiful rests, however, in the *composition*.

Beauty of *action* subsists in the mode of acting, in the character, not in the result.

The worth of *decorations* can either rest merely in their *form* or they please only through the *material*, as *ornament*, and can in the latter case often do damage to the beauty.

## Of the Criterion of the Beautiful
## And of the Aesthetical Ideal

There can be no *objective rule of taste*, rather, only an *empirical* criterion of the beautiful, in that one consults that, wherein all ages have come to an agreement.

There can be a *moral* ideal, because it grounds itself upon a concept. An *aesthetical* ideal is only possible for the *adhering*, not for the *free* beauty. Beauty, for which one wants to establish an ideal, must be contained in the boundaries of a *purpose*. Only that, which is determined through itself, is capable of an ideal of beauty; therefore only man as *moral being* is so capable. To the ideal of beauty belongs first the *normal idea*, which merely takes into consideration the physical purpose of man, the purpose of his structure, the idea of *correctness*; second, the *idea of reason*, which is determined by the expression of the moral. *Freedom* in the presentation of the physical and moral purposes of man could supply a true ideal of beauty, if, of course, all regularity in the presentation vanishes.

## Universal Validity of the
## Judgment of Taste

How can a judgment simultaneously be reached *a posteriori* and yet only be possible *a priori*? Or how can the judgment of taste be empirical and at the same time *a priori*? It is, namely, composed from two judgments. First it is *empirical*, in so far as it expresses something from an object given by experience; it is *a priori*, however, in so far as a universal validity, a universal communicability of pleasure is expressed by the object. Indeed, we judge the beautiful object through a feeling of pleasure; yet this combines itself at first not with the sense perception, but rather with the reflection. The feeling of pleasure presupposes an *a priori* valid frame of mind. As soon as we are conscious of no *material* source of our pleasure, must it be a *formal* source and therefore the pleasure universally communicable: we then relate to the object as *men in general*. The ground, wherefore we assert, that the object must be *universally* pleasing, is there before all experience; we rely upon an *aesthetical common sense*. Such a common sense can be presupposed and is presupposed, in that we ascribe to others a similar capacity of feeling.—All grounds for judgment of the beautiful we take from the characteristics of the objects, which we perceive; this occurs through a feeling of pleasure. Beautiful is namely that, which is pleasing *a priori* in the mere intuition.

Kant makes the beautiful also into a *symbol of the morally good*. The morally good pleases *immediately* through the mere concept, like the beautiful in the mere *intuition*; the satisfaction in both rests upon no interest, and not the content, but rather the form of the representation determines the judgment.—The beautiful is the middle term between morality and sensuousness. Taste accustoms us, to ennoble also the sensuous.

## ON THE OBJECTIVE CONDITIONS OF BEAUTY

The Kantian Critique denies the objectivity of the beautiful for no sufficient ground, since the judgment of beauty would ground itself namely upon a *feeling* of *pleasure*.— The objective constitution of the objects held to be beautiful must be examined and compared. The observation of proportion does not constitute beauty itself, but rather an indispensible condition of the same. It cannot do without correctness.—Free effectiveness of the disposition is essential to the effect of the beautiful. According to Kant, the beautiful is the effect of inner freedom, according to Burke the cause of the same. Observation of regularity is not natural to all objects and impedes the natural freedom in those, which it does not suit. Regularity can thus not have value as the universal grounding concept of beauty, but rather *freedom*, that is, the characteristic self-determined through the nature of a thing. Kant says: Art is beautiful, if it looks like nature and vice versa. It is the *nature* of the imitated, which we expect in a work of art; the matter must lose itself in the form, the reality in the appearance. The form of the statue may lose nothing through the nature of the marble. The artfulness only serves to make *freedom* visible, also in the natural objects, which ought to be judged as beautiful: the recollection of a rule should merely make apparent to us the independence of an object from the same.—A design is beautiful, if its purposiveness looks voluntary.—Architecture can never be an entirely pure beautiful art, since it cannot conceal the purpose of regularity.

*Technique* is the combination of the manifold according to purposes and necessary to beauty, although this does not ground itself upon the judgment of technique, as Sulzer assumes.

Every *formation* or *form* subsists in the *boundary* and is therefore to some extent a *limitation*, which originates either through a rule or through accident. In all products of nature, which refer to a technique, we find the mutual dependence of the part in its constitution upon the other. Beauty, however, is freedom in boundedness, nature in artfulness; it adheres only to the immediate intuition; natural beauty grounds itself on no concept; the technique of a natural product strikes the eye immediately.

Also unaffectedness, easiness and freedom in the technique of the *animal body* is beautiful: its beauty decreases, the more it draws near to ungainly mass, heavy motion. Here, however, we perceive beauty, where the bodily mass is overcome by living powers, where the power does not succumb under the pressure of the mass—for this reason, the winged animals, which are as it were symbols of freedom, most excite sentiments of beauty; on birds the neck is one of the most beautiful parts, its smooth flexible form is beautiful.

In the *human form* the most complicated technique shows itself; there appear in it the most manifold aims. Observation of proportion is presupposed of beauty.—The human form is capable of a double beauty. The one is a mere *gift of nature* and awakens *love*, the other rests upon *moral properties* and at the same time obtains *respect*.— All outlines must show boldness and easiness; free and open must the brow arch itself; the nose must form almost no angle downward from the forehead and not leap out severely. The entire lower face must be light and not pressed down by the weight of the mass and seem enlarged. All excessive tensions must be removed. Dominion of organic power over the animal mass distinguishes man from the animal. Man is beautiful through *freedom in strength*; woman through *freedom in weakness*. Freedom of the form, the result of the self-limiting power, constitutes beauty. So *soars*, as it were, the Vatican Apollo; for no mass hinders him, to use his entire power.—The coarse execution of mass is *clumsiness*. Power, which makes itself visible in *rest,* is *constrained* power. *Weakness*, that is pliancy for impressions, befits chiefly *womanly* beauty. Then she is beautiful, if she is *free*, if she does not go up to *suffering*, does not degenerate into grimaces and demonstrate force. The beautiful does not have need of the expression of suffering, and the not-beautiful becomes through it only ugly.

There is at the same time an *organic* and a *moral* beauty. The former and latter are, with regard to respect, which we have for both, to be compared to genius and industry, to the gift of nature and to merit. Organic beauty can indeed not harmonize with moral depravity, but yet easily with an emptiness of the spirit. *Self-acquired* beauty outlives youth by far and betrays its traces yet in old age; in it is reflected inner peace and benevolence; it is the effect and the expression of moral ideas.

Beauty is freedom in appearance. An action according to the law of reason is then beautiful, if it appears, as if it occurred out of inclination and without all force. The basis of all beauty is *simplicity*; but not all simplicity is beauty.

In nature, violated freedom offends us. However what in nature is ugly, can become beautiful in art. Yet, actually, not the object, but rather only its *presentation* can become beautiful.—Beautiful is a natural product, which in its artfulness appears free. There are now presentations for the *senses* and for the *imaginative power. Free* were the presentation, where the presented seemed *itself to take action* and to have fully exchanged the matter with that to be presented. Of course here only *appearance* can take place. The nature of the medium, of the matter, must be fully overcome; so must, for example, the marble not be visible in the statue, in the actor, not his own natural character. The poet must seek to overcome the striving for universality, which lies in the nature of his language, antagonistic to individuality, therewith the presented appears in its true *characteristic. Presented free self-action* in nature through language is beauty in poetry. Beautiful is the presentation then, if it has suffered the fewest limitations from the characteristic of the presentor. The purpose of the presentation *for others* brings *heteronomy* into the work of art and does easy harm to its beauty.—The *freedom* of the poetical presentation rests upon the independence of the presented from the characteristic of the language, of the presenting and of the external purpose of the work of art. To the first dependence, of the abstract constitution of the language, the poet gives way, in that he seeks to *individualize* the object, for example, often places the part for the whole, the effect for the cause, and thus much is thereby won to perspicuity. So also visualization of the distant is useful to the vivid presentation of self-acting nature. Furthermore, the analogy of representations and sentiments is of this kind, above all with non-sensuous objects. Here rules the freedom of likenesses. The poet links image to image, wherein Homer was the most lavish; Virgil selected likenesses, with more sparing use, more successfully. So arises the most lively expression.—The poet holds himself to the sensuous, in order to make the not sensuous vivid, and seeks through similar images to arouse similar states of mind, as for example in Haller's *Eternity.—Personality* is furthermore the replacement, which is given to the natural object for that, which it loses through the abstract nature of language. The language, which is rich in such personifications, is a *poetical* language. So the Greek mythology presented almost all actions of nature as actions of free beings and has become almost indispensible to poetry. Also the expression in the language itself contributes to the making sensuous of the objects. The rules of grammar restrict the poet less; he offers it up to nature; his sentence construction becomes more irregular; so is, for example, sometimes the more frequent use, sometimes the omission of conjunctions natural and purposive. At times the language paints even the object itself. Often the objective of an object is animated by the subjective of the expression in the language, for example through the climax.—

Works of art are regarded in the imitating presentation as *works of free nature,* for example, a building in a painting, a comedy in the comedy, as in Hamlet. It is a question in the province of art, not of the constitution of the presented object, but rather of the relationship of the presentation to its constitution. The artist does not have to answer for the ugliness of the form of *nature.* The story of Laocoon, presented by a poet and a sculptor, offends in the *object* our feeling of beauty; in *nature,* the group would fill us with indignation; in the *presentation,* however, the offended suffering nature is not held against the peaceful, but rather against the presentation. In nature itself we want to see *free* nature, in art, however, *in general,* to see nature. The freedom, which nature also asserts in the chains of the meter and the language, the truth and liveliness of the image, exacts from us the statement about such a presentation (as that of the Laocoon): that be terribly beautiful. So has Goethe in his *Iphigenia* presented the beautiful in the terrible, which approaches the horrible.—Not because our moral feeling, but rather because our taste is offended, does a presentation displease us, in which the *freedom* of presentation is not at hand. Shakespeare and Goethe are great masters in presentation of nature, with which they are so confident, that they lose themselves entirely in it.

Among the talents of the poet must the imaginative power occupy the highest rank.—The *Sorrows of Young Werther* is a beautiful example of the presentation of passion. The nature, the passion itself it is, which we see take action, and yet everything is the purposeful presentation of the poet, who saw entirely into his object. How true and lively did Shakespeare portray the passions in their most savage aberrations, for example in Lear, Othello, Macbeth, Hamlet!

But nothing, which is adverse to the senses, which makes physically disagreeable impressions, may either the poet or the plastic artist present. Of this kind are Polyphemus, the Harpies of Virgil, the paintings of the Savior with the crown of thorns or of Lazarus covered with abscesses. The senses act too passively toward such impressions, and the body can also be drawn into the play by representations of fantasy and be moved adversely. The impression of the painting is immediately livelier than that of the poem; what good taste forbids the painter, is still more forbidden the actor, who is not permitted to bring the vulgar (like the beggars scene in *Child of Love* by Kotzebue) before the eye. The repulsive is immediately contrary to the senses: it forces itself, as Kant very aptly says, upon our enjoyment, mixes in with the enjoyment. That the repulsive physically resists us, completely excludes its use from art. The displeasure arises not from the supposition of reality, but rather from the mere representation, even the mere fantasy. Only when the poet has need for the *dreadful* and *terrible*, may he employ it. The *repulsive-terrible* is the *ghastly* (so is Homer's Polyphemus portrayed ghastily). The ghastly and the vulgar, the most extreme boundaries of taste, are very carefully employed. The ghastly, where it ought to be allowed to the poet, must be justified by a considerable purpose.

## THE RELATIONSHIP OF THE BEAUTIFUL TO REASON

The fact, that the beautiful is merely *felt*, not actually known, makes the derivation of beauty from principles *a priori* doubtful. It seems, that we must satisfy ourselves with the pluralistic validity of judgment in respect to beauty.

We either *observe* or *contemplate* the natural phenomena: *contemplation* alone befits beauty. The manifold gives *sense*; the form gives *reason*. Reason combines representations to *cognition* or to *action*. There is *theoretical* and *practical* reason. Freedom of appearances is the object of the *aesthetical* judgment. Freedom of a thing in the appearance is its self-determination, in so far as it strikes the senses.

The aesthetical judgment excludes all regard to objective purposiveness and regularity and is devoted merely to the appearance; a purpose and a rule can never appear. A form appears then *freely,* if it explains itself and does not oblige the reflecting understanding to search for a ground outside it. The moral is in conformity with reason, the beautiful is *like* to reason. The former arouses *respect*, a feeling, that arises through comparison of sensuousness with reason. Freedom in the appearance awakens not merely pleasure about the object, but rather also *inclination* to the same; this inclination of reason, to unite with the sensuous, is called *love*. We contemplate the beautiful properly not with *respect*, but rather with *love*; excepting *human* beauty, which however, includes expression of *morality* as object of respect in itself.—Should we at the same time love that which is worthy of respect, so must it be by us achieved or for us achievable. Love is an enjoyment, respect, however, is not; here is tension, there relaxation.—The pleasure of beauty arises, therefore, from the observed analogy with reason and is united with love.

## THE VALUE OF THE BEAUTIFUL AND OF ART

The indictments made of art do not concern it itself but rather its misuse. The beautiful is concerned with and cultivates reason and sensuousness, promotes humanity through contraction of their bond, establishes union between the physical and moral nature of man. Nonetheless, the greatest advantage is still on the side of *sensuousness*; through the beautiful we widen the field of our *sentiments*, but do not become richer in *concepts*. It protects us before the rawness of sensuousness. Hence, for the man of coarse sensuousness beauty is the greatest benefit. However, to the manly sense the too great attachment to the beautiful can become detrimental; he is easily satisfied merely with the superficial contemplation of things; but every path to excellence passes through labor. Genius selects the steepest path to perfection. The *exclusive* culture of the feeling of beauty seduces us easily to superficiality, brings us enervation, softness and aversion to diligence; for we accustom ourselves thereby, to look always merely at the *treatment*, not at the *contents*.

The beautiful ennobles sensuousness, and makes reason sensuous. It teaches, to place a value upon form. With the beautiful one learns to love things without self-interest, merely on account of their form. Moreover, reason is done a service, if sense and phantasy are cultivated in its interest; but truth and goodness win no profit through the aesthetical form. But also virtue may not despise a tasteful form, even though taste does not determine the value of virtue. Only it must be concerned for matter and form in like degree. Union of truth with beauty, of the inner content with the charm of form, is the requirement of true perfection.

# KALLIAS,
## *or, On the Beautiful*

### Letters to Gottfried Körner

**Jena, January 25, 1793**

The investigations of the beautiful, wherefrom almost no part of aesthetics is to be divorced, leads me into a very wide field, where for me entirely foreign lands still lie. And yet I, at the very least, must have taken possession of the whole, if I shall perform something gratifying. The difficulty, to advance a concept of the beautiful objectively and to fully legitimize it a priori from the nature of reason, so that experience indeed confirms it throughout, but that this utterance of experience is not necessary to its validity, this difficulty is almost incalculable. I have really attempted a deduction of my concept of the beautiful, but it is not to be achieved without the evidence of experience. This difficulty always remains, that one will merely acknowledge my explanation to me, because one finds, that it is in keeping with the individual judgments of taste, and does not (as should be with a cognition from objective principles) find his judgment on the individual beautiful in experience to be right, because it agrees with my explanation. You will say, that this be somewhat much to demand; but as long as one does not bring it forth, so will taste always remain empirical, just

---

In a letter to his friend Christian Gottfried Körner on December 21, 1792, Schiller first indicated his intention to put forth his ideas on Beauty in a work to be entitled *Kallias, or, On the Beautiful*. Between January 25 and February 28, 1793, Schiller and Körner engaged in a dialogue on the subject in the form of an exchange of letters. Schiller's letters, which are translated here, prepared the way for his writing *On Grace and Dignity*, which he began in May of 1793, and the letters *On the Aesthetical Education of Man*, which were written in the late autumn/winter of the same year.

as Kant held it to be unavoidably. But precisely of this unavoidability of the empirical, of this impossibility of an objective principle for taste, I cannot yet persuade myself.

It is interesting to observe, that my theory is a fourth possible form, to explain the beautiful. Either one explains it objectively or subjectively; and indeed either sensuous-subjective (as Burke among others), or subjective-rational (as Kant), or rational-objective (as Baumgarten, Mendels-sohn and the entire flock of perfection men), or finally sensuous-objective: a term, whereof thou wilt now of course not yet be able to think much, except if thou comparest the three other forms with one another. Each of these preceding theories has a part of experience in favor of itself and obviously contains a part of the truth; and the error seems merely to be, that one has taken this part of beauty, with which it agrees, for beauty itself. The Burkian is perfectly correct in regard to the Wolffian, that he asserts the immediacy of beauty, its independence of concepts; but he is wrong in respect to the Kantian, that he places it in the mere affect-ability of sensuousness. The circumstance, that by far most beauties of experience, which soar to them in thought, are not fully free beauties, but rather logical beings, which stand under the concept of a purpose, like all works of art and most beauties of nature, this circumstance seems to have misled all, who place beauty in a perceptual perfection; for the logical good would now be mistaken for the beautiful. Kant so wants to cut through this knot, that he assumed a *pulchritudo vaga and fixa*, a free and intellectual beauty; and he asserts, somewhat strangely, that each beauty, which stands under the concept of a purpose, be not a *pure* beauty: that therefore an arabesque and what is like to it, regarded as beauty, be purer than the highest beauty of man. I find, that his observation can have great use, to divide the logical from the aesthetical, but in reality it seems to me to miss fully the concept of beauty. For precisely therein beauty shows itself in its highest radiance, when it overcomes the *logical* nature of its object; and how can it overcome, where there is no resistance? How can it impart its form to the fully formless matter? I am at least convinced, that beauty is only the form of a form and that that, which one calls its matter, must by all means be a formed matter. Perfection is the form of a matter, beauty, on the other hand, is the form of this perfection; which stands thus to beauty as matter to form.

### Jena, February 8, 1793

With regard to thy letter, which I received a few hours ago, I am very much joyed, and it has placed me in a state of mind, where perhaps I shall succeed in the brief presentation of my idea of beauty. How near to one another we have come in our ideas, thou wilt soon see, and perhaps thou findest indeed, more ideas merely *suspected* by thee made clear in *my* representation of the beautiful. Thy expression: *life* in the external objects, *ruling* power and *victory* of the ruling power, *heterogeneous* powers, *resisting* powers and the like, are too undetermined, than that thou surely couldst be, to place therein nothing capricious, nothing accidental: they are more *aesthetically* than *logically clear* and, for that reason, dangerous.

Thereupon can a Kantian always drive thee into a corner with the question, according to which principle of cognition does the taste proceed? Thou groundest thy idea of a ruling power upon that of a whole, upon the concept of the unity of the bound, of the manifold; but by what does one recognize this unity? Clearly only through a concept; one must have a concept of the whole, to which the manifold shall agree. Thy *ruling power* and the *sensuous perfection* of the Wolffian school lie not so far from one another, for the process of judgment is with both logical. Both assume, that one imputes a concept to the judgment. Now Kant is clearly right, when he says, the beautiful pleases without concept; I can have found a beautiful object beautiful, long before I am only remotely able, to indicate the unity of its multiplicity and to determine, what the ruling power is in respect to the same.

For the rest, I speak here more as Kantian, for it is possible in the end, that even my theory does not remain entirely free of this reproach. I have a double path before me, to introduce thee to my theory: a very entertaining and easy one, *through experience,* and a very unattractive one, through the conclusions of reason. Let me advance the last; for if *it* be once traversed, then is the *remainder* the more pleasant.

We conduct ourselves toward *nature* (as appearance) either *passively* or *actively,* or passively and actively *simultaneously.*

*Passively*: if we merely *perceive* its effects; *actively,* if we determine its effects; both *simultaneously* if we *represent* it.

There are two different ways, to *conceive* appearances. Either we are directed deliberately to their cognition: we *observe* them; or we are invited by the things themselves to their *representation.* We merely *contemplate* them.

With *contemplation* of appearance we conduct ourselves *passively,* in that we receive its impressions: *actively,* in that we subordinate these impressions to our *forms of reason.* (This sentence is postulated from logic.)

That is, the appearances must arrange themselves in our representation according to the formal conditions of representative power (for just that makes them into *appearances),* they must obtain the form from our subject.

All representations are a manifold or matter; the manner of combination of this manifold is its form. The *sense* gives the manifold; reason gives the combination (in the widest meaning), for reason is the capacity of combination.

Therefore, if a manifold be given to the senses, then reason attempts to give the same its form, that is to combine it according to its laws.

Form of reason is the kind and manner, as it expresses its power of combination. There are, however, two different main expressions of the combining power; therefore, also in the same way, as many principal forms of reason. Reason combines either representation with representation to cognition (theoretical reason) or it combines representations with the will to action (practical reason).

Just as there are two different forms of reason, so are there also two kinds of matter for each of these forms. Theoretical reason applies its form to representations, and the latter are divided into immediate (intuition) and mediate (concepts). The former are given through the senses, the latter through reason itself (although not without assistance of the senses). In the first, the intuition, it is accidental, whether they shall agree with the form of reason; in the concepts it is necessary, if they shall not dissolve themselves. Here, therefore, reason finds agreement with its form; there is it surprised, when it finds it.

It is just so with the practical (acting) reason. The latter applies its form to actions, and these are regarded either as free or as not-free actions, actions through or not through reason. The practical reason demands from the first just what the theoretical does from concepts. Agreement of free actions with the form of practical reason is therefore necessary; agreement of *not-free* with this form is accidental.

Therefore, one expresses oneself more correctly, if one calls those representations, which are not through theoretical reason and yet agree with its form, imitations of concepts, those actions, which are not through practical reason and yet agree with its form, imitations of free actions; briefly, if one calls both kinds imitations (analogues) of reason.

A concept can be no imitation of reason, for it is through reason, and reason cannot imitate itself; it can not merely be *analogous* to reason, it must be actually in congruence with reason. An action of will can not merely be analogous to freedom, it must—or should at least—be actually free. On the other hand, a mechanical effect (any effect through natural law) can never be judged as actually *free*, but rather merely analogous to freedom.

Here I want to let thee take a break for a moment, especially in order to make thee attentive to the last paragraph, because I will probably have need of it in the following, in order to answer an objection, which I expect from thee against my theory. I proceed.

The theoretical reason is aimed at cognition. In that it therefore subjects a given object to its form, so it tests, whether cognition be constituted therefrom, i.e., whether it can be combined with an already existing representation. Now, is the given representation either a concept or an intuition. If it be a concept, then it is already through its origin, through itself, necessarily related to reason, and a combination, which already is, is merely affirmed. A clock, for example, is such a representation. One judges it merely according to the concept, through which it arose. Reason, therefore, needs merely to discover, that the given representation is a concept, so it decides just thereby, that it agrees with its form.

If, however, the given representation be an intuition, and should reason nevertheless discover an agreement of the same with its form, so must it (regulative, not, as in the first case, constitutive) and for its own purpose *advance* a source through theoretical reason to the given representation, in order to be able to judge it according to reason. It places therefore a purpose in the given object from its own means and decides, whether it conducts itself conformably to this purpose. The latter happens with every *teleological*, the former with every *logical* judgment of nature. The object of the logical is *congruence with reason*, the object of the *teleological* is *similarity to reason*.

I surmise, thou *wilt be surprised*, that thou dost not find beauty under the rubric of theoretical reason and that thou become properly alarmed therefor. But I cannot help thee, it is certainly not to be found with the theoretical reason, since it is absolutely independent of concepts; and yet it *must* be sought reliably in the *family of reason*, and outside of the theoretical reason there is none other than the practical, so we will indeed have to seek it here, and also find it. Also, I think, thou shouldst, at least in the following, convince thyself, that this kinship causes no disgrace to it.

The practical reason abstracts from all cognition and has to do merely with determinations of the will, inner actions. Practical reason and determination of will out of mere reason are one. *Form* of practical reason is immediate combination of the will with representations of reason, therefore, *exclusion of every external* ground of determination; for a will, which is not determined through the mere form of practical reason, is determined from outside, materially, heteronomically. To assume or imitate the form of practical reason is therefore merely: to be determined not from outside, but rather through itself, to be determined autonomously or to appear so.

Now the practical reason, even as the theoretical, can apply its form not only to that, which through itself is (free actions), but also to that, which is not through it (effects of nature).

If it be an action of the will, whereto it relates its form, so it determines merely what is; it declares, if the action is that, which it *wants* and *should be*. Every moral action is of this kind. It is a product of the pure, i.e., of the will determined through mere form and therefore autonomously, and as soon as reason recognizes it therefor, as soon as it knows, that it is an action of the pure will, then it is already evident by itself, that it is conformable to the form of practical reason: for that is fully identical.

If the object to which the practical reason applies its form does not exist through a will, not through practical reason, then the practical reason treats the object just as the theoretical did the intuitions, which displayed similarity to reason. Practical reason lends to the object (regulative, and not, as with the moral judgment, constitutive) a capacity, to determine itself, a will, and regards the object then under the form of this *its* (own) will (indeed not *practical reason's* own will, for otherwise the judgment would be a moral one). That is, it declares of it, if it is *that*, which it is, through *its own pure will*, i.e., through its own self-determining power; for a pure will and form of practical reason is one.

From an *action of the will* or moral action it demands *imperatively,* that it be through pure form of reason; from an *effect of nature* it can (not demand) but wish, that it *be through itself,* that it show autonomy. (But here must once again be observed, that the practical reason cannot thoroughly demand from such an object, that the object be through it, namely through practical reason; for then were it not through itself, not autonomous, but rather determined through something external [because each determination through reason conducts itself toward it as something external, as heteronomy], therefore through a foreign will.) *Pure self-determination* overall is form of practical reason. Therefore, if a being of reason acts, so must it act out of *pure reason,* if it shall show pure self-determination. If a mere being of nature acts, then must it act out of *pure nature,* if it shall show pure self-determination; for the self of the being of reason is reason, the self of a being of nature is nature. Now, if the practical reason discovers in contemplation of a being of nature, that it is determined through itself, it ascribes to the same (as the theoretical reason conceded *similarity to reason* in the similar case of an intuition) *similarity to freedom* or, for short, *freedom.* However, because this freedom is merely lent to the object by reason, *since nothing can be free except the supersensible, and freedom itself can never fall as such into the senses*—briefly—since it is here merely a matter, that an object *appear* free, not actually *is*: so is the analogy of an object with the form of practical reason not freedom in action, rather merely *freedom in the appearance, autonomy in the appearance.*

Herefrom ensues therefore a fourfold kind of judgment and a fourfold classification of the represented appearance corresponding to it.

Judgment of *concepts* according to the form of cognition is logical; judgment of intuitions according to this same form is teleological. A judgment of free effects (moral actions) according to the form of the pure will is moral; a judgment of not free effects according to the form of the pure will is aesthetical. *Agreement* of a concept with the form of cognition is *congruence with reason* (truth, purposiveness, perfection are mere relationships of this latter), *analogy* of an intuition with the form of cognition is *similarity to reason* (teleophany, logophany I would call them), agreement of an action with the form of the pure will is *morality*. Analogy of an appearance with the form of the pure will or of freedom is *beauty* (in the broadest meaning).

Beauty therefore is nothing other than freedom in the appearance.

## Jena, February 18, 1793

I see from thy letter, which I just received, that I have actually only to raise misunderstandings, no actual doubts against my explanation of beauty with thee, and the mere pursuit of my theory will probably bring us into agreement thereon. For the present I only observe:

1) that my principle of beauty is until now certainly only subjective, because I have indeed so far brought forth arguments only from reason itself and did not involve myself with the objects at all. But it is no *more* subjective, than everything which is derived a priori from reason. That in the objects themselves something must be encountered, which makes possible the application of this principle thereto, goes without saying, as also, that it is *my* duty, to indicate it. However, that this something (namely the state of being determined through itself in the things) is observed by reason, and is indeed observed favorably, this can be set forth according to the nature of the thing only from the essence of reason and to that extent therefore only subjectively. I hope, however, to prove sufficiently, that beauty is an objective property.

2) I must note, that I hold as two entirely different things *to give a concept of beauty* and *to be moved* through the *concept of beauty*. That a concept of beauty can be given, it cannot occur to me at all to deny, because I myself give one thereof; but that I deny with Kant, that beauty pleases through this concept. To please through a concept assumes

the preexistence of the concept before the feeling of pleasure in the mind, as is always the case with perfection,
truth, morality; although with these three objects not with
equally clear consciousness. But that no such concept pre-
dates our pleasure in beauty, is certainly evident for among
other reasons, because we still seek it.

3) thou sayest, that beauty be not deduced from morals,
but rather both from a commonly held higher principle.
This objection I have not any more expected after my recent
premises, for I am so far distant from deriving beauty from
morals, that I hold it rather nearly incompatible therewith.
Morality is determination through pure reason, beauty, as
a property of *appearances*, is determination through pure
nature. Determination through reason, perceived in respect to an appearance, is rather nullification of beauty; for
the determination of reason is in respect to a product that
appears, true heteronomy.

The higher principle, that thou desirest, is found and
incontestably set forth. Also it subsumes, as thou demandest
of the same, beauty and morals. This principle is none other,
than existence out of mere form. I cannot stop now with the
elaboration of the same, which will be richly elucidated
anyway in the course of my theory. Only that I yet take
note, that thou must rid thyself thoroughly of all incidental
ideas, wherewith the present religionaires in the moral
philosophy or the poor bunglers, who dabble in the Kantian
philosophy, mutilated the concept of morals—for thereupon wilt thou become completely convinced, that all thy
ideas, so as I can surmise them from thy remarks so far,
stand in a greater agreement with the Kantian foundation
of morals, than even now perhaps thou dost suspect. It is
certain no greater word has yet been spoken by any mortal
man than this Kantian one, which is at the same time the
content of his entire philosophy: Determine thyself from
thee thyself; just as that in the theoretical philosophy: Nature stands under the laws of the understanding. This great
idea of self-determination is reflected back toward us from
certain appearances of nature, and these we call *beauty*.

There is, therefore, such a view of nature or of appearances, where we demand nothing further from them than freedom, where we only look up, whether they are that, which they are, through themselves. Such a kind of judgment is only important and possible through the practical reason, because the concept of freedom is not to be found at all in the theoretical and only in the practical reason does autonomy surpass all. The practical reason, applied to free actions, demands, that the action occur only for the sake of the manner of action (form) and that neither matter nor purpose (which is also always matter) have had influence thereon. If an object in the world of sense be shown now to be determined only through itself, if it presents itself so to the senses, that one observes in it no influence of the matter or of a purpose, so is it judged as an *analogue* of the pure determination of will (indeed not as product of a determination of will). Now because a will, which can determine itself according to mere form, is called *free,* so is that form in the world of sense, which appears determined only through itself, a *presentation of freedom*; for presented is an idea, which is so combined with an intuition, that both share with one another *one* rule of cognition.

Freedom in the appearance is therefore nothing other than self-determination with regard to a thing, in so far as it reveals itself in the intuition. One opposes to it any determination from outside, just as one opposes to a moral kind of action any determination through material grounds. An object, however, appears even less free—it may have received its form either from a physical force or from a rational purpose—so soon as one *discovers* the ground of determination of its form in one of these two; for then, the same does indeed not lie *in it*, rather outside it, and it is just as little *beautiful,* as an *action from purposes* is moral.

When the judgment of taste is fully pure, so must be entirely abstracted therefrom, what for a (theoretical and practical) value the beautiful object have for itself, out of which matter it be formed and to which purpose it be present. May it be, what it will! So soon as we judge it aesthetical, so we merely wish to know, whether it be that, which it is, through itself. We ask so little about a logical constitution of the same, that we credit it rather "independence of purposes and rules to the highest advantage."— Not indeed, as though purposiveness and regularity were incompatible as such with beauty; each beautiful product must rather be subjected to rules: but rather, because the *observed* influence of a purpose and a rule is proclaimed as force and carries with it heteronomy for the object. The beautiful product is permitted and must even be regular, but it must *appear free of regulation*.

Now, however, no object in nature and yet far fewer in art are free of purpose and rules, *none is determined through itself*, so soon as we reflect upon it. Each is there through another, each is there for another's sake, none has autonomy. The single existing thing, that determines itself and is because of itself, one must seek outside of appearance in the intelligible world. However, beauty dwells only in the field of appearances, and there is therefore no hope at all, by means of merely theoretical reason and upon the path of reflection to come upon freedom in the world of sense.

However, everything becomes different, if one lets go of the theoretical investigation and takes merely the objects, *as they appear*. A rule, a purpose can never *appear*, for they are concepts and not intuitions. The real ground of the possibility of an object, therefore, never strikes the senses, and it is as good as not at all present, "so soon as the understanding is induced to seek out the same." It depends here, therefore, exclusively upon the complete abstraction of a ground of determination, in order to judge an object in the appearance as free (for being not determined from the outside is a negative representation of being determined through oneself, and indeed the only possible representation of the same, since one can only think freedom and never perceive it, and even moral philosophy must make do with this negative representation of freedom). A form, therefore, appears free, so soon as we find the ground of the same neither outside it, *nor are led to seek outside it*.

For were the understanding led, to ask about the ground of the same, then would it have to find this ground *necessarily* outside the thing; since it must be determined either through a *concept* or through an accident, both, however, conduct themselves toward the object as heteronomy. One will therefore be able to advance the following as a principle: that an object is freely presented in the intuition, if the form of the same does not necessitate the reflecting understanding to search for a ground. Beautiful, therefore, is a form, which explains itself; to explain oneself is, however, here, to explain without aid of a concept. A triangle explains itself, however, only by means of a concept. A wavy line explains itself without the medium of a concept.

Beautiful, one can therefore say, is a form, which *requires no explanation,* or also such an one, which explains itself *without concept.*

I think, some of thy doubts should now already begin to disappear, at least seest thou, that the subjective principle can yet be led over into the objective. If we come, however, first into the field of experiences, then an entirely different light in respect thereto will become apparent to thee, and thou wilt only then correctly grasp the autonomy of the sensuous. However further:

Each form, therefore, which we only find possible on condition of a concept, shows heteronomy in the appearance. For each concept is something external as against the object. Such a form is each strict regularity (whereunder the mathematical stands in the first place), since it *forces* the concept upon us, from which it has arisen: such a form is each strict purposiveness (especially that of the *useful,* since this is always related to something different), since it brings the determination and the use of the object to our recollection, whereby of necessity the autonomy in the appearance is destroyed.

Now granted, we realize a moral purpose with an object, then will the form of this object be determined through an idea of practical reason, therefore not through itself, hence will we meet with heteronomy. Thence comes it, that the moral purposiveness of an art work, or even of a mode of action, contributes so little to the beauty of the same, that the former must rather be very concealed and appear from the nature of the thing completely free and unrestrained, if the latter, beauty, shall not thereby be lost. A poet would therefore in vain be excused with the moral intent of his work, if his poem were without beauty. The beautiful is indeed related every time to the practical reason, since freedom can be no concept of the theoretical—but merely in respect to the *form*, not the *material*. A moral *aim* belongs, however, to the material or to the content, and not to the mere form. In order to place this difference—upon which thou seemst to have stumbled—yet more in the light, I add yet the following. Practical reason demands self-determination. Self-determination of the rational is pure determination of reason, morality; self-determination of the sensuous is pure determination of nature, beauty. If the form of the not rational be determined through reason (theoretical or practical, that is here all the same), then its pure determination of nature suffers compulsion, therefore beauty can not take place. It is then a *product*, no *analogue*, an effect, no imitation of reason, for a thing belongs to imitation, that the imitating have in common with the imitated merely the form, and not the content, not the matter.

For this reason will a moral behavior, if it be not simultaneously united with taste, be presented in the appearance always as heteronomy, precisely because it is a product of the autonomy of the will. For just therefore, because *reason* and *sensuousness* have a different will, so is the will of sensuousness broken, if reason pervades it. Now unfortunately, the will of sensuousness is precisely that which strikes the senses; precisely, therefore, if reason exercises its autonomy (which never can come forward in the appearance), so our eye is offended through a heteronomy in the appearance. Nonetheless, the concept of beauty is also applied in a different sense to the moral, and this application is nothing less than empty. Although beauty only adheres to the appearance, so is *moral beauty* nonetheless a concept, to which something in experience corresponds. I can advance to thee no better empirical proof for the truth of my theory of beauty, than if I show thee, that even the different use of this word only takes place in such cases, where freedom is shown in the appearance. I will for this reason, contrary to my first plan, spring ahead to the empirical part of my theory and tell thee a story for recreation.

"A man has fallen among robbers, who have stripped him naked and cast upon the street in a severe cold.

"A traveller comes upon him, to whom he complains of his condition and implores him for help. 'I suffer with thee,' the latter, moved, calls out, 'and I will gladly give thee, what I have. Only demand no other service, for thy look seizes me. There come men, give them this money purse, and they will give thee help.'—'Well meant,' said the wounded one, 'but one must also be able to *see* suffering, if human duty demands it. The grasp on thy purse is not worth half so much as a small power over thy feeble senses.' "

What was this action? Neither useful, nor moral, nor generous, nor beautiful. It was merely impassioned, good-hearted out of emotional habit.

"A second traveller appears, the wounded one renews his plea. To this second one is his money dear, and yet he would like to fulfill his human duty. 'I miss the gain of a guilder,' said he, 'if I pass the time with thee. Wilt thou give me so much, as I miss, from thy money, so I load thee upon my shoulders and provide quarters for thee in a cloister, that lies only an hour distant from here.'—'A clever piece of information,' replied the other. 'But one must acknowledge, that thy readiness to serve does not stand high with thee. I see there a rider come, who will provide me the help for nothing, which is to thee to be sold for a guilder.' "

What was then this action? Neither good-hearted, nor in conformity with duty, nor generous, nor beautiful. It was merely useful.

"The third traveller stops quietly by the wounded one and lets the story of his misfortune be repeated. Reflecting and fighting with himself, he stands there, after the other has finished speaking. 'It will become difficult,' he says finally, 'to separate myself from the coat, which is the single protection to my sick body, and to give up to thee my horse, since my powers are exhausted. But duty bids me, to serve thee. Therefore, mount my horse and cover thyself with my coat, then will I lead thee thence, where thou canst be helped.'—'Thanks to thee, excellent man, for thy honest opinion,' rejoins the latter, 'but thou shouldst, since thou thyself art needy, suffer no privation on my behalf. There see I two strong men coming, who will be able to provide me the service, which is sour to thee.'"

This action was *pure* (but also not more than) *moral,* because it, as against the interest of sense, was undertaken out of respect for the law.

"Now the two men draw near to the wounded one and begin to question him about his misfortune. Scarcely does he open his mouth, so both shout with astonishment: 'It is he! It is the one whom we seek.' The latter recognizes them and is frightened. It is disclosed, that both recognize in him their declared enemy and the author of their misfortune and after whom they have travelled, in order to take a bloody revenge upon him. 'Now satisfy your hatred and your revenge,' the latter begins, 'death and not help it is, which I can expect from you.'—'No,' rejoins one of them, 'Now that thou seest, who *we* are and who *thou* art, so take these clothes and dress thyself. We want to take thee between us into the center and bring thee thence where thou can be helped.'—'Generous enemy,' shouts the wounded one full of emotion, 'thou makest me ashamed, thou disarmest my hate. Come now, embrace me and make thy good deed perfect through a hearty forgiveness.'— 'Temper thyself, friend,' rejoins the other coolly. 'Not because I pardon thee, will I help thee, rather because thou art miserable.'—'Then take thy clothing back, too,' calls the unfortunate one, whilst he casts them from himself.

'Become of me, what may. Sooner will I perish miserably, than be indebted to a proud enemy for my rescue.'

"Whilst he stands up and makes the attempt, to set out, a fifth wanderer approaches, who carries a heavy burden upon his back. 'I have been deceived so often,' thinks the wounded one, 'and he does not appear to me as one, who wants to help me. I will let him go by.'—So soon as the wanderer catches sight of him, he lays his burden down. 'I see,' he begins on his own initiative, 'that thou art wounded and thy powers are leaving thee. The nearest village is still distant, and thou wilt bleed to death, before thou arrivest there. Climb upon my back, thus will I set out afresh and bring thee thence.'—'But what will become of thy bundle, that thou must leave behind here upon the country road?—'That I know not, and that does not trouble me,' says the porter. 'I know, however, that thou needst help and that I am obliged, to give it thee.'"

### February 19, 1793

The beauty of the fifth action must lie in that trait, which it does not have in common with the preceding ones.

Now we have: 1. All five wish to help. 2. Most have selected a purposive means thereto. 3. Several wished to charge something for it. 4. Some have proven thereby a *great* self-conquest. One among them has acted from the purest moral impulse. But only the fifth has helped *without being called upon* and without debate with himself, although it was at his expense. Only the fifth has forgotten himself thereby fully and "his duty fulfilled with an easiness, as if merely the instinct had acted from him."—Therefore were a moral action then first a beautiful action, if it appears as an effect of nature arising from itself. In a word: a free action is a beautiful action, when the autonomy of the disposition and autonomy in the appearance coincide.

From this ground is the maximum of the character perfection of a man moral beauty, for it arises only then, *when duty has become nature to him.*

Clearly, the power, which the practical reason exercises in the moral determination of the will against our instincts, has something offending, something distressing in the appearance. We wish to see compulsion nowhere at all, not only when reason itself exercises it; but we also wish that the freedom of nature be respected, because we consider "every being in the aesthetical judgment as a self-aim" and it disgusts us (makes us indignant), to whom freedom is the highest, that something should be sacrificed to the other and serve as means. For that reason a moral action can never be beautiful, if we look on the operation, whereby it is frightened away from sensuousness. Our sensuous nature must therefore appear free in the moral, although it is really not, and it must have the appearance, as if nature merely carried out the instructions of our instincts, in which they bow down, directly opposed to the instincts, beneath the dominion of the pure will.

Thou seest from this small, above-stated demonstration, that my theory of beauty will scarcely have to fear from experience. I call upon thee, to name to me, from among all the explanations of beauty, the Kantian included, a single one, which resolves the selflessly beautiful so satisfactorily, as, I hope, has taken place here.

*Jena, February 23, 1793*

The result of my proofs advanced thus far is this: There is such a mode of conception of things, through which is abstracted from all the rest and is only seen thereby, whether they appear free, that is, determined through themselves. This mode of conception is necessary, for it flows from the essence of reason, which unflaggingly requires autonomy of determinations in its practical use.

That that characteristic of things, which we indicate with the name beauty, be with this freedom in the appearance one and the same, is not at all yet proven; and that shall be from now on my business. I have, therefore, two things to explain: *firstly,* that that objective in respect to things, wherethrough they are placed in the condition, to appear free, also be precisely, that which lends beauty to them, when it is there, and when it is lacking, destroys their beauty; even when they possessed in the first case not one and in the last case all other advantages. *Secondly,* I have to prove, that freedom in the appearance necessarily carries with it such an effect upon the capacity of feeling, which is completely like to that, which we find united with the conception of the beautiful. (Indeed, it may be a futile undertaking, to prove this last one a priori, since only experience can teach, whether we should feel something in a conception, and what we should feel therein. For, to be sure, such a feeling is extracted analytically neither from the concept of freedom, nor from that of the appearance, and a synthesis a priori is just as infrequent; one is therefore herein thoroughly limited to empirical proofs, and what can be accomplished only through these, I hope to accomplish: namely, to demonstrate through induction and by psychological means, that from the composite concept of freedom and of appearance, of sensuousness harmonizing with reason, a feeling of pleasure must flow, which is like to the satisfaction, that is wont to accompany the conception of beauty.) By the way, I will not yet come to this part of the inquiry so soon, since the execution of the first may take up several letters.

## I.

### Freedom in the appearance is one with beauty.

I have recently already mentioned, that no thing in the world of senses really approaches *freedom,* but rather is only apparent. But positively free can it not even *seem,* because this is only an idea of reason, to which no intuition can be adequate. When, however, things, in so far as they come forth in appearance, neither possess nor show freedom, how can one seek an objective ground of this representation in appearances? This objective ground had to be such a property of the same, the representation of which by all means *compels* us, to bring forth the idea of freedom in ourselves and to relate to the object. This is, what must now be proven.

To be free and to be determined through oneself, to be determined from the inside out, is one. Each determination occurs either from outside or not from outside (from inside), what therefore appears determined not from outside and yet appears as determined, must be represented as determined from inside. "*So soon as being determined is thought*, so is the state of not being determined from outside indirectly at the same time the conception of the state of being determined from inside, or of freedom."

Now how will this state of not being determined from outside itself be represented again? Hereupon is everything founded; for if this be not necessarily represented in an object, then there is also no ground at all, to represent the state of being determined from inside, or freedom. However, the representation of the last must be *freedom*, because our judgment of beauty includes necessity and *requires* each man's assent. It may not, therefore, be abandoned to accident, whether we in the representation of an object want to take notice of its freedom, but rather the representation of the same must also utterly and necessarily carry with it the representation of the state of not being determined from outside.

To that end is now demanded, that the object itself invite us through its objective condition, or rather compel us, to notice it in the quality of the state of not being determined from the outside; because a mere negation can be observed only then, *when a need is assumed toward its positive opposite.*

A need toward the representation of being determined from inside (of the ground of determination) can only arise through representation of *being determined*. Indeed, everything is, that can be represented to us, something determined, but not everything is represented as such, and what is not represented, is for us as good as not present at all. There must be something about the object, which lifts it out of the infinite row of insignificance and emptiness and rouses our cognitive instinct, for insignificance is nearly identical to nothing. It must present itself as *determined*, for it should lead us to the *determining*.

Now, however, is the understanding the capacity, which seeks the ground of the consequence, consequently must the understanding be placed in play. The understanding must be induced, to reflect upon the form of the object: upon the *form*, for the understanding has only to do with the form.

The object must therefore possess and show such a form, which permits a rule: for the understanding can only conduct its business according to rules. It is, however, not necessary, that the understanding *knows* these rules (for knowledge of rules would destroy all appearance of freedom, as is actually the case with any strict regularity), it is enough, that the understanding be conducted upon a rule—which is undetermined. If one only considers a single leaf of a tree, then does the impossibility force itself upon one immediately, that the manifold in the same can have been so arranged by accident and without any rules, even if one at once abstracts from the teleological judgment. The immediate reflection on the appearance of the same teaches it, without one needing to inspect these rules and to form a concept of the structure of the same.

A form, which points to a rule (is treated according to a rule), is called artful or *technical*. Only the technical form of an object induces the understanding, to seek the ground for the consequence and the determining for the determined. And in so far therefore, as such a form awakens a need, to question about the ground of determination, so here negation of the *being determined from the outside* leads quite necessarily to the conception of *being determined from inside*, or of freedom.

Freedom can therefore only be sensuously *presented* with help of technique, just as freedom of the will can only be thought with the help of causality, and in contrast to material determinations of the will. In other words: the negative concept of freedom is only thinkable through the positive concept of its opposite, and just as the representation of natural causality is necessary, in order to lead us to the representation of freedom of the will, so is a representation of technique necessary, in order to lead us in the realm of appearances to freedom.

Herefrom now ensues a second basic condition of the beautiful, without which the first would be merely an empty concept. Freedom in the appearance is indeed the ground of beauty, but *technique* is the necessary condition of our *representation* of freedom.

One could express this also so:

The ground of beauty is everywhere freedom in the appearance. The ground of our *representation* of beauty is technique in freedom. If one unites both basic conditions of beauty and of the representation of beauty, then ensues the following explanation:

Beauty is nature in artfulness.

Before I can, however, make of this explanation a secure and philosophical use, I must first determine the concept *nature* and secure it before any misinterpretation. The expression *nature* is dearer to me than *freedom,* because it indicates at once the field of the sensuous, whereupon the beautiful is confined, and implies beside the concept of *freedom* also at once its sphere in the sensuous world. In contrast to technique, *nature* is, what is through itself, *art* is, what is through a rule. *Nature in artfulness,* what gives itself the rule—what is through its own rule. (Freedom in the rule, rule in freedom.)

When I say: *the nature of the thing: the thing follows its nature, it is determined through its nature:* so contrast I therein nature to all that, which is different from the object, which is considered merely as accidental to the same and can be dismissed, without at the same time cancelling its essence. It is, as it were, the person of the thing, whereby it is distinguished from all other things, which are not of its kind. Hence are those properties, which an object has in common with all others, not properly classed under its nature, although it can not lay aside these properties, without ceasing to exist. Merely that is indicated through the expression *nature*, wherethrough it becomes the determined thing that it is. All bodies, for example, are heavy, but to the *nature* of a bodily thing belong only those effects of heaviness, which result from its special condition. So soon as the force of gravity works on a thing, for itself and independent of its special condition, *only as universal natural force*, so is it regarded as an alien power, and its effects behave as heteronomy toward the nature of the thing. An example may shed light on this. A vase, regarded as body, is subjected to gravity, but the effects of the gravity must, if they shall not deny *the nature of a vase*, through the form of the vase be modified, i.e., especially be determined and through this special form be made necessary. Any effect of the gravity on the vase, however, is accidental, which without detriment to its form as vase can be taken away. The gravity works thereupon, so to speak, outside the economy, outside the nature of the thing, and appears at once as an alien power. This occurs, if the vase *comes to an end* in a wide and broad belly, because it appears, as if the heaviness had taken from the length, what it gave to the breadth, briefly as if the gravity had dominated over the form, not the form over the gravity.

Just so is it with movements. A movement belongs to the *nature* of the thing, if it flows necessarily from the special condition or from the form of the thing. However a movement, which is prescribed to the thing independent of its special form through the universal law of gravity, lies outside the nature of the same and shows heteronomy. One places a heavy wagon horse besides a light Spanish palfrey. The weight, which the former has become accustomed to pull, has taken from the naturalness of his movements, so

that, even without a wagon to drag behind him, it trots just
so tiresomely and ponderously, as if it had one to pull. Its
movements arise no more from its special nature, but rather
betray the dragged weight of the wagon. The light palfrey in
contrast has never become accustomed to employ a greater
strength, than he even in his greatest freedom feels instinct-
ively to express. Each of his movements is therefore an
effect of his nature left to itself. Hence he moves himself so
easily, as if he were no load at all, across the same surface,
which the carriage horse treads with lead-weight feet. "One
will not recall at all in respect to him, that he is a *body,* so
much has the special horse-form overcome the universal
bodily nature, which must obey gravity." To the contrary,
the ponderousness of the movement makes the carriage
horse momentarily in our representation into mass, and the
*characteristic* nature of the horse is suppressed in the same
by the *universal* bodily nature.

If one casts a fleeting glance through the animal realm,
one finds, that the beauty of animals declines in the same
proportion, as they approach mass and seem to merely serve
gravity. The nature of an animal (in the aesthetical meaning
of this word) expresses itself either in its movements or in
its forms, and both are restrained by the mass. If the mass
has had influence upon the form, we call this plump; if the
mass has had influence upon the movement, this is called
awkward. In the build of the elephant, of the bear, of the
steer and so forth is it the mass, which participates visibly
in the form as well as the movement of these animals.
However, the mass must always obey the force of gravity,
which behaves toward the *characteristic* nature of the organic body as an alien potency.

On the contrary, we observe beauty everywhere, *where
the mass is fully dominated by the form* and (in the animal
and plant kingdom) by the living powers (in which I place
the autonomy of the organic).

The mass of a horse is, as everyone knows, of unequally
greater weight than the mass of a duck or of a crab; nonetheless is the duck heavy and the horse light; merely because

the living powers behave quite differently to the mass in both. There it is the matter, which rules the power; here is the power, lord of the matter.

Among the animal species, the bird family is the best evidence of my thesis. A bird in flight is the happiest presentation of matter subdued by form, of gravity overcome by force. It is not unimportant to observe, that the capability to triumph over gravity, oft is employed as the symbol of freedom. We express the freedom of fantasy, in that we give it wings; we let the psyche rise above the earthly with the wings of butterflies, when we wish to indicate its freedom from the fetters of matter. Clearly the force of gravity is a fetter for everything organic, and a triumph over the same supplies therefore no unbecoming emblem of freedom. Now there is, however, no more suitable presentation of defeated gravity than a bewinged animal, that is determined from inner life (autonomy of the organic) directly in opposition to the force of gravity. The force of gravity conducts itself approximately just so against the living power of the bird, as—in the pure determination of the will—the inclination conducts itself in respect to the law-giving reason.

I resist the attempt, to render the truth of my assertions still more visual to thee by discussing human beauty; this material demands a separate letter. Thou seest now from that previously said, what I consider as the concept of *nature* (in the aesthetical meaning) and wish therefrom to have excluded.

Nature in the way of a technical thing, in so far as we contrast it to the nontechnical, is its technical form itself, against which everything else, which does not belong to this technical economy, is regarded as something foreign, and when it has had influence thereon, as heteronomy and as violence. However, it is not yet enough, that a thing only appear determined through its technique—be purely technical; for such is also every strictly mathematical figure, without for that reason being beautiful. The technique itself must again appear determined through the nature of the thing, which one could call the voluntary assent of the thing to its technique. Here is therefore the nature of the thing again distinguished from its technique, since it was shortly before explained as identical with the same. But the contradiction is only apparent. In relation to external determinations, the technical form of the thing acts as nature; but in relation to the inner essence of the thing, the technical form can again behave as something external and alien; for example, it is the nature of a circle, that it be a line, which stands equally distant at every point of its direction from a given point. If, now, a gardener cuts a circular figure out of a tree, then the nature of the circle demands, that it be cut perfectly round. As soon, therefore, as a circular figure is *indicated* in respect to the tree, then must it be fulfilled, and it offends our eye, if it is sinned against. But what the nature of the circle demands, clashes with the nature of the tree, and because we cannot help conceding to the tree its own nature, its personality, so this violence annoys us and it pleases us, when it negates from inner freedom the technique forced upon it. The technique is therefore everywhere something alien, where it does not arise from the thing itself, is not one with the entire existence of the same, does not enter from the inside out, but rather from the outside, is not necessary and innate to the thing, but rather is given it and is therefore accidental.

Yet another example will completely inform us. If a mechanic constructs a musical instrument, it can still be purely technical, without making claim to beauty. It is purely technical, when everything is form in respect to the same, when throughout only the concept and never the matter or the lack on the part of the artist determines its form. Also can one say of this instrument, it has autonomy; as soon, namely, as one places the self in the thought, which was here fully and purely lawgiving and overcame the matter. However, if one places the self of the instrument in that, which is nature in it and whereby it exists, the judgment is changed. Its technical form is recognized as something different from it, independent of its *existence* and accidental and regarded as external violence. It is disclosed, that this technical form is something foreign, that it is violently forced upon it through the understanding of the artist. Therefore, although the technical form of the instrument, as we have assumed, *contains* and *expresses* pure autonomy, it *is* itself nonetheless heteronomy toward the thing, in which it is found. Although it *suffers* no compulsion, neither on the part of the matter nor of the artist, it does *exercise* it nonetheless toward the characteristic nature of the thing—as soon as we regard this as a natural thing, which is compelled to serve a *logical thing* (a concept).

What, therefore, were nature in this meaning? The inner principle of existence in respect to a thing, regarded at the same time as ground of its form; *the inner necessity of the form*. The form must be self-determining and self-determined simultaneously in the truest sense; not mere autonomy but rather heteronomy must be there. However, wilt thou here object, if the form must together with the existence of the thing amount to one, in order to bring forth beauty, where remain the beauties of art, which can never have this heteronomy? I want to answer thee thereupon, when we have first come to the beautiful of art, for this requires an entire chapter of its own. Only so much can I say to thee in advance, that this requirement may not be dismissed by the art, and that also the forms of art must amount to *one* with the existence of the formed, when they shall make claim to the highest beauty: and since they are not able to do this in reality, because the human form in marble always remains accidental, they must at least appear so.

What, therefore, is nature in artfulness? Autonomy in the technique? It is the pure harmonization of the inner essence with the form, *a rule, which is at the same time followed and given by the thing itself.* (From this ground, in the world of sense, only the beautiful is a symbol of the completed in itself or of the perfected, because it does not need to be related as the purposive to something outside itself, but rather at the same time commands and obeys itself and carries out its own law.)

I hope, to have placed thee by this time in the condition, to follow me unhindered, when I speak of nature, of self-determination, of autonomy and heteronomy, of freedom and of artfulness. Thou wilt also be of one mind with me, that this nature and this heteronomy are objective properties of objects, to which I ascribe them, for they remain to them, even when the representing subject is entirely dismissed. The difference between two natural essences, in which the one is entirely form and shows a complete rule of the living power over mass, but the other has been subjugated by its mass, remains, even after full dismissal of the judging subject. Just so is the difference between technique through understanding and a technique through nature (as in everything organic) entirely independent of the existence of the reasoning subject. It is therefore objective, and therefore it is also the concept of a nature in the technique, which grounds itself thereupon.

Of course reason is necessary, in order to make precisely such an use of this objective property of the thing, as is the case with the beautiful. However, this subjective use does not cancel the objectivity of the ground, for this is also done with the perfect, with the good and with the useful, without therefore, that the objectivity of these predicates were less grounded. "Of course the concept of freedom itself, or the *positive*, is only projected onto the object by the reason, whilst it regards the same under the form of the will; but the *negative* of this concept reason does not give the object, but rather it already comes upon it in the same. The *ground* of the freedom granted to the object lies, therefore, for all that in *it* itself, although the *freedom* lies only in the reason."

Kant advances in his *Critique of Judgment*, page 177, a thesis, which is of uncommon fruitfulness and which, as I think, can only obtain its explanation from my theory. Nature, he says, is beautiful, when it appears as art; art is beautiful, when it appears as nature. This thesis, therefore, turns the technique into an essential requisite of the naturally beautiful and freedom into the essential condition of the artistically beautiful. Since, however, the artistically beautiful already includes in itself the idea of technique, the naturally beautiful the idea of freedom, so, therefore, Kant himself admits, that beauty is nothing other than nature in the technique, freedom in artfulness.

We must *first* know, that the beautiful thing is a natural thing, i.e. that it is through itself; *secondly,* it must appear to us, as if it were through a rule, for he says indeed, it must appear as art. Both representations: *it is through itself,* and *it is through a rule,* are, however, to be united only in a single way, namely when one says: *it is through a rule, which it has given itself.* Autonomy in the technique, freedom in artfulness.

It could seem from the preceding, as if *freedom* and *artfulness* would have a completely identical claim to the satisfaction, that beauty instills in us; as if *technique* stood in the same line with freedom and, in that case, I had surely been very wrong, that in my explanation of the beautiful (autonomy in the appearance) I merely took freedom into consideration and did not mention technique at all. However, my definition has been very exactly weighed. Technique and freedom do not have the same relationship to the beautiful. *Freedom* alone is the ground of the beautiful, technique is only the ground of our representation of freedom, the former, therefore, the immediate ground, the latter only mediately the condition of beauty. Technique contributes, namely, only in so far to beauty, as it serves, to arouse the representation of freedom.

Perhaps I can elucidate this thesis further—which moreover is already rather clear from the preceding—in the following way.

In the naturally beautiful we see with our eyes, that it is from itself; that it be through a rule, the sense does not speak to us, but rather the understanding. Now, however, the rule is related to nature as compulsion is to freedom. Since we now merely *think* of the rule, but *see* nature, so we

think of compulsion and see freedom. The understanding
expects and demands a rule, the sense teaches, that the
thing is through itself and through no rule. If we are now
concerned about technique, then the disappointing expectation must have annoyed us, which on the contrary gives
us pleasure. Therefore, we must be concerned about freedom and not technique. We had reason, from the form of
the thing to infer a logical origin, therefore heteronomy,
and against expectation we find autonomy. Since we are
happy about this find and feel ourselves relieved thereby,
as it were, of a concern (which has its seat in our practical
capacity), so this demonstrates, that we do not win so much
with regularity as with freedom. It is merely a need of our
theoretical reason, to think of the form of the thing as
dependent upon a rule; but that it is through no rule, but
rather through itself, is a fact for our sense. But how could
we place an aesthetical value upon technique and yet perceive with satisfaction, that its opposite really is? Therefore
the representation of technique merely serves to call the
non-dependency of the product of the same to our mind
and to make its freedom the more vivid.

This leads me now automatically to the difference between the *beautiful* and the *perfect*. Everything perfect,
with the exception of the absolutely perfect, which is the
moral, is contained under the concept of the technique,
because it consists in the agreement of the manifold to the
one. Now, since the technique merely contributes mediately to the beautiful, in so far as it makes freedom notice-
able, but the perfect is contained under the concept of
technique, therefore one sees at once, that it is only *freedom
in the technique*, which distinguishes the beautiful from the
perfect. The perfect can have autonomy, in so far as its form
has been determined purely by its concept; but heteronomy
has only the beautiful, because only in respect to this is the
form determined through its inner essence.

The perfect, presented with freedom, is immediately
transformed into the beautiful. It is, however, presented
with freedom, when the nature of the thing appears harmo-

nizing with its technique, when it looks as if it were flowing forth voluntarily from the thing itself. One can also briefly express the preceding so: An object is perfect, when everything manifold in it accords with the unity of its concept; it is beautiful, when its perfection appears as nature. The beauty increases, when the perfection becomes more complex and the nature suffers nothing thereby; for the task of freedom becomes more difficult with the increasing number of compounds and its fortunate resolution therefore, even more astonishing.

Regularity, order, proportion, perfection—properties, in which one so long believed to have found beauty—have nothing to do with the same at all. However, where order, proportion, etc. belong to the *nature* of a thing, as with everything organic, there they are also by this itself inviolable; but not on account of themselves, but rather because they are inseparable from the nature of the thing. A grave violation of proportion is ugly, but not because observation of proportion is beauty. Not at all, but rather because it is a violation of nature, therefore indicates heteronomy. I observe in general, that the whole error of those, who sought beauty in proportion or in perfection derives therefrom: they found, that the violation of the same made the object ugly; from which they drew the conclusion against all logic, that beauty is contained in the exact observation of these properties. But all these properties make merely the *material* of the beautiful, which can change in any object; they can belong to the truth, which also is only the material of beauty. The form of the beautiful is only a free utterance of the truth, of regularity, of perfection.

We call a building perfect, when all the parts of the same are arranged according to the concept and the purpose of the whole and its *form* has been purely determined through its *idea*. We name it beautiful, however, when we need not take this idea as help, in order to understand the form, when it seems to spring forth voluntarily and unintentionally from itself and all parts to be confined through themselves. A building can for this reason (to speak parenthetically) never be an entirely free art work and never achieve an ideal of beauty, because it at the least is impossible, in respect to a building, that needs steps, doors, chimneys, windows and ovens, to suffice without help of a concept and therefore to conceal heteronomy. Therefore only that beauty of art can be completely pure, whose origin is found in nature itself.

A vessel is beautiful, when it, without contradicting its concept, looks like a free play of nature. The handle to a vessel is merely there due to the use, therefore through a concept; however, should the vessel be beautiful, then this handle must spring forth therefrom so unforced and voluntarily, that one forgets its determination. However, if it goes off in a right angle, if the wide belly narrows suddenly to a narrow neck and the like, then would this abrupt change of direction destroy all appearance of voluntariness, and the autonomy of appearance would disappear.

When indeed does one say, that a person is beautifully clothed? When neither the clothing through the body, nor the body through the clothing suffers anything in respect to its freedom; when it looks, as if it had to change nothing with the body and yet fulfills its purpose to the completest. Beauty or rather taste regards all things as *self-aim* and by no means tolerates, that one serves the other as means or bears the yoke. In the aesthetical world, every natural being is a free citizen, who has equal rights with the most noble, and may *not once be compelled for the sake of the whole,* but rather must absolutely *consent* to everything. In the aesthetical world, which is entirely different than the most perfect Platonic republic, even the coat, which I carry on my body, demands respect from me for its freedom, and desires from me, like an ashamed servant, that I let no one notice, that it *serves* me. For that reason, however, it also promises me reciprocally, to employ its freedom so modestly, that mine suffers nothing thereby; and when both keep their word, so will the whole world say, that I be beautifully dressed. If the coat *strains*, on the other hand, then do we both, the coat and I lose our freedom. For this reason are all *quite tight* and *quite loose* kinds of clothing equally little beautiful; for not considering, that both limit the freedom of movements, so shows the body in tight clothing its figure only at the expense of the clothes, and with loose clothing the coat conceals the figure of the body, in that it blows itself up with its own figure and diminishes its master to its mere bearer.

A birch tree, a spruce, a poplar is beautiful, when it climbs slenderly aloft, an oak, when it grows crooked; the reason is, because the latter, left to itself, loves the crooked, the former, on the contrary, loves the direct course. If the oak show itself slender and the birch bent, then are they both not beautiful, because their directions betray alien influence, heteronomy. If the poplar, on the contrary, be bent by the wind, then we find this beautiful again because it expresses its freedom through its swaying movement.

Which tree will the painter like most to seek out, in order to use it in a landscape? Certainly that one, which makes use of the freedom, which is permitted it with all the technique of its construction—which does not act slavishly in accordance to its neighbor, but rather, even with some boldness, ventures something, steps out of its order, turns wilfully hither and thither, even when it must right here cause a breach, there disarrange something through its stormy interference. To that one, on the other hand, which always perseveres in the same direction, even when its species allows it far more freedom, whose branches remain in rank and file, as if they were pulled by a string, will he pass over with indifference.

In respect to any great composition, it is necessary that the individual be limited, in order to let the whole take effect. If this limitation of the individual at the same time be an effect of its freedom, i.e., if it set this limit itself, then the composition is beautiful. Beauty is through itself subdued power; limitation out of power.

A landscape is beautifully composed, when all individual parts, of which it consists, so play into one another, that each sets its own limits, and the whole is therefore the result of the freedom of the individual. Everything in a landscape should be referred to the whole, and everything individual should seem nevertheless to stand only under its own rule, to follow its own will. It is, however, impossible, that the agreement to a whole require no sacrifice on the part of the individual, since the collision of freedom is unavoidable. The mountain may want, therefore, to cast a shadow on many, which one wants to have lighted; buildings will limit the natural freedom, curb the view; the branches will be burdensome neighbors. Men, animals, clouds want to move, for the freedom of the living expresses itself only in action. The river will accept in its course no law from the bank, but rather follow its own; in short: each individual desires to have its will. Where, however, remains now the harmony of the whole, when each concerns itself only for itself? Just therefrom does it follow, that each out of inner freedom directly prescribes itself the limitation, which the other needs, in order to express *its* freedom. A tree in the foreground could cover a beautiful part in the hinterground; to *compel* it, that it not do that, would be to violate its freedom and betray bungling. What, therefore, does the intelligent artist do? He lets that branch of the tree, which threatens to cover the hinterground, *of its own weight* sink down and therethrough make room voluntarily for the rear prospect; and so the tree accomplishes the will of the artist, in that it merely follows its own.

A versification is beautiful, when each individual verse gives itself its length and brevity, its movement and points of rest, each rhyme offers itself out of inner necessity and yet comes as called—briefly, when no word takes notice of the other, no verse of the other, merely seems to be there, on account of itself and yet everything so turns out, as if it were agreed upon.

Why is the naive beautiful? Because the nature therein asserts its right over affectation and disguise. When Virgil wants to let us cast a glance into the heart of Dido and wants to show us, how far it has come with her love, so had he been able to say this quite well as story teller in his own name; but then this presentation would also not have been beautiful. However, when he lets us make this discovery through Dido herself, without her having the intention, so as to be upright toward us (see the discussion between Anna and Dido at the beginning of the fourth book), then we name this truly beautiful; for it is nature itself, which gives away the secret.

Good is a mode of teaching, where one advances from the known to the unknown; beautiful is it, when it is Socratic, i.e., when it asks the same truths from within the head and heart of the listener. With the first, its convictions are *demanded* from the understanding formally, with the second, they are *enticed* from it.

Why is the wavy line held to be the most beautiful? I have especially tested my theory in respect to this most simple of all aesthetical tasks, and I hold this demonstration for this reason to be crucial, because with this simple task no deception can take place through incidental causes.

A wavy line, the followers of Baumgarten can say, is for this reason the most beautiful, because it is sensuously perfect. It is a line, which always changes its direction (multiplicity) and always returns again to the same direction (unity). Were it, however, beautiful from no better ground, then the following line would also have to be so:

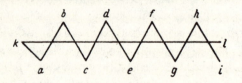

which certainly is not beautiful. Also here is alteration of direction; a manifold, namely a, b, c, d, e, f, g, h, i; and unity of direction is also here, which the understanding thinks into and which is represented through the line KL. This line is not beautiful, even though it is sensuously perfect.

The following line, however, is a beautiful line, or it could surely be, if my pen were better.

Now is the entire difference between this second and the former merely this, that the former changes its direction abruptly, however, the latter unnoticeably; the difference of their effects upon the aesthetical feeling must therefore be grounded in this single observable difference of their properties. What, however, is a suddenly altered direction other, than one violently altered? Nature loves no jump. If we see it make one, then it shows, that violence has occurred to it. On the contrary, only that movement appears voluntary, to which one can assign no determined point, in which it changed its direction. And this is the case with a wavy line, which is distinguished from the above-portrayed merely through its *freedom*.

I could accumulate sufficient further examples, in order to show, that all, that we call beautiful, gains this predicate merely through the freedom in its technique. But in respect to the proof advanced, it may by now be enough. Because *beauty* therefore adheres to no material, but rather consists merely in the treatment; however everything, which represents the sense, can appear technical or not technical, free or not free: so follows therefrom, that the region of the beautiful extends quite far, because reason in everything, which sensuousness and understanding immediately represent to it, can and must ask about freedom. For this reason, the realm of taste is a realm of freedom—the beautiful world of sense is the happiest symbol, of how the moral one shall be, and every beautiful natural being outside of me is a happy citizen, who calls out to me: Be free as I.

Therefore, we are disturbed by every forcing trace of the despotic hand of man in a free region of nature, therefore, by all compulsion of the dancing instructor in the walk and in the posture, therefore, by each affectation in customs and manners, therefore, by any roughness in behavior, therefore, by each offense to natural freedom in constitutions, habits, and laws.

It is striking, how good fashion (beauty of behavior) is developed from my concept of beauty. The first law of good fashion is: *Spare others' freedom.* The second: *Show freedom yourself.* The punctual fulfillment of both is an infinitely difficult problem, but good fashion requires it continuously, and it alone makes the complete man of the world. I know no more suitable image for the ideal of beautiful behavior, than a well performed English dance, composed from many complicated figures. A spectator from the gallery sees innumerable movements, which cross one another most vividly and alter their direction briskly and playfully and yet *never knock into one another.* Everything is so ordered, that the one has already made room, when the other arrives, everyone fits so skillfully and yet again so artlessly into one another, that each seems to follow only his own head and yet never steps in the way of the other. It is the most suitable emblem of the asserted self-freedom and the spared freedom of the other.

Everything, which one usually calls *harshness,* is nothing other than the opposite of the *free.* It is this harshness, that often deprives intellectual greatness, often even the moral of its *aesthetical* value. Good fashion does not forgive even the most magnificent merit this *brutality,* and virtue itself is only worthy of love through beauty. However, a character, an action is not beautiful, if it show the sensuousness of man, whom it befits, under the compulsion of the law or constrain the sensuousness of the spectator. In this case they will merely instill *respect,* but not *favor,* not inclination; mere respect abases him, who feels it. Hence Caesar pleases us far more than Cato, Cimon more than Phocion, Thomas Jones far more than Grandison. Hence it follows, that often merely *emotional* actions please us more than purely moral ones, because they show voluntariness, because they are achieved through nature (the emotional state), not through the categorical reason against the interest of nature—hence may it be, that the mild virtues please us more than the heroic, the womanly so often more than the manly; for the womanly character, even the most perfect, can never act other than from inclination.

*Jena, February 28, 1793*

### The Beautiful of Art

It is of two kinds: a) beautiful of choice or of matter—imitation of the naturally beautiful. b) beautiful of presentation or form—imitation of nature. Without the last there is no artist. Both united, makes the great artist.

The beautiful of form or of presentation is *characteristic* of art alone. "The beautiful of nature," says Kant very correctly, "is a beautiful thing; the beautiful of art is a beautiful representation of a thing." The ideally beautiful, one could add, is a beautiful representation of a beautiful thing.

With the beautiful of choice is seen, *what* the artist presents. With the beautiful of form (of the beauty of art strictly speaking), is merely seen, *how* he presents. The first, one can say, is a free presentation of beauty, the second, a free presentation of truth.

Since the first is more limited to the conditions of the naturally beautiful, the latter, however, befits art exclusively, so I treat of the latter first; for first must be demonstrated, what makes the artist in general, before one speaks of the great artist.

Beautiful is a natural product, if it appears free in its artfulness.

Beautiful is an artistic product, if it presents a natural product freely.

Freedom of presentation is therefore the concept, with which we are here dealing.

One *describes* an object, if one transforms the features, which make it known, into concepts and binds them into unity of knowledge.

One *presents* it, if one places the combined features immediately in the intuition.

The capacity of the intuition is the imaginative power. An object is therefore called presented, when the representation of the same is brought immediately before the imaginative power.

Free is a thing, that is determined through itself or appears so.

An object is therefore called freely presented, if it is held up before the imaginative power as determined through itself.

But how can it be held up before it as determined through itself, since it is not there at all, but rather is merely imitated in an other, since it is not represented in person, but rather through a representative?

Namely, the beautiful of art is not nature itself, but rather only an imitation of the same in a *medium*, that is materially entirely different from the *imitated*. *Imitation* is the formal similarity of the materially different.

N.B. Architecture, beautiful mechanics, the art of gardening, the art of dance and the like may be looked upon as no objection, for that these arts are also subject to the same principle, although they either imitate no natural product or need no medium thereto, will become very evident in the following.

The nature of the object, therefore, is represented in the art not in its own personality and individuality, but rather through a *medium*, which again

a) has its own individuality and nature,

b) depends on the artist, who likewise is to be regarded as a nature of his own.

The object is placed, therefore, through the *third* hand before the imaginative power; and, since both the matter, wherein it is imitated, and the artist who works on this matter, possess their own nature and work according to their own nature—how is it possible, that the nature of the object can be represented all the same as determined purely and through itself?

The object to be presented lays aside its liveliness, it is not itself present, but rather its cause is conducted through a foreign matter entirely dissimilar to it, on which depends how much it shall save or forfeit of its individuality.

Now, therefore, the alien nature of the matter *intervenes*, and not this alone, but rather also the just as alien nature of the artist, who has to give this matter its form. All things, however, work necessarily according to their nature.

There are here, therefore, three kinds of nature, which wrestle with one another. The nature of the matter to be presented, the nature of the presenting matter and the nature of the artist, who shall bring those both into agreement.

It is merely the nature of the imitated, which we expect to find in an artistic product; and that is what the expression actually means, that it is represented to the imaginative power as determined through itself. So soon, however, as either the *matter* or the *artist* interfere with their natures, so appears the presented object no longer as determined through itself, but rather heteronomy is there. The nature of the represented suffers violence from the representing one, as soon as this one advances its nature thereby. An object can therefore only be called *freely presented*, if the nature of the presented has suffered nothing from the nature of the presenting.

The nature of the medium or of the matter must therefore appear completely defeated by the nature of the imitated. Now it is, however, merely the *form* of the imitated, which can be conferred upon the imitating; therefore, it is the form, which must have conquered the matter in the artistic presentation.

With a work of art, therefore, the *matter* (the nature of the imitating) must be lost in the *form* (of the imitated), the *body* in the *idea*, the *reality* in the *appearance*.

*The body in the idea:* For the nature of the imitated is to the imitating matter nothing bodily; it exists merely as an idea in respect to the same, and everything bodily in this belongs merely to it itself and not to the imitated.

*The reality in the appearance:* Reality is called here the *real*, which is always only the *material* in respect to a work of art and must be set against the *formal* or the *idea*, which the artist executes in this material. The form is to an art work merely appearance, i.e., the marble *seems* to be a man, but it remains, in reality, marble.

Free, therefore, were the presentation, if the nature of the medium appears fully destroyed through the nature of the *imitated*, if the imitated asserts its pure personality also in its representative, if the representing seems to have been completely interchanged through complete rejection or rather *renunciation* of its nature with the represented— briefly—if nothing is through the matter, rather all is through the form.

If there be in a statue a single trait, which betrays the stone, which therefore is grounded not in the idea, but rather in the nature of the matter, so suffers beauty; for heteronomy is there. The marble nature, which is hard and brittle, must in the nature of the flesh, which is flexible and yielding, be completely submerged, and neither the feeling nor the eye may be reminded thereof.

Is there in a drawing a single trait, which the pen or the stylus, the paper or the copperplate, the brush or the hand, which led it, makes distinct, then it is *hard* or *heavy*; if the *peculiar taste* of the artist, the nature of the artist be visible in it, then it is *affected*. If, namely, the mobility of one muscle (in a copperplate engraving) suffer through the hardness of the metal or through the heavy hand of the artist, then the presentation is ugly, because it has not been determined through the idea, but rather through the medium. If the characteristic of the object suffers to be presented through the mental characteristic of the artist, then we say, the presentation is affected.

The opposite of *manner* is *style*, which is nothing other than the highest independence of the presentation from all subjective and all objective accidental determinations.

*Pure objectivity* of presentation is the essence of the good style: the highest principle of art.

"Style is related to manner, as the mode of action from formal principles is related to a mode of action from empirical maxims (subjective principles). The style is a complete elevation above the accidental to the universal and necessary." (But under this explanation of style, even *the beautiful of choice* is already included, the discussion whereof shall now not yet be.)

The great artist, one could therefore say, shows us the object (its presentation has pure objectivity), the mediocre shows himself (his presentation has subjectivity), the bad, his matter (the presentation is determined through the nature of the medium and through the limits of the artist).

All these three cases become very vivid in respect to an actor.

1. When Ekhof or Schroeder played Hamlet, so were their *persons* related to their *roles* as the matter to the form, as the body to the idea, as reality to the appearance. Ekhof was, as it were, the marble, from which his genius formed a Hamlet, and because his (the actor's) person was completely submerged in the artificial person of Hamlet, because only the *form* (the character of Hamlet) and never the *matter* (never the actual person of the actor) was to be noticed— because everything was to him only form (only Hamlet), so one says, he played beautifully. His presentation was in great style, because *firstly* it was completely objective and nothing subjective was mixed with it; *second*, because it was objectively necessary, not accidental (whereof the elucidation at another opportunity).

2. When Madame Albrecht played an Ophelia, so did one indeed not behold the nature of the matter (the person of the actress), but also not the pure nature of that to be presented (the person of Ophelia), but rather—a capricious idea of the actress. She had, namely, made it a subjective principle—a maxim—to represent pain, madness, noble behavior just so, without being concerned, whether objectivity is due this representation or not. She has therefore shown only *manner*, no *style*.

3. When Mr. Brueckl plays a king, then one sees the nature of the medium rule over the form (the role of the king), for from each movement the actor (the matter) shows

through repulsive and bungling. One sees at once the base
effect of the *deficiency,* because the artist (here the understanding of the actor) is wanting in insight, to form the
matter (the body of the actor) according to an idea. The
presentation is therefore miserable, because it simultaneously reveals the nature of the matter and the subjective
limits of the artist.

With drawing and plastic arts it strikes one easily
enough, how much the nature of that to be presented suffers, when the nature of the medium is not completely
subdued. But more difficult might it be, to apply this principle now also to the *poetical* presentation, which must be
absolutely derived therefrom. I wish to attempt, to give
thee a concept thereof.

Also here, obviously, the discussion is not yet of the
*beautiful of choice,* but rather merely of the *beautiful of
presentation.* It is therefore assumed, the poet has comprehended the entire objectivity of his object *truly, purely and
fully* in his imaginative power—the object stands already
*idealized* (i.e. transformed into pure form) before his soul,
and it is merely a matter of it *being presented outside itself.*
For this reason it is now demanded, that this object of his
disposition suffer no heteronomy from the nature of the
medium, in which it is presented.

*Words* are the medium of the poet; therefore, abstract
signs for kinds and species, never for individuals; and whose
relationships are determined through *rules,* thereof *grammar* comprises the system. That between the things and the
words no *material* similarity (identity) takes place, makes
no difficulty at all; for this is also not found between the
*statue* and the *man,* whose presentation it is. However, also
the mere *formal* similarity (imitation) is not so easy between
words and things. The thing and its verbal expression are
merely accidental and capricious (except for a few cases),
merely bound with one another through agreement. However, this also would not be of much importance, because
it is not a question of what the word is to itself, but rather
which representation it awakens. Were there in general

only words or word phrases, which represented to us the most individual character of the thing, its most individual relationships, and briefly, the entire objective characteristic of the individual, so it would not depend at all on whether this happened through *convenience* or from inner necessity.

But it is wanting precisely in that. Both the words, and their laws of declension and combination are entirely universal things, which do not serve to indicate *one* individual, but rather an infinite number of individuals. It is even more critical for the indication of *relationships*, which are achieved according to rules, which are applicable at the same time to countless and entirely heterogeneous cases and are only suitable through a special operation of the understanding to an individual representation. The object to be presented, therefore, before it is brought before the imaginative power and transformed in intuition, must *take a very wide detour* through the abstract region of the concepts, upon which it loses much of its liveliness (sensuous power). The poet has overall no other instrument, in order to present the special, than the artificial *composition of the universal*. "The candlestick even now standing before me falls down" is such an individual case, expressed through combination of many universal signs.

The *nature* of the medium, of which the poet makes use, consists, therefore, "in a tendency to the *universal*," and lies hence in conflict with the denotation of the individual (which is the task). The language places everything before the *understanding*, and the poet shall bring everything before the *imaginative power* (present); the poetical art wants *intuitions*, language gives only *concepts*.

Language, therefore, deprives the object, whose presentation is entrusted to it, of its sensuousness and individuality and impresses on it a property of its own (universality), which is alien to it. It mixes—to make use of my terminology—into the nature of that to be presented, which is sensuous, the nature of the presenting, which is abstract, and therefore brings heteronomy into the presentation of the same. The object is therefore not represented to the imaginative power as determined through itself, hence not free, but rather shaped through the genius of language, or it is brought only before the understanding; and so is either not freely presented or not presented at all, but merely described.

Shall, therefore, a poetical presentation be free, then the poet must "*overcome the tendency of language to the universal through the greatness of his art and triumph over the matter* (words and their laws of inflection and construction) *through the form* (namely the application of the same)." The nature of the language (precisely its tendency to the universal) must be fully submerged in the form given to it, the body must lose itself in the idea, the sign in the indicated, the reality in the appearance. Free and victorious must that to be presented stride forth from the presenting and, despite all fetters of language, stand there in its entire truth, liveliness and personality before the imaginative power. With one word: The beauty of poetical presentation is "*free self-action of nature in the fetters of language.*"

# ON SCHILLER
## and the Course
## of His Spiritual Development

### by Wilhelm von Humboldt

TRANSLATED BY JOHN CHAMBLESS

My close association and correspondence with Schiller fell within the years from 1794 through 1797; earlier, we were only slightly acquainted; later, when I lived mostly abroad, we corresponded less frequently.* Precisely the time referred to, however, was, without a doubt, the most important in Schiller's spiritual development. It came at the end of a long period, from the appearance of *Don Carlos*,[1] in which Schiller rested from all dramatic activity, and immediately preceding the period, from the completion of *Wallenstein*, in which he, as though in presentiment of his approaching death, distinguished the last years of his life with almost the same number of masterpieces. It was a

---

Wilhelm von Humboldt (1767–1835) was one of the most extraordinary men of an extraordinary time. As politician, diplomat, reformer, and pedagogue, von Humboldt's work was part of the foundation for the flowering of German science and culture in the nineteenth century; as a student of languages, he helped create the field of scientific philology.

The following essay on Schiller was originally published in 1830, as the introduction to the correspondence between von Humboldt and Schiller. The publication of the letters was inspired in part by the prior publication by the poet Wolfgang Goethe of his own correspondence with Schiller.

crisis, a turning point, possibly the most singular that a human being ever experienced in his spiritual life. The inborn, creative poetic genius, like a long-swelling flood, broke out through the obstructions that had been placed in its way by an all too powerfully maturing preoccupation with ideas and an all too clearly developed consciousness, and brought forth, out of this struggle itself, the form of ideal necessity, more clearly and more purely. Schiller had the purity of his nature to thank for the felicitous outcome of this crisis, and the inexhaustible labor that he applied, in the most varied ways, to the single task of uniting the most exuberant vitality of subject matter with the purest lawfulness of art. He needed simultaneously the formative powers of creativity and judgment; he could be so certain, however, that the first would never arise in him, that there were hours, days of doubt, of despondency, an apparent faltering between poetry and philosophy, a lack of confidence in his poetic calling, as a result of which, those years developed into such a decisive epoch in his life: For everything that made the successes of poetic work difficult for him in those years magnified the perfection of that which finally blossomed into maturity.

It was in the spring of 1794 when Schiller returned from one of his journeys home to settle again and live in Jena. Along with the journey, the terrible illness that had shaken his whole health—and from which, in fact, he never fully recovered—had had the result of interrupting all his work, and Schiller returned with the doubly intense efforts to activity which such an interruption and a new home commonly produce. The association with Goethe, just beginning at this time, contributed even more to stimulate his spiritual vitality. The question now arose, what should he undertake? What could he undertake with hope of success? Other than the *Letters On the Aesthetical Education of Man*, he had no work already begun before him. He had made no efforts in poetry since 1790. The interest in history had cooled; on the other hand, he felt himself drawn toward philosophical investigations. And in the background was always *The Knights of Malta*† and *Wallenstein*, but both were, under the then prevailing circumstances, as though separated by a great chasm even from the decision to make definite plans concerning either.

I had, in order to be near Schiller, taken up residence in Jena, arriving there a few weeks before him. We saw one another twice daily, especially evenings alone, and for the most part late into the night. All that just touched upon, naturally came into our discussions, and those conversations formed the basis for the correspondence here shared with the public, which, in large part, treats of these topics and allows, progressively, an insight into the way along which Schiller approached his last great productive period. For that reason, and without taking into consideration certain brilliant and wonderful formulations in those of Schiller himself, the letters which follow can perhaps hope to arouse the interest of those who wish to follow the mind of a great man beyond that which is impressed upon his works.

There is a more direct and fuller influence which a great mind has than through his works. These show but a portion of his being. In the living presence, it overflows purely and completely. In a manner which permits of no detailed demonstration or investigation, which thought itself is not able to follow, it is assimilated by his contemporaries and passed on to succeeding generations. The quiet and, as it were, magical influence of great spiritual natures is that in particular which allows ever developing thought to germinate, ever more powerfully and extensively, from generation to generation, from people to people. Written works and literature carry it, so to speak, locked away and mummified, over great chasms which the living potency is unable to span. Peoples, however, always made the principal steps in their spiritual progress before writing, and in those darkest, but most important, periods of human creation and formation, only living potency is possible. Nothing, therefore, attracts consideration more than any attempt, however weak in itself, to investigate how one of the remarkable men of the century permeates in his individual way the course of all thought: Uniting law with appearance, striving out from the finite to the infinite. This task has often occupied my reflections on Schiller, and our time has no one to offer, whose inner spiritual development in this respect would be more remarkable to pursue.

Schiller's poetic genius announced itself immediately in his first works; disregarding all deficiencies of form, disregarding many things which must have even appeared as crude to the mature artist, *The Robbers* and *Fiesco* testify to an unquestionable force of nature. It revealed itself afterward in Schiller's yearning for poetry, as though for the true home of his spirit, ever erupting into his quite varied philosophical and historical activities, and so often suggested in these letters. It proclaimed itself, finally, in the masculine power and the refined purity of the works which will most certainly remain, for a long time to come, the pride and the glory of the German stage. But this poetic genius was joined in the most intimate way to thought in all its profundity and sublimity; it manifested itself quite literally on the foundation of an intellectuality that would, probing, analyze everything, and, connecting, bring everything into unity. Therein lay Schiller's individual essence. He demanded a more profound participation of thought in poetry, and subjected poetry more rigorously to a spiritual unity, and this in two ways, in that he bound it to a more substantial artistic form, and in that he treated each poem in such a way that its subject matter was expanded, naturally and of itself, from its individuality into the universality of an idea. From these particular characteristics springs the excellence which typically distinguishes Schiller. From these arose the fact that Schiller first needed a period of time in which to bring forth the greatest and most sublime of which he was capable, in which his entire intellectuality, indissolubly united with his poetic genius, might work through to the clarity and definiteness he demanded. These characteristics finally explain the carping judgments of those who, denying him the spontaneity of the gift of the Muses, think they see in his works less the easy, happy creations of genius than the self-conscious work of the mind, whereas the truth is, of course, that only the real intellectual greatness of Schiller could offer the inducement for such a criticism.

I would consider it superfluous to undertake an analysis of Schiller's works in justification of these assertions, since those works are too current for anyone, whatever his opinion, not to be able to use them for himself. On the other hand, perhaps it will be agreeable to the reader of the correspondence if I briefly attempt to develop how my view of Schiller's essence arose, in particular from my association with him, from recollections of his conversations, and through the comparison of his works in their chronological order and investigations into the progress of his spirit.

What must have struck any observer as characteristically distinguishing Schiller was that, in a higher and more pregnant sense than perhaps with anyone else, thought was the element of his life. Constant, self-active engagement of his mind seldom deserted him, and weakened only during the most severe attacks of his physical illness. To him, it seemed recreation, not exertion. This revealed itself most in conversation, to which Schiller seemed truly born. He never sought an important topic for conversation, leaving it rather to accident to contribute the subject, but from any topic he led the conversation to a universal point of view, and, after a bit of preliminary talk, one found oneself transposed into the center of an intellectually stimulating discussion. He always treated thoughts as something to be achieved in common, and seemed always to need the one with whom he was talking—even if the latter deliberately persisted in receiving the idea only from him—who thus was never allowed to remain idle. In this lay the greatest difference between his conversations and those of Herder. Perhaps no man ever spoke as beautifully as Herder, if one were able to find him in the properly elevated mood, which was not difficult, if one touched one of the easily evoked chords within him. All the rare qualities of this man, so rightly admired, seemed to double their power in conversation, so appropriate were they for it. Thought was united to expression with a grace and dignity which seemed to come only from the subject itself, though in truth it belonged only to the person. And so the conversation flowed on uninterruptedly into a clarity which still left some personal unease, and into that chiaroscuro which yet did not prevent definitely recognizing the thoughts. And when one topic was exhausted, then one went on to another. One would gain nothing from objections; they would rather be a hindrance. One had listened, one could also speak, but one missed the reciprocal activity of conversation.

Schiller did not speak in a truly beautiful manner. But his mind, sharply and definitely, strove always for a new intellectual acquisition; he mastered the struggle, and soared in perfect freedom above his subject. Accordingly, he employed, with a light serenity, any incidental connections that presented themselves, and thus his conversation was so very rich in words that carried the mark of a happy birth in the moment. This freedom, however, was in no way detrimental to the course of the investigation. Schiller always held firmly to the threads which must lead to their end point, and were the conversation not disturbed by some accidental occurrence, he was not easily diverted from reaching the goal.

Just as Schiller always attempted in conversation to gain new ground in the realm of thought, so, in general, his intellectual work was always one of strenuous self-activity. His letters also show this clearly. He simply knew no other way. Mere reading material he relegated to late evenings and to his, unfortunately, so frequent sleepless nights. His days were taken up by his work, or definite studies pertaining thereto; thus his mind was kept taut by work and research together. He knew nothing of, and did not respect enough, those pure studies that are directed to no other immediate goal than knowledge, studies that have such a charm for those familiar with them, that one must guard oneself in order not to be too much distracted from more defined activities. Knowledge seemed to him to be too raw, and the powers of the mind too noble, to see anything more in the material than something to be processed.

Only because he more valued the higher exertions of the mind, which self-actively creates out of its own depths, could he so little content himself with anything lesser. But it is also remarkable, that Schiller created, out of such a small store of material, with such bare tools which others provided him, an extremely complex world view that, when one became aware of it, was startling in its inspired truth; it can only be called that, for it arose in absolutely no external way. He had seen only a portion even of Germany, and nothing of Switzerland, of which his *Wilhelm Tell* yet contains so many vivid descriptions. Whoever stands at the Falls of the Rhine will involuntarily recall the beautiful stanzas of *The Diver*, which portray this spectacle formed by the confused swirl of water that, as it were, captivatingly absorbs one's eye, yet there was, even here, no personal experience as the basis for his description. But what Schiller did gain through his own experience, he grasped with a vision which then made graphic whatever was given him from others' descriptions. For that reason, he never neglected studying reading material for any work; even what he accidentally found to be useful to his purpose was firmly stamped into his memory, and his restless, intense imagination, by reworking into permanent vivacity, now this, now that part of any material collected, supplemented the imperfections of such an indirect apprehension.

In a quite similar way he appropriated for himself the spirit of Greek poetry, without ever having known it except in translations. To that end, he spared no pains; he preferred translations which disclaimed any value for themselves; his favorites were literal Latin paraphrases. Thus he translated scenes and *The Marriage of Thetis* from Euripides. I confess that I reread this chorus each time with greater satisfaction. It is not merely a translation into another language, but into another genre of poetry. The rapture into which the imagination, from the first verse on, is transposed, is a different one, but precisely that constitutes the pure poetic effect. For this can only be ascribed to the general attunement of imagination and feeling that the poet, independently of any thought content, calls forth in the reader merely through the breath of inspiration contained within his work. Like a shade, the ancient spirit shows through the borrowed garments in which it has been arrayed. But in each verse, some touches of the original are brought out so significantly that one is, nonetheless, gripped from beginning to end by antiquity.

I did not primarily intend, however, these translations when I spoke of Schiller's immersion in the spirit of ancient poetry, but rather two of his later works. Schiller also made important advances in these. *The Cranes of Ibycus* and *Victory Feast* carry the hues of antiquity more purely and truly than one can possibly expect from a modern poet, and, indeed, in the most beautiful and brilliant way. The poet has taken the soul of antiquity up into himself, and he moves with freedom within it, and thus a new poetic work arises which breathes only of that soul in each of its parts. The two poems, however, stand in a notable contrast to one another. *The Cranes of Ibycus* permitted a wholly epic development, and what made the subject of intrinsic value to the poet was the idea arising there from of the power of poetic representation over the human heart. This power of poetry, an invisible force created only through the mind, evaporating in harsh reality, belonged essentially to the sphere of thought with which Schiller was actively employed. Eight years before he shaped it within himself into a ballad, this material was present to his mind, as is clearly revealed by these verses from *The Artists*:

Vom Eumenidenchor geschrecket,
Zieht sich der Mord, auch nie entdecket,
das Los des Todes aus dem Lied.[2]

(Terrified by the chorus of Eumenides, the murderer, still not revealed, drew the lot of death from the song.)

This idea, however, permitted a perfectly ancient development; antiquity possessed everything needed for it to emerge in its complete purity and power. Thus everything in the entire narrative is taken directly from antiquity, especially the vision and chorus of Eumenides. The chorus, familiar from Aeschylus, is interwoven so artistically within modern poetic form in rhyme and meter, that nothing of its quiet grandeur seems lost.

*Victory Feast* is of a more lyrical and contemplative nature. Here the poet could, and had, to supplement what did not lie in the thought and feeling of antiquity from the fullness of his own heart, but, otherwise, everything is as equally pure, in the spirit of Homeric poetry, as in the other poem. The whole is, however, stamped with a higher, more abstract spirituality than is characteristic of the ancient singer, and receives its greatest beauty precisely through that.

Schiller's earlier poems are also rich in single expressions taken from the ancients, but to which a higher meaning is often attached. I chose here only the portrayal of Death from *The Artists*,

den sanften Bogen der Notwendigkeit

(the gentle bow of necessity)[3]

which so beautifully recalls the ἀγανὰ βέλεα (the gentle arrow) of Homer, where, however, the transposition of the adjective from the arrow to the bow gives the thought a more delicate, deeper sense.

The confidence in the efficacy of the power of the human mind, elevated into a poetic image, is expressed in the distich entitled *Columbus*, which belongs to the most characteristic Schiller ever created. This belief in the invisibly indwelling power of man, this view, so sublime and deeply true, that there must be an inner, secret agreement between this power and that which orders and directs the entire universe, since all truth can only be a reflection of the eternal and original, was a characteristic feature of

Schiller's system of ideas. To that also corresponded the
tenacity with which he pursued every intellectual problem
until it was satisfactorily solved. Already in the *Letters of
Raphael to Julius*, published in *Thalia*,[4] in the bold but
beautiful expression "when Columbus made the dangerous
wager with the unnavigated sea," the same thought is found
united with the same image.

In both form and content, Schiller's philosophical ideas
were an altogether faithful model of his total spiritual potency in general. Both always moved along the same track
toward the same goal, but in a manner in which the more
vital appropriation of even richer material, and the power
of thought which ruled him unceasingly determined one
another in reciprocal intensification. The final point, to
which he connected everything, was production of the *totality* in human nature through the harmonizing of the different forces in their absolute freedom. Both belonging to the
self, which can only be one and indivisible, but, the one
seeking multiplicity and matter, and the other, unity and
form, they were to point, through their spontaneous harmony here, to an origin which lies far beyond all finitude.
Reason, ruling unconditionally in knowledge and in the
determination of the will, should treat intuition and perception with considerate regard, and should nowhere encroach
upon their domain; on the other hand, these should rise up,
out of their essential being, in their self-chosen way, to a
condition in which each, with all the differences of principle,
might find itself again, according to form. To mediate this
astonishing harmony, which arises in no discoverable way,
but rather as by sudden miracle, to annul the *per se* absolute
contradiction of both natures through a semblance
grounded in their mutual relation to one another, and thus
to give humanity, within the phenomenal realm, an image of that which lies outside of all phenomena—this is
made possible only by that tendency in humanity we call
the *aesthetic*: for it treats matter with a self-activity that

arises out of the realm of the sensuous, not borrowed from the idea, and that yet emerges as freedom.

In *On Grace and Dignity,* and in the *Letters On the Aesthetical Education of Man,* this mode of conception is presented in detail. I doubt if these works, filled with substantial ideas and expressed in a uniquely beautiful way, are still frequently read, which is regrettable in a number of respects. Indeed, neither work, and, in particular, the *Letters,* can be absolved of the reproach that Schiller, in order to firmly establish his assertions, selected a method too strict and abstract, and too much neglected to treat the material in a manner admitting more fruitful application, without in so doing, really having satisfied the demands of a deduction purely from concepts. But, concerning the concept of beauty, concerning the aesthetic in creation and action, and thus the foundations of art, as well as art itself, these works contain everything essential in a manner which can never possibly be excelled. In this whole area, there will hardly be a question which can arise, the right answer to which could not be derived from the principles put forward in these treatises. This stems not merely from the sharp differentiation and delimitation of concepts, but rather flows from the much more unusual merit of having produced everything in its full scope, in its full content, and with the suggestion of having drawn all of the consequences which follow therefrom. Generally, concepts in these essays are not so much dissected and analyzed as, if I may be allowed the simile, chiseled and faceted, of which each receives and reflects a new light. This is particularly true of the last half of *On Grace and Dignity,* where distinctions between different types of states of mind and of conduct are portrayed.

Never before were these questions discussed in such a pure, such a complete and illuminating way. Infinitely much was thus gained, not merely for the positive analysis of concepts, but also for aesthetic and moral education. Art and poetry were directly joined to that which is most noble in humanity, were presented as that by which humanity first awakens to the consciousness of its indwelling nature, which strives to transcend the finite. Thus, both art and poetry were placed at the pinnacle from which they truly derive. This placement, protected from desecration by any petty and degrading opinion, from any sentiment not derived from their pure elements, was, in the truest sense, Schiller's constant endeavor, and appears as his true destiny in life, given him by the original direction of his life. The primary and most stringent demands were therefore made on the poet himself, from whom he demands not merely a genius and talent working, as it were, in isolation, but rather a total attunement of mind fit for the high elevation of his vocation, not merely a momentary sublimity, but one that has become character.

"Before he undertakes to deal with excellence, he is to make his first and most important task the refinement of his own individuality to the purest and most glorious of humanity." *The Review of Bürger's Poetry*,[5] from which this quotation is taken, has drawn upon Schiller the charge of injustice against this rightly beloved poet. By all means it is severe. For, as long as approximately the same condition of the language allows general appreciation of the poetry of our time in Germany (a condition on which the effects of all poetry is dependent), Bürger will incite every imagination most poetically, and will affect any mind with the truth and inwardness that is uniquely his own. Schiller himself confesses in one of his later letters to having applied the ideal too directly to a particular case in this criticism. But he certainly would have foregone nothing of the general demands stated there, and those deserve to be emphasized here precisely as truly Schiller's individual and personal view. He applied those demands to no one more rigorously than himself. One can truthfully say of him that, whatever even remotely resembled the vulgar, even the ordinary, never touched him at all, that he carried over entirely into his whole mode of experience, and into his life, the noble and elevated views that filled his thoughts, and, when writing, he was always, even in his lesser works, fired with the same vital exertion toward the ideal. For that reason, so little is found in his work that must be called feeble or mediocre, and this certainly contributes much to what I touched on before, namely, that his spiritual powers always worked with the same exertion, and that it was thoroughly alien to him to let them find relaxation in, as it were, recreational work. There may be individual passages which correspond less to his total way of writing and his complete philosophical view. But only a few isolated passages will be thrown out as unworthy of him, while the rest is enthusiastically extolled, and the criticism itself, just to note this in passing, will concern precisely his most individual aspects, and thus place the lofty unity of his nature into a yet brighter light. The severity of his judgment on his own earlier productions is expressed clearly and forcefully in one passage in the review of Bürger, and even more clearly in the introduction to a collection of his own poetry, written two years before his death. But what there offended his grand and delicate sensibility—which, in what can be called the second period of his life, comes to prominence so brilliantly in *Don Carlos,* and which thereafter was never marred by a blemish—did not concern the individuality, the personality of the poet. His elevated, pure view of human nature and human life, striving toward wholeness, also speaks out of those works. That which is offensive in them required only an artistic correction, and arose out of misconstrued concepts of poetic truth, out of a yet insufficient appreciation of the necessity of subordinating the parts to the unity of the whole, and, in individual cases, out of a not yet sufficient purification of taste. At the same time, the material selected contributed as well.

In *Don Carlos,* Schiller found himself as though in another realm. Here he was presented with the great contradiction between the broad cosmopolitan view and the narrow diplomacy that fancies itself so profound, and was shown the conflict between ideas which disregard all experience, and a limitation made possible by experience without ideas. Directly involved was the fate of provinces, which, violated in their human rights and the rights of their conscience, had justifiably rebelled and were laid waste, and interwoven within this great political interest was the first emotion of pure and enthusiastic love, innocently and delicately reciprocated. This material thus surrounded the poet, as with an atmosphere which elevated him ever higher. By all means, the choice of this material sprang from the attunement of mind that preceded it. This is also shown in the changed external form, in the abandonment of prose, to which he returned in the first draft of *Wallenstein,* but, inspired by poetry, soon recognized his error, this time permanently. The first scene between Max and Thekla, worked out earlier than those which precede it, resisted the form of prose; it was the first in verse.

The assignment of poetry to the position of the elevated and serious among human endeavors, to which I referred above, and of defending poetry against petty and dull views, the first which fails to recognize poetry's dignity, the second its essential characteristic, the former making it into a trifling decoration and embellishment of life, the latter expecting from it direct moral effects and teaching, is, as cannot be repeated enough, deeply grounded in the German mode of perception and experience. Thus Schiller expressed, but in his individual way, that which his being German implanted in him, that which resonated to him out of the depths of the language, the hidden workings of which he perceived so magnificently and which he likewise knew how so masterfully to employ. There lies in the great economy of spiritual development, which makes up the ideal aspect of world history, as opposed to the actions and events, a certain proportion by which an individual, certainly only the most privileged, is able to raise himself above his nation, so that what the nation has unconsciously bestowed upon him can, cultivated by individuality, flow back to the nation. To consider art, then, and all aesthetic activities, from their true standpoint, no modern nation has succeeded to the extent that the German has, not even those glorified by poets who will be recognized as great and preeminent for all time. The more profound and true attunement of the German lies in his greater inwardness, which keeps him closer to the truth of nature, in his inclination toward the employment of ideas and the experiences related to them, and in everything dependent thereon. Thus, Germany distinguishes itself from most modern nations, and, in its more precise determination of the concept of inwardness, from the Greeks as well. It seeks poetry and philosophy, not intending to separate them, but rather striving to combine them, and as long as this striving for philosophy—even completely abstract philosophy, which is misrecognized and misinterpreted in its indispensable effects even among us—survives, then so, too, will continue the impetus which the powerful minds of the last half of the preceding century unmistakably provided, and will win new force for itself. Poetry and philosophy stand, by their nature, at the center of all spiritual endeavors; only they can unite in themselves the individual results, only from them can unity and inspiration flow over into everything individual, only they represent essentially what man is, since all the other sciences and accomplishments, could they ever be entirely separated off, merely show what he possesses or has appropriated. Without this simultaneously enlightening and fiery focus, even the most encompassing sciences remain too fragmented, and their reacting back upon the ennoblement of the individual, on the nation, and on humanity—which can be the only goal of all inquiries into nature and into humanity, and into the inexplicable connection between both—is restricted and rendered impotent. The search for truth, and the forming and creation for the sake of beauty become mere empty names, if one flees from seeking truth and beauty there, where their kindred natures are not dissipated among separate objects, but reveal themselves as pure objects of spirit. Schiller knew no other preoccupation than precisely that with poetry and philosophy, and the essential characteristic of his intellectual endeavor consisted precisely in comprehending and portraying the identity of their origin. The observations above are thus directly relevant to him.

One idea Schiller especially enjoyed working with was that of the education through art of the crude, natural man, as he assumed him to be, before he could be entrusted with culture by reason. He developed it many times in both poetry and prose. His imagination also lingered with particular pleasure on the beginning of civilization in general, with the transition from nomadic life to agriculture, and with, as he so beautifully expressed it, the pious bond of loyalty established with gentle, motherly Earth. He eagerly seized upon whatever mythology offered that was relevant here; remaining totally faithful to the intimations of fable, he molded Demeter, the principal figure in this realm, into a vision as wondrous as it is deeply moving, marrying human feelings to the divine within her breast. For a long time, it was one of Schiller's favorite plans to treat the first civilizing of Attica by foreign immigration in an epic manner. The *Eleusian Festival* took the place of this uncompleted plan.

Had Schiller lived to see the revival of Indian literature, he would have learned of a closer coupling of poetry with the most abstract philosophy than Greek literature has to offer, and this phenomenon would have gripped him most deeply. Indian poetry, particularly in its earliest period, generally has a more solemn, pious, and religious character than that of the Greeks, without thereby standing, as it were, under alien rule and sacrificing its own character. Only the merit of being graphic was perhaps thereby lost.

It is regrettable to a high degree, and to a certain extent surprising, that Schiller, in his reasoning on the course of human development, never once referred to language, on which is stamped precisely the double nature of man, and, indeed, not separately, but fused into a symbol. It unites, in the most precise sense, a philosophical and poetic activity within itself, the latter simultaneously in the metaphor embedded in the word and in the music of its sounds. At the same time, it presents in general the transition to the infinite, since its symbols excite to activity, but set no limits to this activity, and the highest degree contained within it can always be exceeded by a yet higher degree. It would, therefore, have to have appeared as a welcome subject in Schiller's system of ideas.

Language, of course, belongs to the nation and the species, not to the individual, and humanity can, before learning to understand it, long use it as a dead instrument without being moved by its penetrating life. It cannot, therefore, be unconditionally considered as an instrument of education. There is, nonetheless, a further influence which men, although certainly not originally creating, but still quietly perfecting, can have on their language, and languages always have their highest poetic and musical content in their earlier formation, then connected with the special vigor of imagination of the peoples which speak them. They lose this content in the course of time, but the ascent to that level is at best only seldom visible to us, and thus remains problematic. If one, therefore, gives oneself over, from the contemplation of the wonderful construction of the languages of nations totally without culture—devoted to their analysis, with an open and unbiased mind, as with a natural object—to consider the original condition of the human species, eternally hidden in darkness, so one should expect that, since language is given with humanity, and before it nothing human can be imagined, this original condition may have been more peaceful, more reflective, and one not closed to deep and delicate experiences, and that social bestialization belongs only to a later period, where the struggle of adverse events with wild passion drowned the voice within their own breast. At the very least, Schiller would have hardly considered the view which he held in the *Letters* as necessary, and would generally have less sharply distinguished that which appears as unified and intimately fused in the unquestionably most primitive emanation of human nature, in language.

The drive toward occupation with abstract ideas, the striving to capture everything finite in one grand image, and to join it to the infinite, came from within Schiller himself, and was inspired by no external stimulus; it was given with his individuality. It developed most freely and in the liveliest way in the second and third periods of his life, if the first is taken to include the first three of his tragedies, and the fourth, the final tragedies from *Wallenstein* on. I have already spoken of *Don Carlos* in this regard. The *Philosophical Letters,* published in *Thalia*, with which the poem *Resignation,* a product of the same year, has such a striking kinship in the bold sweep of its passionately philosophical reason, should have marked the beginning of a series of philosophical clarifications for Schiller. But the sequel was not forthcoming, and a new philosophical period began for Schiller in *On Grace and Dignity*, principally founded on his acquaintance with Kantian philosophy. Those two pieces could be regarded only with injustice, as expressing the writer's actual opinions; they belong, however, among the best we have from him. The *Letters* are written with an overpowering fire and a spirit untouched by even a trace of the compulsion of any philosophical school. *Resignation* carries Schiller's most characteristic stamp in the direct coupling of simply expressed, profound, great truth with incomparable images, and in the wholly original language which encourages the boldest combinations and constructions. The principal thoughts developed in the whole can only be seen as a transient mood of an emotionally charged mind, but it is so masterfully depicted that the passion is quite taken up into contemplation, and the expression seems to be solely the fruit of reflection and experience.

Kant undertook and completed perhaps the greatest work ever accomplished by an individual man for philosophical reason. He tested and secured the entire philosophical enterprise in a direction in which he necessarily had to come up against the philosophers of all times and all nations; he measured, delimited, and smoothed out the road in that direction, destroying the houses of cards built there, and established, after completing his work, firm foundations

upon which philosophical analysis could come together with
the natural sense of mankind, often led into error and deadened by earlier systems. He led philosophy, in the truest
sense, back into the depths of the human heart. He possessed everything in the highest degree which distinguishes
the great thinker, and he unified within himself what otherwise seems incompatible: Depth and rigor; a perhaps never
surpassed dialectic, in which the mind does not become lost
in also grasping for *the* truth that cannot be reached in this
way; and a philosophical genius which spins out the threads
of a vast fabric of ideas in all directions, and holds everything
together by means of the unity of the idea, without which
no philosophical system would be possible. Of the traces of
feeling and heart which one meets in Kant's works, Schiller
rightly remarked, that the highest philosophical vocation
requires both qualities (thought and feeling) in combination.
But if we leave him on the path where his mind points
in but a single direction, then we learn to recognize the
extraordinary genius of this man in its full range. Nothing,
either in nature or in the realm of knowledge, leaves him
indifferent; he draws everything into his sphere, but there,
the self-active principle of his intellectuality visibly asserts
its superiority, so that his character shines forth more
brightly where, as in his views on the structure of the
starry heavens,[6] the material, nature sublime in itself, of the
imagination, under the guidance of a grand idea, offers a
vast expanse—for the greatness and power of imagination
directly supports Kant's rigor and depth of thought.

How much or how little of the Kantian philosophy has
remained to the present, or will remain in the future, I do
not presume to decide, but if we wish to determine the
glory which Kant bestowed on his nation and the usefulness
he bestowed on speculative thought, then three things remain unmistakably certain. Some of what he demolished
will never rise again; some of what he established will never
pass away; and, what is most important, he instituted a
reform, the likes of which is hardly equaled in the entire
history of philosophy. And so, speculative philosophy,

which on the occasion of the appearance of his *Critique of Pure Reason* had hardly given even weak testimony of its existence among us, was awakened into an activity which will continue to animate the German spirit, we hope, for a long time. Since he taught, not so much philosophy as philosophizing, and less communicated discovered truths than provided a spark for the torch of one's own search, he indirectly caused the rise of systems and schools which more or less diverge from him, and it characterizes the noble freedom of his mind, that he was able to awaken philosophers again into complete freedom and continuing activity along their own self-created paths.

A great man is a phenomenon in any generation or age, for which always at best only a very partial accounting, or none whatsoever, can be given. Who perhaps would undertake to explain how Goethe was suddenly there, equally great, in the fullness and profundity of his genius, in his earliest work as in his latest? And yet, he founded among us a new period in poetry, transmuted poetry into a new form, impressed his own form onto the language, and gave the spirit of his nation a decisive impulse for all coming generations. The genius, always new and setting the rule, first announces his coming to be by his very existence, and his reason for being cannot be sought in one previously, already known; as he appears, he himself establishes his own direction. Out of the miserable state of eclectic bumbling in which Kant found philosophy, he was able to draw no inspirational spark. Also, it might be difficult to say whether he owed more to ancient or later philosophy. He himself, with that rigorous criticism that was his most salient feature, was obviously more closely related to the spirit of modern times. Also, one of his characteristic traits was to progress with all the advances of his century, even to take a most lively part in all the events of his day. While he, more than anyone before him, isolated philosophy in the depths of the human heart, at the same time perhaps no one used it in such manifold and fruitful ways. These passages, richly scattered passages throughout all of his works, give them an entirely singular charm.

Such a phenomenon could not go unnoticed by Schiller. To him, who always stood above whatever activity was then occupying him, who still aspired to something higher to which to connect even the poetry to which nature had intended him and which permeated his life, a theory, whose nature it was to contain the roots and the end point of the object to which his reflection was constantly directed, was necessarily attractive. Arising suddenly but ignored for years, this theory was seized upon, in precisely that time and region[7] in which Schiller was then found, with an enthusiasm which is still a joy to remember. Schiller showed the way in which he honored Kant in many passages of his works, but nowhere more than in his actions. He appropriated the new philosophy according to his own nature. He hardly entered into the actual structure of the system; he riveted himself, however, on the deduction of the principles of beauty and of the moral law, where it must have powerfully moved him to find natural human feeling restored to its rightful place and philosophically justified in all its purity. It was precisely here that the theories dominant immediately before had dislocated the true point of view and degraded the sublime. On the other hand, Schiller found that, according to his way of thinking, the sensuous powers of man were in part offended against, in part not sufficiently recognized, and the possibility in those powers of voluntary harmony with the unity of reason, through the aesthetic principle, was not sufficiently emphasized. So it happened that, when he first expressed Kant's name in print, in *On Grace and Dignity*, Schiller appeared as Kant's opponent.

It was in Schiller's essence never to be drawn over into the orbit of a great mind near him, but rather to be stimulated in the most powerful way within his own self-created sphere by such an influence, and we can perhaps remain equivocal whether this should be admired in him more as greatness of mind or as profound beauty of character. Not to subordinate himself to another individuality is the characteristic of every superior mental power, every more potent mind, but to see completely into the other individuality, and to honor it in its difference, and out of this admiring view to create the power to direct one's own even more decisively and directly toward its goal—this belongs to few, and was Schiller's outstanding trait of character. Of course, such a relationship is only possible between kindred spirits, whose divergent paths come together in a higher point, but it presupposes from the intellect a clear recognition of that point, and from character, that any consideration of the person must remain totally subordinate to the interests of the matter at hand. Only on this condition do humility and self-feeling, as it is the determination of their ideal working together, go truly over into openness. And this was Schiller's relationship to Kant. He took nothing from him; there were seeds already present in that which he wrote before his acquaintance with Kantian philosophy for the ideas worked out in *On Grace and Dignity* and the *Aesthetic Letters*; they represent merely the inner, original structure of his spirit. Nevertheless, that acquaintance became a new period in Schiller's philosophical exertions, and Kantian philosophy gave him both aid and stimulation. Without a great prophetic spirit, we are able to see how, without Kant, Schiller would have developed his own quite characteristic ideas. Freedom of *form* would probably have been gained in that case.

When I speak here of form, I do not mean, of course, style. The latter Schiller created quite individually in his historical and philosophical as well as his poetic works. What he says in a passage in his writings of the way in which language is to envelop expression, he himself attained to the highest degree. Whoever knows how to appreciate a style which does not strive, as it were, to dryly express already completed thoughts (a necessarily futile exertion, since thought first receives its completion *in* expression), but rather a style which seems to spring into being, self-actively produced *in* the moment, *he* will admire that of Schiller. For, while Schiller carried the stamp of originality on himself, at the same time he gives the rule to anyone who struggles, but to each in his own way.

What I will say here of Schiller's style concerns, in a still more pregnant sense, those of his poems which are devoted in particular to exposition of philosophical ideas. They produce the idea, not merely decorate it with poetic trappings. They met, thus, the challenge of this species of poetry. The reader gains the conviction that the ideas there portrayed for him stand on the far side of a chasm over which the understanding is unable to throw a bridge, a chasm over which only the poetically inspired power of the imagination is able to spring. The poet, who always expresses only that which he has himself experienced, must, in order to effect that conviction, first produce within himself the appropriate attunement of mind, he must possess the power to let the idea, as it is thought, merge into the poetic representation, and to carry his material over into the infinite, where alone, and not in realm of the understanding, poetic powers coincide with knowing. Schiller complains somewhere that there is as yet no truly didactic poem. But some of his can qualify as that in precisely the sense he intends. Of these, perhaps *The Stroll*, in which Schiller surpasses even himself in graphic natural depiction, speaks most to the imagination and universal feeling. Otherwise, some earlier works in this genre, *The Gods of Greece* or *The Artists*, might be preferred to the later, in which the working out of the ideas inspired within are pursued along philosophical lines. For, with Schiller himself, as it cannot be otherwise with a poet, philosophical ideas are developed out of the medium of imagination and feeling.

Schiller's historical writings are perhaps regarded by some as accidental in his life, as produced merely by external circumstances. Such factors undeniably contributed to the fact that these studies received a greater extension in time, but Schiller *per se* was necessarily drawn to historical, as to philosophical studies by the very essence of his spirit. I touch on this point here only to sketch it in a few words. Whoever, like Schiller, is challenged by his most inward nature to seek mastery and spontaneous harmony of sensuous material through and with the idea, cannot withdraw where precisely the richest multiplicity of an enormous field reveals itself; anyone whose constant concern it was, in composing, to infuse the material shaped by the imagination into a form breathing of necessity, he must be eager to investigate what form this be, since that which is representable is such only through some form, is permitted and demanded by the material given by reality. The talent of the writer of history is closely related to the poetic and philosophical, and the profession of historian would appear doubtful for anyone who has within himself sparks of neither. This is true not merely for the writing of history, but also for historical research. Schiller used to say of the writer of history that, after he had taken up into himself all the factual material by means of exact and thorough study of the sources, he must still build, out of himself, the collected material into a history, and Schiller was completely right in that, although his assertion could also be fundamentally misunderstood. A fact can be merely transcribed into a history, as little as a facial expression of a human being into a portrait. As in organic structure and the expression of the soul in external form, there is a living unity within the interconnections of even a simple event, and it can be comprehended and represented only from this center outward. Also, whether intentionally or not, the conception of the historian steps between the event and its representation, and the true connection of events will be recognized with most certainty by those who have exercised their vision on philosophical and poetic necessity. For, here, too, reality stands in a mysterious bond with the mind.

In the collection of facts and in the study of sources, insofar as he was allowed to immerse himself in them, Schiller was very exact and careful. He also never neglected to procure the historical or specialized information necessary for his poetic works. If he failed to achieve something in this area, it was certainly not for lack of diligence in his efforts, but rather the lack of means, his illness, and other accidental circumstances. But we should not always view single factual inaccuracies as instances against the generality of this assertion. Of course, he appropriated for himself, in connection with these studies for poetic work, primarily the totality of the impression. With what love he dedicated himself to the field of history is revealed in one of his letters to Körner.[8] Only in those cases in which he had to take on historical work for merely external reasons, as in connection with the *Die Horen*,[9] did it become a burden to him. Otherwise, even in his last days, the joy in history was not extinguished in him. When I saw him for the last time in the fall of 1802, he told me with passionate warmth of a plan for a history of Rome which he was saving for his later years, after the fire of poetic art had perhaps deserted him. In fact, no other history equals that one in dramatic grandeur. Schiller was especially gripped by the idea of how the greatest world-historical disasters of antiquity and modern times are tied precisely to the locale of this city. We are reminded of Goethe's beautiful remark that, from Rome, history reads differently from any other place in the world. "Elsewhere, one reads from the outside inward; in Rome, one believes that one reads from the inside out; everything settles in around us here, and goes out again from us."

What constitutes genius in a representation of this sort is the concentration of the whole intellect on the single point assigned to it by nature. Two determinations, necessary to any intellectual characterization, are dependent on the nature of this whole: the special stamp of genius, since it can form itself again very differently in every genius, and the freedom of the spirit, alongside and in addition to that, for a more general overview of the intellectual standpoint. Within the boundaries of this type, and the proportion of the powers working together within, lie all the varieties of human intellectuality—a point not otherwise to be developed here—the intellectuality that, within every man, no matter how obscure it may be, is particularly applied to one point. Therefore, it seemed necessary to me, with Schiller, whom everyone feels to be a poet, to speak principally of his entire bent of mind, and particularly of his philosophical bent, in order to portray him as a poet, insofar as that is possible according to the concept. Precisely in order to characterize his poetic genius, I have spoken of those things in which he seems to have abandoned the poet's path. The portrayal of a great intellectual nature presupposes a brilliant insight into the essence and the interaction of the totality of his individually apportioned intellectuality. I may not, therefore, nurture the hope of truly having brought the reader completely to the standpoint of seeing Schiller's essential qualities, as the reader has previously experienced them, henceforth clearly and distinctly in all their interconnections. If I have been successful here even to a certain extent, then Schiller's philosophical exertions cannot appear merely as a many-sided cultivation of the mind, and still less as the uncertain searching about for his true profession, but rather, as bursting forth, with the poetic, from one and the same deep, rich, and powerful source. Just as matter enters into various combinations in physical bodies according to elective affinities,[10] so in Schiller, poetry was intimately connected to the power of thought. But it streamed forth no less freely on that account out of perception and feeling. From just this connection, which intensified the power of imagination through the contrasts to be overcome, the poetry created a fire and a profundity and a power which is manifested in this way by no other poet, ancient or modern. Thought and image, idea and experience, always enter in him into mutual interaction, interpenetrating one another in successful passages without losing their essential qualities. We can imagine nothing in the mind as at rest, only occasionally going over into activity, nothing as separately and abstractly in interaction. What is in the mind *exists* only through activity; what is contained within it is *one*, distinguished only through tension and direction, which is often produced by the impulse of different, even opposing forces. The thought of each moment contains the whole mind, diffused within this formation. This energetic appearance of the entire intellect in the individual thought, which arose only from the energy of the real combination within himself, was particularly evident to Schiller. The beautiful image by which he characterized poetry in general in *The Power of Song*—"a flood of rain from rocky fissures"—stood in a special relation to his own method of thought. What distinguished him, moreover, even if it might also appear as quite unrelated to his career as a poet, is the distance he maintained above any single striving within himself, even over his own poetic genius, one of the mightiest and most powerful which ever moved within the human breast. This was not freedom alone, but a totally authentic superior power.

While this obviously also enhanced him and elevated him as a poet, so it had to be just for that reason that his poetry undeniably arose out of a doubly energetic force. Everything artistic and poetic, of course, carries within itself the character of spontaneity, but this happy lot does not fall to the artist and poet entirely without toil. They too need work, but a work of a quite singular nature, and this was made difficult for Schiller by the very excellence of his nature. His goal was set higher, because he himself saw more clearly the goal of all poetry; he carefully surveyed its various paths, and clearly perceived the total machinery of spiritual activity, if such an expression can be applied to the governance of supreme freedom. He recognized the ideal in its total grandeur, a recognition that always stimulated and never depressed him, and while he, to use his own illuminating distinction, belonged completely to the class of sentimental poets, his individuality elevated the concept of the entire class. Soaring simultaneously over his own works and those of others, he was not merely creator, but also judge, and demanded justification of poetic work in the realm of thought. It is therefore doubly admirable that the truly natural power carrying, unconsciously and inexplicably, the poet along with it, lost nothing of its power in him. Here, however, as in everything, the *totality* of his nature was at work. No one insisted as much as he on the absolute freedom of sensuous material, on its perfect formation, totally independent of the idea, through perception and imagination, and that he did this was not in the least the consequence of theoretical ideas. Rather, he created this for himself, out of the same powerful, inner compulsion that ruled him. What occurs with other sentimental poets, precisely because of this, that their works are less graphic, giving their poems less of sensuous formation, could never have been a hindrance to him. He was, rather, naive in a high degree, more than would seem allowable, given his decisive inclination toward the sentimental class. His nature, given over to itself, led him more to the higher idea, where the distinction between the two types melts away again of itself, as it bound him in one of the two, and if he shared this prerogative with some of the greatest poetic geniuses, with him there was the additional advantage, that he placed in the idea itself the demand of absolute freedom of the ideally forming sensuous material.

The merely touching, sweet, simply descriptive, in short, the genre of poetry which derives directly from perception and feeling, is found in Schiller in countless single passages and in whole poems. I need here refer merely to *The Maiden's Lament, The Youth at the Brook, Thekla: A Spirit-Voice, To Emma, Expectation*, among many others, which seem only to reproduce an experienced impression, and in which we detect Schiller's intellectual essence only as a pale reflection. But the most wonderful authentication of his perfect poetic genius is contained in *The Song of the Bell*, which, in changing meter, in depictions of the greatest vivacity, where briefly suggested expressions produce the total image, goes through all the activities of human and social life, expressing feelings arising out of each, and connects all this each time symbolically to the sounds of the bell, the continuing work on which accompanies the poetry in its different moments. In no language do I know of a poem which opens up such a vast poetic panorama in so brief a space, running through the scale of the deepest human experiences and showing, in a completely lyrical way, life with its most important events and epochs as an epic contained within natural limits. The poetic clarity is, however, increased the more, in that every event, held at a distance from the imagination, corresponds to an actually portrayed object, and the two series thereby formed, continue in parallel to one another toward the same goal.

If one makes real to oneself what has been presented here of Schiller's restless spiritual activity and the close connection of his poetic genius with the mightier force which drew everything within him into the realm of thought, then one will better understand the period in which the following correspondence takes place, which, as I indicated in the preceding, was the critical period in Schiller's life. Every great poetic work requires an attunement and concentration of the whole mind, which Schiller, as he returned to Jena, had lacked for years. In part, the fault for that probably lay in the plan for *Wallenstein,* which he carried around within himself for a long period before actually putting his hand to the work. This material was too immense in its extent, and too delicate in its constitution, not to require the greatest preparation for its execution. Whoever properly appreciates this creation will recognize it as a truly gigantic poetic work; even Schiller's formative genius was able to master the vast material only in three connected works. But the demands which Schiller made on his works for the theater had been heightened; since the creative genius momentarily rested, the stern critic took its place all the more actively, and not without apprehension. In all artistic production, confidence requires the example of successes already achieved. Schiller lacked these now, not according to the judgment of his nation, but according to his own. His earlier pieces could not count for him as a confirmation for talent whose development now seemed worthy of him and his art. *Don Carlos* was composed over a long period of time, because of external circumstances, and the unity and fervor of the first conception did not survive the duration of the period of composition. Thus

Schiller believed himself to stand at the beginning of a new career, and he actually stamped a character on this tragedy, once he had dealt with the barriers which hindered his new conception, the like of which had never appeared before on the stage. Further, this fell at a time in which Schiller's inner aspiration was primarily philosophical. For it should not be mistaken that he, in the time shortly after *Don Carlos,* was greatly concerned with bringing the philosophical ideas which had been excited in him to clarity and definiteness. The choice itself of *Don Carlos* as the subject of a tragedy was not free from a contribution of this inner drive toward ideas—as can be seen from his letters on the play—and the work, unique of its kind, which is furnished in its way individually, in separate details with the entire fullness of Schiller's genius, even if it does not, in the form and arrangement of the whole, betray traces of its origin equally with the later successful works. It was, in fact, a more inward striving toward ideas; since, however, he found nourishment in the publication of Kantian philosophy, and, after he began in *On Grace and Dignity* to speak out in definite clarity, the final construction of the system suggested and partly worked out in this essay, was posed as an inner task for Schiller that, in conformity with his individuality, had to be completed before he could go on to another topic. For it was impossible for him to let any unclarity or uncertainty remain in his mind—until he was forced to give up the hope of bringing it to clarity and certainty—and the ideas which formed the supporting pillars of his intellectual endeavor, with which he saw his poetic production—the element of his life—indissolubly united, as soon as that had become an object of study and reflection for him, had to be purely spun out before his eyes to their final point. Perseverance to the end was a characteristic feature in Schiller with every work, and so he did not rest before the problem set for him by his most inner nature was solved in *The Letters On the Aesthetic Education of Man.* Until then, however, he could take up nothing else. Whatever attracted his mind always occupied it completely and exclusively.

It is quite remarkable how, in the period of which we are speaking here, the longing for dramatic composition, always enduring in Schiller, slowly but continuously emerged, and won the upper hand over philosophical activity. In the first year of his return to Jena, he still worked continuously on the *Aesthetical Letters* and occasionally on historical works. Then poetry blossomed, at first in small lyrical and narrative poems, and philosophy, in the essays *Concerning Naive and Sentimental Poetry,* approached in easier and brighter form the work of the imagination already becoming dominant. Finally *Wallenstein* was begun. Thus Schiller entered, as though into a brighter, for him characteristic element, into the brilliant poetic period of his last years, which was not further interrupted. His death, great and beautiful, however painfully it moved us, snatched him from amid an already gloriously achieved life's work, still being pursued with ever striving force.

In that period of Schiller's return to dramatic composition also falls his intimate association with Goethe, certainly the most important and powerful contributory cause. The mutual influence of these two great men on one another was most powerful and most noble. Each felt inspired, strengthened, and encouraged on his own path, each saw more clearly and correctly how the same goal united them, but via different roads. Neither drew the other over to his way, or caused the other the least hesitation in pursuing his own goal. As in their immortal works, they offered a model in their friendship never seen before, in which their spiritual striving together was interwoven indissolubly with the disposition of their characters and the feelings of their hearts, and they thus honored the name German. To say more on this, however, would be partly superfluous, and is partly forbidden by a natural and justified reserve. Schiller and Goethe expressed themselves so clearly and openly, so intimately and brilliantly in their letters on this unique relationship, that no one can be tempted to add anything to what has been said in such a way.

In the correspondence with me, there are passages where Schiller seems to doubt his poetic vocation, and similar points are given in Körner's description of Schiller's life. I also referred to this earlier at the beginning of this introduction. Such momentary attacks, as well as his extraordinary misconception of being born more for epic than dramatic composition, will mislead no one who is an intimate of the human heart and mind. Never has anyone, if we disregard moments of isolated distemper, known so clearly and decisively what he, through his nature, had to will and seek, never anyone who so rightly and naturally appreciated his own endeavor and successes as Schiller, never was fumbling around in uncertainty for one's naturally determined destiny more alien and odious to anyone than to him. His destiny, however, was clearly dramatic composition. The sharpness of his imaginative powers, which concentrated everything onto a single point, the ability to work toward a powerful effect, the production of the highest tension of reality, joining it to the most sublime denouement of the idea—all of this, which was given directly through Schiller's individuality, particularly suited this mode of composition, whose character, in Goethe's striking remark, derives from the fact that it translates its object into the present moment. For it concentrates its entire effect toward a single end point, moving more along a straight line than by spreading itself through a plane, and stands, as does thought, in closer relation to *time* than to *space*, which is more appropriate to perception. If Schiller momentarily seemed to misrecognize this, and even the poetic genius within him, then it was, in the best of these moments of doubt, because of the grandeur of the ideal which dizzied his vision, and of the intensity of his deepest longing, despairing of the attainment of the goal sought.

I have purposely not referred at all to the influence which external circumstances may have exerted on the changes of Schiller's occupations. To be sure, the prose essays were largely generated for *Thalia* and *Die Horen*, as was poetry for the *Musenalmanach*." The first, from 1796, occasioned almost everything which it received from Schiller; nothing stemmed from an earlier period. Nevertheless, the varying transition from the poetic to the philosophical, from prose to rhythmic work, was derived principally and totally only from Schiller's spiritual attunement portrayed above. Only because the greatness which he carried in yearning expectation within himself had not yet grown to maturity, because the concentration and attunement of his mind, which is the only preparation possible for artistic production and creation, were not complete, did he allow himself undertakings of that sort, which, of course, afterward occasionally seemed to him disruptive, but this was more semblance than was actually the case. It remains highly admirable how these external incentives were never the occasion for mediocre work, and how the compulsion (for thus such works must be characterized which are promised for a certain time) was transformed into a beautiful spontaneity as soon as the idea, happily received, presented itself to the mind, thus obliterating the external origin of the work itself. For no one is able to deny the stamp of authentic genius on even the least important of the *Almanach* and *Horen* poetry.

What particularly distinguishes the later dramatic works is, first, a more careful and correctly understood striving toward the totality of the form of art; then a deeper cultivation of the subjects, through which they enter into a greater and richer global environment, and more sublime ideas are connected to them; and, finally, a more complete effacement of everything prosaic through a more pure poetic sweep in representation, thought, and expression. At every point, the concept of art demanded for an individual poem is elevated within it, and the living poetic form completely penetrating the material then becomes, in a higher sense, nature. In many passages in his letters, Schiller suggests, that his greater regard for the *whole* is the most essential advance made by him, and criticizes the fixation on details, and the direct cultivation, by preference, of parts. Much earlier, however, he had expressed this highest demand of a work of art in a way both wonderfully clear and beautiful in *The Artists*. What he understood by such a treatment of a dramatic subject he showed immediately in that most difficult of works in this respect, in *Wallenstein*. Everything of such an infinitely comprehensive event was to be rescued from reality and appear as bound together by poetic necessity; all the foundations on which the bold hero intended to base his dangerous undertakings, all the obstacles on which they were wrecked, the political position of the princes, the course of the war, the condition of Germany, the mood of the army—all these were to be brought poetically and graphically before the eyes of the audience. Seldom has a poet made greater demands on himself or his material, and excepting Shakespeare, there is scarcely anyone else who encompasses in one tragedy such a world of objects, movement, and feeling.

The works which follow *Wallenstein* show, that Schiller continued to work in the same way. In fact, his life consisted in the fact that, as a poet, he practiced what he said somewhere of the ideally educated man in general, that he draws as much of the world, with the total multiplicity of its phenomena, into himself as his imagination is capable of conceiving, and there fuses it into the unity of the form of art. Therefore, his tragedies are not repetitions of a talent which has become a manner, but are each the birth of an ever youthful, ever new struggle with the demands of art, rightly perceived and sublimely conceived. It is not my purpose to go more deeply into those works. The observations made in this *Introduction* have the goal solely of fitting the following letters into the total context of Schiller's course of development. They find, therefore, their natural end at the unquestionable beginning of the period of his last tragedies. These long ago received the judgment of the world; they can await with tranquility that of future generations. They will continue to occupy the stage for a long time to come, and then take their place in the history of German poetry.

The poet does not bring new truths to light, does not collect new facts. He has an effect just as he creates; he brings his figures, which educate and edify, before the imagination of all times; he produces this in the form in which he clothes his subjects, in the characters with which he ideally enriches mankind, in his own image, which radiates forth from all of his works. Thus, inspiring and educating, through exaltation and emotion, Schiller will continue, for a long time, powerfully to affect his nation.

He was torn from the world in the perfect maturity of his spiritual power, and would have yet been able to create an infinity. His goal was so fixed that he could never have attained an end, and thus his continually progressing powers could never have been brought to a standstill; for a long time still, he could have had the joy, the rapture, and even—as he inimitably put it in one of the letters following here in connection with the plan for an idyll—the blessedness of poetic creation. His life was cut short, but as long as it lasted, it was exclusively and unceasingly occupied in the realm of ideas and imagination; perhaps of no one can it be said with so much truth that "he had thrown away the fears of the earthly, and had flown up out of the narrow, dull world into the kingdom of the ideal"[12] he lived, always surrounded by the highest ideas and the most brilliant images that a human being is able to take up within himself and bring forth from himself. Whoever thus leaves the Earth can only be styled happy.—Tegle, May 1830.

## AUTHOR'S NOTES

*The present collection contains all our letters that are still extant, except for some few which are totally uninteresting. A good number, however, are lacking. Schiller must not have preserved all of my letters, and a good number of Schiller's to me were lost at the country estate, where I am writing this, during the unfortunate events of the war of 1806.

†A play which Schiller considered for quite some time, of which there is discussion in the following letters.

## TRANSLATOR'S NOTES

1. Schiller began work on *Don Carlos* in 1785; he completed it in 1787.

2. *The Artists*, line 229.

3. *The Artists*, line 315.

4. *Philosophical Letters*, an uncompleted work which appeared in 1786 in the *Thalia*, a literary journal founded and edited by Schiller in 1784, when Schiller was 25. Its full title was *Rheinischen Thalia*. Schiller published many of his poems, including *To Joy*, in its pages.

5. *On Bürger's Poetry* was written in 1791 as a review of a new edition of Bürger's poetry. Schiller particularly attacks Bürger's view that the artist must in part sacrifice the integrity of art to gain popularity. Goethe was highly impressed by the review, and expressed the wish to have written it himself.

6. The reference is to the famous passage from the *Critique of Practical Reason*, "Two things fill the mind with ever new and increasing admiration and awe . . . the starry heavens above me and the moral law within me."

7. Humboldt is referring to Schiller's tenure at the University of Jena, where he became a professor of history in the spring of 1789. At Jena, he was close to Professor Reinhold, one of the leading Kantians of the time, and was thus introduced to the study of Kant's philosophy.

8. Christian Gottfried Körner (1756–1831) was a friend of Schiller from 1785. Körner wrote an eighteenth-century-style biography of Schiller, *Account of Schiller's Life*, published in 1812.

9. *Die Horen* was established in 1795, and was the original place of publication of his *Letters On the Aesthetical Education of Man*.

10. The idea of "elective affinities" (*Wahlverwandtschaften*) was of great importance in Goethe's thought, and the term served as the title of one of his novels.

11. *Die Musenalmanach* was a poetry journal founded in 1796, and lasted until 1800. In it, Goethe and Schiller published their jointly written *Xenien*.

12. Compare verse 28 of Schiller's *The Ideal and Life*.